The Cathedral Towns and Intervening Places Ireland and

A Description of Cities, Ca   ais, Lakes, Mountains, Ruins, and Watering-places.

Lee L. Powers, Thomas W. Silloway

Alpha Editions

This edition published in 2024

ISBN : 9789366389356

Design and Setting By
Alpha Editions
www.alphaedis.com
Email - info@alphaedis.com

As per information held with us this book is in Public Domain.
This book is a reproduction of an important historical work. Alpha Editions uses the best technology to reproduce historical work in the same manner it was first published to preserve its original nature. Any marks or number seen are left intentionally to preserve its true form.

Contents

INTRODUCTORY. ....- 1 -
IRELAND. ....- 3 -
CHAPTER I. ....- 5 -
CHAPTER II. ....- 18 -
CHAPTER III. ....- 33 -
CHAPTER IV. ....- 51 -
ENGLAND. ....- 65 -
CHAPTER V. ....- 67 -
CHAPTER VI. ....- 85 -
CHAPTER VII. ....- 101 -
CHAPTER VIII. ....- 114 -
CHAPTER IX. ....- 143 -
CHAPTER X. ....- 148 -
CHAPTER XI. ....- 166 -
SCOTLAND. ....- 175 -
CHAPTER XII. ....- 177 -
CHAPTER XIII. ....- 189 -
CHAPTER XIV. ....- 207 -
ENGLAND. ....- 215 -
CHAPTER XV. ....- 217 -
CHAPTER XVI. ....- 226 -
CHAPTER XVII. ....- 241 -
CHAPTER XVIII ....- 252 -
CHAPTER XIX. ....- 264 -
CHAPTER XX. ....- 282 -
CHAPTER XXI. ....- 293 -

CHAPTER XXII. ....- 306 -
FOOTNOTE: ....- 317 -

INTRODUCTORY.

The Authors, having travelled somewhat leisurely over important parts of Ireland and Scotland, and in a yet more deliberate and critical manner over the principal parts of England,—observing not only salient points in the life of each country, but at the same time passing in review their history and work,—and believing that a synopsis of what their New England eyes, ears, and minds saw, heard, and discovered, would be acceptable to the public, one of them prepared a series of articles which were published in one of the weekly papers of Boston. The interest awakened, and a belief that these reminiscences should be put into a more permanent form, have inclined the authors to amend the articles as the case seemed to demand, and they are thus presented in this volume.

When the original papers were prepared, a departure from the usual custom of writers on travel was made. Instead of simply recording personal observations, the labor was extended by the incorporation of historic and biographic facts, the authors hoping that, while their work would be valuable and interesting as a compend to those familiar with the facts, it would also be entertaining and instructive to that large class, in all communities, who are without the means of obtaining such information. Care was therefore exercised to obtain data verified by the testimony of various authors.

The articles having been published in narrative style, it has been thought well to present them again in that form; and the authors wish to say by way of apology, if one be needed, that the opinions and criticisms expressed are such as impressed their own minds, and are not reflections of the minds of others. With this explanation, and craving the indulgence and patience of the reader, they send forth their volume.

IRELAND.

CHAPTER I.

NEW YORK TO QUEENSTOWN—CORK.

On Saturday the 12th day of April, 1878, at half-past 3 P. M., the good Inman steamer City of Richmond, with us on board, loosed her cables, and the floating palace moved out into North River majestically,—as only such vessels can move,—passed the forts, and sailed on, till at dusk, yet before dark, the Highlands of Neversink—a misnomer to us then—retired from view, and, Byron-like, we felt and said,

"My native land, good-night."

Suppered, and enjoyed the look of that waste of sky and waters till ten o'clock, and then consigned ourselves to the embrace of

"Tired nature's sweet restorer, balmy sleep."

The morrow was Sunday. We were up betimes, and on deck for new views, fresh air, and to see how things compared with those of last night. All was well,—comparatively smooth sea, and good breeze. We had sailed 224 miles, and so were that much from home. Breakfasted, and on deck again,—this time to see nearly all our cabin passengers, about one hundred complete. They appeared well, and we thought our lot had been cast in a pleasant place; and so it proved. There were conspicuous the essentials of comfort for the voyage,—among them inclined-back, cane-finished lounging-chairs, and good blanket robes, brought by providential people who had travelled before, or who had friends who had journeyed and in whose advice they had confidence. No matter if it be July or August, it is a good friend who effectually advises one to carry a great coat, shawl, or blanket robe.

The sun shone bright, and the inhabitants of the City of Richmond were happy. At 10 A. M. came the roll-call of sailors and table-waiters, arranged in squads at special points. An officer and the captain passed in front, the name of each was distinctly called, the old, old response, *Here*, passed along the line, and the work was done. Of course a large part of the passengers were near by, inspecting, and they were presuming enough to think all was going on right, and the work well done.

Next came an officer giving information that divine service was to be held in the cabin at 11 A. M., and inviting singers to be at a certain location. One of our party, having before tried the ship's piano, was installed as pianist. At the hour appointed, nearly all on board, including the sailors, had assembled, and it seemed very like a church meeting. The pulpit was a desk placed on a common table, covered with a cloth; a Bible and prayer-book were on it, and our captain officiated,—a man of fine physique, apparently about sixty years old, and, but for the absence of clerical robes, very bishop-like in appearance.

He went finely through the service of the Church of England, employing about an hour, and concluded by saying: "I am now to preach my usual sermon, which is to take up a collection for the widows and orphans of sailors." A good charity,—and a befitting response was made.

At one o'clock, dinner; next, various methods of using the time, the principal of which was reading or lounging about decks.

Soon came a change in conditions. Wind breezed up and we had more than a fifteen-mile power; and so sails were in order—our first sight of operations of the kind. Next came white-capped waves; and at 5 P. M. had come those indescribably hateful movements of the ship, that many a one has felt before,—down first at bow, and next up at stern, and *vice versa* continuing. "Confound," said they of the physically weakening brigade, "the deliberation, yet fearful determination and success with which these movements are made,"—as though transforming us first into lead and then into feathers; and soon follows an aggravating roll, playing with us as though we were alternately puff-balls and cannon-shot. But neither waves nor ship were to be *confounded* to accommodate us. Instead, both ship and sea appeared to be in league with the old-fashioned adversary. It seemed, to the subjugated ones, as though his Satanic Majesty was down under the propellers, with a mighty power straightening himself up, and lifting as only he could do; and then, as aid, there appeared to be an imp scarcely less powerful, pulling down at the bow, and in addition, many a fellow of like nature under each side of the ship, lifting up and letting go alternately. What masters of the art! How easily they did it!

Disgusted with the company and their doings, one after the other of our associates paid tribute to whom tribute was due; and what was left of our disgusted organisms went below as best they could. And here the curtain drops; for, though the spirit was willing, the flesh was weak.

It is 6 P. M., Sunday. We were told that the winds increased to a gale; rain, snow-squalls and hail came into the fray. The vessel staggered; the stanch bulwarks were but a partial barrier to that fury-lashed sea; and the decks were often swept with the newest of new brooms.

Next in our record is Friday P. M. Fair weather. Ship has come out ahead. Imps and their master are defeated and gone; the decks, as by talismanic transformation, are peopled again with the old brigade; and then for hours is in order a statement of what each has done and has not done. Well, the history of one lot of mortals, conditioned thus, is that of all.

It is a question often arising with people who have never been to sea, how passengers manage to occupy their time and break up the monotony of the passage. On a long voyage, days and hours doubtless move sluggishly, but on a simple passage to England this is not so. A thousand things, that on land would be of no account, on shipboard attract attention and please. "Men are but children of a larger growth," and there are playthings in abundance. There's a discount on reserve, and at sea a general freedom in conversation obtains; aristocracy is at a discount, and democracy at a premium. Reading, lolling around in a delightfully don't-care sort of a way, are done in first-class manner; smoking, cards, and checkers occupy some, while others are busy lookers-on. Talking things over,—politics, religion, science, and a large amount of nothing in particular; promenading; watching steamers and sailing vessels; observing schools of fish, or single ones, ocean currents, peculiar clouds, and work the sailors are doing; eating four meals, or eating none, but instead hating the thought of increasing one's self,—these and like things fill the eight or ten days. And so we were entertained and employed to the journey's end,—greatly interested in the chart at the head of the companion-way, which at noon daily had marked upon it a distinct line showing the direction and extent of sea passed over the preceding twenty-four hours.

So our voyage continued till the next Sunday, at 6 P. M., when the monotony was broken by one of the officers confidentially saying he thought he saw land. Of all intelligence to a tourist this is most welcome. One of the passengers—nameless here—looked to the left far ahead, and really saw what the officers did; but to his less disciplined or sea-educated eyes it appeared to be a ship, and so he declared; but in a half-hour more sounded from stem to stern the intelligence of discovered land, and then the fancied ship had been transformed into a dim-appearing, small mountain. It was the Skellig Rocks, the first-seen land of Ireland, fifty miles from Cape Clear. Passing on came to view Dursey Island, with its Bull, Cow, and Calf rocks, and then—alas for us waiters and watchers!—night came and we must forbear.

At 4 o'clock A. M. on that fine Easter Monday morning, April 21, a good company on deck saw plainly on the left, and not far away, the veritable land. There lay in the distance the old mountains of Munster, and Fastnet Rock, a pyramidal formation standing majestic in the water five miles or so out from the high, dark, rocky coast. Next a lighthouse came into view, desolate but surrounded by an indescribable beauty.

Soon we pass into George's Channel. The land is treeless, but clothed with elegant verdure. The surf beats wildly and unhindered against its rocky ramparts. Here and there, nestling cosily on the hillsides, are small Irish cabins, one-story high, built of stone, plastered and whitewashed, having thatched roofs, a few small windows, and a single door. Next appear a few Martello Towers of stone, some twenty-five feet in diameter, and perhaps forty feet high,—designed as fortresses, having formerly, if not at present, cannon on their level, and, it may be, revolving tops. And now appear fresh evidences of civilization, in the fishing-boats with tan-colored sails; and next we arrive at a little hamlet, Crooked Haven, the seat of the telegraph to Queenstown. We next pass Kinsale Head; in less than an hour more Daunt's Rock, with its bell-buoy; and after that a sail of five miles carries us to the opening into Queenstown Harbor, and we are at the end of the voyage.

It is now 5 o'clock A. M. Our ship for the first time in eight days shuts off steam; her pace slackens; and—as though while not tired, yet willing to rest—she floats leisurely. How majestic and calm! The small "tender" steamer is alongside, and now what scenes begin! How others retire before the hurry, the bustle, the good-nature everywhere manifest. A veritable "Paradise Regained." No matter for corns trodden upon, nor lack of respect for dignity or age. Every one destined for a landing minds his own business. Never was work of the kind done better. All the Queenstown passengers on board, the tender starts for the desired haven.

The City of Richmond starts her machinery, and is soon lost to view on her journey of eighteen hours to Liverpool; but we on board the small steamer are full of admiration for the new sights and sounds. Have just passed through the great opening two miles across, and one mile deep or through, and so are inside the harbor lines. In passing, on our left were high, verdant hills. On the right were higher hills, crowned with a few chalk-white buildings,—the lighthouse and its keeper's dwelling, the grounds enclosed with a wall, white like the buildings, resembling fairy-work in that setting of emerald. And now has opened an expanse of great extent and rare beauty. "No finer harbor in the world can there be," think and ejaculate all, at that early day, when few if any of the party have travelled; and "No finer in the world is there," say we now, when we have gone a good part of the world over.

To the right, encircling and on a magnificent scale, stretch the green hills on a curved line, half enclosing a basin five miles long and three wide. As before named the hills are grandly verdant, and dotted over here and there with single stone shanties, as white as snow. Scattered about promiscuously in profusion is the Furze—a shrub from two to six feet high, in general appearance not unlike our savin—in full bloom, with a profusion of chrome-yellow blossoms, fragrant and like the odor of a ripe peach. A few groves intermingle, and thus a finished look is given, inclining the beholder to call all perfect and needing no change. To the left is a scene more broken in outline and less elevated and extended. There is a sublime repose and feminine beauty to the right and around the shore to the town; but on the left is a masculine effect, and a sort of vigorous business air obtains. In the foreground of this side of the harbor, and not far from the shore, are three islands, on which are the barracks, the penitentiary for eight hundred convicts, and the naval storehouses, four or five stories high. These are modern and appropriate-looking stone edifices, built, as all such establishments are, "regardless of expense." In front of the opening to the harbor, and two miles away, lies the town itself, containing 10,039 inhabitants, and till 1849 called the Cove of Cork. In that year, in commemoration of a visit of Queen Victoria, it took the name of Queenstown.

We are for the first time inside a harbor of the land of the shamrock, and beholding the soil of the Emerald Isle. Only one who has sailed and waited and, Columbus-like, watched the approach to land, and has read and thought well about the Old Country, can know the feelings that fill the breast of one about to land. This pleasant anticipation is here, for fancy resolves itself into reality and fact. He is about to "know how it is himself," and as no one can know it for him.

The town lay stretched out in front, right and left, rising by abrupt terraces or cross streets—parallel to the water—to a great height, with a few streets leading upward. The wharves are of wood; and these, which partake largely of the nature of a quay along the line of the water, are old and more or less decayed in appearance, as are many of the buildings in the vicinity. The houses to the right of our landing and along the shore, and continuing up quite a distance on the hill, are of the usual stone construction, being mostly one or two stories high. The streets are very narrow, and far from being cleanly kept. The rear yards of the houses, as they back up against the hill, are very small; and as one walks through an elevated street, and looks down into these contracted and filthy back-yards and on the roofs of the houses, he is led to pity the occupants, for there is presented the evidence of poverty and wretchedness. To the left of the landing, and above this portion of the town, is a better population and condition. The principal avenue and business portion of the place is at hand. A wide, clean, and properly built thoroughfare, used more or less as a market-place and stand for teams, stretches for a fourth of a mile, with stores of fair capacity and good variety, and a few are of more than average style. The buildings are nearly all of stone, light in color, and three or four stories high.

From the nature of the land, and intermingled as the buildings above the main street are with gardens and trees, a picturesque appearance is presented; and the view of the great basin or harbor, from these elevated streets is indescribably grand. The streets here, and especially the continuing roads, are well macadamized and clean.

At the centre of the town a large and elegant Roman Catholic Cathedral, built of dark limestone and in the decorated Gothic style of architecture, is about finished.

One peculiarity of the place is a lack of fruit-trees in the gardens. The common dark-leaved ivy abounds, and is found growing wild on road-walls, and along the roadsides in profusion. As a front-yard or lawn shrub, fuchsias, such as are raised in America in pots, are common, and often in large clumps like our elder, six or eight feet high.

Another peculiarity is an absence of clothes-lines. Instead, the practice prevails of spreading newly washed clothes on the grass, with small stones to keep them from being blown away.

Another thing of interest is the common and general use of diminutive donkeys to draw small carts, used by boys and girls, from eight to sixteen years old, for common porterage. They are also used for milk-wagons. Each wagon has an oaken tank, holding about half a barrel; straight-sided, larger at the bottom than at the top, having a cover and padlock; the measure hanging on one side. There is straw behind, and at the front end the boy or girl is driving. These donkeys are usually of a cream-color or gray. All are cheap and coarse-looking, and a majority of them are aged, with their hair two thirds worn off. They are the very personification of good-nature, and do their work well. So far as value is concerned they are "worth their weight in gold," but they cost, when in best condition, not more than ten dollars each. Witnessing their patience, the great services they render, and the small amount of recompense they have while living, we incline to the opinion that, as a result of the working of the laws of cause and effect, there may be expected for them good conditions in their Hereafter. They are angels in disguise, and we wish they were in use in America as commonly as they are here.

Other objects that attracted attention were the public wells built in especial parts of the town. They are enclosed springs of water, or it may be reservoirs supplied by pipes; the places are from six to ten feet square, and only a few feet deep, a descent to which is made by stone steps into the small, stone-covered rooms. The people using them for the most part carry the water to their houses in earthen jars holding two or three gallons each. The water is carried by girls and women, seldom by boys and men; at least we could see none engaged in the service. As may be imagined, considering the filthy nature of some of the people who thus obtain the water, it is necessary to have a placard declaring the enforcement of law on any one who dips a dirty or questionable article into one of the wells, or interferes with the purity of the water.

Signs render a large service in the place, and some of them make queer statements,—at least so they appear to Americans. For instance, one reads:

Here Margaret Ahearn is Licensed to sell Tobacco.

The street letter-boxes had this inscription:

Cleared at 8 a.m. and 6 p.m., and on Sundays at 5 p.m.

At 2 p. m. this same day with some reluctance we left what was to us a place of interest, and took the nice little black-painted steamer Erin, for a sail from this Lower Harbor of Cork, as it formerly was called, to the city itself.

The journey, covering a distance of eleven miles, may be made by rail or steamer. The wise, pleasure-seeking tourist goes by river. On board the little steamer, having paid a shilling (twenty-four cents) for the passage, valises at our side,—and that is all of our baggage, or as we ought now, being in foreign lands, to term it, *luggage*,—we take our last admiring look at this queen of harbors, and with inexpressible reluctance bid adieu to its beautiful scenery, submitting to our fate in anticipation of another visit, as the steamer that takes us to America will be here for a day to receive the mails. We steam to the left end of the basin, and, rounding to the right, pass into the lovely River Lee,—an extremely picturesque stream averaging here perhaps a quarter of a mile in width.

The weather is cool, but pleasant for the season. Vegetation in certain respects is three or four weeks in advance of that about Boston. This applies to grass, lilacs and shrubs of the kind, and spring flowers; but garden vegetables, from planted seeds, are not at all in advance. In fact, up to this time, April 22, little planting has been done. The atmosphere of the southern parts of Ireland and of England being very damp, and the entire winter mild, certain kinds of vegetation advance; but cultivated work has no especial advantage over New England, where the first fruits of the gardener's labor are gathered as early as in those islands.

But to return from our digression, we proceed on our short voyage to Cork, and are now on our passage up the River Lee. The scenery on the right bank, on the Queenstown side, is somewhat hilly and of pleasing aspect, though not especially striking or unusual; but that of the opposite shore is elegant and picturesque in the extreme. About a mile from the mouth of the river is the beautiful village of Monkstown, a semi-watering-place, having tourists' hotels and a castle. Monkstown Castle is in ruins, having been built in the year 1636. It is related that Anastatia Goold, a woman of masculine qualities, during the absence of her husband in Spain, conceived the idea of building this as a family mansion, and to pay for it, hit upon the scheme of supplying her workmen with their family stores. She purchased them at wholesale, and retailed them at a profit which paid the entire cost of the castle, with the exception of a single groat (eight cents of our money).

The river above this widens into a small lake, and is called Loch Mahon. Three and a half miles farther up we arrive at the smart little village of Glenbrook; and one and a half miles farther, we come to another pretty town, called Passage.

Soon appears Blackrock, a small promontory, on which is a structure suggesting an ancient castle, built on a tongue of land extending into the clear water of the river. The mansion, however, is old only in style and outline, for it is of modern construction. Blackrock is supposed to be the place from which William Penn, the founder of Pennsylvania, set sail, A. D. 1682, landing after a passage of six weeks.

We were for the hour sumptuously entertained. Small castles, coves, headlands, near and distant scenery, and a luxurious vegetation lent a fascination and charm, which was but the beginning of a series of similar entertainments, not to end till after the first of September.

CORK.

Arrived at the castle, not far in the distance is seen, through the opening of the hills making the river banks, the shipping of the city of Cork, which is practically the capital of South Ireland. We find it a large commercial metropolis, built closely on both sides of the River Lee. The latter is parted at the city, and thus the left side of Cork stands mainly on an island, connected with the other side by nine stone or iron bridges. It has in all a population of 97,887, and is the third city of Ireland in importance and commerce, being excelled only by Dublin and Belfast.

On one side of the river as we pass into the city, at our left hand, are shipyards, repair and dry docks, and a vast amount of work of the kind is done. It may be added, there is presented to view in the harbor a forest of masts, and here may be seen the shipping of all nations. Near these and just above them, up along farther in the city and bordering the river, are fine Boulevards,—narrow parks or promenades well graded, called the Mardyke, and set out with shade-trees. The opposite side of the river, at the entrance of the harbor proper, is occupied by elegant lawns, with shrubbery and shade-trees in front of fine mansions and villas; and again, along the river above these, begins the business part of the city.

A good quay extends half a mile on both sides of the river. These have walls of cut, dark limestone, crowned by a substantial railing as a protecting balustrade. The larger part of the place, so far as its business portion is concerned, is built on level ground, and here the streets are wide, well paved and clean, and with the buildings, all of which are of brick or stone, a majority of the latter being painted in light colors, present a pleasing and finished appearance. All things seen are anything but what is imagined by a stranger when he hears one speak of Irish Cork.

Here and there, as at Queenstown, may be seen some of the old Irish male stock, with corduroys and long stockings, velvet coats, peculiar felt hats, heavy shoes—strangers to Day and Martin's specialty; but these are exceptions, about as much so as they are in the Irish sections of New York or Boston. Generally speaking, the dress of the people, male and female, of Irish cities is not peculiar, and aside from these exceptional instances they do not vary from those of London or Boston.

As regards a good civilization—everywhere in the business parts of the city, manifested by large and well-filled stores and fine warehouses, and by well dressed and industrious people—our impressions were very favorable.

The city in this region, like all large places, has its quota of men loafing about its bridges and wharves, waiting, Micawber like, "for something to turn up." So has Atlantic Avenue, Boston. In these respects Boston is Corkish, or Cork is like Boston. About the steamer wharves and at the railway station (we don't now talk of *depots*, for to be true to foreign dialect, we must say *station*) it is the same. At these, and along the thoroughfare from it, are boys, Yankee-like, ready to turn an honest penny or to earn one; and very demonstrative they are, and the cabmen as well. Americans are often outdone by them. One of these boys, at the moment of our landing from the steamer, seized our valises and *would* carry them. He *in*sisted and we *re*sisted, and at length the American element in us—"the spirit of '76"—was aroused, and in the ascendant; and to convince him that he ought to let go his hold, down came a hand on his arm with a force, and accompanied by a tone of voice and ejaculation, that meant business. "Keep off! Let go!" was the order and advice, and he did both.

Here, as at Queenstown, the little donkeys were on hand, and rendering a large and patient service. The public buildings are not very important, but substantial and good of their kind. Conspicuous among the new edifices is the Episcopal Cathedral now being erected. It is of stone, very imposing, with three towers, and in the Romanesque style of architecture. The Roman Catholic Cathedral, SS. Peter and Paul, also of dark limestone, having cut or hammered dressing, is a Gothic structure of considerable size, with a good tower at the centre of the front end, crowned with four turrets, and having a neat but small lawn, surrounded with an iron fence, about the cathedral's front. It was erected after designs by the celebrated F. W. Pugin, and cost $150,000. The interior, although not old, was dirty and presented a dingy appearance. We were told by the verger (sexton) that times being hard, business dull, and the people poor, accounted for the condition. We differed in opinion in other respects than theologically, but made no mention of the fact, and passed out.

Of course we must see, and soon at that, the church of St. Ann's, Shandon, and so made for that. It ought before to have been said that soon after crossing the river the land rises quite fast; so that as one stands in the business part, and in the thoroughfare along the line of the river,—and looks across the entire section of the city from the river backwards, the distant parts are seen towering much above the business portion. High up, along from the centre to the right, appear shade-trees and good gardens, with other evidences of a better civilization; but from these along to the left is presented a view quite the opposite of the front, or harbor, view of Queenstown. There, the low population is to the right and near the water; while here it begins half-way up the hill at the centre, and extends a half-mile or more to the left; and, as we leave the centre named, the buildings on the hillside, and the group or lot widening till they reach from the river to the top of the hill, are so arranged that, with houses of several stories and of remarkably quaint design, the high roofs appear in ranges one above the other, and the great hillside presents a strange, antique, thoroughly European appearance. They are of stone, built in the most substantial manner, and are unlike anything that can be found in America.

But we resume our journey to St. Ann's, Shandon. As observed from the river streets, it stands not far from the Catholic Cathedral, nor far from the centre of the hillside, as regards extent right and left, or elevation. The edifice was built in 1722. The tower was built of hewn stone, taken from the Franciscan Abbey—where James II. heard mass—and from the ruins of Lord Barry's castle. It is of dark limestone on the three principal sides, and, like the body of the church, with red sandstone on the rear side above the church roof. The edifice is made celebrated by what are termed and somewhat well known as The Sweet Bells of Shandon, made conspicuous by the poem of Father Prout:—

"Sweet Bells of Shandon,
That sound so grand on

The pleasant waters of the River Lee."

The church is Protestant Episcopal, and is of a debased Roman architecture. It has a square tower rising a proper distance above the roof, and this is crowned by a series of three square sections of somewhat ill proportions as regards their low height; and the top one is finished with a small dome surmounted by an immense fish as a vane, the tower and steeple being perhaps one hundred and twenty feet high. We did not hear the bells, save as they played a few notes at the quarter-hours. The one on which the hours are struck is probably the largest tenor bell, and weighs perhaps 2000 pounds.

What we did hear of them did not arouse enthusiasm. We simply thought them good average bells, and made more than that, in song and story, simply by Father Prout's poem. One thing about the tower struck us forcibly, and that was the monstrous dials, full twelve feet in diameter, painted directly on the stonework of the tower, with a rim of stone at the figure circle.

Next, a few words in relation to the population and condition of this part of the city. It will be remembered that we are now in the centre of the hillside, as seen from the business parts of the place, and at an elevation of full sixty feet,—in the conspicuous, and what ought to be aristocratic, quarter of the metropolis. But alas for what "might have been." The street in front, and the passage along the side of this building, are ill cared for and filthy in the extreme. A burial-ground forms part of the premises on both sides of the edifice, and is as neglected and disgraceful as one can well imagine. On the right is a thoroughfare alongside of the church, leading through the cemetery to some institution—perhaps a parish-school or hospital—in the rear of the church, and fronting on this passage-way. Here are cast-off shoes, broken crockery, stones thrown about by the boys, and unmentionable filth in abundance. At the right are broken monuments, badly defaced gravestones, and half-dilapidated tombs, all betokening a general lack of care over the premises.

Walking from the front of the church to the narrow and filthy streets that compose the neighborhood, we noticed such odors, sights, and conditions as we had before erroneously associated with all of Cork. We here saw a low Ireland at its best—or worst, as we may choose to term it; for here abounded dirt, degradation, poverty, and general squalor, up to the height of our early imagination. The houses are of stone, plastered and whitewashed, most of them one or two stories high, with roofs covered with very small and thick slates. We soon had enough of this kind of "Erin go bragh." If we did not know all that was possible to be known, imagination would, in spite of us, aggravatingly supply what was lacking.

As we passed out of this "Paradise Lost," or at least the one not regained, we could but feel that to make less display of service within their churches, depend less for good fame on the Sweet Bells of Shandon, and render a more reasonable and practical service, would be more rational, Christian and right.

We are told that the ancient Pharisees made the outside clean, and the inside was full of dead men's bones, and all manner of uncleanness. These people have reversed this, and without visible improvement.

Next must be named a thing of interest, and that is the Bazaar. It is a one-story building of immense size, and in appearance like a railway freight-house. Built of stone, and centrally situated, it is filled with every conceivable kind of second-hand goods. Separated, market-like, into stalls, it is so arranged and confusing as to make a labyrinth of avenues and divisions. Here are such things as old hardware, boots and shoes,—some as poor and valueless as we throw away, some better and newly blacked,—clothing for both sexes, crockery,—and we might continue the list. The Bazaar is managed by women, and the place and its commodities are as indescribable as the nationality of the Man in the Moon.

As at Queenstown, we saw much drunkenness, and often met, singly or in squads, the Red-coats, or English soldiers; but more concerning these will be said in another place.

The space we devote to this city is perhaps more than its share, but less can hardly be said, and our references to it are ended by a quotation or two from its history.

It is said that Cromwell, during his short sojourn in Cork, caused the church bells to be cast into cannon. On being remonstrated with against the profanity, he replied that as a priest had been the inventor of gunpowder, the best use of the bells would be to cast them into *canons*.

It was here that William Penn, founder of our Pennsylvania, became a convert to Quakerism. He visited the place to look after his father's property, changed his religion under the preaching of Thomas Loe, and on Sept. 3, 1667, was apprehended with others and taken before the Mayor's Court, charged with "attending unlawful assemblies." Refusing to give bonds for good behavior he was imprisoned, but wrote to the Lord President of the council of Munster, who ordered his discharge. He was identified with the Quakers from this time till his decease, at Ruscombe, England, July 30, 1718, at the age of seventy-four.

Cork has an interesting ancient history. It was long the seat of a Pagan temple, on the site of which St. Fionn Bar, the anchorite, founded a monastery in the beginning of the seventh century. The Danes in the ninth century overran the kingdom, and were probably the real founders of the city, and they surrounded it with walls; though the St. Fionn Bar monastery had continued through the centuries, and it is recorded that, on the intrusion of the Danes, the seminary had full seven hundred scholars "who had flocked there from all parts."

The inhabitants, under the Danes and their successors, frequently devastated the entire vicinity, and were in turn punished by the neighboring chiefs.

In 1493 Perkin Warbeck, the impostor king and pretender to the throne of England in the reign of Henry VII., was received here with great pomp and display. In consequence of participation in this act, the mayor was hanged and beheaded, and the city lost its charter, which was not restored till 1609.

An ancient historian, Ralph Holinshed, whose works were published in 1577, thus describes this city. "On the land side they are encumbered with evil neighbors—the Irish outlaws, that they are fein to watch their gates hourlie, to keep them shut at service time, and at meales, from sun to sun, nor suffer anie stranger to enter the citie with his weapon, but the same to leave at a lodge appointed. They walk out at seasons for recreation with power of men furnished. They trust not the country adjoining, but match in wedlock among themselves onlie, so that the whole citie is well-nigh linked one to the other in affinite."

In the War of the Protectorate, Cork maintained its condition as a loyal city till 1649, when it was surprised and taken by Cromwell, whose acts and cruelties are well known the civilized world over.

CHAPTER II.

BLARNEY—KILLARNEY—THE LAKES.

At 9 A. M. Tuesday, April 23, we took a jaunting-car for famed Blarney Castle. Before proceeding with our story we must speak of our team, for it is the mode of conveyance for tourists over the Emerald Isle, and Ireland would hardly seem like Ireland without the jaunting-car. It is a vehicle with two wheels and a single horse. The driver is mounted up, sulky-style, in front. There are two seats, lengthwise and back-to-back, for a couple of adult persons, facing outwards, and most of the time *holding on*, though a little practice convinces one that the danger of falling is less than anticipated. Large numbers of these teams are in the main streets of all the principal Irish towns, waiting for employment. The usual price for a jaunt is eight shillings, or about $2.00 of American money. The one selected, whose driver was over anxious to carry the two Amirikins, as he called us, offered to do the job for 7*s.* 6*d.* Yankee-like, having made a good bargain,—and the driver, unyankee-like, having as at an auction bid against himself,—we mounted, and were soon on our way to the place so renowned in history. First, we will consider the roads.

The ride is exceedingly pleasant, and over one of the smooth and hard roads which are everywhere to be found in Ireland. We go out of Cork southwardly, and pass through a small and not over-nice settlement called Black Pool, by no means inaptly named. The scenery is very pleasing, and so is the road we travel. The view on the north side of the river, though not wild or romantic, has beautiful landscapes, made up of fine hills and valleys, streams and groves, with, now and then, unlooked-for ruins of a monastery or small castle, or of distant round-towers.

There are no long straight roads, but there is an ever varying aspect, and the ways are clean to a fault. It is a characteristic of Ireland, England, and nearly all European countries, to have well-built faced-stone walls along the roadside, and an entire absence of the random weeds and bushes which so commonly grow along the walls and sides of the roads in America. It is a disgrace to our Young American civilization that it should be an exception, where the sides of our roads, and especially in the vicinity of farmhouses, are clean, and in lawn-like condition, as is always the case abroad. We have much to learn from Ireland,—a deal of our practice to unlearn, and considerable to do,—before we can compare favorably with Europe in this respect. A waste of acres exists in consequence of this neglect on nearly all New England farms. In the aggregate there are hundreds of thousands of acres which, if kept clean and cultivated for grass, would be profitable. Even if done at the town's expense, the income would go far towards paying the cost of keeping in repair the adjoining highway. The State should pass a law making this neglect a finable offence; and the sooner all States do this the better our civilization will be.

We continue on our way enjoying inexpressibly the exhilarating air and sunny, May-like day, and entertained somewhat by the clack of the driver, who, as best he can, tries to make his old story appear to us as new as possible, but, in spite of our or his efforts, we get the impression that he has told that story before.

We next get a good but distant view of Carrigrohan Castle, belonging to one Mr. McSwiney—the name of both castle and owner Irish enough. It is situated on a precipitous limestone-rock formation on the opposite bank of the river. At length—one hour passed, and about four miles traversed—we arrive at the old, dirty, low, dilapidated, Irish town of Blarney, which, for situation and surroundings, is as beautiful as every place in Ireland can't help being. Blarney has been immortalized in song by Millikin, Croker, and old, peculiar Father Prout.

A ride of two miles, and we are at the grounds of the castle itself. It was built in the fifteenth century by Cormac McCarthy, or possibly by the Countess of Desmond, and became the home of the famous family of McCarthys. It is now a magnificent old ruin, well situated near a little lake, and surrounded by grand old trees. Admission to the premises is readily gained, as the grounds are open to the public free, such small, optional fee being given to the guide as the tourist may incline to present.

The castle consists mainly of the massive Donjon Tower, about forty feet square, and one hundred and ten feet high, and some ruined walls of less height, once part of adjoining apartments. Much of the tower and lower walls is completely covered with ivy, and most of the foliage is from twelve to sixteen inches thick. There is a picturesqueness about such a place that is indescribable. The grand and colossal scale on which it is constructed; the rich greenness of the lawns; the shade of portions of the immediately adjoining groves; the sombre hue of the stonework, and the dark green of the mantling ivy; the gleam of the little lake as discovered through the vistas; the age of the edifice, so apparent; the consciousness that this is a veritable ruin, and what is left of an unparalleled splendor of other days, now calm as if resting fixed in its immortality,—these combine to resolve imagination into reality, and produce sensations that are felt, but never transferred from one mortal to another. Perhaps there enters into emotion a suggestion of decline and decay still operating. "The vulgar crowd," as old English expression would put it, are possessed not by the finer æsthetic conditions, but by those more tangible and material.

The famed Blarney Stone is one of the coping-stones of the outside projecting cornice, near the top of the tower, and resting on large, but plain, stone corbels, or brackets. In appearance from the ground, it is six feet long and eighteen inches thick, and projects two feet or so. Many years ago it appeared to be insecure, and two iron bars were put on the outside, securing it in its position. There are courses of stone upon it, falling back from the front surface, and making a parapet to the tower. It was over this parapet that persons, head downwards, held and aided by others, performed the task of kissing the stone. A stairway on the inside leads nearly to the top of the tower; but now, for a more convenient and safe way of performing the operation, another stone, bearing date 1703, is kept within the tower. Its magic is as effectual, while it is reached with comparative safety.

It is indeed marvellous that a few lines of worse than doggerel poetry have materially aided in giving this stone a notoriety that is world-wide, and which, but for this aid, would hardly have been heard of outside of its neighborhood. It was long a superstitious belief that whoever kissed it would ever after be in possession of such sweet, persuasive, and convincing eloquence as to put the listener entirely under the control of the speaker. Rev. Father Prout's allusion to the stone is in part as follows:—

There is a stone there that whoever kisses,
Oh! he never misses to grow eloquent;

'Tis he may clamber to a lady's chamber,
Or become a member of Parliament.

A clever spouter he'll sure turn out, or
An out and outer, to be let alone!

Don't hope to hinder him or to bewilder him,
Sure he's a pilgrim from the Blarney Stone.

The grounds by which the castle are surrounded were once adorned with statues, bridges, grottos, but all are now gone, and Father Prout deplores the condition as follows:—

The muses shed a tear,
When the cruel auctioneer,

With his hammer in his hand to sweet Blarney came.

Blarney Lake is a beautiful piece of water, set in a charming framework of trees and natural shrubbery, and is about five minutes' walk from the castle. Tradition, handed down through many generations, has it that at certain seasons a herd of white cows come up from the centre of the lake, look admiringly but with a melancholy pleasure on the ruined castle, for a few moments' graze on the lawns near it, and then with a soldierly march retire to their oblivion-like resting-place, there to remain till the time comes next year for their weird and fairy-like visit. Another legend is—and this country abounds with them—that the Earl of Chantry having forfeited the castle, and having had it confiscated and ruined at the Revolution, carried his plate and deposited it in a particular part of the lake, and that three McCarthys, and they only, are in possession of the secret of the place where it was cast in. When either of the three dies, he communicates the intelligence to some other member of the family, and thus the secret is kept, never to be publicly revealed till a McCarthy is again Lord of Blarney.

Within the castle grounds runs the small River Coman, and on its banks is an old Cromlech, or druidical altar; and there are also a number of pillar-stones, similar to those at Stonehenge, on which are worn inscriptions of ancient Ogham characters.

Differing as the place did from anything yet seen by us, and our anticipations more than fulfilled, we, after a two hours' sojourn, reluctantly mounted the jaunting-car and took our way back to Cork. After dining at the Victoria, at half-past three of this same day, we took steam-cars for the town of Killarney; and here we must speak of the railroads.

As this was our first experience in travelling on one of them, we may with propriety say something of them once for all; for one statement applies to railroads, not only in Ireland, England, and Scotland, but in all those parts of Europe where we have travelled. Solid are the roadbeds, not troubled by frosts as ours are. Stone or iron are the bridges, and of the most durable kind, often with brick abutments and arches. Of course, at times, there are the bridges for common roads that pass over them. The substantial tunnels are sometimes miles long. There are well-made grass enbankments, nicely kept. The stations are quite good and cleanly, and there is invariably an exquisite neatness about the outside, where flower-patches and borders are carefully cultivated. The restaurants are poor and uninviting. Especially is this description true of England. Large and strong engines, on which is an absence of superfluous decorations of brass, or costly-to-keep-clean finish, are universal. The cars, as we say, but *coaches* as they term them, are of three classes, first, second, and third. The best of them are undesirable to Americans, but submitted to in the absence of those with which they are familiar.

Prices for travel vary. That of first-class is slightly more per mile than in ours. The second-class is something less, or, on an average, two thirds the cost of ours. Two cents per mile is the usual tariff. Perhaps one quarter of the people ride first-class, and the remainder are about equally divided between the second and third. The first-class are what we may describe as from four to six common mail-stages, built together as one, but wide enough for five persons on each seat. There is a door in the middle, opening on the platforms, and of course half of the passengers must ride backward. This is true also of the other classes, with slight exceptions in some of the cars of Switzerland; and even these, at their best, make an American homesick, and sigh for those of his native land. A light, or window, in the doors, and a small one at the end of each seat, is the universal rule. Second and third-class cars are nearly alike, save perhaps that there are cushions in the former, while there are none in the latter; though by no means does the purchase of a second-class ticket ensure cushions. The cars of these classes are straight-sided, like our freight cars, with side doors and small windows like those of the first-class. There are no fires, poor lights for night travel; no toilet saloons, nor any conveniences as in ours. Once in, the door is shut by an official, and usually locked till we land at the next station. In the cars of the first two classes the partitions extend from floor to roof, with seats against both sides; but in a few of the third-class there is simply a wide rail for resting the back, or a partition of the same height. When we saw any of these, though having it may be a second-class ticket, we would, to be as homelike as possible, avail ourselves of them. One does not object to second-class passage; and even the third is far from being as questionable as at first thought, to one unused to travelling, it might seem. It is generally the intensely aristocratic class, of the *noli-me-tangere* kind, who ride first-class,— or Americans inexperienced in travel.

Officials are at all stations in abundance. They are ready cheerfully—but in their own way, to be sure—to give any information a traveller may require. In all parts of the Continent over which we journeyed, we had no special trouble in understanding them, or in making them understand us. So many English and Americans travel that the employees soon learn how to reply to the usual questions put to them. A little knowledge, however, of German and of French—as much as applies to common things, and as may with a little exertion be learned from most of the guide-books—helps the tourist amazingly. As regards the time made by these railroads, we rode on some of them faster than on ours at home, and are justified in saying that their promptness of arrival at stations is incredible. The roads with which we are conversant are in advance of ours in this respect. In but one instance did we find a train late; and waiting at junctions for other trains was apparently unknown. The conductors are expected to run their trains on time, and they do so unless prevented by accidents. We have been thus minute in stating the facts, as they are sure to be of interest to persons contemplating a journey.

And now we pursue our way, having left Cork at 3 o'clock P. M., towards Killarney and its famed lakes, which to us have all the charms of the best Castles in the Air; for who that has thought of the famous Lakes of Killarney has not fancied something good enough for a place in the neighborhood of

Eden in its palmy days? Tickets in first-class cars cost us $2.25 each. After a ride of two hours we arrive at Mallow, and after three hours more, at Killarney. The first look of the town indicates a village well shaded with trees, and one is led to anticipate anything but the reality.

The houses are built in the usual Irish style,—that is, they are of plastered and whitewashed stone, and the roofs are thatched. Generally they are not over one story in height, and a low story at that. They stand on crooked and narrow streets—or alleys, rather. There is an absence of cleanliness, and little to sustain distant impressions. One of the things that early attract the tourist's attention is the general poverty of many of the inhabitants, their lack of employment and visible means of support. Beggars are bold and used to their calling; and both they and the swarm of would-be guides are annoying if treated with common civility. There is an ancient look about buildings and people, and we get the suggestion that we see things as they were a century ago. Nothing is new and fresh but the foliage. Everything has the old odor of an ancient place.

The town has a population of 5,187, exclusive of 400 inmates of the almshouse—one to every thirteen of the population. Killarney is situated about a mile and a half from the nearest of the three lakes. There are two or three streets of some pretensions, on which are buildings three or four stories high, used as stores and hotels. Our hotel, the Innisfallen House, was kept, as all such small taverns are, by a woman. It was a thoroughly antiquated Irish institution, and for this reason we selected it. Experienced by long years of practice, our hostess was the *man* of the house, and had an eye to business that would do honor to the manager of the Vendome or the Brunswick at Boston.

There are few public buildings. The newish Roman Catholic Cathedral is a large structure of limestone, of good early English architecture, built from designs by Pugin. It is hardly in keeping with the town as it is, and only the eye of faith can see its harmony with the Killarney of the future.

Here may be related an incident illustrating a custom which is doubtless a relic of other days. After our visit to the cathedral, at about 7 P. M., we were surprised by the sight of a peculiar crowd of people coming up the street we had entered. It was a procession, numbering some hundred or more, carrying a coffin to the cathedral. The coffin was oaken, moulded at the top and bottom edges with black, and having three ornamental, black, iron plates— eight inches square, with rings in them—on each side. Black, round-headed nails ornamented the ends. The coffin was not covered, and rested on the shoulders of six men, three on each side. As by magic, three bearers would occasionally step out, and others take their places. Back of those who headed the procession were two rows of women, from fifty to seventy years old, with black dresses, and shawls over their heads. These were howling, two or more at a time keeping up the noise; and thus, without break or intermission, there was a continued wailing, in syllables of a slow but measured and distinct utterance, sounding like "Ar-ter-*ow*-ow-*ow*-er." This was repeated till the perfection of monotony was attained.

When near the cathedral the procession halted and the wailing ceased. The crowd numbered, it may be, a hundred. Arriving at the side door the coffin was carried in, and about twenty persons, probably the near relatives, entered. The remainder, including the Americans,—who, now "being in Turkey, were doing as the Turkeys do,"—remained outside, and stood or knelt uncovered. In a few moments all was ended; the friends came out of the cathedral, the crowd dispersed, and "rag, tag, and bobtail" resumed their usual vocations, the dead man having been left in the building, with the approved and requisite number of candles "to light him to glory."

Turning into another street, another and similar crowd was encountered. This time the coffin was covered with black cloth, but decorated like the other, with mouldings, nails, and iron plates. In five minutes more came another. We were told the bodies were to remain in the cathedral till tomorrow, when mass could be held and they would be buried. This is a custom of the place each evening, and has been continued from time immemorial. It results from bad judgment as to what is a good use of the present, or what is a befitting preparation for the hereafter. It is a type of superstition gone to seed, and shows a love for sitting in "the region and shadow of death."

Now we ramble over the town, and through some of the well-kept and stone-walled roads. In spite of the condition of the most populous parts, there is a delight and charm in these suburbs. In that pleasant evening air, within sound of the vesper bells, enveloped in the general stillness of that village atmosphere, there came good and vivid impressions of the antiquity of the place. Without an effort came the remembrance that, through the past centuries, thousands and tens of thousands of sight-seers, poets, historians, and people of great and of small renown, had walked these streets, meditated, used the time as we were doing, and passed on,—their feet never to press this historic soil again,—

Like the snow-fall in the river,
A moment white, then melts forever.

The next morning we took a jaunting-car, and began our tour of the lakes. A most elegant day it was, like good old George Herbert's Sunday—the "bridal of the earth and sky." Admirable in all respects were the roads and their surroundings,—a perpetual reminder of worse kept ones at home. We pass an elegant stone building, the Union Workhouse and County Lunatic Asylum, on the right, leaving the cathedral on our left, and ride on through that lovely scenery. It is not wild or romantic, in the common signification of those words.

On our right, off in the fields and on elevated ground, are the ruins of Aghadoe, overlooking an immense valley, where reposes—out of sight to us at our left, Lough Leane, the lower and largest of the three celebrated lakes.

Next, three miles out, are the ruins of Aghadoe castle and church. All that remains are the fragments of a tower thirty or forty feet in height. Of its history, or the date of its foundation, no records are extant. The church is a fine ruin, and shows the remains of a long low building, consisting of two chapels, joined at their rear ends. The easterly chapel is in the Gothic style, bearing date A. D. 1158, and is dedicated to the Holy Trinity. Full seven hundred years are gone, more than a third of the Christian era, since that stone pile was placed where it is. The other chapel is older yet, of a rude, Romanesque architecture, and was built under the patronage of St. Finian. The two are separated by a solid wall, through which there was once a communication, closed up long before the vacating and destruction of the building. The roof and woodwork being gone, nothing but stone remains. The two chapels, extending to the east and west, are eighty feet long and twenty feet wide.

Continuing our ride a mile farther, we turn to the left, and pass the Aghadoe House,—a fine and well-kept estate, the residence of the Dowager Lady Headley. Next, we turn sharp to the right, and are at the estate of James O'Connell, Esq., brother of the late distinguished agitator, Daniel O'Connell. Continuing, we pass the Killalee House, and the ruins of its church. Six and a half miles now from Killarney, we have on our left, the elegant estate of Beaufort House.

We cross the little River Laune, which is filled with surplus water from the small, or upper lake, and here appears to view Dunloe Castle, the seat of Daniel Mahoney, Esq. The building has a modern look, and was originally the residence of the powerful and noted O'Sullivan Mor. We must not fail to notice the Cave of Dunloe. It is situated in a field some distance off, is of great antiquity, and was discovered in 1838. It contains peculiar stones, which are presumed to belong to an ancient Irish library; and, strange to say, the books are the large stones composing the roof. Their angles contain the writings, which are simple, short, vertical lines, arranged, tally-like, above and below a horizontal one. Special numbers or combinations of these lines designate letters. It is the Ogham alphabet.

We are now near the cottage of the celebrated Kate Kearney, whom Moore has immortalized in his "Sweet Innisfallen,"—

"Kate Kearney,
Who lives on the banks of Killarney."

The house is solitary, and stands on the left of the roadside, with high hills about it. It is but one story high, and is some forty feet long, and twenty wide. It is made of stone, plastered and whitewashed, has a thatched roof, and is occupied by the reputed granddaughter of the famous Kate, and of course she bears the same name. On our arrival, she appeared at her door as usual—an old woman of sixty years, of small stature. She wore a short dress, heavy shoes, the inevitable kerchief, or miniature shawl, folded diamond-ways over her shoulders, and a frilled white muslin cap on her head. She held a mug in one hand, and a common wine bottle in the other, with glass tumbler to match. She poured out the goat's milk, and then naïvely, with an almost young-maidenly tone of voice, asked: "And will ye not have put into it a drop of the mountain dew?" We must, though total abstinence men, run a bit of risk now, to do all that curious tourists do, so we said Yes. A drop or two mingled with the milk, when the thought instantly came that at home the dew would have been so like whiskey that we couldn't convince ourselves it was not, and so we cried "Hold! Enough!" She held, and it *was* enough. A shilling was presented; but no, she had done business too long, and her distinguished grandmother before her, to be outgeneralled by Yankees, and so came a demand for more, which was refused. Her maiden-like demure condition changed, and we left, thinking discretion and valor were synonymous terms; and she, probably of the same opinion, retired to try her luck with the next comer that way.

And now we enter the Gap of Dunloe, one of the notable places of Ireland. It is a narrow, wild, and romantic mountain pass, between highlands known as Macgillicuddy's Reeks on the right, and Purple Mountain on the left. The length of the pass is about four miles, and the road is circuitous and hilly. At the side, and at times crossing it, is a narrow stream called the Loe, at as many places expanded into five small lakes, or pools. The mountain-sides are rocky and often precipitous, and the road is here and there little more than a cart-path, winding right and left romantically between these hills, from which echoes finely the sound of our voices, or the bugle blown or the musket fired by peasants for the tourists' amusement. The journey is one thrillingly interesting, and about the only one of the kind that can be made on the island.

One of the five lakes, each of which has a name, is called Black Lough; and it is in this—a basin some one hundred feet long and thirty feet wide, with walls of stone, partially filled with a dark water—that St. Patrick is said to have banished the last snake. The guides have the story at their tongue's end, and glibly relate it in a schoolboy-like fashion, never tripping, nor leading one to so much as surmise that they have not told the story before.

The team takes us but a short distance into the gap, and we avail ourselves of animals called horses, who are ever on hand for the purpose. The guides owning them have followed us for a mile or more, in spite of our protestations, acting as though they knew we should hire their beasts, although we had with business-like earnestness told them that we thought we would walk. These animals were of a doubtful nature, that would confuse Darwin. They were either high-grade mules with short ears, or low-grade horses with long ones. We finally agreed with the owners, paying fifty cents each for the *what-is-its*, the guides engaging to take the animals back when we were done with them.

Emerging from the gap we come out at the Black Valley stretching away to our left, and hemmed in, amphitheatre-like, by the base of the hills. The first view of this sombre moor reminds one of the heath-pictures in "Macbeth." Kohl says of it: "Had there been at the bottom, among the rugged masses of black rock, some smoke and flame instead of water, we might have imagined we were looking into the infernal regions." We ride down a winding road in the great amphitheatre, and along to its extremity, and are at the end of our journey with the horses; and now we are to walk a half-mile through a footpath, over fields and through pleasant groves, to the once fine garden and present ruins of Lord Brandon's Cottage. Here, we are at the upper lake; and our boatmen, by arrangement of the hostess at Innisfallen House, were there awaiting our arrival at 1 P. M. They had, as usual, gone direct from Killarney to the lower lake, and had rowed over that and the two others to this point, having made, in reversed order, the tour over the lakes we are to take.

At 1.30 P. M., Thursday, April 25, we are in the row-boat with our two oarsmen, starting from the shore of the upper lake which is the smallest of the three,—a sheet of water two and a half miles long, three fourths of a mile wide, and covering 430 acres, being about two thirds as large as the middle lake, and only a little more than a twelfth as large as the lower one. And here we must say, what of choice we would not say, that in most instances, where the imagination has free play, realities do not fulfil anticipations.

The fulsome and unqualified praises which have been bestowed on these really beautiful and justly celebrated lakes incline one to expect too much, and to overestimate their sublimity. This element, so ever present on the lakes of Scotland, is here often lacking. There is, however, a cleanliness in the remarkably irregular outline of their shores, and a beautiful decoration made by varying tinted and luxuriant vegetation, that largely compensates for a lack of vast boldness, and of great and precipitous rocky walls; and enough mountain views are in the near distance to give the scenery a majestic appearance, at times even grand in general effect. The heavy woodlands, with here and there a craggy cliff, as at the Eagle's Nest, combine to produce a charm not found about ordinary lakes. Yet it must in justice be said that our Lake George, and parts of Winnepiseogee, are their equals.

The upper lake, at its westerly end, contains twelve islands, which in the aggregate cover six acres,—none of them, however, containing more than one acre, and some of them less than a quarter of one. McCarthy's is the one first reached. Arbutus is another, and the largest in the lake. It takes its name from the shrub, *arbutus unendo*. The leaves are a glossy green, and so arranged at the ends of the branches, that the waxen, flesh-like blossoms, as they hang in graceful racemes, or the later crimson fruit, seem embraced by a mantle of the richest verdure. All the islands abound in ivy, and the rocks and trees are often thoroughly bedecked with it. This lake is surely the finest of the three, and is so mainly from the fact of its having these islands and the great irregularity of the shore, embellished by the beautiful accompanying foliage. Being more immediately in the vicinity of the highlands, it has much of stern mountain effect and grandeur. From some points of view this little sheet of water appears to be entirely land-locked. Towards the lower end it becomes narrow, and is only a strip of water half a mile long. This is called Newfoundland Bay. On from this it is a yet narrower stream, varying from thirty to one hundred feet wide, and two miles long, which is the connecting part with the middle lake. To add a fascination, and intensify the interest of the tourist, every rock of respectable dimensions, and every island or cove, has its high-sounding name; for we pass Coleman's Eye, the Man of War, the Four Friends. We now arrive at the Eagle's Nest, a craggy formation 700 feet above the water, in the rugged clefts of which the eagle builds its eyrie. The young birds are taken from the nest between the middle of June and the first of July, and the rocks are so precipitous that the nests are only reached by means of ropes let down from above.

The echoes from this and the surrounding rocks are very fine, and we hear them grandly repeated from hilltop to hilltop—ever continued, and passed on with a clearly perceptible interval, till, weaker and weaker by their long, rough travel, they grow fainter, and at last melt away in some unknown cavern, or, as it were, infinitely distant glen, and are lost in the great realm of nothingness from whence they came.

Continuing on, we reach a fairy-like place, the Meeting of Waters, where our river, arriving at the middle lake, glides to the left around the end of Dinish Island, which reaches from, and is bounded by, this and the lower lake. Now we are at the Old Weir Bridge, very antiquated,—consisting of two unequal arches, through which the water rushes with great earnestness and force. The boatmen do nothing but guide the boat, and it is a moment of intense interest to the novice, as we dash under one of the arches. Soon we are in the middle, or, as it is called, the Mucross, or Torc Lake.

This contains 680 acres, or forty more than a square mile. The principal islands are the Dinish and the Brickeen, and these are in fact the side and end walls, or the dividing barrier between it and the lower lake. There are three passages between them. This lake is oblong and narrow. In a line nearly straight we pass to the high, Gothic, single-arched bridge connecting it with the lower lake. Brickeen contains 19 acres, and is twenty or more feet up from the lake, and well wooded. Dinish is also well wooded. It contains 34 acres, and is a sort of watering-place. It has a small, rough, rustic stone wharf; also a cottage-hotel with pleasure-grounds; and by making previous arrangements dinner may be had.

Our provident hostess, having an eye to our comfort and another to her income, had sent by the boatmen a basket of luncheon, and so we dined on the lake itself, and not on the shore of it. Of the beauty of Torc Lake much may be said. It has a charm peculiarly its own. Shut in with a considerably uniform wall-work of islands, it is an immense pool of clear water, in which the overhanging shrubbery is finely reflected. Its air of repose and quiet beauty makes it of interest to persons of a retiring nature, and those to whom the vastness of mountain scenery does not so pleasantly appeal.

We now pass under the great Gothic arch of Brickeen Bridge, and are in Lough Leane, or the lower lake. It has an area of five thousand acres, being five miles long, and three wide, with a very irregular shore, comprising, high and low lands, coves and inlets, a few mountain recesses, and a great variety of pleasing scenery. Its islands are thirty in number, few of which, however, measure more than an acre in extent. The largest are Rabbit Island, of more than twelve acres, and Innisfallen, of twenty-one acres. Many of them have a fancied resemblance to particular things, and so are named Lamb, Elephant, Gun, Horse, Crow, Heron, Stag. The chief beauties of this great sheet of water are its generally placid surface, the mountains bordering it on the south and west, and its unlikeness to either of the others, in its low lands, and its estates stretching off to the north and east. It abounds in quiet nooks, bays, and inlets, breaking its margin; and the barren rocks on one side contrast finely with the verdure of the shore on the other.

Sir Walter Scott has given a magic charm to Loch Katrine by reciting its legends; but, had he been so disposed, he could have given a like halo to these lakes, for legends of O'Donoghue and of the McCarthys abound, and supply such romantic materials as few countries can boast. As a sample we quote but one:—

Once in seven years, on a fine morning, before the sun's rays have begun to disperse the mist from the bosom of the lake, O'Donoghue comes riding over it on an elegant snowwhite horse, with fairies hovering about him, and strewing his path with flowers. As he approaches his ancient residence, everything resolves itself into its original condition and magnificence; the castle itself, banquet halls, library, his prison, and his pigeon house, are as they were in the olden time. Any one who desires, and is courageous enough to follow him over the lake, may cross even the deepest parts dry-footed, and ride with him into the caves of the adjoining mountains, where his treasures are deposited and concealed; and the daring visitor will receive a liberal gift for his company and venture, but before the sun has arisen, and in the early twilight, O'Donoghue recrosses the water, and vanishes amid the ruins of the castle, to be seen no more till the next seven years have expired.

The part of the lake first entered is called Glena Bay, and as the opposite shore, some three miles away, is low, the distant surface of the lake seems to melt into the horizon, producing an effect not made by either of the other lakes. Here on the little bay's shore is the picturesque cottage of Lady Kenmare; and in the woods and highlands, which for a couple and more miles bound the western shore of the lake, are red deer, and the place was once a famous hunting-ground.

We pursue our course, not stopping at O'Sullivan's Cascade, a waterfall consisting of three sections, situated a short distance back in the forest; nor do we go over to Innisfallen Island, distant but two miles to our left and in full view, though it is remarkably interesting on account of historical associations.

Of all the islands of the lakes it is the most picturesque and beautiful. It contains glades and lawns, thickets of flowering shrubs and evergreens, with an abundance of arbutus and hollies of great size and beauty, and also oak and ash trees of magnificent foliage and growth. Innisfallen contains about twenty-one acres, and commands one of the most desirable and lovely views of the entire lake and surrounding mountain scenery. The most interesting object on it, however, is the grand ruin of the ancient abbey, founded in the year 600, by St. Finian.

In this celebrated place the strange and interesting "Annals of Innisfallen" were composed. They contain fragments of the Old Testament, and a compendious, though not very valuable, annual history down to the time of St. Patrick, and one more perfect from the fourth to the fourteenth century. The originals, written more than five hundred years ago, are now in the Bodleian Library at Oxford. A translation of this work has been repeatedly attempted, but has never been far enough advanced to issue from the press. The Annals are a special record of Munster, but are filled with a dry record of great crimes and their punishment, wars, lists of princes and clergy, and elaborate accounts of the disputes and violent deaths of the ancient kings of

Kerry. They record that in 1180, seven hundred years ago, the abbey was the place of securest deposit for all the gold and silver, and the rare and rich goods of the country; that it was plundered by Mildwin, son of Daniel O'Donoghue, as was also the church of Ardfert; and that many persons were slain in the cemetery of the McCarthys.

In parting, the temptation is resistless to quote the lines of Moore relating to this renowned and beautiful place:—

Sweet Innisfallen, fare thee well,
May calm and sunshine long be thine;
How fair thou art, let others tell,
While but to *feel* how fair be mine.

Sweet Innisfallen, long shall dwell
In memory's dream that sunny smile,
Which o'er thee, on that evening fell,
When first I saw thy fairy isle.

We next pass on towards our place of landing. Before us and not far off is Ross Island, situated on the eastern shore of the lake. It is not really an island, but a peninsula, which at times of high water, however, is difficult to reach without crossing a bridge. The place has a finished look, having good lawns and many well-kept avenues and walks. In 1804 a copper mine was opened on it, and for a time afforded a large quantity of rich ore. Croker asserts that during the four years it was worked, $400,000 worth of ore was disposed of at Swansea, at a valuation of $200 per ton, and he informs us that "several small veins of oxide of copper split off the main lode and ran towards the surface. The ore of these veins was much more valuable than the other, and consequently the miners—who were paid for the quality as well as quantity—opened the smaller veins so near the surface that water broke through into the mine, in such an overwhelming degree that an engine of thirty-horse power could make no impression on the inundation." The work was then abandoned. No doubt exists that these mines had been worked in times of antiquity, perhaps by the Danes; for while working them in 1804, rude stone hammers were found, and other unequivocal proofs of preoccupation at an early time.

Ross Castle is a commanding and conspicuous object, standing isolated near the shore, on comparatively level land. It is visible from almost every part of the lake. This castle is generally visited from the land, and is less than two miles from the town of Killarney. Though now in ruins, it has a massive square tower and appendages of considerable size, and is of pleasing outline. The dark stone walls are in good preservation, and well decorated with ivy, which gives the ruin a most stately, yet romantic and picturesque effect.

The grounds are well kept, and are free to the public; though a small optional fee is in order to the lass who comes out of her cottage near by, unlocks the door of the great tower, and, with a tongue not very glib, tells what little she knows of local history. The castle was built by the O'Donoghues, and was long occupied by that celebrated family. In 1652 it was well defended; at the Revolution it held out long against the English invaders, and was the last one in Munster to surrender. On the 26th of July of that year Lord Muskerry, then holding a commission of colonel under the Irish, being hard pushed, occupied the castle, and defended himself against Lord Ludlow; and it was not until he brought vessels of war (in history called *ships*) by the lake, that the surrender was made. An old legend existed,—and legends are powerful for good or for ill,—that Ross Castle was impregnable till ships of war attacked it. These were brought, it may be, to take advantage of the superstition. When they were in view, the heart of the inmates of the fortress failed; they were paralyzed with superstitious fear, and could not be induced to strike another blow. Lord Ludlow, in his Memoirs, thus tells the story:—

We had received our boats [these were probably the *ships*], each of which was capable of containing one hundred and twenty men. I ordered one of them to be rowed about the water, in order to find out the most convenient place for landing upon the enemy, which they perceiving, thought fit, by timely submission, to prevent the danger threatened them.

After the surrender five thousand Munster men laid down their arms, and Lord Broghill, who had accompanied Ludlow, received a grant of £1,000 ($5,000) yearly out of the estate of Lord Muskerry, the defender of the castle.

We have ended our tour over the lakes, and have visited these justly celebrated ruins, and are now ready for a walk of three quarters of an hour to our hotel at Killarney. To say that we enjoyed the day, even beyond our most sanguine anticipations, would not overcolor the picture. The drive of the morning through that sublime old scenery, to us so new; the ever fresh and pleasing emotions continually awakened; the romantic ride through the Gap of Dunloe, where the mountains are so near us, and we so near them; Kate's cottage; the Inferno-like look of the Black Valley; the walk to the upper lake, and the fairy-like sail over its waters,—all these recollections are enough for one day. At 6 P. M., as the sun declined, and the mellow tints of its evening rays were thrown aslant the waters, we wended our way home. Yet were we not entirely content, but must make one more tour, this time to Muckross Abbey.

CHAPTER III.

MUCKROSS ABBEY—LIMERICK—DUBLIN.

The time for visiting Muckross Abbey is most auspicious, the sun being still above the horizon; and the approaching tranquillity befits a trip of the kind. The ruins we have before inspected have been castles, or fort-like structures, designed as a home for some royal family, yet sufficiently strong and impregnable to ward off the attacks of a formidable enemy. What we are now to see is not a place designed for ease, comfort, and defence against ill conditions in this life, but rather to ensure pleasure and safety in the life to come.

The spot is about five miles from Killarney, and owned by Mr. Herbert, a gentleman held in the highest esteem by rich and poor. There is a neat gate-lodge, beyond which the visitor finds gratuitous admission at any hour before 6 P. M.; after that, and properly enough, a shilling is due to the gatekeeper. Our team left outside the gate, we pass through a grand avenue, and soon opens to view one of the finest and most enchanting mediæval ruins to be found in Ireland,—exquisitely interesting in every part, and beyond the power of any one to adequately describe. The ruins are on a large knoll, surrounded by trees, conspicuous among which is the yew. These trees are formed much like large cedars, and resemble them in general outline; but the foliage is dark-green, so dark as at first sight to appear almost black. The branches are very large, and spread out into flat or fanlike masses, to near the ground.

The abbey was founded in 1140, and is now 742 years old. As we examine it, and more especially an ancient yew-tree, surrounded by the cloisters, known to have been there for more than 600 years, we are deeply impressed with the thought that we are communing with things relating to long past generations. It had its last repairs in 1602, was soon after abandoned, and is now without a roof, but is otherwise in good preservation. The ruins are very large and varied. They consist of both an abbey and a church. The cloisters belong to the former, and form a stone colonnade, some ten feet wide, connected by the arches with the open-to-the-sky area, some seventy-five feet square, in the centre of which stands the venerable yew already mentioned.

In the retirement and obscurity of these cloisters, walked and meditated and prayed hundreds,—and in the large aggregate of years it may be thousands,—to whom no other spot on the broad earth was, in their judgment, so good and befitting for their pious purpose. Here for centuries piety intensified, was transformed into superstition, germinated, blossomed, and fruited.

The different rooms of the abbey are still in good preservation, the entire structure being of masonry. The kitchen, with its immense fireplace, appears as it was centuries ago; and a little room about six feet square in one of the towers, and opening out of the kitchen, was occupied for eleven years as a sleeping-room by the hermit, John Drake, a hundred or more years ago. His patriarchal demeanor and solemn yet cheerful aspect obtained for him a people's veneration, and his piety and general seclusion excited general interest. To this day he is spoken of with scarcely less esteem than would be one of the early monks of the abbey itself. The floors of the rooms in the second story, the building being roofless, are well overgrown with the finest lawn grass. As one walks thoughtfully up the narrow, winding, stone stairs, into the dormitory, hospital, lavatory and other apartments,—in all but few in number,—the solid and venerable walls, the open sky above him, and the green grass (emblematic of human life in its best estate) beneath his feet,—under the influence of these, in spite of himself he becomes absorbed in meditation, and holds communion with those who lived and labored here centuries ago, and at length passed on to "the house appointed for all the living."

Reluctantly we left the abbey, and walked through the antique passage-ways and cramped stone stairway down into the church, where, in the midst of singular beauty, were the unwelcome evidences of inevitable decay. Here are the roofless walls of the nave, choir, and transept; here are windows elegant in design, with their stone traceries yet perfect. In places, the friendly, sombre ivy is spread, like a kind mantle of charity, covering defects of broken wall, and disguising the empty place of some fallen stone.

"How old all material is," we instinctively say; and yet how new the results of labor,—the vine, the shrub, the tree. How velvety and carpet-like is the grass on parts of this very floor, once pressed by the toil-worn, blistered feet of pious penance-doers, and even now a place of deposit for their mouldering bodies. Instead of desk or altar or font, of kingly stall or peasant's seat, are ancient mural stones. Here are monuments, the outward tokens of reverence and respect for the blue blood of royalty, or the saintship of those who hundreds of years ago—their work done, the checkered scenes of life over—went down to the "silent mansions of the dead."

In the piscina, in the lavatory, in the place for sacred vessels, the swallow unscared builds its nest; and along the altar-steps the lizard crawls, or basks in the sunshine unalarmed. Here sleep in their low, common—and yet *uncommon*—resting-places, they of the old dispensation, side by side with men of the new. O'Sullivan, O'Donohue, Mc'Carthy—nobles and kings of Munster, before whom the multitude trembled and reverentially bowed—mingle their dust with nineteenth-century leaders.

An incident, showing a notable instance of faithfulness in the performance of an agreement, may be related. At the time of the surrender of these ruins, it was stipulated that, in consideration of the fact of their being the repository of dust so peculiar and sacred, no Protestant should ever be buried within these walls; and while it would otherwise have been the choice of the late owner of the premises—Mr. Herbert the elder, Member of Parliament for Kerry and Chief Secretary of Ireland—to be here buried, this was not done. On elevated grounds outside the abbey precincts, a very large, ornamental, mediæval, granite cross was erected by subscription of both Catholics and Protestants as a mark of love and esteem for him whom they call "One of the best of men."

Muckross Abbey Mansion, not far away, the seat of H. A. Herbert, Esq., the present owner of the grounds, is a fine stone building, of Elizabethan architecture. We knew of the Torc Cascade not far off; but as darkness had imperceptibly come upon us, and we were informed that little water was then passing over the fall, we did not go there, but listened to a description from our guide, who told us that the waters are precipitated in a sheet of splendid foam over a ledge of rocks, breaking into mist and spray; that the volume of water then resumes its hurried course through a deep ravine, narrow and irregular, through groups of fir and pine trees, and at last crosses the beautiful pleasure-grounds, till it falls into Muckross Lake.

At no time shall we probably have a more appropriate place to speak of the mountains of Ireland; and, at the risk of being charged with digression, we make the venture. Ireland is not a prairie-like country; yet, though for the most parts hilly and undulatory, it cannot be called mountainous. In this vicinity are the principal mountains of the Emerald Isle. It was for a long time thought that Mangerton, of the Macgillicuddy's Reeks, was the highest peak in Ireland, but a late survey makes Carrantual, of the same range, the highest. They are respectively 2,756 and 3,414 feet high. For the aid of those who may not be able to judge heights readily, yet are familiar with our New England mountains, we will say that the Grand Monadnock, at Jaffrey, N. H., is 3,186 feet high, and the Wachusett, at Princeton, Mass., 2,018 feet. The distance from Muckross to the summit of Carrantual is not far from five miles. The ascent is easy, and may be made with horses. Four miles from Muckross is what is called the Devil's Punch Bowl, a tarn or mountain lake, 2,206 feet above the level of the sea, and more than two thousand feet above the surface of the lakes, they being not far from two hundred feet above sea-level. It is an ovalish basin containing about twenty-eight acres, being two thirds the size of Boston Common, the latter having within its fence lines an area of a few feet over forty-three and three fourths acres. On all sides of the tarn are shelving cliffs. History has it that C. J. Fox swam entirely around it in 1772. Purple Mountain, opposite Macgillicuddy's Reeks, with the Gap of

Dunloe between, is somewhat lower than these, but we have not the figures of its elevation. After our visit to the abbey, we returned to the hotel—in name only, Innisfallen—and remained over night. Having breakfasted, valise in hand we wended our way back through the village streets to the railroad station, and took passage to Limerick.

"And sure," says the reader, "that is another Irish city, and no mistake," and you are right. Our ride was exceedingly pleasant. The country was at its best, so far as vegetation was concerned,—especially its grass, for cattle-raising is the general farm occupation of the people. Here and there was a patch of potatoes, but no fruit-trees, and few good vegetable gardens. There were no stone walls or fences; if there were any land divisions they were hedges, and few at that.

The more one travels in foreign countries, the more he is convinced of the folly of so much fence-work as we have on New England farms. It is a waste of labor and material, an abuse of the ground itself, and a loss of the land, usually uncultivated, lying close against the partitions; and, in addition, the shade is objectionable. Of course some divisions are needed; but many of them exist, as a necessity, only in the farmer's imagination. There are but few New England farms where a large amount of labor and time are not worse than wasted in repairs of cross walls, set up by our fathers and grandfathers, which would be used to a much better purpose if employed in their demolition.

LIMERICK.

After a ride of five hours, having on the way passed back through Mallow, we arrived in Limerick, where we took rooms at the Royal George Hotel. Valises deposited, and the usual toilet operations gone through with, we walk out to see this place, so like Cork and Dublin. Limerick is the capital of the county of Limerick. It is on a narrow arm of the sea, or mouth of the River Shannon, with a population of 49,670. It consists of an English town, built on an island of the Shannon, and also an Irish one; and it has a suburb called Newton Perry, on the left bank of the river. These three portions are connected by five bridges, one of which, the Wellesley Bridge, cost $425,000.

We were pleasantly surprised with the appearance of the place, with the cleanness of the streets, and their good pavements, and the general order and substantial condition of all we saw. We speak now of the English portion, which is in fact the larger and principal division of the place. The surface is level, and the buildings are mostly of dark-colored brick. They are generally three or four stories high, without decoration, save simple brick cornices and arched doorways to the houses. There are solid and plainly finished fronts to the stores. The streets are of strikingly uniform appearance, presenting only here and there anything to attract notice. It has its slums like Cork; but of these we need not speak now.

We next begin our walk to the cathedral, for this was the first of the cathedrals we had reached. The greater part of the edifice, as it now stands, was built during the twelfth and thirteenth centuries, and so is six hundred years old. We readily found it, and came to one of the iron gates leading to the burial-ground in front of it. The dark and antiquated look of the old, massive structure impressed us favorably, and touched the right chord. We had seen castles and abbeys in fine ruin, but they belonged to a dead past. We were hungering for something ancient in which the living present was playing its part, and nothing feeds this hunger so well as a cathedral, especially those that, at the Reformation, passed over from Catholicism to Protestantism, as this has done.

After demonstrations at the iron gate the verger soon appeared, coming from the cathedral tower some hundred or more feet away. This burial-ground is the principal way of access to the cathedral, and has good walks from the gates to the edifice. The entire ground, perhaps a half-acre in extent, is neat and well kept, and has many ancient-looking gravestones and low slab-monuments. Our verger was a portly man of some sixty years, a master of the situation. An adept at the business, he soon understood our case and our nationality, and we thought we understood him. Both parties being in good humor and knowing their business, we proceeded from point to point over the edifice, he all the time trying to earn his fee of a shilling each, and we aiding him as best we could, by seeming to pay respectful attention, yet doing as much thinking outside of his thoughts as we chose, and in our own way.

The cathedral is large and imposing to view from the outside, irregular in outline, and antique-looking in the extreme. It is built of a dark-dinged, brownish colored stone, and is of Gothic architecture. It has a tower one hundred and twenty feet high, but no spire above it. At the time of our visit the building was under process of extensive restorations of the interior.

There are many ancient monuments in the various parts of the building, some of them centuries old. It would be interesting to allude freely to them, but our limits will not permit. One illustration must suffice, and that is quoted for its simplicity and quaintness. It was read off by our guide with a promptness and precision, both of words and declamation, that suggested familiarity, and that we were by no means the first who had heard it.

MEMENTO MORY

HERE LIETH LITTELL SAMVELL
BARINGTON THAT GREAT VNDER

TAKER OF FAMIOVS CITTIS
CLOCK AND CHIMS MAKER
HE MADE HIS ONE TIME GOE
ERLY AND LATTER BVT NOW
HE IS RETVRNED TO GOD HIS CREATOR
THE 19 OF NOVEMBER THEN HE
SCEST AND TO HIS MEMORY
THIS HERE IS PLEAST BY HIS
SON BEN 1693.

After a good examination of the venerable edifice and its appendages below, we ascended the tower, our verger accompanying,—for which an extra shilling each must be paid. From here we had an admirable view of the city; but nothing seen from above, or inside the cathedral below, interested us more than the chime of bells in the tower. Wherever the English language is spoken, these bells receive honorable mention, for it is these to which reference is made in that plaintive but sweet poetry,—and who has not sympathized with its sentiment?—

"Those evening bells, those evening bells,
How many a tale their music tells."

There are eight of them, each hung with a wheel to aid its ringing. Four of them are old, and the others comparatively new. The largest weighs about three thousand pounds.

Having said something in regard to the business part of the city and cathedral, we next take a look at other parts of the former, and consider a few items of history. Newton Perry, the new section, contains wide streets and promenades, and on these are fine residences of wealthy inhabitants, many of whom are merchants doing business in the city proper, which we will now speak of. George Street, a grand thoroughfare, continues on one side through Richmond Place to the Military Walk, and on the other along Patrick Street, through Rutland Street, to Matthew Bridge—named in honor of Father Matthew, the apostle of Temperance. Henry and Catherine streets are also important. In Perry Square is a column surmounted by a statue to Lord Monteagle, and in Richmond Place there is a bronze statue of Daniel O'Connell. St. John's Cathedral, Roman Catholic, completed in 1860, is a Gothic edifice, erected at a cost of $85,000.

The principal industries of the place are the manufacture of flax, army-clothing, lace, and gloves. The city carries on an extensive traffic, and, having hundreds of well-stocked stores, it is the wholesale as well as retail market for towns of the vicinity. There is at the border of the city the remains of a castle built in the time of King John, a somewhat dilapidated, but still noble structure. It has seven massive towers, which are connected by a wall of great thickness, and affords an example of the best Norman strongholds of the country, if not of the world, and inside the castle walls are buildings used as barracks.

The castle is situated in the Irish part of the city. Here are narrow and unclean streets, and a low grade of population, many of whom live in destitution; though, so far as degradation is concerned, we found less than in Cork. What struck us forcibly in this section was the number of buildings—one or two, and even three stories high—dilapidated, abandoned, and without roofs. They were the rule and not the exception. There seemed to be a dislike on the part of owners to take down an old house; but when, in the last extremity, it became absolutely unfit for a day's more occupancy, they preferred to abandon it, and let it tumble down piecemeal. On the floors, in holes in the walls, about the chimneys, weeds were growing, and especially the not inappropriately named snapdragon. Fine specimens of these, of all the usual colors, were in full bloom and growing luxuriantly.

Having spoken of the Irish and English parts of Ireland, an explanation may be in order. Soon after the union of the two countries at the beginning of the present century, English people of wealth and influence established themselves in the principal cities of Ireland. They built stores and dwelling-houses, and it is safe to say that now two thirds of each large city are occupied by English people, the Irish inhabitants remaining in their old quarters. This large preponderance of English influence and life gives to Ireland's large cities an English look, and it is only when one enters the Irish part that he feels he is not in an English town. This is notably true of Cork, Limerick, Dublin, and other southern cities; while Belfast and Londonderry, at the north, have had so much commerce and exchange of thought with Scotland as well as England, as almost to transform their citizens into English people.

In Limerick may be seen Norman walls and remains in abundance, some of them a thousand years old. The harbor is sufficiently capacious to accommodate a large amount of shipping, and extends a mile along the river, which has a breadth of four hundred and fifty feet, with here and there a semi-basin or dock.

Limerick was the last place of Ireland which surrendered to English rule, and only submitted to the Parliamentarians, under Ireton in 1651, after a determined resistance and gallant defence. During a siege in 1691 a large gun was planted on the top of the cathedral tower, and rendered most effectual service. "Muscular Christianity" was then at a premium. The old city has experienced and withstood many sieges, the last of which were those under Cromwell and William III. After several repulses, William, in 1691, offered advantageous terms to the besieged which were accepted by the troops then under the command of Sarsfield, Earl of Lucen, and the surrender was made to General De Ginkle. Part of the treaty was signed here, on a stone now called the Treaty Stone which, for safety and as a monument of interest, is now kept on a pedestal at the end of Thomond Bridge. The treaty guaranteed to Roman Catholics certain religious privileges and rights, and promised amnesty to all who took the oath of allegiance; but it was afterwards, to the disgrace of the victors, recklessly broken, especially in regard to the points first named, and to this day the place is called "the city of the broken treaty."

Limerick has from time immemorial been a military seat, and is now the headquarters of the southwest military district. Anciently it was the royal residence of the Irish kings.

There are within the limits of the city over twenty places of worship. It has many charitable and educational institutions, and much enterprise and business activity. Save the old and slummish portion, which is not of very great extent, and is under comparatively good control, it has a thoroughly English look, or, perhaps we may say, an old American look. We greatly enjoyed our visit, and were happily disappointed; for our minds were disabused of opinions we before erroneously entertained, and supposed to be true, concerning this famous city.

DUBLIN.

At 1.30 P. M., on Friday, April 26, we left for Dublin, and after a ride of four hours reached that city. The landscape on the way was interesting, though not presenting anything very picturesque or romantic. We were, however, continually impressed with the fact that Ireland is well named the Emerald Isle; for not a bare acre is to be seen, and over hill and dale luxuriant vegetation is found.

We could but feel sorry that the laws of primogeniture and entailment of property yet prevail, and that England thus deprives herself and poor Ireland, her disconsolate child, of the rich blessings of an interested and land-loving, as well as soil-working people. The land is owned by a few lords. Estates must be kept entire, and so handed down through the male heirs from generation to generation. No absolute sale is possible, and a homestead can rarely be bought. The farm, be it little or great, cannot be owned by the tiller, but is held by the lord of the domain. An estate may not be divided among his descendants, but must pass to each successive heir in its entirety. It cannot be sold to those who would use it and improve its value. Without homesteads, with no prospect of anything but unsatisfying labor, with scarce the surety of earning a scanty subsistence,—there is, among the common people, a lack of interest in agricultural efforts. Thousands of laborers leave this land, the fairest on which God's impartial sun shines; few are left to care for the soil; and so, as the shortest cut across this field of deliberately created difficulty, nearly all the land is laid down to grass. In our ride of more than one hundred miles, hardly one fruit-tree was seen, or one nice garden. The country suffers for want of skilled yeomanry, to whom anticipation of ownership of the soil is "a cloud by day, and a pillar of fire by night," to pilot them out of the bondage they are in. The laws of justice and divine compensation are, however, at work, and change for the better is at hand; amendment after amendment, even now foreshadowed, will come, for He who ruleth over all will "turn and overturn," "till he whose right it is shall reign."

But to return to the Queen City of Ireland,—its greatest place socially and commercially speaking.

Dublin is finely situated at the head of Dublin Bay. It is built solidly, on comparatively level land, on both sides of the River Liffey, running from west to east. The city has a population of 242,722; including the adjoining suburb, 295,841. The river is navigable to Carlisle Bridge at the centre of the city, and from the mouth of the river up to the bridge it has good docks and wharves. Its commerce is varied and extensive. Unfortunately there was at the entrance of the harbor a sand-bar, on which, at low water, the depth varied from nine to twenty-four feet. This is now no great source of annoyance, as a portion of it has been removed, and large ships, taking advantage of the tides, may come up to the wharves.

A great part of the city is regularly built, having wide and well-paved streets, and magnificent stores and public buildings. They are of splendid architecture, and of every style and kind, from the classic Greek and Roman, to the elegant Renaissance, and from the Gothic of antiquity to the most refined of our own day. The latter, however, in its best estate,—save perhaps in its new grouping and combination of the best of the old ideas, with a rejection of the questionable features—is not much in advance of its original sources.

Like all large places, there is a slum where the people are poor and low; but in these respects Dublin is not the equal of Cork and some other parts of Southern Ireland.

As we go north towards Belfast and Londonderry we find an advance in what constitutes a higher and better civilization. The influence of the people of the North of England, and more especially of Scotland, has modified it. It may be said that where inflexible Episcopacy, acting on Catholicism, has prevailed, different results have come. While the good but ignorant Catholic has no affinity for Presbyterianism, he has a great respect for the industrious, well-appearing, just-dealing Scotchman, and he entertains an active suspicion in regard to the more formal Episcopalian, who has ruthlessly, as he thinks, appropriated the grand old churches where rest the bones of revered saints, and where his fathers worshipped for many generations. Some especial influence certainly has modified Northern Ireland's action, nature, and life. There is a deal more implied in the phrase North of Ireland, and in its antithesis, Far-downer, than appears to the casual observer. There is no city of Ireland where wealth and poverty are more contiguous, and where aristocracy and democracy are nearer neighbors, than at Dublin.

Nine bridges, two of which are iron, cross the river, and a magnificent avenue nine miles long, called the Circular Road, environs the city. The Bank of Ireland, near the college, is a low but very large building, and was once the House of Parliament. Trinity College opposite—and both are in the very centre of the most crowded business portion of the city—has fine stone buildings, with large and elegantly kept lawns, one opening into the other. The institution was founded by Pope John XXII., closed by Henry VIII., and reopened by Queen Elizabeth, who incorporated it in 1592.

Of the many public buildings, such as hospitals, museums, libraries, it is useless to speak. They are noble institutions, and worthy the capital of even England itself. It has a very large pleasure-ground called Phoenix Park, on the edge of the city. This park is well laid out, and is for Dublin what Central Park is for New York, or Fairmount for Philadelphia. There is in it one of the largest and most admirably kept zoölogical gardens of the world. Glasnevin Cemetery, their Mount Auburn or Greenwood, is an elegant city of the dead. Here repose the remains of Daniel O'Connell, under a high, round tower visible from all parts of the grounds. The profusion of sweet-scented lime-trees, and the taste and beauty of the scenery and artificial work, enable it to vie with any cemetery in Europe. In a city like Dublin, where there is so much that is good and great, one is tempted to enlarge the range of his thoughts, and is loth to leave the spot.

Before speaking of the Cathedral of St. Patrick, we will give a brief history of cathedral service itself. Till the time of Constantine, Christians were not allowed to erect temples. Early, churches meant only assemblies, not buildings; and by cathedrals were meant their consistories, or places of meeting. It was in 312 that this emperor first granted absolute toleration to Christians. In 325 the Council of Nice was convened, and made, under his sanction, an open declaration that Christianity be thereafter the recognized official religion of the land. The earliest record we have of a distinctive cathedral service is near the end of the fourth century; although there are traces of it at an earlier date, too indistinct to be reliable. St. Basil, at the close of the fourth century says:—

The people flocked to the churches before daylight, first to pray on bended knees, then rising to sing psalms, either in alternate chorus, or one chanting, others following in an under-voice; and this was done in all Egypt, Libya, Thebes, Palestine, Arabia, and Syria.

In seventy years the Christians had many church edifices, or *ecclesia cathedralis* (church meeting-places), and a pretty well developed and organized prayer and singing service; but cathedral or church service did not come to great perfection till the days of Gregory the Great, who was born A. D. 540, and died in 604. Chanting had its origin in the church of Antioch during the episcopate of Lontius, A. D. 347-356. Theodoret informs us that Flavianus and Diodorus divided the choir into two parts, and made them sing the Psalms of David alternately, and that this method began first at Antioch. At the Council of Laodicea, held between 360 and 370, it was determined that there should be canonical singers, who should sing out of written books. We may imagine something of the state of affairs before the order passed; for Balsamon says that, prior to the convening of this council, the laity would many times, and at their pleasure, begin to sing such hymns and songs in the church as were crude and unusual. To obviate this the canon was made, ordering that none should begin to sing but those whose office it was to do so, the laity having permission, however, to sing with them in the entire service; and so was inaugurated our modern congregational singing, to be led, however, by an appointed choir. Choir-singing was carried into Rome in 380, under Pope Damasus; and in the time of Gregory the Great, about 620, it was brought to great perfection. Gregory sent Austin to introduce it into England. He found the clergy there unwilling to receive it, and it is said that he caused twelve hundred of them to be slaughtered at once. In 670 Theodore was sent by Vitalian to fill the See of Canterbury, and he succeeded in introducing the cathedral service; and he also has the credit of introducing organs into divine worship. The year 679 is the earliest certain date of cathedral worship in Great Britain.

In France Gregorian chant-work began about the year 787, and was patronized by Charles the Great. In the reigns of Henry VIII. and Edward VI. thirty-two commissioners were appointed to examine all canons, constitutions, and ordinances, provincial and synodal, and they declared against a cathedral service. The judicious and pious Hooker, ceremony-loving, and jealous of the interests of the church, yet under the ban and interdicted, could not suppress his thought, and he says:—

Cathedrals are as glasses, wherein the face and very countenance of apostolical antiquity remaineth, even as yet to be seen, notwithstanding the alterations which the hand of time and the course of the world hath brought.

So the work continued till a final establishment of present customs, and Seymour says of cathedrals and their service as at present carried on:—

They serve as parish churches, only on a more elaborate scale; and there can be no valid objection raised to their maintenance, except by those who condemn an intoned service, and the introduction of a highly cultivated musical choir. The canons preach in turn, and, provided the preaching is orthodox and purely evangelical [a hit this, undoubtedly, at Dean Stanley, Canon Farrar, and others of like sentiment], and the old story of Christ's blood and righteousness and substitution is set forth as enough for all the spiritual necessities of mankind, there can be no just grounds of complaint against the peculiar mode of our present cathedral worship.

St. Patrick's being the first cathedral in which we attend services, the foregoing statement is made, preparatory to a consideration of this and other cathedrals we are to visit. It should be remembered that in all of them the service is intoned or sung, with the exception of the sermon itself, that being a part of the service only on Sundays or other important days. So strong is the force of habit, that the sermon also is generally delivered in a drawling, monotonous tone. This was a marked feature of the style of Dean Stanley in sermons delivered during his visit to America. Very strange did his elocution sound to American ears, and it was only tolerated because it came from a man so really great and truly honored.

St. Patrick's Cathedral is one of the most interesting churches in Ireland, and hours can be spent with pleasure and advantage in the grand old structure. It is said that St. Patrick here erected a place of worship, and baptized his converts with water taken from a well in the floor of the present cathedral, which is still shown to the visitor. As evidence of its antiquity as a place of worship, and of the importance and character of the original building, we have it as a well attested fact that in 890—almost a thousand years ago, and four and a half centuries after the establishment of worship here by St. Patrick, and the building of his church—Gregory of Scotland, with his adherents, attended worship here.

The present edifice, the seat of the Bishop of Dublin, was begun by Archbishop Comyn in 1190. It was doubled in its capacity by Archbishop Minot, who held the See in 1370, repairs on the old cathedral, and the extension, being necessitated by a fire which destroyed a large portion of the building in 1362. The edifice is of dark or blackish stone. It is irregular in outline, being cruciform in plan, with nave, choir, transepts, lady-chapel and porch.

A number of monuments are scattered about the interior, among them a tablet to the memory of the Duke of Schomberg, with an inscription by Jonathan Swift, at one time Dean of the cathedral. In another part are mural tablets, high up from the floor, to the memory of the Dean, who died Oct. 19, 1745, and was here buried. Near by is the monument to Mrs. Hester Johnson, the *Stella* of his poetry. A monument of note near the door commemorates Boyle, Earl of Cork, who died 1629. It is of a peculiar design, and attractive by its quaint oddity. It is of black marble, ornamented in parts by wood mouldings and carving, which were painted in positive colors, but are now dull and somewhat obscured. It represents the earl and his wife in recumbent positions, surrounded by their sixteen children. These figures are of wood, and carved in a grotesque style, barbaric enough to be pleasing examples of sculpture to a "Heathen Chinee."

The exterior of the cathedral presents a very aged appearance, and the two parts of the structure, erected by the two bishops in 1190 and 1370, are distinctly marked. The tower has plain buttresses at the corners, each ending in embattled turrets. A low, stone spire above this is attached to the section built by Bishop Comyn, and was erected some time after the other parts of the cathedral. Each part is of Gothic architecture, and is of the style prevailing at the period of its erection. Elaborate decoration does not appear in any part, and as the edifice fronts on a cramped, narrow street, and is near the surrounding buildings, no extended view of it can be obtained.

In 1860 the late Sir B. L. Guinness,—the noted brewer of Dublin, whose celebrated ales and porter are known the civilized world over,—at his own expense, undertook a complete restoration of the cathedral; and after years of continued labor, by a large body of workmen, the whole was finished at a cost of $720,000. Changes were made in the interior by the removal of modernish screens, and the exterior, while it has the same antiquated look, is in perfect repair. The interior with its lofty groined ceiling and arches, its stately columns, its rich oaken stalls, its beautiful stained glass windows, the great organ at the left of the communion table, the rich pulpit,—especially dedicated by Mr. Guinness to the late Dean Peckham as a memorial,—these combine to make the venerable structure rank well with many of the cathedrals of England. We hardly need to say that it is under the administration of the Church of England.

This was our first Sunday on land, April 28, and we decided that we would attend worship here in the forenoon. The Bishop of Dublin, and his canons, curates, and robed adult choir, were in attendance, and the cathedral was about one third filled. The service, as we afterwards found to be the universal custom in England, was intoned instead of read. It was disturbed, too, by the constant echoes; and, being unfamiliar with an intoned service, we were but poorly interested, and hoped for better things in the sermon, which was by one of the canons. It proved to be a weak statement of common things, a labored effort to prove what all admitted at the start. We would, however, speak lightly of no religious work, and were thankful for the treat we had enjoyed of seeing this time-honored sanctuary in use, and that we had listened to its grand music, and also to even a poor rendition of its beautiful service.

At 2 P. M. we are out again for a ramble, this time to visit the fine grounds and buildings of the Royal Hospital, built by the celebrated architect of St. Paul's Cathedral at London, Sir Christopher Wren, in 1669. The building is large, though but two stories in height, and has ample grounds, and two-hundred-year-old avenues, well shaded by large trees. The institution is now used as a military station. We were freely admitted to the principal parts, were delighted with the old and good portraits in the ancient dining-hall,—and inexpressibly so with the chapel, for here are to be seen transcripts of the mind of Wren. He appears to best advantage as a designer, when he undertook to make pulpits and altar-pieces; and here, about the large circular-headed altar-window, he has almost excelled himself. This, like all the stall work, is finished in oak, and is as elaborate and as perfect as though of modern construction, though it is more than two hundred years old.

Reluctantly we left these hallowed premises for a walk in the great Phoenix Park near by, and in the Zoölogical Garden. On our walk home to the hotel, we made it in our way to pass the companion church of St. Patrick, the other cathedral; for, incredible as it may seem, Dublin has another Protestant Episcopal cathedral-church, one scarcely inferior to St. Patrick's in renown. It is the venerable Church of the Holy Trinity, more commonly known by the name of Christ Church Cathedral. As is well known, a cathedral is so called because it is the seat of a bishop. Of course Dublin has but one bishop, and he is at St. Patrick's. The edifice we are to describe has, in turn with St. Patrick's, been the bishop's church, and from that circumstance the name has obtained its present use.

This edifice is of great interest and antiquity. According to the "Black Book of Christ's Church," a very ancient record, its vaults, or what is now the crypt, were built by the Danes before the first visit of St. Patrick to Dublin in the fifth century, but who is erroneously reported to have celebrated mass in them. The present edifice, in comparison with these vaults, is quite modern, for it was not built till five hundred years after; but enough of antiquity remains to excite our admiration, for this building was begun in the year 1038,—845 years ago, 152 years before the building of St. Patrick's, and about half-way between the date of the birth of Christ and our own day.

The statement that St. Patrick said mass in the crypt of this cathedral is simply a legend, for he had ended his ministry early in the fifth century. A sort of tavern was kept for centuries in this crypt; while services were being performed above, the votaries of Bacchus were adoring their god beneath. It was no uncommon thing in that age for churches to provide accommodation for the tramps and bummers of the time. As late as the close of the sixteenth century, the benches at the door of Old St. Paul's, London, were used by beggars and drunkards to sleep on, and the place was surrendered to idlers of all descriptions.

Christ Church Cathedral was greatly enlarged by Lawrence O'Tool, who, in 1163, changed the canons, originally secular, into the regular canons of Arras, as they were termed. Next, Strongbow, the Earl of Pembroke, and Fitzstephen, both Norman adventurers, made repairs and additions about the year 1170; and again Raymond le Gros, at a yet later day, added the steeple, choir, and two small chapels. In 1190, but twenty years after, it was practically rebuilt by John Comyn, who at the same time was building St. Patrick's; and about the year 1360 John de St. Paul erected the chancel. With occasional repairs the edifice remained as it was, 523 years ago, till a few years since, when great dilapidation had taken place, and extensive restorations were needed. Not to be outdone by Mr. Guinness at St. Patrick's, Henry Roe, Esq., the well-known distiller of Dublin, emulating the example of his friend, ordered, at his own expense, complete repairs on both the exterior and interior, costing a full million of dollars. The work was done under the architectural supervision of G. A. Street, and paid for by Mr. Roe as the work proceeded. At the time of our second visit, May 2, although not entirely finished, the building had been reopened, and an assemblage of the most distinguished prelates of the Episcopalian order held a four days' service, largely musical, at the grand opening, of which we speak hereafter.

The building, though very massive and suggestive of strength, is not beautiful in proportions or decoration. It has a clumsy look, but is consistent in design throughout. The interior has the same appearance. While it is finished in the highest style of workmanship, and in the best possible imitation of the original plan, it is mainly pleasing in variety of design, its thoroughness of work, and in the faithful representation it probably gives of the cathedral as it was centuries ago. When one looks at the nicely cut stone and fine finish, he can but believe that it is a vast improvement in workmanship on its original self. It has many ancient monuments of the quaintest sort, often with rude and grotesque designs.

Conspicuous among these is one of the Earl of Pembroke, or, as he is more commonly called, Strongbow, the Norman invader, who died in 1166. It represents the renowned warrior in a recumbent posture, clothed in mail armor, with his wife Eva by his side. Reasonable doubts exist of the authenticity of the monument. Its honors are divided between him and the Earl of Desmond, the Lord Chief Justice, who was looked upon with suspicion and jealousy on account of his kindness to the Irish people, and in consequence of this jealousy was beheaded at Drogheda in 1497. This monument was removed from its original location, by order of Sir Henry Sidney, in 1569.

This cathedral is a place of resort for those who are interested in the elaborate service performed every Sunday forenoon. It has a lawn on one side of it, somewhat larger than any at St. Patrick's. This is well fenced in from the side street, and parallel with the side of the cathedral; but the rear end and side are in close contiguity to common buildings, and the neighborhood is entirely made up of ordinary houses of brick or stone, which are filled with tenants, often having families on each floor. The streets are narrow, and while not remarkably dirty, they are anything but tidy in appearance. This portion of the city, and St. Patrick's neighborhood—which is not more than a five minutes' walk away—are probably the oldest settled parts of the city; a low population having taken possession still retain their foothold, as they do about the great churches at Cork and Limerick.

There are many interesting facts shown on the ancient records of this cathedral. In 1434 the mayor and some distinguished citizens of Dublin did penance, by walking barefoot through the streets to the cathedral, for having committed manslaughter; for taking the Earl of Ormonde prisoner "in a hostile manner;" for breaking open the doors of St. Mary's Abbey, dragging out the abbot, "and carrying him forth like a corpse, some bearing him by the feet, and others by the arms and shoulders."

In 1450 a parliament was held in the cathedral by Henry VI.; another was held in 1493. In 1497 liberty from arrests, and all other molestations, was granted, by the city of Dublin, to those who should come to visit any shrine or relic of this edifice. In 1528 the prior of this cathedral, with the priors of St. John of Jerusalem and of All Saints, caused two plays to be acted, on a stage erected by Hoggin Green, representing the Passion of the Saviour, and the several deaths the apostles suffered. This was a sort of Irish Oberammergau play.

Seven years later, in 1535, a great change in public sentiment had come; for in this year George Brown, an Augustin friar who had been consecrated bishop, removed all images and relics from this and the other churches of the diocese, and in their stead placed the Creed, the Lord's Prayer, and the Ten Commandments in gilded frames. In 1538 the *Baculus Jesu*, or holy staff, said to have belonged to St. Patrick, and deposited here in 1180, was publicly burned. In 1554 Bishop Brown, who was the first Protestant prelate of Dublin, was deprived of his office by Queen Mary. Four years later another reaction had taken place. In 1559 Parliament was held in the cathedral; the Act of Uniformity was passed; the Litany was sung in English, for the first time in Ireland, before the Earl of Sussex, the Lord Lieutenant; and a large English Bible was chained in the middle of the choir, free for the people to read. By order of Queen Elizabeth, Thomas Lockwood, the dean, removed all Popish relics and images, that had been restored in the days of Queen Mary in 1570. Penance was performed here by Richard Dixon, Bishop of Cork, who was also deprived of his See for gross immoralities. In 1633 the Lord-deputy sent an urgent letter to the Archbishop of Canterbury, asking him to prevent a longer use of the vaults under the cathedral as ale and tobacco shops.

In 1738 a peal of bells was cast by Abel Rudhall of Gloucester, England, and placed in the tower. He had cast the Sweet Bells of Shandon at St. Ann's, Cork. He was also the maker of the bells at Christ Church, Boston, which were cast but six years later, in 1744. There were at the cathedral originally but eight bells. Five have recently been added. In 1821 George IV., and in 1868 the Prince and Princess of Wales, attended service in the cathedral.

All cathedrals have a similar history. A cathedral's history is but a record of humanity's march through the centuries, through superstition, blood, and contest, onward and upward to advanced and yet advancing conditions, till finally—if there be truth in divine writ or the aspirations of humanity—"the kingdoms of this world shall become the kingdoms of our Lord, and of his Christ."

Sackville Street is a splendid business avenue leading from Carlisle Bridge. It is full one hundred feet wide, and filled with a hurrying, Broadway or Washington Street-like population. On the left stands the classical portico of the post-office, composed of six large Ionic columns, and their entablature and pediment. It is surmounted by figures of Hibernia, Mercury, and Fidelity. In front, at the centre of the street, is Nelson's monument, a splendid column 112 feet high,—exclusive of the crowning statue of the hero of Trafalgar, which is in itself 13 feet in height. This is a fine piece of sculpture, and is from the studio of a native sculptor, Thomas Kirk. The monument was erected by public subscription and cost over $34,000. In consequence of the general levelness of the city of Dublin, from the top of this column, though not of very great height, may be seen almost the entire surrounding country, from the Mourne Mountains in the county of Down on the north, around to the Wicklow Mountains on the south. Spread out before the observer are the plains of Meath and Kildare, extending far westward, and parted by the hills of Dublin and its bay; and to the eastward appears the Irish Sea.

The Custom House and the Four Courts of Dublin are immense structures, of classical architecture, and well decorated with statuary. On the former are statues representing Navigation, Wealth, Commerce, Industry, Europe, Asia, America, and Africa. Other parts have the arms of Ireland. There is a fine allegorical representation of Britannia and Hibernia in a great marine shell, with a group of merchantmen approaching, and Neptune driving away Famine and Despair.

The Court House has on the upper angle of its great portico pediment a statue of Moses, and at the lower ends statues of Mercy and Justice. On other parts are Wisdom and Authority. The great entrance hall is 64 feet in diameter; at the centre stands a colossal statue of Truth, bearing in her upraised hand a torch, from which issue gas jets for illuminating the rotunda.

We attended a court session. The rooms were cramped in size, and dark from the few smoked and unwashed windows. A peculiar impression was made, reminding us of a by-gone custom and age, when we saw the lawyers,—or barristers as they are called,—old and young, arrayed in loose black alpaca robes, open in front and flying as they walk, and wearing gray wigs of scrupulously curled hair. These are for sale in especial stores, and their use is imperative when one addresses the judge of any save the lowest common police court.

Previous anticipations of what was to be seen in Ireland's great metropolis were in the main realized. We expected, however, to see more Irish and less English elements. The city is quite American in appearance. Except for a more durable and classical look to its buildings, and the cut-stone embankments on both sides of the river; excepting also its heavier horse-cars and their roads,—*tramways*, as they are called,—little is seen that may not recall our large cities, especially Buffalo and Cincinnati. In fact, we were strongly reminded of these by the stores, houses, and streets, the quantity of business doing, and the average appearance of the people. Sunday was observed, much as it is in Boston or New York, by a general suspension of business, the streets being filled with well-dressed, orderly people. Bells often saluted the ear, horse-cars and omnibuses were well patronized, and the parks were visited by thousands, all in a state of sobriety that we are not sure of seeing in a large American city. We now for a time leave the city, but in another chapter shall speak of it again.

CHAPTER IV.

WATERFORD—CARRICK-ON-SUIR—KILKENNY—DUBLIN AGAIN.

Business now called us back to the lower part of Ireland, and we will here take a look at Waterford and other places.

Waterford is one of the most noted places of Southern Ireland, and has for centuries played an important part in history and commerce. We arrived here at 6.30 P. M., after a ride of five and a half hours from Dublin. The city is situated on the right bank of the River Suir, nine miles from its entrance into Waterford Harbor. It has an extensive suburb, with a pleasant settlement called Ferrybank, on the other side of the river, opposite a part of the city. The population of Waterford proper is 23,349. The quay is the finest in Ireland. It is 120 feet wide, extends for three quarters of a mile along the river, and is well built of stone. Bordering this, on the land side, are stores of various kinds. It looks like an old commercial place, and the general dingy look of everything suggests great dampness of atmosphere. There are not many buildings of importance. Few of the streets are wide, but most of them are narrow and crooked, and lanes and alleys abound. We were impressed with the aspect of poverty. The shore opposite is bold, rocky, and precipitous, and, at the lower end, about the bridge and railway station, is romantic and picturesque.

The old, long bridge is a structure of stone, and of considerable consequence. It was erected in Ireland's memorable year, 1798, and near this place one of her most important battles was fought, which ended to her disadvantage, and resulted, in 1801, in the surrender of her power, and the establishment of English rule. It is too much to expect that England, who so long ago established its authority in India, and in our time in Cyprus, thousands of miles away, should resist the temptation of subjugating a land so indefensible as Ireland, which lay at her very door. The bridge having been built in her last great battle year, a stone slab in the parapet records the fact.

Here are the inevitable barracks. They are of stone, three stories high, and very extensive. There were evidences of military rule in every place yet visited. The soldiers are all young. None are over thirty years of age, and many not more than eighteen. All are stout and robust, and each is a picked man. The uniform coats are red, with gilt buttons, the pants are a dark plaid; they look dandyish. These men are the best physique of the nation, and, as a whole, put to a bad use. They are always to be found on the street, either singly, by twos, or in squads, each with a switch-cane, said to be furnished by the government.

The police are English, for no Irish person is trusted, and they are finely dressed in dark clothes. They are very civil and gentlemanly, and, like the soldiers, are picked men. Save on a single occasion in Dublin, we saw no disturbance of any kind, nor any service rendered by the police.

What interested us most was an old tower on this main thoroughfare, situated at the extreme end of the quay on the land side, and just out to the sidewalk line, in close contiguity with the surrounding buildings. It is fifty feet high, and about thirty-five feet in diameter, and is built of irregular ledge stone, of a dark gray or brownish color; is very plain, as far as a projection near the top, of a few inches; above this it is continued up plain some two or three feet higher, having a conical roof which comes down apparently inside of the stone work. There is a single door in the first story. Just above this, to the left, is a stone tablet, about two and a half feet wide and five feet high, with pilasters and pediment top,—the whole much like a dormer window. The inscription is as follows:—

IN THE YEAR 1003
THIS TOWER WAS ERECTED
BY REGINALD THE DANE.
IN 1171 IT WAS HELD AS A FORTRESS
BY STRONGBOLD, EARL OF PEMBROKE.
IN 1463 BY STATUTE 3D, EDWARD IV,
A MINT WAS ESTABLISHED HERE.
IN 1819 IT WAS REEDIFIED IN ITS
ORIGINAL FORM AND APPROPRIATED TO
THE POLICE ESTABLISHMENT
BY THE CORPORATION BODY OF
THE CITY OF WATERFORD.
RT. HON. SIR JOHN NEWPORT, BT., M. P., MAYOR,

HENRY ALCOCK, ESQ.,
WILLIAM WEEKS, ESQ. } SHERIFFS.

The city is very old, and was founded about the year 850, or more than one thousand years ago, at which time Sithric the Dane made it his capital. In 1171 Strongbow and Raymond le Gros took the place, and put to death most of the Danish inhabitants. King John gave it its first charter, and resided here for some time. The place was unsuccessfully besieged by Cromwell, but was afterwards captured by the intrepid Ireton. There are remains of old fortifications and monasteries.

Curraghmore, the seat of the Marquis of Waterford, containing four thousand acres, is near the city. After a stay till 9 P. M. of this day, we took train for the town of

CARRICK-ON-SUIR,

where we arrived at 9.45, and took room at Madame Phalan's Hotel. It is a very comfortable place, and thoroughly Irish, but of a good sort,—a little old inn of the first water; and, as usual, a woman sixty years old was the "man of the house." A good night's rest, and, next morning a tramp over the town, and the business for which we had come was attended to. The place was very clean and neat, the buildings being of stone, with slate roofs. Many were plastered on the outside, painted in tints of cream-color or gray, and blocked off to represent stone. They are generally two or three stories high. We have spoken of the slate roofs. Some were new and clean, like the best in Boston. Others were ancient, and made of thick slates, little better than thin stones of small size, and often mortared up so as to give a very clumsy appearance. On many of them were large patches of thick, green, velvety moss, and not unfrequently growing in it, and in the roof-gutters, were specimens of snapdragon in full bloom. The people refrain from removing these excrescences, unless for repairs which compel them to do so.

We were delighted with the old market-place, and with the thoroughly Irish houses, one story high, built of stone, plastered and whitewashed, and situated in narrow lanes, which were paved with round cobble-stones, and kept remarkably clean. The place shows cultivation and a good civilization. It is a market-town, and a parish of Tipperary, and is situated on the pretty River Suir, crossed by a bridge built over five hundred years ago. It has a population of 8,520. It was formerly enclosed by walls, and has a parish church of great antiquity. A fine Roman Catholic Church has lately been built, and a large school is connected with it, having an elegant building of gray limestone. There is a castle of some repute, formerly belonging to the celebrated Ormonde family. The town also has a prison, a hospital, and barracks.

Improvements in the river, made in 1850, rendered it navigable for vessels of considerable capacity, which can now come up to the town, which has quite a trade in cotton, corn, and general produce. Monthly fairs are held in the market-place. There are some shade-trees, and the town in many parts has a rural look. But few very Irish-looking people are seen. While the town is unmistakably Irish, it is of a high grade; and, notwithstanding many of its buildings are quaint and old, for the most part it is modern, though not of course like New England. The place has two banks, and a number of good stores. We had seen no place quite like Carrick, but, as we aftewards found, it anticipated Kilkenny.

The good wine was, however, kept till the last, for we had an exquisite suburban trip. At 1.30 P. M. we took a team, standing in the street for hire, for our journey to Pilltown. We didn't care to inquire where the village got its name, and doubt of success had we made the attempt. A half-mile out, and we were in love with the scenery. There presented itself every kind of view imaginable,—hills, fields, groves, and mountains in the distance. We thought then, and we think now, that little section is the garden of Ireland. How fine the landscapes! how balmy and clear the atmosphere! what good vegetation, and what sleek horses, beautiful healthy cows, and splendid sheep! and how very civil they were, and how confiding, when we strangers came near them! We were so full of satisfaction that we had but little real ability to appreciate what we saw next,—a street as wide and clean as can be desired, some of the neatest possible one-story stone houses, with appropriate front-yards with flowers in them; and nowhere to be found, in either street or yard or house, so far as we could see, a thing to amend or alter. Well, we almost knew there was an especial cause for all this. No lot of mortals, fallen from the assumed high plane of Adam and Eve, ever existed,—at all events that we have heard of,—who would of themselves get into this Eden-like condition. We inquired the cause, and soon the mystery was at an end, for we were told that Lord Bestborough,—we hope that name is given right,—a much beloved landholder, owned all, and gave annual prizes for the best kept houses and grounds. A committee of ladies and gentlemen have the matter in charge; they make two especial visits, and award five prizes in all, the largest being two pounds, or ten dollars.

We rode on, and were soon at the original Purcell estate, which has for some hundreds of years been occupied by the family of that name, from which one of the writers came in the course of human progress. In talking of our own company, we are not inclined to say *descent*, and especially in these days of Darwinism; so we draw it mild when we refrain from saying *ascent*, and are contented with suggesting that we have advanced or progressed.

We may have been prejudiced, but very delightful was the scenery in this region. The river took a grand quarter-circle sweep just back of the old farm, and was here a quarter of a mile wide, with remarkably fine English grass-meadows, half a mile wide, bordering it. The distant hills were irregular and well wooded, and over them was a fine haze, like that of our Blue Hills at Milton. The great ravines had dark places of interest, and made all very picturesque. Not more than two or three scattered farmhouses were in view.

No noise was heard save that of the small birds; but conspicuous was the song of the Irish Thrush.

Two coal-vessels were at anchor in the river, and these added a strange element to the scene. We hallooed to one vessel and beckoned, and a boat was put out to ferry us over. In making for Purcell's we had mistaken the road, and so had walked a mile or more out of the way, and were on the wrong side of the river. It wouldn't be Yankeeish to go back, but rather to go ahead, especially when, Davy Crockett-like, we were sure we were right,— for, to use an Irishism, we were right when we were wrong. The boat came, and we, like the two kings of ancient Munster—Strongbow and Raymond le Gros—stepped in and were rowed over. We gave a shilling to the boatman, and landed, and were now all right. It would not be becoming to tell all that we saw, said, and did. We had never seen one of that family, nor they us; nor had they seen any other Yankees; and if any mortals were surprised, they were. Photographs of some kindred were, however, in that very house. The whole matter of relationship was thoroughly talked over, and in the room where the great-grandfather died, we took tea. We stood in front of the large kitchen fireplace, where for almost a century he used to sit, and were delighted with a sight of old New-Englandish pots, kettles, trammels, hooks, and large high andirons, about which the burning furze crackled. Keats has it, "A thing of beauty is a joy forever." This is a joy forever,—that old fireplace; but the beauty is nowhere, not even, thought we, in the "mind's eye Horatio." To leave a cathedral or a fine old ruin, a picture gallery or museum, caused less trouble than our parting with this good old Irish homestead; but the spell must be broken.

As we walked through the long, winding lane, each side well hedged, we were delighted anew. In what profusion were the modest daisies in the pathway; how many, many snails, their houses on their backs, were on the bushes; and then, those exquisite primroses, in such vast numbers,—of the most delicate, refined straw-tint imaginable. The entire vegetation was so clean! And then the stillness—nothing but sweet-singing birds to make a noise. Half a mile off, on a rise of land to our right, was a little village of perhaps twenty houses,—and the church, the mother building of them all. Here, once a Purcell was the priest. He built the house we had visited, and was a brother of the great-grandfather. *Advanced* as we are, and removed from Romanism, yet there was a charm about that old spot. Though dead a century, that venerable priestly ancestor yet speaketh.

We wended our way to Fiddown Station. How refinedly Irish that name is, and also that of the village Polroon; but alas, the euphony had become exhausted before we went in imagination a half-mile back from Polroon, and over to Purcell's Village, for that has the æsthetic name of Moincoin. Our walk from this place was three miles, but the distance was short enough amidst such air and scenery.

A ride in the steam-cars, of an hour from Fiddown, and at 9 P. M. we were back, not in Carrick-on-Suir, but in Waterford, at the Imperial Hotel, near the old Strongbold Tower before described. Not much of Irish about the hotel! Next morning breakfast was ordered at 6 A. M. Then we went out and copied the tower inscription before given. At 7.15 took cars for Kilkenny, where we arrived at 8.30.

The general look of the landscape between the places, and in fact all the way down from Dublin, was very like that of New England along shore. Trees and woods are in about the same proportion as with us, and, excepting the houses, we saw nothing that we might not have seen in a similar ride at home.

KILKENNY.

"Kilkenny is sure another of the Irish places," says the reader; and it is hardly less so by reputation than Sligo, Dundalk, and Drogheda. It is the shire town of the county of Kilkenny, and a county of itself, situated on the River Nore, 63 miles from Dublin, and 30 miles from Waterford, having a population of 12,664. It is divided by the river into an Irish and an English town, the former in the vicinity of the cathedral, and the latter near the castle. In ancient times the place figured largely as a seat of parliaments, and was often the scene of stirring events. As viewed from the railway, which is one of the best points of observation, Kilkenny is one of the most picturesque rural places that can be imagined. On the left of the centre, and on low ground, is the castle. The original was built by Earl Strongbow in 1172, and, destroyed by Donald O'Brien soon after. The present structure was built in 1195. In 1319 James Butler, third Earl of Ormonde, purchased the estate of the Pembroke (or Strongbold) family, and with his descendants it has since remained. It is in perfect condition, and occupied by the Marquis of Ormonde. It is a very large edifice, of an old granite appearance, is situated on a slight elevation, and the river runs rapidly by its base. The location is at the centre of population, the main avenues adjoining the grounds. The general effect reminds us of Warwick Castle. Richard II. spent two weeks here on a visit to the Earl in 1399. In March, 1650, Cromwell, having invested the place, opened a cannonade on the castle and made a breach in its walls; but the attackers were twice repulsed, and the breach quickly repaired, Cromwell was traitorously admitted by the mayor and a few of his townsmen; and as he was in company with Ireton, Sir Walter Butler, who was in charge of the place, deemed it expedient to capitulate, and did so on honorable terms. He and his officers were highly complimented by Cromwell, who informed them that he had lost more men in storming the town than he did in taking Drogheda, and that but for treachery he should have retired from the siege.

To the right of the centre and on very high ground we see the Cathedral of St. Canice, one of the most interesting ecclesiastical structures of Ireland. It was begun in 1180 by Felix O'Dullany, who transferred the See of Sagir from Aghabo to Kilkenny. So extensive was the design of the building that its projectors, never expecting to see it finished, contentedly covered in the choir and consecrated it, leaving to others the task of consummating the work. It is cruciform in plan, 226 feet long, and 123 feet wide at the transepts. It has a low and long look, and the tower, which is also low, gives the structure a depressed appearance. The interior, however, is grand and imposing. The pillars are of plain black marble, surmounted by high Gothic arches. The arches under the tower, which is at the intersection of nave, choir, and transepts, rest on four massive marble columns. The great western window is triplicated, and a large cross and two Gothic finials crown the centre, angles, and apex of the great gable. The exterior is in tolerable repair, and the interior is in perfect condition, having been fully restored by Dean Vignolles.

The monumental remains are numerous and interesting. Among them is that of Peter Butler, the eighth Earl of Ormonde, and his Amazonian Countess, known by the Irish as Morgyrhead Ghearhodh. Irish enough the name is, and for that reason we quote it. They died in the sixteenth century. The Countess was of the family of Fitzgerald, and did not dishonor her blood, for she was masculine in organization, and as warlike as any of her race. History says of her that "she was always attended by numerous vassals, richly clothed and accoutred, the whole forming a gay pageant and formidable army;" and it was more than whispered, by the gossips of her day, that, like Rob Roy, she levied blackmail on her less powerful neighbors.

Near the cathedral is one of the finest monumental round-towers of Ireland, 108 feet in height and in perfect preservation; though like all these solitary towers, its use is yet enveloped in mystery. No place of Ireland presents a better opportunity of research for the lover of antiquities than the county of Kilkenny, for it is not too much to say that here ruins abound. A writer in "Hall's Hibernia" says:—

So numerous are church ruins in this region, that on our way we were guided through numerous alleys and by-lanes, to examine relics of the olden time. We found wretched hovels propped up by carved pillars; and in several instances discovered Gothic doorways converted into pigstyes.

This was not quite our experience. Our impressions were that the town, in the English part, was business-like and attractive, the streets clean and well paved, and the inhabitants well dressed. In the Irish portion there was the usual quota of one-story houses, and a poor population.

The Roman Catholic Church, recently built, is an elegant structure, with lofty towers and spires above them, and stands, as viewed from the railroad, at about the centre of the place.

Kilkenny is celebrated as the seat of witchcraft trials. One of the most remarkable was that of Lady Alice Kettel in 1325. There were, however, but three executions. It should in justice to Ireland be said that, with all its superstitions, it had comparatively few inhabitants who were barbarous enough to force presumed witches to trial. New England was more than her equal. Aside from these three at Kilkenny, there was but one such execution in all Ireland; and that was at Antrim, in 1699, seven years after the first appearance of the delusion in New England, which occurred at the house of Rev. Mr. Parris, in Salem, in 1692. The Antrim trial was the last, and was told as a story in pamphlet form, entitled, "The Bewitching of a Child in Ireland." It had a large circulation, and was foolishly copied by Professor Sinclair into his work entitled "Satan's Invisible World Discovered;" and is frequently referred to by Sir Walter Scott, in his "Letters on Demonology." While speaking of Sir Walter, we are reminded of the fact that Kilkenny, as well as Melrose had its Sir Walter. His name was John Banim. He wielded a facile pen, had a peculiar temperament, and represented the character of his country and its people with more fidelity and interest, if not romantic effect, than any other Irish novelist.

We are admonished that we must here end our talk about this lovely Kilkenny; and, as we turn once more for a final view as our train moves away from the station, it is not without feelings allied to those which Longfellow describes in his own sweet way:—

A feeling of sadness and longing,
That is not akin to pain,

And resembles sorrow only
As the mist resembles the rain.

We are fully aware that we have not often spoken of Roman Catholic churches, cathedrals, nunneries, and schools; and at first sight it would appear that in this Catholic country more attention should have been paid to these things; but recognizing the narrow space that could with propriety be devoted to any one place, we have reluctantly had to forego the pleasure of describing many points of interest. The reader may rest assured that it would have given us unalloyed pleasure to speak of hospitals, charity-schools, asylums, almshouses, and a thousand charitable institutions we saw and heard of. All these abound. That kind-heartedness, so characteristic of the Irish nature; that hospitality which is part of their being, making their houses, large or small, in Ireland or America, hospitals, asylums, or hotels,—these qualities show themselves, in constant and varying forms, in buildings designed as comfortable retreats for the unfortunate.

Descriptions have been given only of such buildings as are of remarkable antiquity, and possessed of more than ordinary interest. At best, these chapters can only be a brief and meagre synopsis of an inexhaustible store; but perhaps they will tempt the reader to consult the more elaborate thought of others, as found in histories and gazetteers. No more comfortable road up the hill of general knowledge exists, than that which one travels while reading such works. In the former, and measurably in the latter, he finds truth stranger than fiction, and romance supported by an obscured reality, at once enchanting and almost incredible.

In passing over the roads from place to place there is one continual panorama of interesting objects, each of which is out of the usual line of observation of such travellers as ourselves,—Americans, Yankees, with New England lineage and descent through a line of more than a hundred years. These scenes are so interesting that hundreds of chapters might be written about them; and when the work ended, description proper would be just begun.

What novel can be more interesting, or what entertainment more enchanting, than to read about Galbally, where a monastery was founded, as early as 1204, for the Grayfriars, by a member of the celebrated family of O'Brien. It justly boasts of its beautiful Glen Aherlow, eight miles long and two wide, which truthful descriptions say, is not surpassed in interest by anything in the country. It has also a Druidical Temple, consisting of three circles of stone, the principal one of which is 150 feet in diameter, consisting of forty stones, of which the largest is 13 feet long, 6 feet wide, and 4 feet thick!

The Rock of Cashel, but twelve miles from Limerick,—a large lone rock, rising boldly out of a plain,—is of world-wide celebrity, by reason of its association with one of the most interesting ruins in the kingdom, which still repose on its summit,—those of a grand castle, held by the chiefs of the family Hy Dunnamoi, now called O'Donohue. They consist chiefly of a round-tower, ninety feet high; a small church in the Norman style, with a stone roof; a cathedral church, in Gothic style; and a castle and monastery; and yet in addition, are the fine ruins of Hore Abbey at the base of the rock. Let the intelligent reader know of these, and he has at hand strange and enchanting romances in no way inferior to "Kenilworth," or "The Lady of the Lake."

We shall be pardoned for seeming egotism when we name Loughmore Castle,—a fine old building in ruins, showing yet a massive castellated front, with strong square towers at each end, the one at the right being of great antiquity, the remainder having been built in the sixteenth century. On the opposite side are the church and chapel of Loughmore. The estate was long the seat of the Purcells, from whom, in a maternal line, has probably descended one of the authors of this volume.

Let our investigator continue his research, and he will be informed of the remarkable ruins of Kildare, thirty miles out from Dublin, among which is the Chapel of St. Brigid, called the Firehouse, it being the locality of the perennial fire which the nuns maintained day and night, during a thousand years, for the benefit of strangers and the poor. A thousand years of never extinguished charity-fire! How incomprehensible the fact and story!

Ireland is indeed a land of romance, which is merged in the obscurities of a time which the records of man do not reach or measure. Superstition and general ignorance long prevailed, but the temperament and organism of the race have made a history peculiar to itself. There's a deal of strength and nationality in the blood. Dilute it, generation after generation, and its idiosyncracies are still there. Where can romance inhere, if not in conditions like these? What, if not legends of fairies, visions, miracles, could result from the operations of this religious turn of mind, and its accompanying superstitious beliefs? Castle, church, monastery, abbey, tower, must come into being; and their convictions were so influential that these people "builded better than they knew."

We arrive at Maryboro at 7.30 P. M., and here we meet with our first and last experience of a tardy train, which is an hour and a half late at a junction. We remained over night at Borland's Hotel, paying for supper, lodging, and breakfast, $1.50 apiece. At 8.40 A. M. next day, May 2, took train for Dublin again, arriving at 11 *A. M.* This was to be our last day in Erin, and so we went directly to the steamer Longford and engaged "passage out of Ireland," paying for the passage to Liverpool $2.37 each. And now for one more tramp over the Irish metropolis.

We had been informed of the completion of Christ Church Cathedral, and that on this day the great public opening was to take place. We soon discovered that we were unfortunate in not being one of the dignitaries, as they only had tickets of admission. But no Yankee of good blood would be three thousand miles from home, and lose a sight on which a million dollars had been expended; and so, with as much faith that we should gain admission to their building, as most of the prelates perhaps had of one day entering "the house not made with hands," we made our demand, and were of course repulsed. Remembering the daring of Strongbow, whose bones were reposing inside the cathedral, and that *we* were of Irish extraction, we were emboldened, and bethought ourselves of who we were; for, like one of old, we were citizens "of no mean country," and were ready to fight spiritually with the beasts of Ephesus. We made an effort, and came off conquerors. "Americans," said we. That was the charm which held the attention of the official, robed and consequential, with whom we talked, and who was moved by that talismanic word. Although he had refused, and with righteous indignation declared he could not—and perhaps felt that he would not—let us in; yet, as soon as he knew who we were, he came down from his lofty position and the cathedral door swung open. His whole being was filled with a consciousness of the good of which he was the happy author. We complacently bowed our compliments, as all triumphing Americans should do; then we went in and surveyed everything, and in due time were out and taking our last look of the city.

At 6 P. M. we were on board our steamer; and soon she steamed out of the harbor and into the bay and channel, and we were once more on the briny deep. A pleasant sail, and a comparatively quiet one, landed us at 7 A. M., on Saturday, May 3, on the soil of Old England.

We have with comparative thoroughness—that is, for a tourist's statement—given an account of Old Ireland; and now, before we begin our similar account of Old England, we think it well to add a page or two more, and give a few leading points in regard to Ireland as a whole; for in these chapters, be it anew remembered, we are to try and give such incidental information as will be useful as well as entertaining to the general reader, so that he will know more of the country than he would learn from mere statements about a few things we chanced to see.

As is well known, the Emerald Isle—so called from the luxuriance of vegetation induced by a mild and moist climate—is one of the four divisions of Great Britain, England, Wales, and Scotland being the others. It is separated from England by the Irish Sea and St. George's Channel, and contains an area of 32,531 square miles. This is not far from the size of the State of Maine, which contains 35,000. Ireland is divided into four provinces, Leinster, Munster, Ulster, and Connaught, and these comprise thirty-two counties. Its greatest population was in 1841, when it amounted to 8,199,853. During the next ten years, owing to famine and emigration, it decreased 1,600,000, that is to 6,599,853; and this was about 200,000 less than in 1821, when the first census was taken. The number of inhabited houses in 1861 was 995,156; in ten years they decreased to 960,352. The average number of persons to a house was seven, giving for 1871 a population of 6,722,464. This is not far from the present population, which is more than ten times that of the State of Maine, 626,915, and twice that of all New England, 3,487,924. As New England has 68,460 miles of surface, and Ireland 32,531, it follows that the latter has about four times as many persons to the square mile as the former.

Ireland has ninety-two harbors and sixty-two lighthouses. There are in all 2,830,000 acres of bog land that is available for fuel, or about one seventh of all the island. At Dublin the mean temperature for the year is fifty degrees, which is seven degrees warmer than the average of Boston; and there is an average of but three degrees of difference between the extreme northern and southern parts. There is a perpetual moisture, which induces vegetation and maintains unfailing pasturage. This is due to the prevalence of westerly winds, which bring with them the warm moist atmosphere of the Gulf Stream. The average rainfall is thirty-six inches, or about six inches less than at Boston.

Ireland boasts of great antiquity. We will, however, speak of it only from the time of St. Patrick, who was sent here by Germanus of Rome, to convert the people to Christianity. He arrived about the middle of the fifth century, and died in 493, leaving the island nominally Christian. Schools and monasteries were established; and so noted did the country become for the learning and piety of its ecclesiastics, that it was called *Insula Sanctorum*, Isle of Saints. In the year 646 many Anglo Saxons settled on the island, and in 684 it had become of sufficient importance to be invaded by Egfrid, king of Northumberland, who destroyed churches and monasteries. From this time invasions were common. In 1002 Brian Boru, who was king of the province of Munster, was powerful enough to expel the Danes who had come in, and was crowned at Tara, "King of all Ireland." Hence Moore's poem, "The Harp that once through Tara's Halls."

Brian Boru wrought great reforms, for he founded churches and schools, opened roads, built bridges, and fitted out fleets. He introduced surnames, heretofore not in use, and made the marriage contract permanent. The Danes again invaded Ireland in 1014; and on Good Friday—April 23, of that year—Brian, an old man of eighty years, was killed in his tent, although his party had triumphed.

Internal dissensions and civil wars followed. The island soon fell into a state of degeneracy, and lost its good character as the Isle of Saints. St. Bernard called the attention of the Church authorities of Rome to its condition, and Pope Eugenius III. sent Cardinal Papiron to restore discipline. In March, 1152, a synod was held at Kells, when the supremacy of Rome was acknowledged, and the archbishoprics of Dublin and of Tuam were established. In 1155 a bull is said to have been issued by Pope Adrian IV. conferring the sovereignty of Ireland on Henry II. of England. Next came invasions by two bands of Normans, one under Robert Fitzstephen in 1169, and another under Earl Pembroke (Strongbow) in the same year. Henry II. issued a proclamation recalling Strongbow, and all Englishmen, under pain of outlawry. Then there was a series of interesting battles, sometimes one party being successful, and sometimes the other.

In 1341 Edward III. ordered that all offices held by Irishmen, or by Englishmen who had estates or wives in Ireland, should be vacated, and filled by Englishmen who had no personal interest whatever in the Green Isle. Great resistance and trouble followed, and the English triumphed.

A parliament was held in Dublin in 1537, when the Act of Supremacy was passed, declaring Henry VIII. supreme head of the Church, prohibiting intercourse with the court of Rome, and making it treason to refuse the oath of supremacy. Then began a new series of wars and troubles. Each subsequent page of history is stained with blood. Insurrections and resistance were oft repeated. Finally, in 1798, new battles were fought, the English being in the end victorious. The next year a bill of amnesty was passed, and the country settled down into comparative quiet. Jan. 1, 1801, Articles of Union were agreed upon, and from then till now, with occasional outbreaks and riots, England has maintained her hold. Much of the work done by Henry VIII. has been good in its results; but much has proved to be wrong in the extreme. The principle of entailing landed estates tends to impoverish the people, drive them to emigration, and so depopulate the country. These are the seeds of decay for not only Ireland, but for England herself. It is a wrong "so rank it smells to heaven," and deliverance is sure to come. And now, we bid adieu to Ireland, where we have enjoyed so much, and for whose good time coming we watch and wait in sympathy with her sons.

ENGLAND.

CHAPTER V.

LIVERPOOL—CHESTER—SHREWSBURY—WORCESTER—HEREFORD.

Steamers leave Dublin every week-night for Liverpool, as they do Fall River for New York, and the distance is about the same. It involves a trip of a few miles out of Dublin harbor and bay, across St. George's channel, and four miles up the River Mersey at the other end. It is an English custom to put the name of the river last, while Americans put it first. It would sound very odd to an American to hear the remark River Ohio or River Mississippi; and so it would to an Englishman, to hear the expression Thames River.

Every wise tourist, on visiting New York for the first time, is on deck early to see the approaches to the harbor, and the scenery below the city. One visiting Liverpool will do likewise; for this is to be his first view of the Mother Country. We were on our steamer's deck at 5 o'clock A. M., on Friday morning, May 3. In the distance, on our right, towered up, though somewhat obscurely, the bold headland of Holyhead, a part of Wales. As we approach it we discover the great gorge in the rock, and the bridge over it, and also the white lighthouse and long, substantial breakwater for the defence of the harbor. Sweeping in a curved course to the southeastward we see the Welsh high uplands, with their thrifty farms and many windmills. Behind these, as a splendid background, the Welsh mountains loom up, and the peaks of Snowden and other highlands show themselves.

We now pass an interesting object,—an assemblage of rocks called the Skerries, three miles or so distant from the Welsh shore. They are very dangerous, and are lighted, being directly in the way of passage to the River Mersey. Next we arrive at Point Lynas, the pilot-station for Liverpool. Near it is Orme's Head, a rough promontory on which is a lighthouse, having a Fresnel light, one of the most powerful in the world. To add to the picturesqueness of the scenery, here and there are little Welsh villages, cosily situated, and nestling at the base of the hills. Among them is Llandudno and the watering-places; and so we anticipate a higher type of civilization, signs of which are on every hand.

Not far from the mouth of the Mersey, fresh evidences of commercial life present themselves. Steamers, pilot-boats, and tugs thicken, and we know we are nearing a port of no ordinary importance. We pass the Northwest Lightship, and soon after hear the bell-buoy on the bar sending out its plaintive warning as it pitches and rolls. Like faithful sentinels are Formby and Crosby lightships; and at the right is Rock Light, at New Brighton.

This place is the end of the peninsula, which for five miles stretches down the river, and is the shore opposite Liverpool and its suburbs. It is a pleasant and cheap watering-place, and one much sought by the common people. Steamboats from Liverpool run half-hourly between the places. New Brighton has a good beach, and there are many restaurants along the upper side. An old stone fort is one of the objects of interest, and free to visitors. On any fair day may be seen thousands of people promenading over the beach, or riding in teams or on Irish donkeys, which are at various stations ready for hire, most of them owned by aged men and women, and let for a single ride or by the hour. Here are stands for the sale of round clams (*quahaugs*, as we call them), muscles, periwinkles, and, it may be, a few poor oysters. There are also cheap refreshment tables, and facilities for the entertainment of children, such as Punch and Judy, swings, revolving horses. From this place, along the right bank of the river, the landscape is diversified with low hills, clean fields, woods, and groves, with here and there a little settlement. Opposite the city proper lies Birkenhead, a busy place, with docks and shipping, of its own, and a population of 65,980. In 1818 Birkenhead had but fifty inhabitants, but they have trebled since 1851, a rapidity seldom witnessed in the Old World.

Up the Mersey on the left side, the landscape is picturesque and rural. Along the river, on comparatively level land, with a slight rise at the rear, and some especially elevated points at the extreme upper end, lies the substantial and sombre city of Liverpool. It has literally forests of masts. There are no wharves extending into the river, but at stated intervals are openings into the famous docks. These are controlled by oaken gates, of which there are eight in all, some of them a hundred feet wide. They are opened and closed twice daily, at turns of the tide. The docks are built of hewn stone, the oldest of a perishable sandstone, but the newer of granite. They are built somewhat in the rear of the outer or river docks, and open into each other. The spaces between them are used like our wharves, as sites for large warehouses and sheds of deposit. These docks and landing-places extend five miles on the Liverpool side of the river, and two miles on the Birkenhead side. In the aggregate, the docks cover 404 acres, or about two thirds of a square mile. The aggregate length of the wharf space is sixteen miles on the Liverpool side, and ten miles at Birkenhead. The cost was $50,000,000, $35,000,000 of which was expended at Liverpool. The Landing Stage, as it is called, where passage is taken to the steamers, is an enormous floating platform, supported on iron tanks, and is along the business centre of the city, outside of the main street or sea-wall, which is five miles long, eleven feet thick, and forty feet in average height from its foundations.

At the beginning of the eighteenth century Liverpool had but one dock; but between 1830 and 1860, over twenty-five new ones were opened.

The place is of considerable antiquity, and is first spoken of, in any authentic record, in a charter of Henry II., bearing date 1173, by which document the privileges of a seaport were secured; and in 1207 King John granted it a municipal charter. Henry III. constituted it a free borough in 1229. It made but little progress for centuries, and was a scene of sanguinary conflict in 1644, for during the contest between Charles I. and his Parliament, this place resisted the King. After a month's determined opposition, it was taken by Prince Rupert, and was soon afterwards largely reduced in population by pestilence and famine. In 1699 it had not more than five thousand inhabitants.

There is no other foreign city so influenced by the United States. Its condition, advancement, and progress have been in proportion to our advancement; for upon the fluctuations of trade it has, for a third of a century, been somewhat dependent. The general look of the city is like that of the older parts of New York or Boston, which it resembles more than it does any place in Europe.

Its streets are generally wide, clean, and are always well paved. Its buildings are very substantial. They are of brick or stone; but from the large amount of smoke from the bituminous coal, and the damp, and—in winter—foggy atmosphere, they have an old and dingy appearance. Particularly is this true of most of the churches, with their square towers. The city proper has few very good church edifices; but it has many old ones, some of them surrounded by burial-grounds, in the very heart of the city. These churchyards are not only treeless, but they are without shrubs, or even grass. An acre is sometimes covered with slabs of stone, level with the ground. They are about three feet wide and six long, set close together, with hardly a crevice, and on them are cut the epitaphs.

St. George's Hall, a colossal and superb structure, has one of the largest organs in the world, and exhibitions of it are given two or three times a week for the small admission fee of a sixpence (twelve cents). At the time of our visit, there were full one thousand people present. It has a good art-gallery, in which are many fine paintings by the Masters.

Drunkenness abounds. In no other place did we see so much drunkenness or so many rum shops. A visit to the police court, and a stay of a couple of hours there, exhibited more inebriation, poverty, and destitution than we could imagine as existing as we walked through the streets of the city. We were informed by the judge that he had on his book one hundred and ninety-four cases for drunkenness alone, or crimes growing immediately out of it; and that in some way all must be disposed of that day, as to-morrow was likely to bring as many or more. Some offenders had been before his court over sixty times. Such victims were released, as would be so many wild animals or lepers, the kind-hearted judge simply lecturing them, and expressing his sorrow for what in these years he had been compelled to witness daily. He was humane in all his considerations. We could but tell him that he was a remarkable man, to be able for years to be in the presence of this mass of evil and degradation, and not become hardened in feeling, but retain a sympathetic yet judicious determination and manhood. Never did a case occur where with more propriety the old remark might be justly made, "the right man in the right place." We went away somewhat sad, as we thought of the upright judge's remark, made so innocently, that we intelligent Americans prohibited this evil and governed it better than did the people of England. Said he: "Close up the rum shops as your people do, and my occupation would end." Alas! Would that we did thus close them, for so would most of our judges' occupations be gone. But no! In enlightened Boston there are churches, schoolhouses, and asylums,—and thousands of vile rum-holes sandwiched between, making void the good done by the former, and furnishing inmates for station-house and prison.

The suburbs of Liverpool are very fine, and in appearance much like those of Boston. Horse-cars and omnibuses constantly ply between the city and these places. Sefton Park is inexpressibly fine in itself, and in its distant rural scenery; and Toxton (Brookline, we might consider it) is of great rural beauty. The distant view of the old red church tower, cathedral-like and grand, situated on elevated ground, peering up out of shade-trees that obscured other parts of the building, and even the larger portion of the village itself; small lakes gleaming in the sun; the evidence of high civilization,—made us long to see more of Old England,—of these "sweet Auburns," lovely villages of the plain; and we were soon gratified, for at 2.20 o'clock P. M., Saturday, we took cars for the city of

CHESTER.

Who that travels would risk his reputation as a person of taste, and not go to Chester? A fare of $1.50 each brought us to this Mecca; for as the Jews of old must go to Mt. Zion, so must the England-visiting American go to Chester. First, a few words about the city itself; and here the brain acts sluggishly, and the pen rebels at the thought of describing what has been described so many times before. We arrived after an hour and forty minutes' ride from Liverpool.

Chester is the capital of Cheshire, and is situated on the River Dee, with a population of 35,701. It was a Roman station known as Deva Castra. It is nearly surrounded by the river, and the original portion of the city is encompassed with an ancient wall having low towers at special points. This wall is in perfect condition, and is the best specimen of its kind in all England. The foundations are Roman, and part of this work is visible, and is an item of much interest. The upper portions, resting on the Roman base, date from the time of Edward I., who was born at Westminster in 1239, and died 1307; and so the wall is nearly six hundred years old. It is about eight feet thick at the top, and varies in thickness at the bottom according to its height, which, of course, is determined by the irregular surface of the land. The space enclosed is a parallelogram, planned like all Roman camps, with a gate or entrance in the middle of each of the four sides, the main streets intersecting at the centre of the town.

There are at stated intervals stone stairs, leading up to the walk at the top of the wall, and this is a common promenade for the public, and more especially for strangers, as from this elevation, a large portion of the entire city is seen, and the view of the outside scenery is most enchanting.

There are streets, and a busy population of dwellers on both sides of the walls. Here, too, is a noble field called Grosvenor Park, many acres in extent, used as pleasure-grounds for the public, or as a parade for soldiers, whose barracks are near. As a background, bordering it, half a mile away, are the grounds of fine mansions, half embowered with trees. As we pass around to the left, we see the muddy banks and meadow-like borders of the River Dee. Opposite this, making the other shore, is a dirty fishing-town, with its principal street extending up from the river. This is called Sty Lane,—at least by some people. Here we saw from the walls, where we were walking, a Hogarthlike nest of dilapidated buildings and destitution. There were the sights and sounds of a veritable Saturday-night row, in which men, women, and children were promiscuously mingled. It was a good specimen of a bad original. After a sight like this, we were inclined to give Hogarth less credit as an inventor than we had before done; for he had sights worthy his pencil at hand, without an effort of his imagination.

Continuing our walk along to where the river runs sluggishly beside the walls, we extend our delightful tramp. Encircling the old town thus, occupies us nearly an hour. On our way, just inside the walls, are ruins of small lodges, antique and ivy-clad; and on the top of the wall itself is a little tower, on which is an inscription, cut in a stone tablet, telling that from its floor King Charles I. beheld the defeat of Rowton Moor, in 1645. These walls are built of a dark-reddish stone, well laid in white mortar, and have a very antiquated appearance. There is a breastwork, or parapet, three feet high on each side for protection, and capped with long, rough-cut stones. Having finished our circuit we, much against our inclination, go down one of the stairways, and into the street within the walls, where we continue our explorations, confessing that our early dislike of the task of writing up this city has about vanished. So marked was the early impression of peculiar interest and novelty, and so fully satisfying to our anticipations, that when we finally left the city we could not help feeling as did one of old when he said, with the change of but one word,—"If I ever forget thee O Chester, may my right hand forget her cunning." We were not the first Americans who have thought and felt thus; no one who has ever seen Chester will or can forget her. The cry once was, "Great is Diana of the Ephesians." We ejaculate "Great is Chester of the Britons."

The queer old streets are interesting in the extreme. Narrow and short, but clean, they are said to be at right-angles with each other; and perhaps they are. The buildings are quaint, antique, and of all designs, the second story often projecting beyond the first, and the third beyond the second, and the gable end out over that. Their general appearance so attracts attention that nothing in particular is noted, so far as relates to the arrangement of the city itself. The Rows, as they are called, that is, the covered sidewalks in the older and business streets, are built in under the second stories, and are paved. The different store-sections are out of level, each with its neighbor, though tolerably level through the length of the entire streets. Often the ceilings of these walks are low enough to touch with the hand; generally the floor, or pavement, is raised from two to four feet above the grade of the street. Of course the shops are back of these. The idea is not a bad one. In times of foul weather or of strong sun, the Rows are protections. The entire width between the buildings being given to teams, renders it much safer for pedestrians.

The majority of the buildings are built with their ends to the street, showing gables with the high roof or attic ends, with elaborate decorations, and these afford a fine opportunity for a display of quaint finish. Many of these buildings have a framework of oak, more or less carved, with brickwork fitted into the frame, and plastered and painted, generally with subdued tints. The people are to be commended for the good taste and judgment displayed in their rebuilding; for when a new edifice takes the place of one removed, the new design, while it may increase the height of the stories, and add other real improvements and conveniences, yet preserves the old style. Chester is a lively, bustling, and enterprising business place—a gem in its way.

Of course the cathedral comes in for early attention. So long as Charles Kingsley—Canon Kingsley, for here he was made canon in 1869—is remembered, so long will the cathedral be of interest. It is situated in the very centre of the city. Jammed in among other buildings, with no quiet grass and aged trees about it, the pavements lead up to its very doors. It is irregular in outline, dark-reddish-brown in color, aged in appearance, with a massive low tower, but no spire above it. The transept, choir, and nave windows are of monstrous size, not much higher than wide, filled with elegant perpendicular Gothic tracery, and divided into many compartments. The interior is in good repair,—*restored*, as it is termed. Here, as in all cathedrals, there is a stone floor, and hundreds of inscriptions that tell of those who are quietly resting beneath.

"Their labors done, securely laid
In this, their last retreat,

Unheeded o'er their silent dust
The storms of life shall beat."

The building was originally the abbey of St. Werburgh, built for the Benedictines,—begun in 1095 by Hugh Lupus, assisted by St. Anselm,—and retains its original design.

The next object of interest, and one truly remarkable, is the church of St. John, once the cathedral. It is situated about five minutes' walk away from the cathedral proper, and, unlike that, stands in a large green, or close, for centuries used as a burial-ground. The red tower is very high, yet without a spire, and partly in ruins. It stands almost alone in solitary beauty, with picturesque ivy-clad cloisters and arches, presenting a striking and wonderful group, which tells of the remote past. The old tower, colossal and grand, but in such decay as to make it dangerous to ring the bells (and fallen since we saw it), is connected with what was formerly the nave of the church; and this is now, with slight additions for a chancel, all that is used, a new end having years ago been put on at the line of transepts. St. John's is of early English architecture in some parts, and late Norman in others, having large, plain, round columns that carry the arches of the clerestory. These columns lean outward from the perpendicular, making the nave wider at the top, and the widening was thought to have been caused by a settling of the old stone groining. On making repairs a few years since, the height of the clerestory walls was foolishly reduced some four feet, and a lower wood ceiling put in to lessen the weight on the columns; but it was at length discovered that the original was built for effect,—whether for good or for ill, we will not decide. In picturesqueness never excelled, St. John's Church, with its grounds and accompanying ruins, not only divides the honors with the cathedral, but by many would be named first.

Chester is the seat of rare monuments of the past. The castle, built by Lupus, Earl of Chester, seven hundred and more years ago, while it has been largely re-constructed, is used as the shire hall, and contains many portraits of noted men who have been distinguished in the city's history. Near the castle is a fine old stone bridge crossing the Dee, with a single arch of two hundred feet. There is, in the suburbs, a curious manorhouse, once belonging to the abbey of St. Werburgh; Eaton Hall, the seat of the Marquis of Westminster; and a ground where famous races are held. Cheese fairs occur once a month, promiscuous fairs three times a year, and markets twice a week; and the city gives the title of Earl to the Prince of Wales.

At 10 A. M. we visited the military barracks, and in the parade-ground, with thousands of other spectators, witnessed the usual Sunday drill, and also the military evolutions, such as striking tents and stacking arms. Some five hundred soldiers were engaged in these operations on this Christian Sunday, made especially sacred by its associations with the Prince of Peace. At this hour, amid the sound of innumerable chimes of from three to five bells each, were the intermingling sound of trumpets and the clamor of war,—so confused yet each so prominent as to make one doubt which had the inside track, church or army, God or Satan.

In the afternoon we were at the cathedral, and, the service being intoned, the echoes made confusion worse confounded. We finally saw more clearly than ever before the force of the remark of one of old, when he said: "In the church I had rather speak five words with my understanding, that by my voice I might teach others also, than ten thousand words in an unknown tongue." We have thought, while enveloped in this confusion, that it would be well for the managers of cathedral services everywhere, to be thoughtful as St. Paul was, and say: "Whether pipe or harp, except they give a distinction in the sounds, how shall it be known what is piped or harped?"

There is one especial object of American interest. In the chapter-house there hang over the doors two flags that were carried by the Cheshire Regiment— the 22d—at the Battle of Bunker Hill in our American Revolution; and they were also carried by General Wolfe at the taking of Quebec in 1759, sixteen years before. It will thus be seen that soldiers from this county were at Charlestown, June 17, 1775.

There are some very ancient houses of particular note. They are of the old timbered and panel-plastered fashion, with very fine specimens of profuse and sometimes grotesque carving. Among them is God's Providence House. Its three stories and gable project over each other as before described. The historical fact is that, when the plague prevailed, there were deaths in every house on the street save this one, and after all was over, the owner put this inscription upon it, which remains to this day:

GOD'S PROVIDENCE IS MY SALVATION.

Of bold and high decoration, by carving of the wooden parts, is Stanley House, with its three gables. This is one of the best specimens of ancient timber and plaster-work to be found in England.

On Bridge Street there is an ancient Roman bath that well repays a visit, for we are there permitted to look upon work a thousand years old. Do we realize or comprehend the fact? No; but the impression, with a photographic fidelity, has been made on the mind, and will never be effaced. Let what will happen, so long as memory acts and intelligence remains, the good influence of these impressions will endure. The mind is truly, as the poet has expressed it,—

Like the vase in which roses have once been distilled,
You may break, you may ruin the vase, if you will,
But the scent of the roses will hang round it still.

In closing our description of grand old Chester, we will name the fact that in Trinity Church are the tombs of the poet Thomas Parnell, who was born at Dublin, 1679, and died at Chester in July, 1717; and of the eminent commentator, Matthew Henry, born at Broad Oak, Flintshire, 1662, and died at Nantwich, June 22, 1714. He became pastor of a church in Chester—perhaps Trinity—in 1687, and remained till 1702, a period of twenty-five years. The Commentary was the result of his lectures in exposition of the Bible, the whole of which is said to have been thus passed in critical review during his ministry at Chester. He continued the lectures at Hackney, to which place he removed in 1712. The first collected edition was published at London, in five volumes, in 1710, but to Chester really belongs the honor of being the place where this work, so well known the Protestant world over, had its birth.

It would be pleasant to linger in this venerable place. We had enjoyed so much antiquity at Chester that we could hardly endure the shock of being suddenly dropped into some modern spot; and so the place set down in our programme as next in order was the one, of all others, admirably in keeping with our purpose. This was the good old domestic town of

SHREWSBURY,

of well-known Cake notoriety. We took passage at 5.10 P. M. this same Sunday evening; and while the sun was high above the horizon, at 7 o'clock, we were safely landed at Station Hotel. Soon after supper, as English people call it, we were out for a tramp. There's always an indescribable impatience in the tourist to see the place. There's a great deal of the can't-comfortably-wait condition, and it generally has soon to be gratified. We were early in love with the town. How comfortably we had been let down from Chester, and how unharmed we felt! The quaintness discovered in the narrow streets and the ancient buildings made it a second Chester; but we thought we saw in the mansions more of stateliness, costliness, and evidences of a substantial English aristocracy. The better class of houses were like the first-class three-story brick mansions at Salem and Newburyport, making one feel at home. Here and there were newer buildings of modern style, which made a worthy connecting link between the old dispensation and the new; for there were buildings as modern as are anywhere built, and some as ancient as are to be found anywhere, almost equalling those so justly adored at Chester. Shrewsbury is the shire town of Shropshire, and has a population of 23,406. It has the remains of an ancient castle, and some of the old walls of the city are yet standing. The River Severn, a sluggish and muddy stream, some three hundred feet wide, divides the town. The older portion is connected by two bridges, and also by a cheap rope-ferry, with the other side, on which are rural residences and public-entertainment grounds.

When we speak of the River Severn our interest is intensified by the thought of a great historic fact. In 1428, by order of Clement VIII., the body of Wycliffe, which since 1415 had been buried in a dunghill, to which it had been consigned by order of the Council of Constance, was exhumed and burned to ashes, and these were thrown into the little River Swift, a tributary of the Avon. This gave birth to the fine old verse:—

The Avon to the Severn runs,
The Severn to the sea;

And Wycliffe's dust shall spread abroad
Wide as the waters be.

The river curves, and partly encircles the city; and on its banks we found the public park, and near it St. Chad's circular stone church, with its large square tower above a portico, crowned with a belfry, under which are great clock dials. The park is simply an ordinarily well-kept grass ground, of perhaps one third the size of Boston Common. It has three or four superb avenues of old lime-trees, and Quarry Walk is one of the finest in Europe. Tradition has it that all of these linden-trees were set out by one man, more than a century and a half ago. The ruins of Battlefield Church, now little appreciated, roofless and dilapidated, are four miles away. This is famous as being the place where *Sir John Falstaff* "fought an hour by Shrewsbury Clock."

The town was an important one as early as the twelfth century, and prominent at times as being the place of royal residence. Parliaments were held here in 1283 and in 1398. In 1403—ninety years before the discovery of America by Columbus—the famous Battle of Hotspur was fought near here, in which that distinguished soldier was killed. In 1277 it was the temporary residence of Edward I., and to this place he removed the King's Bench and Court of Exchequer during the Wars of the Roses. The inhabitants took part with the House of York, and it was the asylum of the queen of Edward IV. after having given birth to the princes Edward and Richard, the two children who are supposed to have been murdered in the Tower of London by Richard III. As will be seen, the place is intimately connected with historic facts. Remembrance of this contributes a charm not well expressed in words.

As we walked over these streets, through which distinguished personages have walked, and by houses which intelligent people have occupied for a thousand years,—as we thought of many generations who here lived, labored, and died, their dust now mingling with the soil of its ancient burial-grounds, or resting in the tombs of its venerable churches, within sound of the same vesper bells to which we were listening at the close of this pleasant Sunday evening,—as these reflections took possession of our minds, the quiet sanctity of the Puritan New England Sunday was about us, and we felt that we were in a befitting place to end a day so well and interestingly begun at Chester.

Sunday night is passed, and Monday, May 5, is at hand. As usual we are impatient for more experiences. Our thoughts are mingled with regrets, tinted with righteous indignation, that American tourists so neglect these places, and hurry to others of more metropolitan renown, but of less real interest to any one who would see England in her best estate. Their loss—a great one—is nobody's gain. A fine walk this of to-day, through street after street of good business activity.

Now was the time to attend to another duty. In passing a store we saw a notice, high up on a building, that here were made the original Shrewsbury cakes. We found that the recipe had been in use for over one hundred years, dating from 1760; that for as long a time the cakes had been there manufactured, and were now enjoying an enviable reputation the world over; and also that it was not an uncommon occurrence to send them by express to the United States. They are put up in round, blue, paper-covered, pasteboard boxes, about six inches in diameter and four inches deep, the cakes being of a nature that will bear transportation. We are soon in possession of them, but examination does not make us over-enthusiastic. If at home we should be even less so. They are thin cakes, say less than a quarter of an inch thick, and five inches in diameter,—apparently made without spice, but very sweet, fat, and crisp. As nearly as we could judge they are composed simply of flour, sugar, eggs, and butter, the latter in generous proportions. There's a deal in a name, and in the reputation gained through the sluggish lapse of a century's advertising and vigilant attention to business. Our young saleswoman is quite pert in her independence, and scorns the idea of selling or even hinting at a recipe for their manufacture; and we go away consoling ourselves with the idea that we have many times eaten similar things at home, and shall again, and animated by the conviction that,

"A rose by any other name would smell as sweet."

It may be our judgment is at fault, and that they are in possession of a precious as well as a remunerative secret.

Continuing our walk, we met with St. Mary's Church, which has every requirement of a cathedral except a bishop. Had we not seen churches of the kind before, we should have gone deeply into enthusiasm now; for here was a grand structure, thoroughly antique, with nave, choir, transepts, chapels, ancient monuments, and fine windows,—one very large, as good as any in all England, and six hundred years old. It is an inclination of the tourist to ejaculate at every new place, "This is the most interesting we have seen." We are at a loss to know why St. Mary's is not oftener spoken of as among the favored few, for it is all of that.

Shrewsbury, grand old town, full of interest, and antiquities we have not time to name, is itself a museum of antiquity. We know much more than we did when we first surveyed it, but travel and observation have not at all dimmed our admiration. At 11.10 A. M. we move on to our next place, which was the prototype of, and gave its name to, the Heart of our Massachusetts Commonwealth,

WORCESTER.

We arrived at 2 P. M. in a mild rain, the first we had been compelled to walk out in since our journey began. Valises deposited at a hotel, we were, as usual, soon out to survey the place. Like Shrewsbury, it is situated on the River Severn, which runs along the rear part of the place. It contains 33,221 inhabitants, was once a walled city, and vestiges of the walls remain. The Danes destroyed it and rebuilt it about 894, and it was burned by Hardicanute, the last of the Danish royal dynasty in England, in 1041. It suffered from frequent incursions of the Welsh, and was one of the principal cities of the ancient Britons. In the early period of the Saxon dynasty it became the second bishopric of Mercia. Having espoused the cause of Charles I. it was greatly troubled by the soldiers of Parliament; but on Sept. 3, 1651, the final battle, termed by Cromwell "a crowning mercy," was here fought by the Royalists under Charles on the one side, and Cromwell on the other, which resulted in routing the former, and ended in a defeat from which he never recovered.

Samuel Butler the poet, of "Hudibras" celebrity, received the rudimentary elements of his education in the schools here; and the celebrated Lord John Somers was born here in 1651.

The city is built mostly of brick, and, from the number of gardens and shade-trees, has a rural appearance. The river is crossed by an old stone bridge of several arches, and along the bank next the city proper, and below the land elevation, is a promenade, a mile or more long, following the curve of the river. In portions of the place an active business is done, and enterprise is everywhere manifest. Except that the buildings are of brick or stone, it well reminds one of our Massachusetts Worcester. A few of the houses are two or three centuries old.

It is a marked place for antiquities, and foremost among them is the cathedral, which is built of light-drab sandstone, in the form of a double cross, having four transepts. It is 426 feet long; the western transepts are 180 feet through, and the eastern, 128 feet. The tower is at the centre, or at the junction of the nave, choir, and east transepts, and is 193 feet high. It is very elaborately decorated, ending with a rich battlement and lofty turrets. It was founded in 680, but the present edifice dates from the fourteenth century. It has surrounding grounds, and is in most perfect repair, both the exterior and interior having been lately restored.

A few words once for all are needed in relation to this word *restored*. As will readily be conceived, buildings erected of a somewhat perishable material are more or less in constant decay. The degree depends on the nature of the stone, its exposure, and the extent of its elaboration; but all stone is subject to disintegration, and the buildings were so long in process of erection, that the older portions were in need of repair before the newer were finished. In these latter days, being more neglected, much dilapidation existed, and important parts of the edifices were threatened with entire destruction. A new spirit of enterprise has been infused into the people, and repairs have been vigorously prosecuted. In some instances, large portions have been refaced on the outside.

In the instance of Worcester Cathedral, the great tower was nearly rebuilt ten years ago. More particularly has there been an interest in the work of re-decorating the interiors. This has consisted, first of all, in the removal of whitewash, which had been put on. A time has been when the common judgment of all bishops approved its use. It gave a clean look, but injured the general effect. Cathedrals are generally finished over head with stone arches and ribs; and the wooden roof is slated, tiled, or covered with metal. Sometimes the stonework of the ceilings was plastered and blocked off in imitation of stone. The present taste—without doubt largely induced by the late Sir Gilbert Scott—is to clean off this wash and leave the stone as nearly as possible in its natural condition. It was a common practice in olden times to color and ornament stonework, and as the wash has been removed, paintings, often grotesque, are found, and always left as a memento of the past. Eventually, all cathedrals will probably be decorated in high colors and fancy designs. Some such paintings are already begun in unimportant parts by way of experiment. As the walls now look somewhat bare, and as a love for display in service is on the increase, there is a strong desire for new glass of the very highest colors. It is to be expected that the same spirit will not rest till the decoration is also in gorgeous hues. In a few cases the stone is so well put together, and of such a tint, as to make it sacrilege to interfere with it; but in a majority of churches such decorating would harmonize well with the gay windows and rich interior stone finish, and really be an improvement.

Another change is the removal of the organs from the choirscreens, originally located at the line of choir and transepts. They have been removed in a majority of cases to the side of the choir, and much to the improvement of the edifice. All cathedrals that we visited have been restored more or less as described, and a majority of them are finished. When a restoration of stonework has been made of any especial part, as new door-work or a window, the work has been done in the style of the period. Of course all changes since the last period of Gothic architecture—the perpendicular—have been made in that style; so that at times we find in one structure all the styles, from the Norman down through the whole four. This method of operation must receive general, if not universal sanction, since we find it invariably pursued.

On cathedrals generally are chimes of bells, on which the quarter and half hours are struck by a few notes; and in Worcester Cathedral is, also, a large barrel, of music-box construction, by which at especial times in the day, as at 9 A. M., 12 M., 3 and 6 P. M., an entire tune is played on the bells. For every day of the month there is a new tune, a list of the music being at the door. On the day of our visit was played "The Harp that once through Tara's Halls."

It would be an impossibility to describe in detail these great works of art, the cathedrals of England. Little more can be done than name things of especial interest. So far as the interior of Worcester Cathedral is concerned, it is very inviting, and has interesting monuments. The impression is not quite what one would imagine as he thinks of an edifice over four hundred feet long, for sight never conveys an idea of its actual length; but the impression is that you are looking at a colossal church—one larger than you have ever before seen. You admire the lofty tower, think it of elegant design, proportions, and finish, that it looks new,—as it really is,—but get no impressions of the great age of the building.

From the bridge, looking back to the left, you see an elegant picture—the river low down, a terraced walk at its side, the land surface some ten or fifteen feet above. An eighth of a mile or so distant, half embowered in fine trees, is the cathedral. The upper parts loom high above the branches, and the tower rises still higher. The rear end of the cathedral choir, with its great east window, projects beyond the grove, and is in full view from our point of observation. From this place the city has a rural rather than a commercial or manufacturing appearance. Let one stand on the bridge and view this scene, and listen to the sweet notes of the bells. The mellow and refined sound—

we had almost said the intellectual demonstration—of the cathedral bells, as by an intuition of its own, institutes a comparison between this day of civilization and that of the rude savage, and then if ever, one sees and knows that the world moves.

In the cathedral are monuments of marked and distinguished men. Here reposes the dust of King John; and bedimmed with dust, in sombre repose and ancient glory, is an effigy to his memory. He died in 1216, or more than 667 years ago. Here lies the body of Bishop Stillingfleet, who was made Bishop of Worcester in 1689, and died ten years later.

Adjoining the cathedral are fine cloisters, or covered and partly enclosed corridors, for walking and meditation. These on the open side are built with piers and arches, filled with stone tracery. They open into the quadrangle, which is grassed over, but roofless, of which the cloisters form the sides. On the grounds, and in those adjoining, are the residences of the bishop and other dignitaries of the cathedral; also, the Cathedral, or King's School. One can hardly imagine the beauty of these great cathedral grounds,—the grouping of its buildings; the finely kept lawns; the shady walks; the atmosphere of repose, broken only by the sound of the rooks, that are in the ancient tree-tops, or by the quarter-hour bells so sweetly disturbing it, and solemnly proclaiming that a new division of time has been joined to those before the flood. How admonitory the sounds are! Not to all listeners are they thought-hardening, but the reverse. Now and then, by night and by day, all do *think*, and so the inanimate bells preach effectually, and as the living preacher cannot always do.

Among the many interesting churches here is St. Andrew's, with its fine old tower and spire, 245 feet high,—a Bunker Hill monument in height, with 25 feet added.

The pottery manufactories must be named, for their productions are among the finest of our times, competing even with those of Sévres. The management of these establishments kindly opens them to the public, and all parts of the work may be inspected. Their warerooms present a display that is interesting in the extreme. The results of many years of experiment are here on exhibition, and they are remarkable triumphs of mind over matter. The fine blending of tints, the high degree of finish attained in representing fruits, landscapes, and flowers, are truly wonderful. We were informed that our own Boston has its constant share of these products.

Remaining over night, in the evening we are entertained by a thunder-shower, the first we have experienced for the season. Heavy thunder and vivid lightning, accompanied by warm and refreshing rain, remind us of home.

We should have before stated that in this, as in all the English cathedral towns, service is held in the cathedral at 11 A. M. and 3 P. M. daily. There is no sermon, but the regular morning and evening prayers of the Church. We were present and enjoyed the grand organ music and singing; but the intoned services and its accompaniment of echoes, confused and neutralized the spirit of worship. A few persons, perhaps twenty in all, were present, aside from the clergy and choir. Most of them were strangers, as we were, drawn thither by curiosity, but treated in the kindest manner, and every facility given for enjoyment. We were even invited into the stalls, which are the chief seats in the synagogue. We occupied them readily; at the expense of being accused of Phariseeism we may say, in a whisper, that we desired them. We went to the top of the tower and were delighted by the view of highland, vale, river, grove, and the city itself. Here, as in all cathedrals, men are in waiting to show persons over the edifice, and call their attention to things of especial interest. They are dressed in black, with white cravats and flowing black robes, which add much dignity to their appearance. At 10 A. M., Tuesday, we left Worcester for another cathedral town,

HEREFORD.

At 11.30 we have just arrived, and find our pronunciation at fault. *Her*-e-ford, say the people, not *Here*-ford, as we had spoken it. Well, thus corrected, we speak it as well as they to the manner born. Our ride here, and in fact all the way from Liverpool, has been through no very striking scenery. The land is well kept, and about one quarter of it is under cultivation. We notice the absence of land divisions. As few as possible are used, and those are hedges.

Here we call the reader's attention to the plan of travel we are pursuing. We decided not to hurry to London, as most Americans do,—stopping only at Chester, Stratford-on-Avon, and Oxford; we would see Ireland and Scotland well, and England thoroughly. We therefore, on leaving Ireland, went directly to Liverpool, which is on the extreme western side of England, and about two thirds of the way north from its lower coast. Thence we went southerly to Chester, then to Worcester, and now we are at Hereford. It is our intention to work down to Salisbury and Winchester, stopping at other cathedral towns on the way, and thence to take a northerly route to London. This line of travel carries us over the entire western part of the island.

Hereford is a substantial English town. It has many antique buildings, of the jutting-story construction,—good examples of the timber-and-plaster pattern,—and wide streets. There is a thrifty look about the inhabitants, and their number is 18,335,—or was in 1871, for that is the year from which date the statistics.

We could but think of some of the celebrated men who had looked upon these identical scenes. We thought of the Kembles, who here managed the theatre. They are of world-wide celebrity, beginning with old Roger, born in this town in 1721, and dying in 1802,—the father of twelve children, among whom are Sarah (Mrs. Siddons), and John Philip, the eldest son, and Charles, the youngest, born, respectively in 1757 and 1775, and dying in 1823 and 1854. We thought also of David Garrick of histrionic renown, born here in 1716, the personal friend of Dr. Samuel Johnson of dictionary notoriety.

We walk to the River Wye, on which the town is situated, and which is crossed by an ancient, six-arched bridge. The cathedral, as at Worcester, is to the left, and on land rather elevated from the river. Hereford strongly resembles that place, though without the river promenade, and with less refinement.

The cathedral, of course, must have attention. Founded in 1072, it was building during the next two hundred years. Mostly in the Norman style, it is 325 feet long, 110 feet through the transepts, and has a grand old central tower, 160 feet high, ending with a battlement and corner turrets. The color of its stone is light drab, much resembling that at Worcester. Every part is in good repair, and the interior has a very imposing look. We were by no means prepared for the bold finish and fine windows for the chapels and cloisters, and, above all, for the well kept lawn and trees of the Bishop's Palace, and other ecclesiastical houses. The Lady Chapel is one of the finest in England, and the cathedral library has very valuable manuscripts, among them one of Wycliffe's Bibles, very rare. The monuments date back to the eleventh century. In what profusion are the antique slabs, with their great brass crosses. How the very atmosphere of the place is fragrant with the memory of the sainted dead! In visiting these cathedrals, in looking on the ruins of ancient abbey or monastery,—so complete in themselves, and exhibiting such evidence of former grandeur,—one is inclined to feel that each is *the* cathedral of all England,—the Mecca of all the Church; for what is lacking? Not capacity or costliness; not lack of graves of kings, earls, barons, or lords, for here beneath our feet repose the dust of enough such for an entire kingdom. Webster well said of another place: "I do love these ancient ruins. We never tread upon them but we set our foot upon some revered history."

The part the town has taken in the wars gives her renown. How often the Welsh came here and made fearful devastation! Could the sleepers, now at rest forever, speak again, they would tell of the invasions of the Saxon era, and the strange Baronial wars; of the sanguinary conflicts of the Plantagenets, and of the battles of the seventeenth century; of the long siege, when a brave defence of the place was made by the people, their town being one of the very last to submit to the Parliament. All is peaceful now, and we, on this pleasant day, were dreamily wandering along the lines dividing a great past from a greater present, and both from a yet more remarkable future. Without ability to comprehend all this, we were trying to get a little entertainment, if we dared not hope for something greater. A wide door is opened when one in meditative mood goes into a town like this, knows of the great past, sees the present, and then, in spite of himself, projects his thoughts into the future,—the near and the distant blending into one.

The sweet chimes on the bells proclaim the end of an hour; then the short pause,—how still! and now how clearly marked is the new hour. The great diapason bell of the tower solemnly pronounces its four strokes, and we wend our way to the station for Gloucester.

CHAPTER VI.

GLOUCESTER—BRISTOL—BATH—SALISBURY—SARUM—
AMESBURY—STONEHENGE—WILTON.

At 6 P. M., after a scant two hours' ride, we take rooms at the Gloucester House, and are out on a walk in another beautiful town, the River Severn running through it,—a town more like Worcester than like Hereford, though in population (18,330) strikingly like the latter. The city is of British origin, but is very ancient. It was once a Roman station by the name of Colonia Glevum, and under the Emperor Claudius received the name of Claudia Castra. The Saxons, after they had taken it, gave it the name of Glean-ceaster; hence our modern word Gloucester. It had its part in battles, and in the seventeenth century was strongly fortified and took part with the Royalists. The place was of so much importance that Henry VIII. made it a bishop's seat, and so its great abbey church became a cathedral. The edifice is in fine repair, and is noted for its elegant cloisters,—the finest of any cathedral in the world. They are of very liberal dimensions, and adorned with fanlike tracery of extraordinary finish; and the openings into the great courtyard are filled with glass. The cathedral itself is one of rare beauty. It is 423 feet long, and 147 feet wide at the transepts; and the great central tower is 176 feet high to the base of the corner pinnacles, which tower up 49 feet higher. The cloisters are 148 feet long on each of their four sides. We shall not attempt a closer description of this than of other cathedrals, though every part is a study.

It has but a small number of noted monuments, but among them are some of unusual interest. One, always attracting attention, is of Robert, Duke of Normandy. It is a recumbent effigy of bog-oak, covered with wire network. Being a Crusader, the legs are crossed, as is the customary representation. Robert was imprisoned by his brother Henry, his eyes were put out, and for twenty-eight years he continued in this miserable condition till death came to his relief. Another monument is to the memory of Edward II., who was murdered Sept. 21, 1327. Another commemorates Bishop Warburton, who was made bishop of the diocese in 1759, and died here in 1779. Near the entrance is a monument to Dr. Edward Jenner, the discoverer of vaccination, or inoculation, as a preventive of smallpox. He died at Berkley, in the county of Gloucestershire, and was buried in this cathedral in 1823, at the age of seventy-five.

In this city, in 1735, was born Robert Raikes, who in 1781 hired rooms for Sunday-schools, and employed women at a shilling a day to teach poor children, whom he found in the streets, the rudiments of common education. The school was held from 10 A. M. to 12 M. An hour's recess was followed by a lesson in reading, and then they went to church. After service the catechism was repeated till 5 P. M., "when they were charged to go home at once, and quietly." This was the origin of our present system of Sunday-schools, that of Mr. Raikes being the first of which we have any account. Here also, on the 16th of December, 1714, was born the celebrated preacher, George Whitefield, who died at Newburyport, Mass., Sept. 30, 1770, and whose remains are entombed under the pulpit of the Old South (Presbyterian) Church of that place. One mural tablet was of especial interest to us,—a white marble slab, high up on one of the transept walls, thought to be in memory of a relative of the founder of the chimes on Christ Church at the North End of Boston. It reads as follows:—

ABRAHAM RUDHALL BELL FOUNDER
FAM'D FOR HIS GREAT SKILL
BELOV'D AND ESTEEM'D FOR HIS SIGNAL
GOOD NATURE AND INTEGRITY
DIED JAN'Y 25TH 1785-6 AGED 78.

One of the bells at our Christ Church bears this inscription: "Abel Rudhall of Gloucester cast us all, Anno. 1744." As Abraham would have been about forty-two years old at the time, perhaps he was the son of this Abel.

The organ in the cathedral is one of great power and brilliancy of tone. It was built by the celebrated Renatus Harris of London, who built many of the large organs of England.

Reluctantly we left these beautiful grounds, and entertaining a regret unusually deep. The walks are kept scrupulously clean, and the flowers in the vicinity of the student's precincts were charming. As we sauntered about we could not but think of the great who have here held court. Beneath the shadow of these very walls walked Edward the Confessor, and many a Norman lord. In the old abbey Henry III. was crowned three hundred years ago; and who can walk and meditate here and not think of Richard III., Duke of Gloucester? We cannot refrain from quoting the quaint description given of him by Sir Thomas More:—

Richarde, the thirde sonne of Richard, Duke of Yorke, was in witte and corage equal with his two brothers, in bodye and prowesse far under them both, little of stature, ill fetured of limmes, croke backed, his left shoulder much higher than his right, hard favored of visage, and such as in stater called warlye, in other menne otherwise, he was malicious, wrathful, envious and from his birth ever frowarde. It is for truth reported that he came into the world with the feet forwarde, and also ontothed, as if nature changed her course in hys beginnynge, which in the course of his lyfe manny thinges unnaturallye committed.

Just outside the cathedral grounds, in a little park, stands a monument to the memory of John Hooper, who, in the reign of Queen Mary, was one of the first to suffer martyrdom, and was on this spot burned at the stake Feb. 9, 1555. Over three hundred years are gone since the smoke of the martyr arose from this spot. How changed the scene! Over the vast domain, none now for conscience sake have power to destroy.

As reluctantly as can be imagined, we turned away. Very dear to us already had become old Gloucester. With an indescribable feeling we left the hallowed spot, and at 11 A. M., on Wednesday, May 8, took cars for Bristol. Our people do not think enough of the Mother Country. They hurry breathlessly and thoughtlessly, with but confused perceptions, to yet more foreign lands; they do not rest by the way in these fine old towns, drink in the inspiration which pervades their very atmosphere, and so make themselves ever after able better to interpret history. Another has well expressed it: "To him who is of a mind rightly framed, the world is a thousand times more populous than to the men to whom everything that is not flesh and blood is nothing."

BRISTOL.

Arrived at 2 o'clock P. M., after a ride of three hours from Gloucester. First impressions of the place were much like those one experiences at our American Pittsburg, for smoke prevailed, and the dingy appearance of the buildings confirmed the belief, that this condition of the atmosphere was not exceptional. The city is a seaport, situated on both sides of the rivers Avon and Frome, at their confluence, and eight miles from their entrance into the Severn, which is the head of Bristol Channel. The population is 182,524, and the city presents a bustling, hurried appearance. It is provided with docks built in the time of George III., at a cost of $30,000,000, and in commercial influence was long the second city in the kingdom. There are five substantial bridges connecting the several portions of the city. Tides rise very high,— those denominated spring tides forty-eight feet, and the neap ones twenty-three feet, compelling the use of a floating landing.

Our luggage left at the station, in anticipation of but a short stay, we walked out in quest of the cathedral, and soon, as we fancied, saw it in the distance. We entered, admiring much about it, yet disappointed in its general appearance, for it looked old but not cathedralish. It didn't seem to have the genuine antique atmosphere. There were old monuments, but not old enough. The color was dark-reddish brown, very sombre, and in places the building was decayed.

At the risk of showing our ignorance we asked the female verger—for it was a woman this time—if this was the cathedral. Lo, our good judgment had prevailed, and we were informed that it was St. Mary Radcliff Church. We were glad of the mistake, for here the celebrated Joseph Butler—author of the renowned "Analogy," who was made Bishop of Bristol in 1738, and died at Bath, June 16, 1752—was buried. Before us was a monument to his memory, the inscription written by the poet Southey. There were other monuments of considerable antiquity, which in number and interest greatly excelled those of the real cathedral. Of most interest to the visitor is the fact that in one part of this structure the wonderful young Thomas Chatterton—who died in this city August 24, 1770, at the age of eighteen—wrote his astonishing literary forgeries.

We were ushered up a flight of narrow stone stairs, from one of the transepts, into a room where yet remains a dusty chest, formerly belonging to a wealthy merchant in the reign of Edward IV. It was in this that Chatterton said he found his manuscripts,—declaring that, after being sealed up for centuries, these documents, among others, were there in 1727 when the chest was opened. It was in this room, with its unglazed openings, with the rooks as his companions, his only light that of the moon,—for he claimed that by her illumination he could write best,—were penned these remarkable impositions. History says that during the entire Sundays he would wander in the fields of Bristol, and lay for hours on the grass, gazing, rapt in meditation, on the tower of this old church.

We can hardly forbear stating briefly the nature of his remarkable deception. Let it be remembered that Chatterton died at the age of eighteen. His father, who was one of the schoolmasters of Bristol, died three months before his birth. At the age of five he was sent to school; so obtuse was his intellect, that in a year and a half "he was dismissed as an incorrigible dunce." His mother finally taught him to read, and to the astonishment of all he became at once an intellectual prodigy. At the age of eight he was again sent to school, and remained till his fifteenth year. He took little interest in his associates, but gave his attention to miscellaneous reading. In 1767, the year he left school, he was apprenticed to a Bristol attorney. Very studious, but remarkably eccentric, he kept his own counsel, employing his leisure time in the study of theology, history, and especially the phraseology of Old English. The next season, when in his seventeenth year, he performed the work which immortalizes his name. The old chest was opened by the proper authorities a half-century before. The parchments were of no especial value, and they remained undisturbed, till Chatterton's father used some of them as covers for schoolbooks. Some of them his son obtained; their curious chirography and phraseology excited his attention, and he conceived the idea of writing something of the kind himself. He asserted that some were written by Canynge, the original owner of the *cofre*, or trunk, and others by Thomas Rowley, the ecclesiastic and poet. He carefully copied the style of writing, followed the phraseology, and, by a process known only to himself, succeeded in giving a stained and timeworn look to his parchments, deceptive to all who examined them.

To Burgam, the celebrated pewterer, ambitious of obtaining the heraldic honors of his family, he gave a full pedigree, tracing his descent directly from the noble family of De Bergham. The historian of Bristol was aided in his ecclesiastical researches, and put in possession of a full account of the churches as they were three hundred years before, according to Thomas Rowley. A theological student was presented with part of a sermon by Rowley. One of the wealthy citizens of Bristol received from him a poem, entitled "Romaunt of the Cnyghte," said to have been written by the recipient's ancestor four hundred years before. To the Town and Country Magazine he made contributions, and Horace Walpole gratefully received anecdotes of eminent travellers and painters. So he continued cultivating, in the singular atmosphere of his temperament, this strange enthusiasm for the antique, and felt most comfortable while deceiving the public; but at length more critical eyes were turned toward him. Walpole, entertaining suspicions, submitted the parchments to Gray, who unhesitatingly pronounced them forgeries. They were returned to young Chatterton, who, indignant, avenged himself by a bitter attack on his antagonist. He led next a singular life of semi-seclusion and misery, writing articles for the reviews, sermons for clergymen, and songs for beer-gardens; all the time maintaining a gay exterior, though very poor, for he had an unconquerable vanity. Confiding in no one, he declined a dinner offered him by his landlady, even when he had been three days without food. Finally he expended his last pennies for arsenic, and was found dead in his room, August, 1770. He was buried in the pauper burial-ground in Shoe Lane, Bristol, and afterwards some of the citizens erected a monument to his memory.

Here, in 1495, and probably for some years before, lived John Cabot, the discoverer of the North American Continent, and while living here, March 5, 1496, he and his three sons obtained a patent from Henry VII., authorizing them, and their heirs and assigns, to go on voyages of discovery; and so we have it that a Bristol ship early touched our shores. Newfoundland was colonized by people from this place in 1610, under the supervision of a merchant by the name of Guy, whose colonists—while not successful in making a permanent settlement of the island, being superseded in 1621 or 1623 by others—were the first among foreigners to make this place their fixed residence.

Bristol was one of the first places in Great Britain, whence regular steam communication was established with the United States. April 4, 1838, the steamship Sirius, of 700 tons burthen, and with engines of 250 horse-power, sailed from Cork for New York. Four days later, April 8, the Great Western, of 1,340 tons, having engines of 450 horse-power, sailed from Bristol. Both arrived in New York on the 23d, the former making the passage in eighteen, and the latter, in fourteen days, arriving respectively on the morning and noon of the day named.

This city is the seat of manufacture of the well-known Bristol Brick, so long used for domestic purposes throughout America. An operative in one of the works visited the United States in 1820, and discovered similar sand in South Hampton, N. H., since which period a brick of equal value has been made in our own country.

The cathedral itself was next visited. It is on the other side of the River Avon, and is not a large structure, but is in good repair within and without. It is built of red sandstone, and has no grounds about it, but is situated in the midst of a populous neighborhood. It was founded in the time of King Stephen, who was born A. D. 1100, and died in 1154. It is 175 feet long, 128 feet wide, and has a large, solid, clumsy tower, 140 feet high. Here, as usual, we were entertained by the three-o'clock service. As an inducement to stay, we were informed by the verger that a new anthem was to be performed. We remained in chairs near the door, and were soon greeted with the usual imposing procession,—the verger with his elevated mace, followed by the robed choir of twelve men and boys, the two canons, and the bishop. With much order and becoming dignity they took their places before an audience of twelve persons. The service was intoned, making an unintelligent jumble of echoes and indistinct sounds, to us annoying in the extreme. We venture to say: "We think it don't pay." At the risk of being dealt with as were some of old for making a similar remark, we are inclined to ask, "Why was this waste of ointment made?" There are some monuments of interest in the cathedral, but none of great renown.

As we walked through the long and many streets, we were impressed with the city's extent. The land rises abruptly from the rivers, making many of the streets quite hard to climb. Very observable was the great number of houses in which the first stories were occupied as shops, the families of their keepers residing in the rooms above. A good idea, and one not practised enough. There were several Tremont and Park streets. Some of the buildings are modern in style, though for the most part they have an old and substantial appearance. Many of the oldest were originally so well built as to need no change, save for trading purposes.

The immediate suburbs are elevated. There are hills, amphitheatre like, on all sides; and on those adjoining the city proper are the fine grounds and mansions of the merchants and wealthier families. It is a place of manufactures and much commerce, and the central part, about the rivers, has the appearance of an American city.

There are many old institutions, and they have venerable buildings. We can only name a few. One of these is St. Stephen's Church, built in 1470, twenty years before the discovery of America. Others are the Old Guild Hall, built in the time of Richard II., who died A. D. 1400; the Corn Exchange, of modern Corinthian architecture, costing $250,000; the Royal Infirmary, which annually treats seven thousand five hundred patients. The city supports six hundred schools, educating twenty-five thousand pupils. Almshouses and hospitals, charity institutions and infirmaries, abound. After a somewhat hurried examination of the place, we took train at 5.30 P. M. for

BATH,

where, after an hour's ride, we arrived at 6.30 P. M. This is situated on the River Avon, and has a population of 52,542. It is one of the most ancient cities of Great Britain, was founded before the Roman invasion, and was an important station on the Roman road, leading from London to Wales. The remains of a Corinthian temple have been found; also many ancient Roman coins, vases, and altars. The city is chiefly built on level ground, or on a gentle slope; but it has along its rear side very elevated land, arranged in terraces and lawns, presenting, with its costly residences, an imposing background, giving to the place an air of consequence and picturesqueness. The city is principally built of brown stone, not at all dingy or sombre in appearance. A short ramble satisfied us that this was one of the aristocratic places of England. Substantial and clean was everything we beheld. Nothing anywhere was new; but the old was of the very best.

It is a fashionable place of resort for invalids, and we saw in the great thoroughfares carriages drawn by men and occupied by invalids of all ages. We said then and say now: "Let all who go to London go also to Bath." It is England's Queen City, and one of which she may well feel proud.

The cathedral is a perpendicular Gothic structure, very old, but in most perfect repair. It is 210 feet long, and has a tower 170 feet high, and is made of the reddish-drab sandstone of which the city is principally built. The stone ceiling of the church is of open fan-work, the finest of the kind in England. The whiteness of the whole interior is very striking, and accords with the neat exterior. There are no grounds about it, or even a fence; the streets are paved with large flagstones, reaching close to the building itself. The church and the world are in intimate proximity.

Here again the cathedral chimes saluted us every fifteen minutes, all day and all night. To the thoughtful their few notes speak with living lips. Sometimes they have two notes, and it requires but slight imagination to interpret them as saying "Quarter hour;" or three notes, and then they say "Quarter hour gone;" or four, and then we have it "Quarter hour more gone." The intervals are but short when the knell of departing time is not thus sounded. The poet Young says,—

We take no note of time,

But from its loss. To give it then a tongue
Is wise in man.

The advice is good, and we gave it a tongue; but it makes a deal of difference what the tongue says. If it waken regrets at the loss of time, when an eternity remains, then it had better have no tongue. These divisions of time are made by men, and are but incidentally a part of the Creator's plan. These sweet sounds are fresh music-flowers, strewn over the graves wherein are buried the new minutes of the quarter-hour just departed.

The city takes its name from its famous hot baths, and was frequented by the Romans for the purpose of using its waters, known to them by the name *Aqua Solis*, (sun-water). Baths were erected here in the time of Claudius, who died A. D. 54. These waters are saline and chalybeate, but they also contain sulphur and iron. The principal ones are called King's, Queen's, and the Cross baths, and the waters are constantly boiling at a temperature of from 109 to 117 degrees Fahrenheit. There are two others though of less note, called the Abbey and the Hot baths. Rooms for drinking the water and for bathing are constantly patronized, and at times the population of the city includes 14,000 visitors. King's Bath is the most popular. It is a fine old classic structure, fronting on one of the principal streets, in which is what is called the Pump Room, a saloon 85 feet long, 48 feet wide, and 34 feet high, elegantly finished and well furnished, where every convenience is provided the invalid for rest and refreshment, and for drinking the water from a constantly flowing fountain. These rooms are attended by matrons who for the small fee of a penny, furnish all the water desired. It is not unpleasant to the taste, though unmistakably impregnated with the materials named. It steams up well from the goblet, and is so warm that one must drink it in separate swallows. The old room was erected in 1760, and has been used by millions of people.

The baths connected with this building were the only ones we visited, and are a sample of the others. The visitor pays his shilling (24 cents), and receives a ticket which admits him to another part of the edifice, where he finds dressingrooms and toilet conveniences. He presently passes out into a small room, about four feet wide by eight feet long, closed on three sides; the fourth partly open, but protected by a screen reaching two thirds up to the top of the opening. The floor is covered with hot water, four feet deep, and stone steps lead into it. The bather can remain inside, or he may enter the great swimming-bath, filled with the same water. That is precisely what we did. Opening the screen, we found the great reservoir to be perhaps seventy-five feet square. Three sides were enclosed by rooms, similar to ours; the fourth side was a very ancient wall of stone, reaching ten feet or more above the water, in which were antique tablets telling of the foundation of the baths. The space was open to the sky. The water was so warm as at first to disincline one to enter it, but by degrees the sensation became far from unpleasant. Steam was constantly arising. The water was not clear, though clean, but had a dull clay-water, yellowish look, and was quiet, except in a space of ten feet square at the centre, where it constantly boiled up, at times with a rushing noise. We remained there nearly an hour, admiring and wondering.

In the great pump-room is a statue of the celebrated Richard Nash, familiarly known as Beau Nash, who died at Bath in 1761. He was at one time the leader of fashion. At the entertainment given by members of the Middle Temple to William III. he was employed to conduct the festivities. So marked was his success that the king offered to knight him, but conscious of his lack of means to support the honor, he declined it. More than any other person he aided in making Bath a place of fashionable resort. By his labors, propriety in dress and civility of manners were enforced in public resorts, till at length he was styled the King of Bath. He was an eccentric, and obtained his living at the gaming-table. He lived in great style, travelled in a coach with six outriders, and dispensed charity in a prodigal and reckless manner. Near the close of his life an act of Parliament was passed prohibiting gambling. Having depended entirely upon that, he afterwards lived in comparative indigence, and died in poverty, Feb. 3, 1761. Strange to say, he was ungainly in person, having coarse and even ugly features, and dressed in a tawdry style. It is remarkable that such a person could induce a system of public refinement, and be honored by this statue. Goldsmith was so interested in his strange career, that he anonymously published a biography of him in 1762, the year after his decease.

We can readily imagine what the place was prior to the time of Nash. Macaulay, quoting from Wood's "History of Bath," written in 1747, says:—

A writer who published an account of that city sixty years after the Revolution, has accurately described the changes which had taken place within his own recollections. He assures us that, in his younger days, the gentlemen who visited the springs slept in rooms hardly as good as the garrets which he lived to see occupied by footmen. The floors of the dining-rooms were uncarpeted, and were colored brown with a wash made of soot and small beer, in order to hide the dirt. Not a wainscot was painted. Not a hearth or chimney-piece was of marble. A slab of common freestone, and fire-irons which had cost from three to four shillings, were sufficient for any fireplace. The best apartments were hung with coarse woollen stuff, and were furnished with rush-bottomed chairs.

Samuel Pepys in his remarkably interesting diary, under date June 13, 1668, gives an account of his visit to the baths, and in his own quaint way tells the story as follows:—

Up at four o'clock, being by appointment called up to the Cross Bath, where we were carried one after another, myself and wife, and Betty Turner, Willett and W. Hewer, and by-and-by, though we designed to have done before company came, much company came; very fine ladies; and the manner pretty enough, only methinks it cannot be clean to go, so many bodies together in the same water. Good conversation among them that are acquainted here and stay together. Strange to see how hot the water is; and in some places, though this is the most temperate bath, the springs are so hot as the feet are not able to endure. But strange to see when women and men, here, that live all the seasons in these waters cannot but be parboiled, and look like the creatures of the bath! Carried away, wrapped in a sheet, and in a chair home; and there one after another thus carried, (I staying about two hours in the water) home to bed, sweating for an hour, and by-and-by comes music to play to me, extraordinary good as ever I heard in London almost, or anywhere.... *Sunday*, June 14: Up and walked up and down the town, and saw a pretty good market-place and many good streets, and fair storehouses, and so to the great church, and there saw Bishop Montague's tomb; and, when placed, did there see many brave people come, and among others, two men brought in, in litters, and set down in the chancel to hear; but I did not know one face. Here a good organ; but a vain pragmatical fellow preached a ridiculous, affected sermon, and made me angry, and some gentlemen that sat next me did sing well. 15th, *Monday*. Looked into the baths, and find the King and Queen's full of a mixed sort, of good and bad, and the Cross only almost for the gentry.

In 1768, Richard Brinsley Sheridan, the dramatist, removed here, where his father's family had previously settled. At the age of nineteen, in conjunction with his friend Hathead, he began his literary career. In 1772, at the age of twenty-one, he fell in love with Miss Linley, the popular singer of Bath. To save her from the persecutions of the libertine Matthews, he fled with her to France, and they were secretly married at Calais.

Delighted inexpressibly with this Queen City of the South of England, the antipodes of everything in the South of Ireland, we left it at 2.30 P. M. for

SALISBURY,

where, after a ride of four hours, we arrived at 6.30 P. M. We found this city possessing something of the look of old Chester, with narrow streets, projecting stories, queer oriel windows, and having 12,903 inhabitants. The clean streets are drained by small brooks running through them. The city was founded at Old Sarum, two miles north of its present location, and removed to this spot in 1217. It stands on a level and fertile plain, and is partially enclosed with the remains of the old walls. Little manufacturing is done, nor is trade followed to a great extent, the community being more inclined to agricultural pursuits.

Of course the cathedral is the great object of attraction, for it is very large and imposing, and has the highest spire in the kingdom, 404 feet in height. Spires are the exceptions on cathedrals, for of all the twenty-nine, only six have spires above their towers,—Salisbury, Litchfield, Norwich, Chichester, Oxford, and low ones on the front of that at Peterboro. The others have towers without the spire, but from association they are looked upon as finished, as in the case of King's Chapel and the old Brattle Square Church in Boston. At Salisbury we have the perfection of a central tower, and a spire, of charming outlines and graceful proportions. The cathedral was erected between the years 1220 and 1260, and is the only one in Great Britain where a single style of architecture was employed, and the pure Early English prevailed throughout. It was completely restored on the exterior in 1868, and the interior was in process of restoration at the time of our visit. In plan it is a double cross, its extreme length being 442 feet. The stone is of a dark soapstone color, and, being partially covered with very thin lichens, it has a dingy look; but the clean-cut outlines and smooth surface of the stone, the unusual height of the building, standing at the centre of a large close, furnishes such a good opportunity for viewing it that it presents an imposing appearance. It has many ancient monuments, and a beautiful altar-piece of the Resurrection. The grounds are walled in, and a half square-mile is within the enclosure. The English oaks are very large, the pathways clean and hard, and the lawn elegant. Rooks were to be seen in large numbers. Their circling flight as they wheeled from tree to tree; the stillness, unbroken save by their incessant cries; the prevailing air of repose; the aristocratic aspect of the Bishop's residence, and those of the other functionaries; the memories that have clustered around the spot, during the six hundred and sixty years since Bishop Poore founded the cathedral,—all conspired to invest the place with sanctity. Here again came the thought, "This is *the* cathedral,"—as though all England were but the diocese, and this the seat of the entire Church.

The great bourdon bell in the tower solemnly proclaims the hour of 8 P. M., and we wend our way over the dike, skirting the narrow river, to get a moonlight view of the cathedral. How often we turn to look anew on that symmetrical tower and lofty spire, and how satisfying the gaze. We turn back again and admire the fields spread around us; we are delighted with the hills, and with the winding river, narrow and clear, whose banks we are treading. The little mill-village ahead lures us on; but the cathedral is more potent. We turn again and gaze, walk backwards and admire, till the little hamlet a half-mile away is reached. We walk over the trembling footbridge and along the rude milldam, and try to be entertained; but no, we must turn our footsteps, for in full view is the "all in all." So we walk back, and think and admire anew, till night comes over us, and we and the cathedral are draped with a common pall. Through the night, as the chimes broke the stillness, and the great bell set its heavy notes as milestones of time, we felt the greatness of our surroundings.

OLD SARUM.

On Friday A. M., at nine o'clock, we took team at Salisbury for this place. Few spots in history are of more interest than this and its neighbor, Stonehenge,—the former two, and the latter a little less than nine miles from Salisbury. Sarum was an important settlement made by the early Britons, which afterwards became a Roman station, and the residence of the West Saxon kings. King Alfred fortified it, and in the eleventh century it was made a bishop's see. In 1217, however, Bishop Poore removed two miles away, and there established what is now Salisbury Cathedral, and so the city itself. As a matter of course, Sarum declined. The people followed the bishop, and what was once a place of note became almost extinct. Only one house remains on the grounds, but there are yet traces of the walls, cathedral, and castle. A more complete ruin is not to be found elsewhere in Great Britain, and a strange enchantment hovers about the scene.

The ride from Salisbury is very pleasant. From the level land on which the new city (though over 660 years old) stands we pass into a very undulating country, a quarter of which is covered with groups of shrubbery and trees. On the greenest of green grass, thousands of sheep and many cows are grazing, but no houses are in sight. A rare beauty exists everywhere, and many evidences of civilization. Salisbury is in our rear. Above all we see the cathedral tower and spire, distinct in outline, like a faithful sentinel standing there and guarding us.

We alight from our team, hitch the horse by the roadside, and turn to our left into a path parallel with the main road, and running a short distance across the field. We walk on along the edge of a grove, and come upon a solitary house, which is the only human habitation at Old Sarum. It is a stone house of moderate size, two stories high, plastered and whitewashed, with a red tiled roof. It is situated back some fifty feet from our path, is well fenced, and surrounded by shade-trees and shrubbery. It has a very English appearance. A sign over the gate informs the traveller that it is a place of transient entertainment. It fronts on the main road, and we are now at the rear entrance. Salisbury itself—or Boston, for a sixpence or a dime—can at a moment's notice furnish better entertainment than can be provided there. Yonder elevated land, in this same field, is our better restaurant. We walk delightedly over the pathway thither. What thoughts take possession of the mind. Here ancient Britons, conquering Romans, and Saxon kings and queens walked a thousand years ago. The same sky bent over them; the same soil was beneath their feet. Odors from flowers and the same balmy atmosphere regaled them. The birds sang to them as they sing to us now.

We approach the venerable enclosure. It is a vast circular enbankment some twenty feet high, with here and there bushes and small trees. The general symmetry suggests the work of human hands, but the abandoned appearance tells of antiquity. Our road leads down over a depression, the old moat,— and then up again, and in through an opening, on both sides of which is ragged masonry of flint, cobble-stones, and white mortar. We now discover that the huge mound is a mortar-wall, overgrown with grass on both sides, this opening having been rudely broken through it. Walls, a thousand and more years old! What desolation; what strange fascination! We enter and go up to the top of the embankment. What tongue or pen can adequately describe the emotions awakened? The views in all directions are charming. No mountains are visible to inspire awe; no great metropolis is to be seen; but "sweet fields of living green" hills innumerable, pleasant groves, feeding sheep, tinkling cow-bells, and air sweet with wild flowers and modest daisies (crushed at every tread beneath the feet) are about us; but we leave these, to study the grand old ruin. At the centre is a hollowed, though comparatively level space, of five hundred feet in diameter, covered with grass, bushes, and small mounds. The depression is not far from twenty feet deep, the earth and grass sloping up to the walk, about ten feet wide, which encircles it. The outer edge is irregularly hemmed in by bushes. Outside of this is a mote fifty feet wide, and thirty feet deep. Encircling all is a plateau two hundred feet wide, and another mote, thirty feet wide and twenty feet deep. The motes were once filled with water, but now grass has superseded it. Instead of being a barrier against approaching foes, they have better uses. In the language of Whittier, applied to an old New England burial-ground:—

There sheep that graze the neighboring plain
Like white ghosts come and go;

The farm horse drags his fetlock chain,
The cow-bell tinkles slow.

With variation of tense another verse of the same poem applies to it:—

It knows the glow of eventide,
The sunrise and the noon,

And sanctified and glorified
It sleeps beneath the moon.

The time has come to leave, and we return to our team. Old Sarum has been seen, and is never to be forgotten. Where are they who here thought and labored a thousand years ago? Gone, without a solitary exception, gone to the silent mansions of the dead.

AMESBURY.

Three miles more and we are at Amesbury, the town for which our Massachusetts Amesbury was named. One of us having been born within five miles of the latter, we must of course see its prototype. We found it to be remarkably neat but queer. The streets and avenues are hard and smooth. There are no modern buildings. It is substantial, not thickly settled, rural to a fault, but bears marks of high antiquity. Here are the remains of a celebrated abbey, now used as the parish church. The outline is varied but low. A mile or two away was born, at Milston in 1672, Joseph Addison. One cannot help being reminded that this was a fitting place for the beginning of such a career. In all our wanderings we have seen no town resembling this,—odd in the plan of the roads, peculiar in its fixed appearance, nothing suggesting change or repair. Most of the buildings are brick, two stories in height, and a market-place is at the centre. How admirable the surroundings,—Salisbury, Sarum, Stonehenge, Wilton, Bemerton.

This ride was, all things considered, the most delightful in our journey through England. The scenery was nowhere wild or romantic, but the reverse. The landscape was undulating, with great valleys well supplied with groves, the whole forming a panoramic view of unsurpassed elegance.

STONEHENGE.

A ride of six miles, and we reach Stonehenge, on the Salisbury Plain. The plain is three or four miles in extent, comparatively level, well grassed, and surrounded with hills. No house could be seen, nor any sign of civilization save the road and the sheep and the cattle so quietly grazing. A sign at the left of the roadside directed us into a cart-path over the field. Our driver, an old visitor, informed us that yonder, a distance requiring a slow five minutes' ride, were the famed ruins, in the midst of this vast field, without a tree for company. Alighting there we found an elderly man in attendance to describe the ruins, and see that tourists did no harm. We were informed that the present owner of the domain, Lord———, was pleased to have visitors come, and that all were welcome, but strictly prohibited from removing fragments or defacing the stones. Two large ovals are inside of two circles. On these, or lying about them, are large rough-squared oblong stones, many of them four feet wide, two feet thick, and fifteen feet long. While keeping the same general form, the others vary in size down to half these dimensions. All have a blackened grayish appearance, with spots of thin moss on them. Several of them are set like posts in the ground, some perpendicular, others aslant.

Some rest on the top of these, reaching from one to another. Some stand alone; others have fallen, and lie flat. Some of them are broken or lean against others. To complete the scene is a flat stone called the altar, inside of the inner oval. This is a slab about fifteen feet long and four feet wide. The grass growing about them is well trodden down and cropped by the sheep. There were originally one hundred and forty stones, and they varied in weight from six to seventy tons. They are much weather-worn, though many of them retain sharp angles; and on the top of the pillars are small rude tenons, with corresponding mortices in those that once rested upon them. The large ones appear to be about twelve feet high, and they stand four or five feet apart. The outer circle has seventeen stones remaining out of the original thirty; the inner has but eight whole stones, and fragments of twelve others. The inner oval consisted of twenty smaller stones, of which eleven are yet standing. The other oval had ten stones, of which eight remain.

Scattered over the plain, in sight of these ruins, are about three hundred mounds or tumuli, varying from six feet to forty in diameter. They are conical in form, and well grassed over. Some of these have been opened, and they prove to be places of sepulture; for in them were charred human bones, fragments of pottery, and British and Roman ornaments and weapons. On making excavations at the altar, remains of oxen, deer, and other animals were found, mingled with burnt wood and pieces of ancient pottery.

Evidence tends to show that this was a Druidic temple. Geoffrey of Monmouth assumes that it was built by order of Aurelianus Ambrosius, the last British king, in honor of four hundred and sixty Britons slain by Hengist the Saxon. Polydore Vergil declares that it is a monument to Hengist, who died about A. D. 488. The temple theory has more evidence in its favor, and finds the largest number of supporters.

WILTON.

After a stay of an hour we ride on, not over the road we came by, but first by a cart-path over the field among the mounds, and afterwards for a half-mile out into another road. We now go back through the nice little town of Wilton, where carpets of that name were first manufactured. The excellent roads are at times very white, because of the chalkstones which enter into this construction. Halfway from Stonehenge lies Wilton, with a population of less than two thousand. The carpet manufacture has declined till but comparatively few are now made. Most of the houses are of brick, with tiled roofs, having neat flower-gardens in front, and grapevines on the walls. It was once a seat of monastic establishments, but the edifices are torn down with a single exception,—the Hospital of St. John. One place of antiquity yet remains, namely, the Wilton House, the seat of the Earl of Pembroke, which contains a gallery of rare paintings, and stands on the site of the abbey founded by a sister of King Egbert, A. D. 800. The place is open to the inspection of the public on certain days,—uncertain ones to us or our driver,—but we must drive around it. On approaching we saw an old but rich Roman gateway, with the usual porter's lodge, and a fine avenue, short but well shaded, as an approach to the square in front. Alighting, we were informed that this was not Admission Day, and the Noble Lord not being at home could not be appealed to; so we reluctantly departed; but before going, we had through the gateway a good view of the grounds, and of the mansion itself, bowered in trees. Large, of Italian architecture, built of a light-drab stone, it is said to have been designed by the celebrated architect, Inigo Jones—who died in 1652—aided, it may be, by Holbein. As we turned away we could but think of a similar experience which took place just two hundred and ten years before, June 11, 1668. The eccentric Pepys visited the ruins at Stonehenge, Wilton, and this very spot, and with an experience like our own. The record in his Diary is as follows:—

Went to the inne; and there not being able to hire coach horses, and not willing to use our own, we got saddle-horses, very dear, give the boy that went to look for them sixpence. So the three women behind, W. Hewer, Murford, and our guide, and I, single to Stonehenge, over the plain, and some great hills, even to fright us, come thither, and find them prodigeous as any tales I ever heard of them, and worth going this journey to see. God knows what their use was! they are hard to tell, but yet we may be told. Gave the shepherd-woman, for leading our horses, fourpence, so back by Wilton, my Lord Pembroke's House, which we could not see, he being just coming to town; but the situation I do not like, nor the house at present, much, it being in a low rich valley.

CHAPTER VII.

BEMERTON—WINCHESTER—READING—NEWBURY.

In sight of Salisbury Cathedral, and but two miles away, is Bemerton, an ideal spot, combining those qualities that go to make up one of the best specimens of a rural hamlet of Old England,—clean roads, well built walls, highly cultivated land, beautiful trees, grounds with no evidences of poverty or want. A spot that does not appear to have been at all interfered with by any outside trouble, is this little municipality; and how fit a place for "Holy George Herbert" to live and die in. Whoever remembers the hymn beginning,

Sweet day, so cool, so calm, so bright,
The bridal of the earth and sky,

will wish to see the place of the author's labors and final repose. He died here in 1632. Charles I. gave him the living; but only for the two years before his death was he rector of the parish. We rode down a quiet lane, and on the left found the miniature church, the smallest we had ever seen. We didn't measure it, but thought it to be about seventeen feet wide, forty feet long, including the chancel, and not more than ten feet high to the eaves. It is built of stone, with a moderately high roof, covered with old reddish tiles. Of Gothic architecture, it had a modest belfrey, a chancel at the east end, with a colored-glass east window, and all the altar appliances of a miniature church. It is built with its side to the lane, only a few feet back, with an entrance through a porch. There are two windows on each side. There are no pews, but the floor is partly occupied with high-backed, flag-bottomed chairs, of which there is room for but three on each side of the aisle. About the building is an old burial-ground, where "the rude forefathers of the hamlet sleep."

Here the sweet spirit of Herbert was at home; here from choice he did his work. "Having served his generation, by the will of God he fell on sleep," and beneath the altar his ashes repose. To this spot pilgrimages were made by distinguished men in the days of his rectorship, for he was one of the few not without honor in his own country. Sir Henry Wotton, Lord Bacon, Dr. John Donne,—the poet and Dean of St. Paul's at London, who died the year before Herbert,—these were among the companions who received inspiration from the humble rector of this little church. Honest Isaac Walton could not rest till he had written a biography of him, though it was not published till 1670, more than a third of a century after the good rector's decease.

How choice a place is the Bemerton parsonage. If holy ground anywhere exists, this spot has indisputable claims to the title. Across the road, not more than thirty feet away, is the house in which Herbert lived, much in its old condition, though somewhat enlarged. Humble and unpretentious, it is still the Bemerton parsonage, and occupied by Rev. Mr. Piggot, the present rector. The house is a story and a half high, standing sidewise to the road, and parallel to the church, which might be its twin. Mr. Piggot, a gentleman of means and taste, was absent; but with extreme courtesy his man-servant met us at the door, and cheerfully showed us over the house, especially into the study which makes it historic. The efforts he made for our pleasure, the permission granted us to walk at will over the old garden, indicated the present incumbent as one who would do honor to the memory of the sweet singer of that Israel. How charming that Eden! Walks and lawns are as they were in Herbert's day. There is the medlar tree he planted, now more than two hundred and fifty years old,—decrepit, and supported by props. The trunk, six or eight inches in diameter, is protected by thin metal plates, and cared for like an invalid or a pet child. It yet bears a little fruit, and is a living link between the centuries, bridging over the long chasm from George Herbert to ourselves. The little River Avon, at the rear of the garden and washing its banks, still runs as it did then, and every foot of the acre is sacred. In the immediate rear of the old house, opposite from the river, perhaps two hundred feet away, is a beautiful lawn. Vines climb the housewalls and flowering shrubs complete the picture. Inside the house, works of *vertu* and evidences of scholarly life abound. All is befitting to the dear memory of Herbert. Exquisite is the beauty of the road, and perfect the shade of the overhanging trees. What a charm seemed to permeate everything!

"Take it for all in all,

We shall not look upon its like again."

Carrying with us better influences than had come from the hills and on the great plain of Sarum and Stonehenge, we bade Bemerton farewell. Passing through Fisherton, a suburban village of Salisbury,—like Bemerton, watered by the Avon,—we reached Salisbury at noon, and at two o'clock took a train for

WINCHESTER,

where we arrived at four. This is historically of remarkable interest, and may be named as one of the few places the tourist cannot afford to miss. It is built mostly of brick, contains 16,336 inhabitants, and is pleasantly situated on the River Itchen, which, though not itself navigable, is used as a canal to the sea. While the buildings have a modern look, and especially the shop windows, one cannot walk far before he feels that he is in one of the old places of England. This was an important place in the days of the Britons, and the

Romans are supposed to have built its walls. In the year 519 Cerdic, the Saxon chief, captured and made it the seat of government. Under the Danes it became the capital of England, and so remained till after the reign of Henry II., who died in 1189. It was at the height of its glory in the reign of Henry I., who died in 1135, but in the time of Henry VI. it had materially declined. He is believed to have been killed in the Tower at London, A. D. 1471.

Winchester was the principal residence of the sovereigns till the accession of George I., A. D. 1714. Henry III. was born here in 1207, and here Henry VIII. sumptuously entertained Charles V. In this place also Isaac Walton—author of the Complete Angler, and of celebrated biographies—was born Dec. 15, 1683. The atmosphere is surcharged with great events. Every foot of ground is classic, and in nearly every street may be found mementoes of something famous. We Americans, born and educated under new conditions, are poorly calculated to measure these ancient historic remains; yet by kindred and historic associations we are the very people to best get large and just impressions of England's worth.

At Worcester, Gloucester, Bath, Salisbury, we were richly entertained. At the mention of either place, memory is immediately roused to incidents crowding into reconsideration! Either of these places might take its position as chief! So now of grand old Winchester. How hard it is to write and not be intensely eulogistic. It has enough antiquity for a whole country. On one street is a monument commemorative of the plague of 1669. In the distance, a mile or so from the city, may be seen the hospital of St. Cross, founded in the reign of St. Stephen, who was crowned in 1135, and died 1154, nearly eight centuries ago. We come to the venerable St. Lawrence, the mother church of all in the city, into which each new bishop has, for a thousand years, made solemn entry when he took charge of the See.

At the time of the Reformation, there were ninety churches and chapels, besides monasteries where thousands, under a blind religious policy, were being supported at public expense; but the Reformation drove these drones from their seclusion, reduced the churches to but nine, broke up abbeys, and true progress began.

The city was formerly walled in, and had four gates, but all except the west gate have been removed; and that now stands sentinel-like in the midst of a commercial population, which all day, and late into the night, hurries through the old arch. Its durability, has apparently demanded few repairs.

For centuries upon centuries the chamber over it was the deposit for the national standards of weights and measures, as instituted under King Edgar, who died 975. Who has not heard of the Winchester Bushel? Nine hundred years old is the phrase, yet to-day the identical measures are in existence. We found that they had recently been removed from their long resting-place, to the museum of Guild Hall, a place of great interest. Our first request was to be shown the measures, and there before us was the famous bushel, resting on a low stand. It is of brass, or some similar composition, and dark bronze-like in appearance. We guessed it to be nearly a quarter of an inch thick, and, lifting it, found it to be quite heavy, weighing perhaps thirty pounds. It is in form like a shallow kettle, some sixteen inches in diameter, and eight inches deep, with straight sides, well rounded lower corners, the bottom slightly concave; it rests on three small feet, and has stiff pitcher-like handles on each side. The metallic weights are round, and deep as compared to their diameters. They are various in form and decoration, having been altered under different administrations. The measures of length are brass. All these relics are kept in glass cases.

In this museum are other rare antiques, among them exhumed Roman pottery, ancient proclamations, and rare documents,—among which was one relating to the practice of touching for cure of King's Evil, or scrofula. After reciting cures wrought, and the public press on the occasion, it makes proclamation of rules governing the operation, and naming certain times as set apart for the king's visit and work.

Next, we visit the banqueting-hall of the ancient castle, in which the first parliaments of England were held. While the building has been remodelled and extended, for judicial uses, this hall remains unchanged. It is elaborately finished in oak, which is now like ebony in appearance. The room is, perhaps, one hundred and twenty feet long, fifty feet wide, and forty feet high.

At one end, lying flat against the wall, some twenty feet from the floor, is the Round Table of King Arthur, who must have reigned as early as A. D. 525. Much as we dislike to spoil good stories, we ought to say that doubt exists whether this personage ever lived, for the balance is in favor of the theory that the entire story of King Arthur and his knights is only an English legend; but here is the *table*, and the only one that claims to be genuine. It appears like a dial,—a round wooden tablet, three inches thick, and eighteen feet in diameter. At the centre is a circle, some two feet in diameter, in which is painted a flower. From this lines radiate to the circumference, making twenty-four divisions. In one of them is a portrait of King Arthur; the other divisions are alternately white and green.

Not far from this hall was the palace, built for Charles II.,—a tame structure of light-reddish stone, three stories high, and of Italian architecture. The old courtyard is now a gravelled parade-ground, and the palace is used for barracks:—

"To what base uses we may yet return."

The music and revelry of the festive board, conspicuous in which perhaps was the fascinating voice of Nell Gwynn, are now supplanted by the notes of the ear-piercing fife and startling bugle, the clatter of arms and the beat of the drum. The courtly king is two hundred years dead. New people walk these grounds, few ever giving thought to the fact that here the highest of the land once dwelt.

"The cathedral," says the reader, "what of that?" Of course it had an early visit, the first hour after our arrival, and it lives in most pleasant recollection. We have said understandingly what has been written of cathedrals before. We have needed all the adjectives of the language, but at times have felt the poverty of words to express our meaning when a cathedral was under consideration.

Winchester Cathedral! How futile will be the attempt to speak worthily of it; but the reader should have some facts concerning it. The longest of all the twenty-nine cathedrals, it has the finest nave in the kingdom, and a history of more than nine hundred years. It is another of the architectural wonders of Great Britain. The lawn and great trees furnish a befitting environment, and a genuine cathedral atmosphere envelops the venerable ecclesiastical residences near by. The ruins of the monastery and abbey lend their charm, and the grand cathedral stands solemn and majestic in their midst. Founded in 648, in 980 the stones were refashioned into their present forms, which have continued to this day. Centuries have now passed since all was complete; and save for the repair of a crumbling stone, or a restoration of some portions to original conditions, nothing needs to be done. It is 527 feet in length, seven more than Quincy Market in our Boston, and 186 feet wide at the transepts. The low demure-looking tower, only 26 feet taller than the roof, is 130 feet high. In color, it is much like Salisbury Cathedral,—a dark indistinct gray, with thin moss-patches. Parts of the exterior are very rich in decoration, and a feeling akin to admiration is inspired as one gazes at the turreted walls. We enter the nave. This part was built under the administration of William of Wykeham, who was also the architect. He was made bishop of the See in 1366, and died in 1404. It is imposing in its proportions; and simple, though gracefully elegant, is the decoration of columns, arches, and ceiling. White throughout as new-fallen snow, every moulding and carving is of such admirable size as to be clear and distinct in outline. The interior is more than one hundred feet high. The light is solemnly toned down, and everywhere there is an impression of vastness. And how can pen or tongue adequately picture the great reredos, the strange monuments, and the countless mementoes of departed worth? Again comes the impression, this is *the* cathedral.

Here sleeps Isaac Walton. Wood, the historian, says of him: "In his last years he lived mostly in families of eminent clergymen of England, of whom he was much beloved." Dec. 15, 1683, at the age of ninety, he died in Winchester, at the residence of his son-in-law. Who that reads his "Complete Angler, or the Contemplative Man's Recreation," does not admire the sweet temper and good sense, the cheerful disposition and honest purpose of the old saint, enthusiastic in his devotion to his pastime and calling? Nature and his spirit were in remarkable harmony. A large flat stone tells us that here his dust was deposited nearly three centuries ago, but the bookstores of England and America prove that, like the great Webster, he still lives.

"So works the man of just renown,
On men when centuries have flown;
For what a good man would attain,
The narrow bounds of life restrain;
And this the balm of Genius gives:
Man dies, but after death he lives."

On a marble pedestal reposes the effigy of Wykeham, once painted in gaudy colors,—perfect yet in every line of his benignant countenance, of his stole and his canonical robe. Beneath this monument has rested his revered dust for nearly five hundred years.

Forty-three years after the burial of the great bishop, on the 13th of April, 1447, the solemn stillness was disturbed by a procession to deposit the remains of Henry of Beaufort, the successor of Wykeham in 1404, afterward made cardinal of St. Eusebius, by Martin V. This is he of whom Shakespeare said, "He died and made no sign." How unlike John Knox, of whom Carlyle says: "When he lay a-dying it was asked of him, 'Hast thou hope?' He spake nothing, but raised his finger and pointed upward, and so he died."

Beaufort was a remarkable man. He was president of the court when Joan of Arc was on trial; by his countenance and aid she was sentenced to death. What influence this dust once had on kings! Out of Beaufort's vast cathedral revenues, $150,000 was advanced to his nephew, Henry V. To the infant Henry VI., who was brought up under his immediate care, he advanced $50,000. But we must not play the historian now, and only call attention to the fact that, in the play of Henry VI., Shakespeare represents him as dying in great remorse. As a redeeming quality be it said, that when spirit and body must part companionship, the good angel of charity took possession of him, and his great property went to works of charity. The hospital of St. Cross speaks for him more eloquently than monumental stone, or the chantry where he ministered in the great cathedral itself.

Here too is kingly dust, that of William II., son of the Conqueror,—William Rufus, as they called him, because of his red hair. Shot in the New Forest in the year 1100, by Walter Tyrrel, Lord of Poix, he died instantly, at the age of forty-four, and for 783 years his royal body has been mouldering here. But he is only one of many, for over each side range of the choir stalls are oak chests,—containing what? Records of the church or important papers of State? Jewels of deceased bishops, or their robes? No; but the mortal remains of Wessex and Saxon kings. Each chest is perhaps three feet long, eighteen inches square, and bears on its side the name of its occupant. These bones were once buried in the crypt, between the years 1126 and 1171, but were put into these chests by order of Bishop De Blow. Three hundred and eighty-four parishes pay their homage to the Bishop of Winchester. No See in all England is as rich in its revenues as this.

As we pass to other visits the thought comes that, like Newton, we have picked up but a few pebbles on a limitless shore. As the immortal Sumner said, "the description is, to the reality, as a farthing candle held up to the sun." At 12 M. we leave for the old city of Newbury, but on our way to take a look at

READING,

where we arrive May 10, after a pleasant ride of two hours. We found a modern city, more than usually American in general appearance. There are, however, examples of antiquity, and one learns that he is in no new place, but in one modernized from the old. There are 32,324 inhabitants. It is an important railroad and canal centre, and is noted for the manufacture of Reading Biscuits, even now to be found in the large stores of America. Before the days of Bond at Wilmington, Kennedy at Cambridgeport, and the Pearsons at Newburyport, these crackers were common in New England, and in fact all over the United States. Reading is a market for the sale of velvets, silks, and agricultural products and implements, and from it, large exportations are made. The seed-gardens and conservatories of Sutton & Sons are well known throughout Great Britain. On visiting their conservatories we saw the finest collection of calceolaries and primroses that we have ever seen, or ever expect to see. The air of England is especially adapted to the development of these plants, and the firm has made them a specialty. The finely shaded and wide avenues, and the large number of comfortable dwelling-houses with their gardens, and the general look of the business portions, fully reminded us of Worcester, Mass., though unlike the latter, it is built on level ground. Reading has three ancient parish churches, and a grammar school founded by Henry VIII.; also the remains of an abbey founded by Henry I., who died 1135. The ancient grounds now contain a fine public walk. Parliaments were held here as early as the thirteenth and fifteenth centuries, and so the place was notable as being frequently visited by kings and nobles.

An item of interest is that Archbishop Laud, the notorious persecutor of the Non-conformists, who was executed on Tower Hill, London, Jan. 10, 1645, was born here Oct. 7, 1573. One of his infamous deeds was to cause Dr. Leighton, a Presbyterian pastor of Scotland (the author, in 1628, of a book entitled "Sion's Plea against the Prelacy"), to be condemned to pay a fine of $50,000; be twice publicly whipped and pilloried in Cheapside, London; to have his ears cut off, his nostrils split open, and his cheeks branded S. S. (Sower of Sedition); and, in addition, to be imprisoned ten years in the Fleet Prison. This was an exceptional example of his cruelty, but even his *mild* rule was barbaric. He was the son of a wealthy clothier of Reading, and held offices as follows: President of St. John's College at Oxford, 1611, at the age of thirty-eight; Dean of Gloucester, 1616; Prebend of Westminster, 1620; Bishop of St. David's, 1621; Bishop of Bath and Wells, 1626; Bishop of London, 1628; Archbishop of Canterbury, 1633. A reaction in public sentiment took place. The cruelties of the church, instigated by him, had an effect similar to that of the Fugitive Slave Law in the United States. The poison carried with it an antidote. Immediately after the Long Parliament, he was impeached for high treason, and presently we find the archbishop of the realm languishing in the Tower. An imprisonment of three years followed before he was brought to wearisome trial, when he defended himself with distinguished ability, but received a sentence that, in the light of patient investigation, is pronounced unjust and illegal.

One can hardly read the history of these English towns, or walk through their streets, however modern they may appear, and not discover that he is in Old England and not in Young America. We carried away pleasant memories of this place. The modernish brick and stone buildings, with their tiled roofs, many of them new and of a bright-red color; the Avon Canal, with its slowly moving Bristol boats; the sluggish rivers Thames and Kennet, affording avenues of transportation like our great railways,—all conspired to make us think of home; but St. Mary's Church, half a thousand years old, with Norman columns and arches on one side of the nave, and Early English on the other,—with its neat and quaint burial-ground about it,—made us realize anew that we were yet in *Old* England.

At 4.30 P. M. we took train for Newbury. There was never a more desirable country to ride over, or a more delightful season at which to see England to best advantage. What our country shows at this season of the year is here also to be seen.

A general absence of fruit-trees is painfully apparent. A small part of the land only is devoted to cultivated crops. Grass prevails. Beef, mutton, and dairy products absorb the attention. No modern buildings of any kind are to be seen. In the cities are red-tiled roofs, while a few are slated; but thatched roofs abound in the country. The surface of the land is undulating. General comfort prevails; and the impression is that in his way, the English farmer is working to his own advantage and is satisfied. He has no fences to keep in repair,—only hedges as land divisions. When we saw cattle and horses, and even sheep, restrained by these often apparently thin barriers, we got the impression that the animals were more easily managed than are ours in America. It is possible they inherit these traits of obedience. It may be that the long training of their sires and dams has made their offspring tractable also, for like begets like, the world over.

NEWBURY.

This is aside from the main road between Reading and London, and is reached by a short passage over the Hungerford branch. On arrival we went immediately to the Jack House tavern. The present building is a part of the dwelling-house once owned and occupied by the famous Jack of Newbury, who figured in English history. He was a celebrated clothier, or cloth manufacturer, and born at Winchcomb, in Gloucestershire, about 1470. On a slab, in the floor of the parish church of St. Nicholas, are brass effigies and the following inscription:—

OFF YO CHARITIE PRAY FOR THE SOULE OF JOHN
SMALWADE, ALIAS WINCHCOM,
AND ALYS HIS WIFE. JOHN DYDD THE XV DAY
OF FEBRUARY MCCCCCXIX.

He espoused the cause of Henry VIII., and at his own expense equipped 200 men and sent them *towards* Flodden Field. When the company arrived at Stoney Stratford they were met and reviewed by Queen Catharine, who complimented them in the highest terms; but immediately news came from the Earl of Surrey that the soldiers might be dismissed, for a victory had been gained over the Scots, whose king had been slain in battle. Jack was much disappointed, but his feelings were relieved by the promise of a visit from his Majesty, which was made at a later day. We are told that he much enjoyed "showing the king his factory, and that the floor of the room wherein the banquet was held was covered with broadcloth instead of rushes." Jack was very generous, and did much for the poor and for public institutions. The tower of the church, and a large part of its nave, were paid for by him.

In the year 1811 an extraordinary feat was accomplished here. Two sheep were sheared; the wool was carded, spun, warped, loomed, and woven; the cloth was burred, milled, dyed, dried, sheared, and pressed; a coat was made by White of Newbury, and worn by Sir J. Throgmorton, in the presence of five thousand spectators,—all within thirteen hours and twenty minutes. The widow of Mr. Coxter, who had charge of the exploit, completed her one hundredth year, January 1, 1875.

Another important personage here was Rev. Dr. Twiss, rector of St. Nicholas. He was the presiding officer, or prolocutor, of the Assembly of divines at Westminster, when the famous catechisms were compiled, though they were not adopted till after his death. The Larger Cathechism was sent to the House of Commons, October 22, 1647, and the Shorter on November 25 of the same year; but for some reason they were not adopted till July, 1648, two hundred and thirty-five years ago. The shorter catechism soon found its way to New England, and was printed in the New England Primer,—a little educational, but somewhat proselyting work, asserting that "In Adam's fall, we sinnèd all." It became the principal instruction book in New England families and in some of the public schools. In spite of its old and heavy theology, it was the most comprehensive schoolbook then published, and, with all the light and advance of the nineteenth century, has never been excelled. The hot-house system of cramming was not then known; but this concise handbook, well understood, did a masterly work which we can never expect to see excelled, till the child is treated as a human being, and tasks not exacted (irrespective of intellectual capacities) at which parents and teachers would themselves rebel.

Speaking of students,—Mr. Benjamin Woodbridge, of our American Newbury, Mass., the first graduate of Harvard College, went to Newbury, England, and became rector of St. Nicholas, after the death of the celebrated Dr. Twiss, so that our town has double honors. Mr. Woodbridge remained rector more than twenty years,—a learned and eloquent preacher,—till at last, in consequence of his strongly non-conformist doctrines, imbibed partly in New England, he was driven from his pulpit, and suffered great persecution. After this he was an independent preacher for twenty years, and died at the age of sixty-two, in the year 1685. In spite of his doctrines he was buried with honor in the church where he so long ministered. Speaking of him in connection with Harvard College, Cotton Mather says: "He was the leader of the whole company and ... a star of the first magnitude in his constellation." And the historian Calamy says: "He was a great man every way, ... the first graduate of the college, ... the lasting glory as well as the first fruits of the Academy."

Rev. John Cotton, one of the earliest pastors of the First Church in Boston, dying in 1652, was, at the time he left England for America (and had been for twenty years before) the Vicar of St. Botolph's, the great parish church of Boston, England,—a fact that gave our Boston its name. Woodbridge was the personal friend of Cotton, and wrote the following epitaph on the latter's tombstone; and this doubtless suggested to Benjamin Franklin the celebrated epitaph he prepared for himself.

A LIVING BREATHING BIBLE; TABLES WHERE
BOTH *Covenants*, AT LARGE, ENGRAVEN WERE;

Gospel AND LAW, IN 'S HEART, HAD EACH ITS COLUMN;
HIS HEAD AN INDEX TO THE SACRED VOLUME;
HIS VERY NAME A *Title Page*; AND NEXT,
HIS LIFE A *Commentary* ON THE TEXT.
O WHAT A MONUMENT OF GLORIOUS WORTH,
WHEN IN A *New Edition*, HE COMES FORTH,
WITHOUT ERRATAS MAY WE THINK HE'L BE
IN *Leaves* AND COVERS OF ETERNITY!

The town is situated on the River Kennet, which runs through the centre of the business part, and is crossed by a single-arched stone bridge. There are 6,602 inhabitants. It has but few streets, which are well paved, but quiet lanes abound. There is picturesqueness everywhere, and especially in the vicinity of the old St. Nicholas Church, where the grouping of roads, river, canal, meadows, trees, peculiar buildings, produce an effect seldom excelled. The Lombardy poplar is conspicuous, as it often is in these landscapes.

One place of note is Donnington Castle, once the home of the poet Chaucer, to which he retired in 1397. As he died Oct. 25, 1400, this was probably his residence at the time of his decease. The Shaw House, completed in 1581, an elegant structure in the Elizabethan style of architecture, is still standing, with its ample grounds, now as it was nearly three hundred years ago. It was the headquarters of Cromwell during his campaign in the neighborhood, battles being fought here in 1643 and 1644.

A couple of curious incidents are connected with the parish church of St. Nicholas. Some hundreds of years ago a person bequeathed a sum of money, the income to be used for purchasing bread for the poor. While we were in the church on Saturday, the baker brought the lot for distribution on Sunday; and on the morrow, during service, the new bread being piled on a table in the great room, the fragrance of this charity, like sweet incense, permeated the place. The work will continue preaching about "the bread of life" and the practical part of Christianity. This custom is not peculiar to this church. We saw it in some of the old churches of London also, the glass case on the vestibule wall being filled on Saturday, to be delivered on the next day to the worthy poor.

A new rector had been installed over St. Nicholas parish the week before, and the secular paper stated that on the arrival of the incumbent in the city the church bells were rung. On Saturday before the Sunday when he preached his first sermon, he (according to old custom) entered the church, locked the door, rang the large bell, and then unlocked the door and let in the vestrymen, delivering the key to them, and they in turn to the sexton. On the following day, Sunday, he formally read and subscribed to the Thirty-nine Articles. Whether he is to interpret them as would the Dean of Westminster, or the Archbishop of Canterbury, we are not able to say.

A few months ago, in making repairs to the chancel, some brass plates, or mural tablets, were found, which are now placed on the walls with others. Two of them read as follows:—

A MEMORIAL OF MY FATHER, MR. HUGH SHEPLEIGH, SOMETIMES RECTOR AND PASTOR OF THIS CHURCH AND TOWN OF NEWBURY, WHO WAS BORN AT PRESCOTT IN LANCASHIRE 1526 AND BUERIED HEERE THE THIRD OF MAYE 1596 AGED 70 YEARES.

HERE LIES THE BODIE OF FRANCIS TRENCHARD OF NORMANTOWN IN COVENTIE OF WILTS ESQUIRE, WHO DEPARTED THIS LIFE THE SIXT OF NOVEMBER 1635, LEAVING ISSUE ELIZABETH HIS ONLY CHILD.

Finally, a word concerning the old pulpit. It is of stone, octagonal in form, not very large or high, but of somewhat elaborate design. To protect it from injury in the time of Cromwell, the parish officers caused it to be whitewashed, thus making it appear to be a cheap affair and unworthy of attention. It remained in this condition till recently, when its true nature was accidentally discovered. Originally it was gilded in some parts, and painted in positive colors, as red, green, yellow. The wash has been removed, and it is now proposed to restore it to its former condition.

One attempts much when he begins to recite a few among the thousands of interesting facts connected with Old England. We have tried to be judicious, and are entitled to more credit for what we omit than for what we describe. Having gone down the western side of England (with regrets for having passed by Exeter and Wells, at both of which are cathedrals) we continue from the southern part northerly towards London, stopping by the way at Newbury and Reading. We at 10 A. M. on this same Sunday, having attended an early service at St. Nicholas's, take our start for the famed metropolis. Once more we rode over the Hungerford branch, back to

READING.

The day was warm. Probably the mercury stood at about 75 degrees. After a walk over the town we attended divine service. At 2 P. M. we were back in the station, waiting for the train. Having dined we had some time on our hands, and so we took out our notebook and wrote about what follows.

The sermon was extempore, though well thought out, and ingenious and unlooked-for in thought and expression. The elements of good preaching were there, but the theologic atmosphere was bad. There was too much East and too little West in it. The subject was the spies that went up to investigate the Canaan question. Most of the English preachers delight to talk about Moses, Caleb, and Jeremiah, forgetting, or not seeming to know, of men who have lived three thousand years later. It's easy to tell about what *was*, rather than to observe and investigate, and know what really *is*, and is surely *to be*. The best thing about this sermon was that the preacher discovered an inclination to look with leniency on opposing thinkers in the domain of theology, and to treat them as Christians. He didn't *like* the new ideas, but advised his hearers to accept the situation and trust that God would in time tire out the investigators, and so things would relapse into their ancient condition. He was oblivious that his Congregationalism was entirely indebted for its existence to the fact that, years ago, some people did the very thing he condemned, investigate theological questions and ascertain whether their "thus saith the Lord" was real or fancied,—that is to say, discover whether the interpretations of the Word were according to fact and true philosophy, or only traditional. The beam in his eyes disabled him from taking a mote from the eyes of others. He declared that the Israelites had the pillar of fire and the cloud, and so have we the Bible; but the propriety of investigating the true meaning of either was not to be tolerated.

At one o'clock we are just out of church. Have heard an old sermon in Old England,—a good one, however, of the kind. We go on our way rejoicing for many things, but not sorry that the long service is over, though sorry that in the light of the nineteenth-century thought, men of education, watchmen on the walls of Zion, do not better discern the signs of the times. We are, however, inclined to say with Ovid,—

Our bane and physic the same earth bestows,
And near the noisome nettle blooms the rose.

Our seat taken in the railway carriage, we are on our way to great London. We think over our roundabout way to the place, which most Americans reach the first or second day from Liverpool. A *can't wait* condition takes possession of them, and they hurry on. We landed at Queenstown twenty days ago. How long a time to get to London,—twice as long as a passage across the Atlantic Ocean! Yet what a vast experience in the three weeks! What sights we have seen, what thoughts conceived! What seeds of thought have been sown to bear fruit in the future! Into how many new channels has thought been turned! We ride in meditation thus over miles of this good country.

CHAPTER VIII.

LONDON.

At 3.30 P. M. we are in Paddington Station at the West End of London, feeling much at home, for the trainhouse is like the Lowell and Providence depots at Boston, though larger. Our impressions of London are not as anticipated. There is less crowding of the buildings and narrowness of the streets. The houses are neither new nor old. Our older western cities well represent this part of London. Half of Cincinnati and Cleveland, or a quarter-section of Buffalo, typifies this part of London better than do our eastern cities. A native of those cities would feel at home in the vicinity of this railway station, and would hardly imagine, from buildings, streets, teams, or people, that he was not amid scenes familiar from his youth up. By recommendation of a railway companion we took rooms at a lodging-house near the station. After dinner we began our tour. The map was brought into requisition, and—after passing through a few streets, and being yet more impressed with the American Westernish look of everything—we at length, in a half-hour's walk, arrived at Hyde Park. It is "a fine old Common," as Bostonians would call it, containing four hundred acres. It has long been used for public purposes, for it became public property in 1535. It was sold by Parliament in 1652, but was recovered by the Crown after the Restoration in 1660. Like our Common, it was for years a pasture ground; but it was improved, and became a resort for thousands of pleasure-seekers. In 1730-33 a body of water was introduced, arranged in curvilinear outline, and therefore named the Serpentine. Now there are gravelled avenues and groups of trees. While not presenting the uniformity of the trees bounding the principal avenues on Boston Common, it is still an admirable park; and its vast extent, in the very heart of London, makes it a resort for hundreds of thousands. On this fine Sunday afternoon a great number were enjoying it. What struck us forcibly was the general uniformity in the appearance of the people; none were representatives either of a very poor class or of a very rich one.

Parts of the grounds are cultivated with flowers, like Boston Common and Public Garden combined. Near this is Kensington Garden, and other similar places, making the West End of London remarkably favored in these respects. A long walk over one of the principal avenues of this place, and we were in the neighborhood of Buckingham Palace, the Queen's winter residence. It is a large, oblong building, of brown freestone, four stories high, and hotel-like in appearance. Back some hundred or more feet from the square, made by the junction of two or three great thoroughfares, it has a high but open iron fence enclosing the grounds. There are two principal gateways, and an amplitude of rear grounds and gardens. Many shops are within a minute's walk of the premises. Some portions of the vicinity are very aristocratic, like Grosvenor Square and its radiating streets, in which are palatial residences in close blocks. Contiguous to parks, and having the public thoroughfares about it, one hardly feels that this is the famed Buckingham Palace.

We are aware that we have began to talk about London. We will, however, not promise anything like a formal description,—certainly, no complete one. London is great beyond description. All that will be undertaken is a statement of what we saw, with the addition of any fact that history may suggest as immediately interesting. Very clean are the streets. Never were better pavements, especially on the sidewalks. There is no look of the London we had pictured. We had expected too much of a frivolous Parisian look in London's West End. A few avenues were up to our anticipation; but *all*, even here, is not up to this high mark. There is nothing ancient in appearance; and yet nothing looks entirely new. We should judge that everything had been finished twenty years before, and left untouched. Some shade-trees, some flower-yards, a garden here and there, are to be seen; but generally all is solid and rich. A generous number of carriages and people are in the thoroughfares, but no great crowd. Imagine these things, and you have the aristocratic West End of London. We walked on, and soon in the distance caught a view of the towers of Westminster Abbey. We went through street after street, out of right-angles with each other, but not crooked nor very narrow; light and airy was the atmosphere, at this season free from smoke or the London fog. There was a Boston May-day look about everything. It was cool enough to make overcoats useful every day till the first of June. At 6 P. M. we had reached the abbey, and were a mile or more from our lodgings. The roads, or avenues, in the vicinity of the edifice are very wide, and form squares about its venerable grounds, the focus of a business centre. Nowhere, though, was there an over-crowded condition. At times there were crowds,—much more so than at others; but never what might be expected in the neighborhood of the Abbey, Parliament Houses, Westminster Bridge, and other noted places that centre here.

We are really seeing New London. Streets are newly finished, widened, and everything is modern; and yet few things exist that appear to be very new. The smoke subdues all freshness.

England is old. Nature recognizes the fact, and sees to it that an ancient dignity is not disturbed. Nineteenth-century life has asserted its existence, but the old, old fog and smoke are great factors in keeping up the look of dignity that too much new brilliant work might lower. Buildings are mostly of sandstone; some of brick; no trace of wood anywhere. Elegant stores are from three to six stories in height. They vary in architecture as do those of Boston or New York. Think of such a place, and you have the Westminster part of London. But what of the abbey itself? Well, much more than we can tell. Had we not seen grand cathedrals we should probably be more profuse in adjectives in speaking of this edifice. The structure is large and imposing, but does not on the exterior give one an impression of vastness or great antiquity, though it looks anything but modern. It is built of Portland stone, as are all the old churches of London, including St. Paul's Cathedral,—a sandstone of considerable hardness and durability, of a light appearance, approaching white. The general effect is that of white marble, slightly tinged with blue,—a milk and water hue.

Now comes a qualification which applies to all the old buildings of Portland stone; and that is, that parts—which are in shadow, or not exposed to the sun—are either blackened or (as is invariably the case with many prominent parts of each structure) jet-black, and of a solid color. Casual examination would suggest soot, or the results of fog and smoke; but chemical analysis shows it to be a sort of fungi, or deposit of an animal nature,—the shady situation and porosity of the stone, aided by the moist atmosphere, being favorable to its growth. Imagine, then, a large structure, of Gothic architecture, blackened in entire sections, but mostly white. Picture to your mind a large front end, with two square towers, projecting but little from the principal front, and each ending with four turrets, not of great height,—then a side-wall broken by buttresses and transept,—and you have the exterior of Westminster Abbey. Next, think of a good-sized Gothic church, of the same stone, with a square tower at the front end, and this building set at right angles to the great abbey,—the rear end of the former not far from the rear end of the abbey. Picture further to yourself a surrounding iron fence, and a burial-ground, with a graded, gravelly surface, containing many slabs. Combine these pictures in one, and you have St. Margaret's, Westminster, the rectorship of which is in the hands of the celebrated F. W. Farrar, D. D., who is also canon of the abbey.

The interior of the abbey is rather dark and sombre. Its windows are of stained glass, most of which is modern. The columns and arches, the groined ceiling, and all the interior finish is of a dark gray limestone, of dirty soapstone color. The moulding is very rich. On the whole it has a narrow look, is very high in effect in the nave, and has elaborate altar and screen work. There are no pews, of course, but enough flagbottom chairs to cover the floor of the nave. From morning to night visitors are in this venerable place,—hundreds in a day, coming from all parts of the civilized world. This is true of St. Paul's, and of every cathedral. The task would be endless to describe the monuments. The abbey floor is made of monumental slabs, and on many of them are the stories of mortals whose dust is beneath. On columns and walls are mural tablets and monumental marbles. Benedict Arnold, true to English interests, but untrue to American; and John Wesley, faithful to the interests of humanity and God, but uncompromising towards formality, oppression, and sin,—have commemorative tablets, almost near enough to touch each other. It pleased us Americans to see Arnold's near the floor and Wesley's on the wall,—higher, as his spirit always was, and probably now is.

Here is the Poet's Corner, where repose not only tablet and stone, but the precious dust itself of Samuel Johnson, David Garrick, Dr. Barrow, and other notables; and now a bust of our own Longfellow. How subdued the voice and tread of visitor and verger! What propriety every moment and everywhere! The threshold crossed, the hurrying world is left behind. The hum of industry, the subdued noise of carriages and commercial life steal in, but the sound, like the listeners, is toned into accord with the place. The dead control the living. The influence of the venerable pile is potent. That "all who live must die, passing through nature to eternity," is here fully apparent. Dean Stanley and Canon Farrar are not more eloquent than Isaac Barrow. Samuel Johnson, with his ponderous procession of words, and Dickens, his very opposite, though dead, yet speak. Milton, through his elevated bust,—though a paraded advertisement of the egotist who "caused it to be erected here,"—looks down upon a semi-barbaric effigy five hundred years old. Handel, too, is there. They all, a glorious company,—in life divided, but in death associated,—make the place hallowed.

How well, while thus in meditative mood, is one able to realize, and as he nowhere else can, that "in the midst of life we are in death." The impression thus made can never be effaced, for, with the faithful exactness of a photographic process, it is indelibly stamped on the spirit itself.

While these pages were passing through the press, the dearest and best earthly friend of one of the authors passed on to "the city which hath foundations," that "house of God not made with hands, eternal in the heavens." By a strange and interesting coincidence, while this particular chapter was under consideration, there was found in her small pocket-book the appropriate poetic thought of another, which we here append:—

I do not know what sea shall bathe
My tired and earth-worn feet,

When they lay life's soiled sandals off,
And enter rest complete;

But I shall call that still sea, Peace!
And in its limpid tide

Lave all the dust of travel off,
And find me purified!

I do not know what sounds shall greet
My soul's awakening sense,

Nor what new sights await me when
I take my journey hence.

Though folded be my earthly tent,
My soul hath where to stay,

And she shall not be shelterless
One moment of the way!

And I fear no bewilderment,
No shock of sudden change;

To journey to one's home and friends
Will surely not seem strange!

And peace is on the waiting sea,
And rest is on its shore;

And further on—I dare not dream
Of all that lies in store.

How sweet and divine the influence,—in what sublime accord with our theme and place!

To her dear memory, who—with a companion-mother yet in the flesh—of all friends most encouraged our proposed adventure; who more deeply and sincerely than any other mortals were solicitous for our safety and happiness while wandering among strangers and historic shadows in foreign lands; and who welcomed us with inexpressible gratitude on our return,—to them both, with filial affection, we inscribe this chapter; and among the world's great we erect shrine and monument to our own revered dead,—greater, to our hearts, than the monarchs or heroes who beneath cathedral pavements sleep.

We return to the material aspect of the abbey and speak of its history. How full of incident! How long the catalogue of devotees and prelates and crusaders, of monks and nuns, of heroes both of the very old time and of the new.

The abbey was founded near the close of the seventh century, and was in full operation by the middle of the eighth. The larger portion of the present structure was completed in the thirteenth century. It is a coincidence that the years since its completion, and its length in feet, exclusive of the Henry VII. chapel, are equal,—511. The extreme breadth at transepts is 203 feet; and the height of the nave, from the pavement to the highest point of the groined arch, is 102 feet. The towers are 225 feet to top of the pinnacles. This west front, added by Sir Christopher Wren, though of good general outline, is faulty in architectural detail. English sovereigns, from Edward the Confessor to Queen Victoria, have all been crowned here, and the coronation chair, a clumsy, square structure of wood, is shown the visitor. Monuments of Queen Elizabeth and of Mary Stuart—who died respectively March 24, 1603, and December 28, 1684—are in the south aisle. The latter, as well as Mary Tudor, is buried in the Henry VII. chapel, a most elegant example of perpendicular Gothic architecture, at the choir end of the abbey. We left the place after a cursory examination, in expectation of repetitions of the visit.

The Houses of Parliament, only a few hundred feet away, are built of a light-brown sandstone, with an elaborate finish in every part. As we observed the disintegration already at work, we could but deplore the fact that such bad counsel obtained, when the structure was erected, as to be incredibly lavish in working up the outside finish to this extraordinary richness, while unwilling to reduce the decoration, so as to expend the labor on a more durable stone, even at the expense of some extravagance of detail. Attempts at minute description cannot be expected here. The Thames washes the terrace on the rear. The end with the great bell-tower, the most elegant in the world, is but a few feet from the main avenue, and almost at the London end of Westminster Bridge. The premises are enclosed by a grand, cast-iron fence. These grounds, though limited, are ample; and about this end, and its principal front, are thoroughfares of the best parts of the great city. The structure covers eight acres, and contains eleven hundred apartments. There are a hundred staircases, and two miles of corridors. The corner-stone was laid April 27, 1840, and the total cost of the edifice, up to 1874, was $20,000,000. The principal rooms for the House of Lords and House of Commons, compared to the size of the building, are much too small. The former is 100 feet long, 45 feet only in width and height, was opened for use in 1847, and is the most gorgeous legislative hall in the world. The latter is 60 feet long, and 55 feet wide and high. While elaborate in finish, it is not, of course, the equal of its companion. The windows of both, and in fact through the entire building, are of exquisitely stained glass. The Victoria Tower, at the southwest angle, is 75 feet square, and 340 feet high,—a magnificent work finished in 1857. The central octagonal tower, with a spire above it, is 60 feet diameter and 300 feet high. The Clock Tower, at the end towards Westminster Bridge, at an angle of the building, is 40 feet square, 300 feet high, and has four dials 30 feet diameter. The great bell on which the hours are struck is called Great Stephen. It was cast in 1858, and weighs over eight tons, taking the place of a broken one which was called Big Ben of Westminster. There is a chime of bells on which the quarter and half hours are chimed. As may be imagined, frescoes and statuary abound. There is no part of the exterior of the structure where exuberance of carving is not to be found,—all of course in the same stone of which the building is composed.

A minute's walk from the front of the Houses of Parliament, and we are at the London end of Westminster Bridge, looking over the turbid waters of England's celebrated river. How much is implied when one speaks of the River Thames! John Denhan, like all Londoners, was in love with it, and said:—

Thames, the most loved of all the Ocean's sons
By his old sire, to his embraces runs,—
Hasting to pay his tribute to the sea,
Like mortal life to meet eternity.

The river is about fifteen hundred feet wide, and runs with quite a current toward the sea. The muddy water rises and falls twelve or more feet with the tide. Standing at our right are the Parliament Houses, with a vast length of nine hundred feet, their grounds adjoining the bridge. We pass from the bridge to the left, and along the river. Bounding it is the Victoria Embankment, built of finely hammered granite, and finished with a moulded parapet. At proper intervals are pedestals, surmounted by ornamental and appropriate lamp-posts. At especial points are stone stairways down to the floating rafts and steamer landings. This embankment extends between Westminster and Blackfriars Bridges, and is a mile long. It was finished in 1870, at a cost of $10,000,000. It is one hundred feet wide on the roadway, and follows the curving line of the river. Next the sea-wall is a sidewalk of liberal width, with shade-trees. Outside of this, and about sixty feet wide, is the macadamized roadway. Beyond, and extending to the fence lines, is another sidewalk; and bordering this are small public squares fronting important buildings. Prominent among these is Somerset House, with its three thousand windows and one thousand rooms. From Blackfriars Bridge the river is bordered by buildings, wooden landings, and small docks,— continuing thus for a mile or more, to the Tower of London.

The high buildings are built of brick, in a common and cheap warehouse style, hardly in keeping with this important part of the city. London Bridge terminates among these; but it is elevated, so that its entrance is above the waterside buildings, and has a spacious approach, as its importance demands. At Blackfriars Bridge—the end of the Victoria Embankment—the road diverges to the left somewhat, and runs up towards St. Paul's Cathedral, which is on slightly elevated ground, perhaps a half-mile away. It is about two thirds of the way between Blackfriars and London Bridge, and not far from an eighth of a mile from the river. The triangle thus formed is filled with warehouses. The streets are well paved, clean, and full of business. The avenues are not very wide; some of them are quite crooked; and there are many lanes and alleys, or short-cuts across-lots.

Parts of New York, as, for instance, about Williams and Fulton streets,—or even Boston, in North Street,—well represent the vicinity of London Bridge, Paul's and Wharf avenues. We have now traversed the embankment for two and a half miles, and begin our survey of the opposite side. Beginning at the Lambeth end of Westminster Bridge, we have another elegant river-wall,— the southern one, or Albert Embankment,—built like the other, and at a cost of $5,500,000. It extends from Westminster Bridge nearly to Vauxhall Bridge to the right, and opposite the Houses of Parliament. The new St. Thomas Hospital buildings, four or five in number, are of brick with granite dressings, facing the embankment, and of course the Parliament Houses on the other side of the river. Above this is the Chelsea Embankment, opened in 1874. It continues on to the old Battersea Bridge, the whole presenting a massive stone wall. Beyond it, back from the river at this end, is a series of pleasure grounds, Lambeth Place, etc. This is the old Episcopal seat of the Church, and the usual residence of the Archbishop of Canterbury. It is noted as being the place of ecclesiastical councils for many centuries.

From the bridge down to the left opposite the Victoria Embankment, and for the entire distance opposite that part of the city, are wharves, docks, storehouses, such as may be found along the shore of any commercial place; but the shipping proper lies farther down the river, below London bridge. There are the docks, built at enormous cost, and extending for miles below the Tower, which is not far from a mile below St. Paul's. On the opposite side is the city of Southwark, containing a population of 200,000. The shore is lined with quays, and has an unfinished appearance. The tide runs very low, and often the mud is exposed to view against the buildings on both sides of the river, especially on the London side in the vicinity of Blackfriars.

The river is crossed by many fine bridges; among them are London, Southwark, Blackfriars, Waterloo, Hungerford, Westminster, Vauxhall, and Chelsea, besides two or three large ones for the railroads. London and Waterloo bridges are of stone, and are respectively 928 feet and 1,242 feet long, and 53 feet and 42 feet wide. The first has five arches, and the other nine. Built in 1831 and 1817, they cost $10,000,000 and $5,750,000, respectively. Southwark, Blackfriars, Westminster, and Vauxhall are iron bridges. Hungerford is a suspension bridge, and Chelsea is wooden. Blackfriars and Westminster are elegant structures, somewhat recently built.

Steamers in great numbers ply between London and Westminster bridges, and to Chelsea and points beyond. So frequent are these in their passages up and down the river, that the passenger makes no especial calculation as regards time, but goes to the nearest floating-station, and need not wait long for a conveyance. This is a comfortable method of travel, of which hundreds of thousands daily avail themselves. It has been aptly called the Silent Highway, for, in spite of the traffic on the shores, there is a peculiar quiet on the river.

We can hardly think of a subject we should be more pleased to write about, and there are few by which our readers would be more entertained, than these old bridges in London. Only one of them can have attention, and that shall be London Bridge, more especially the old one. A London Bridge is mentioned in a charter of William the Conqueror, granted to the monks of Westminster Abbey in 1067; but the earliest historical account of any is that made by the old chroniclers of its destruction, Nov. 16, 1091, "on which day a furious southeast wind threw down six hundred private houses in the city, besides several churches; and the tide in the river came rushing up with a violence that swept the bridge entirely away."

Next, in 1097, we learn from a Saxon chronicle, the credit of rebuilding it is given to King Rufus. It was of wood, and destroyed in 1136, by a fire which "laid the city in waste from St. Paul's to Aldgate." The historian Stow speaks of it as having been wholly rebuilt in 1163 by Peter Colechurch, priest and chaplain.

The first London Bridge of stone was begun in 1173, or 710 years ago, and finished in 1209. Stow says, "the new stone bridge was founded somewhat to the west of the old timber one." The new one had twenty arches. The road was 926 feet long and 40 feet wide between the parapets,—surely a magnificent structure to be erected six hundred years before the American Revolution. This great thoroughfare was destined to be despoiled of its ample dimensions, for, as soon as 1280, mention is made, on the pay-roll of the ninth year of Edward I., of "innumerable people dwelling upon the bridge." In course of time it was resolved into a complete street, buildings having been built on each side, partly on the bridge and partly projecting over the river, in solid line, with the exception of three openings on each side, at unequal distances, from which might be obtained views up and down the river. Strange to say, on the east side, over the tenth pier, was a fine Gothic chapel, dedicated to Thomas à Becket. It was thirty feet in front on the bridge, and consisted of a crypt, and a chapel above, and was used for divine services down to the Reformation.

Near the Southwark end of the bridge, on the eleventh pier, was a tower, which Stow tells us was begun in 1426. On the top of this tower the heads of persons who had been executed were "stuck up for public gaze." When it was removed in 1577, the exposed heads were taken to the Southwark end of the bridge, and the gate there received the name of Traitor's Gate.

When William Wallace resisted Edward I., his heart was plucked out, and his head placed aloft on this old tower. This was in 1305. There was displayed, in 1408, the head of the Earl of Northumberland, the father of the gallant Hotspur. There also were placed here, in 1535, the heads of Fisher, Bishop of Rochester, and his friend Sir Thomas More. That of the former was first shown to Queen Anne Boleyn, and the next day "parboiled and placed upon the pole." It is related:—

In spite of the parboiling, it grew fresher and fresher, so that in his lifetime he never looked so well, for his cheeks being beautified with a comely red, the face looked as though it had beholden the people passing by, and would have spoken to them; wherefore the people coming daily to see the strange sight, the passage, even the bridge, was so stopped with their going and coming, that almost neither cart nor horse could pass; therefore at the end of fourteen days the executioner was commanded to throw down the head in the night time into the river of Thames, and in place thereof was set the head of the most blessed and constant martyr, Sir Thomas More, his companion in all his troubles.

The German traveller Hentuner, who was here in 1597, records, that he saw above thirty heads at one time; and some old prints of the tower show its roof nearly covered by spiked skulls.

The bridge remained till the year 1832 when the present structure was built. During the long interval it was often endangered by fire,—once in 1212, as Stow relates:—

A great fire enveloped the church of St. Mary Overy's, which extended to the bridge, and, sweeping into it, struck a vast crowd of people who were collected upon it, who were hemmed in thus between two advancing masses of flame, and thus perished miserably above 3,000 persons, whose bodies were found in part or half burned, beside those that were wholly burned to ashes and could not be found.

In 1281 "five of the arches were carried away by ice, and a swell in the river, succeeding a severe snow-storm and great frost." Stow says:—

In 1437, at noon of January, 14th, the great stone gate, with the tower upon it next to Southwark, fell down, and two of the farthest arches of the same bridge, yet no men perished in body, which was a great work of God.

We might continue the record of fires and disasters, of murders on the bridge and in the houses, as well as of tumults and other strange proceedings.

How many remarkable pageants have here taken place. In 1381, on the 13th of June, the celebrated Wat Tyler forced his way over the bridge and into the city, in spite of the mayor, Sir William Walworth, and his military and police, and the "raised draw fastened up with a mighty iron chain to prevent the entry."

On the 29th of August, 1392, King Richard II. passed over it, having come in joyous procession with his consort, Queen Anne, by whose mediation he had just become reconciled with the people of London. The account says:—

Men, women, and children, in order, presented him with two fair white steeds, trapped in cloth of gold, parted with red and white, hanged full of silver bells, the which present he thankfully received, and afterwards held on his way towards Westminster.

Over it, Feb. 21, 1432, young King Henry VI. came, and made a magnificent entry after his coronation at Paris.

But we must forbear. Even a portion of remarkable events, that might be related, would more than fill this book.

The Thames, as before mentioned, has been aptly termed the Silent Highway. For centuries boating and ferriage have been important here. The watermen, as they were called, formed a numerous and somewhat influential body. In our day the horse-railroad companies are thought to be powerful, and Temple Place, narrow Tremont Street, and wide Scollay Square are said to be under their control. The railroad wars of our day (*e. g.*, between the Union and Charles River railways) only remind us of the London conflicts of eight hundred years ago. Bridgemen and watermen were then in opposition, as representatives of elevated and surface railways are at odds now. Great opposition was made by the watermen to the building of bridges over the Thames. "Othello's occupation," they thought, would be gone, and that was, in their estimation, enough to condemn the project. John Taylor, a waterman, lauded the river as follows:—

But noble Thames, whilst I can hold a pen
I will divulge thy glory unto men;
Thou in the morning, when my corn is scant,
Before the evening doth supply my want.

Soon came a new trouble, for then, as now, misfortunes did not come singly. Coaches came into use, and coaches and a new bridge at the same time threatened large invasions on the realm of the watermen, and Taylor was not slow to complain of this. In a poem entitled "Thief," published in 1622, he says:—

When Queen Elizabeth came to the crown
A coach in England was then scarcely known.

He could tolerate coaches for royalty, but their use by common people was more than he could well endure, and so he continues in the following strain:—

'T is not fit that

Fulsome madams, and new scurvey squires,
Should jolt the streets at pomp, at their desires,
Like great triumphant Tamberlaines each day,
Drawn with pamperèd jades of Belgia,
That almost all the streets are choked outright,
Where men can hardly pass, from morn till night,
While Watermen want work.

And he tried his hand at prose as follows:—

This infernal swarm of trade spillars [coaches] have so overrun the land, that we can get no living upon the water; for I dare truly affirm that every day in any term, especially if the court be at Whitehall, they do rob us of our livings, and carry five hundred and sixty fares daily from us.

And he grows earnest, and means business, when he again talks as follows:—

I pray you look into the streets, and the chambers or lodgings in Fleet Street or the Strand, how they are pestered with them [coaches], especially after a mask, or a play at court, where even the very earth quakes and trembles, the casements shatter, tatter, and clatter, and such a confused noise is made, so that a man can neither sleep, speak, hear, write, or eat his dinner or supper quiet of them.

Alas for poor John Taylor, and the occupation of his associates, who longed and sighed for the good old times and customs of the fathers, and deplored these new-fangled notions!

The winter of 1684-5 was very severe; and Sir John Evelyn, in his celebrated Diary, records an unusual spectacle on the famous river. His statement is as follows:—

Jan. 9th I went crosse the Thames on the ice, now become so thick as to beare not onely streetes and booths, in which they roasted meate, and had divers shops of wares, quite acrosse as in toune, but coaches, carts, and horses passed over. So I went from Westminster Stayres to Lambeth and dined with the Archbishop.... 16th. The Thames was filled with people and tents, selling all sorts of wares as in the city.... 24th. The frost continuing, more and more severe, the Thames before London was still planted with booths in formal streetes, all sorts of trades and shops furnished and full of commodities, even to a printing presse, where the people and ladys tooke a fancey to have their names printed and the day and yeare set down when printed on the Thames; this humour took so universally, that t'was estimated the printer gained £5 a day, for printing a line onely, at six pence a name, besides what he got by ballads, &c. Coaches plied from Westminster to the Temple, and from several other stayres to and fro, as in the streets, sleds, sliding with skeets, a bull-baiting, horse and coach races, puppet plays and interludes, cooks, tippling, and other lewed places. So it seemed to be a backanalian triumph, or carnival on the water, whilst it was a severe judgement on the land, the trees not only splitting as if by lightening struck, but men and cattle perishing in divers places, and the very seas lock'd up with ice that no vessels could stir out or come in.... Feb. 5th. It began to thaw but froze again. My coach crossed from Lambeth to the Horse ferry at Milbank, Westminster. The booths were almost all taken downe, but there was first a map or Landskip cut in copper, representing all the manner of the camp and the several actions and pastimes thereon, in memory of so signal frost.... Jan. 10th. After eight weekes missing the foraine posts, there came abundance of intelligence from abroad.

We now take our leave of the Thames. Often shall we sail over it during our stay. It is a highway of nations like the ocean itself. Ideal is the Rhine; matter of fact is the Thames; but it is greater than the Amazon in the best kind of greatness.

We have employed much space in describing the West End of London—the Abbey, Parliament Houses, the River. It will be remembered that these were seen within the first few hours after our arrival. At 6 P. M. of the same day, Sunday, we continue our walk from the river embankment, and up to St. Paul's. This edifice stands on slightly elevated ground, and being very large, with its lofty dome, is of course readily seen from any point along the river for some miles away. It is about a mile from Westminster to the cathedral. The land rises but slightly, but the small elevation was a fact worthy of note; and so in Pannier Alley, a narrow passage some six or eight feet wide, not far from the cathedral, is a stone tablet, which has a rude carving representing a naked boy sitting on a pannier, and on the lower part or pedestal is the following:—

WHEN Y'V SOVGHT
THE CITTY ROVND
YET STILL THIS IS
THE HIGHEST GROVND

AVGVST THE 27

1688.

St. Paul's is located at a business centre. In front of its principal end is a square, out of which runs Fleet Street, from Ludgate Hill. This is one of the busy thoroughfares of the city. About the cathedral, fenced in with an open iron fence not much unlike that of Boston Common, is the burial-ground, enclosing all of it but the Fleet Street end; and the space is not more than fifty feet from the fence to the building. The whole is grassed over, and has gravestones scattered promiscuously about. On either side, and across the rear end, is a street, with a roadway and one sidewalk, with stores bordering it. This space is of the same width as the burial part of the grounds, and the entire place has for centuries been known as Paul's Churchyard; for such it was before the great fire of 1666. For many years it was celebrated for its second-hand bookstores. Newgate Street, Cheapside, and other avenues of trade are at the left and rear, making the situation of the cathedral very much exposed.

In general the buildings of London are modern, the streets are clean, and there is no look of great antiquity or a very cramped condition. A scene is presented to view very unlike what one imagines when he hears of Old London; for so much has been said of its antiquities, great age, its fogs and smoke, that most people entertain ideas which are far from the truth. Speaking of this, it may well be said, once for all, that no great thoroughfare of London is more crowded than Broadway, New York; and none is narrower, unless we except Cheapside, by Bow Church; and that is no worse than our Washington Street, between Court and Milk. Just now we can think of no other street more resembling Cheapside, as regards width, amount of travel, and general variety and style of its buildings.

It must be remembered that, while London has a history of two thousand years, yet most of it has been many times rebuilt, and its streets have been widened. Boston has a history only one tenth as long, 240 years, yet we find in it little evidence of great age. London has however notable examples,— Guild Hall, Temple Church, St. Paul's, and fifty churches built after the great fire of 1666; but these do not probably look older than they did one or two centuries ago. In fact they do not impress one as being of a remarkable age; and, not being seen in a group, the city as a whole looks modern.

The greatest improvements have of course been made in Old London proper,—that part once within the walls, which, compared to the present London, is simply as original Boston is when compared to itself as a whole, and including the annexations. London is indeed vast in dimensions, and has a population of 3,266,987; but outside of Old London are the annexed places. This new territory is built principally of brick, and is in comparatively modern style. Land having been cheap, the streets are of good width; and since the territory has become part of London, it is paved, lighted, and well cared for. So let no one imagine for this, the world's metropolis, a great over-crowded city different from Boston or New York,—a vast labyrinth of narrow and crooked streets, in which are evidences of bad conditions, the results of life in a dark age,—for nothing of the kind is true. In some portions, *e. g.* not far from Covent Garden Market, there are streets where very poor people reside, and are crowded, but not in very old and peculiar buildings. In no way are the conditions worse than in sections of New York and Boston. London is a very large and very fine city, modern in general appearance.

For five months in the year, from May 1 to October 1, the climate is not very different from our own, though it has a slightly lower temperature, and a moister atmosphere. It rains with great ease, unlooked-for showers are imminent, and an umbrella accompanies a man almost as often as his hat. During the remaining portion of the year fog is frequent, and, as the heavy atmosphere prevents smoke from passing off, the difficulties are intensified. At any time in the four winter months this is a serious trouble.

We have wandered from our especial subject to speak of these matters, as we are sure that most people entertain wrong opinions concerning them; but now we go back to the cathedral.

St. Paul's is built of white stone, in general appearance like white marble. Parts of it are as white as ever, and kept clean by sun and storm; other parts are black as soot. This edifice was built to take the place of Old St. Paul's, which was destroyed in the great fire of 1666. The commission for the new building was given under the great seal, Nov. 12, 1673. The first stone was laid with imposing ceremonies under the administration of Bishop Henry Compton, by the architect Sir Christopher Wren, assisted by his master-mason, Thomas Strong. An interesting fact is related in connection with the beginning of an important part of the structure, and the relation is as follows:—

Sometime during the early part of its works, when Sir Christopher was arranging and setting out the dimensions of the great cupola, an incident occurred which some superstitious observers regarded as a lucky omen. The architect had ordered a workman to bring to him a flat stone, to use as a station; which, when brought, was found to be a fragment of a tombstone, containing the only remaining word of an inscription in capital letters: RESURGAM. ("I shall rise again.")

It is possible that this incident suggested to the sculptor, Colley Cibber, the emblem—a phoenix in its fiery nest—over the south portico, and inscribed with the same word. A kindred thought is, that the rising again of the cathedral and the city from their ashes was the hint to the artist, and that he availed himself of the emblem and word as grandly suggestive. The work was continued so that "April 1, 1685, the walls of the choir, with its aisles, being 170 feet long and 121 feet broad, with the stupendous arched vaults below the pavement, were finished; as also the new chapter-house and vestries. The two beautiful circular porticoes of the north and south entrances, and the massy piers which support the cupola, a circle of 108 feet diameter within the walls, were brought to the same height."

In the diary of Sir John Evelyn, under date of Oct. 5, 1694, we have the following: "I went to St. Paul's to see the choir, now finished as to the stonework, and the scaffolds struck both without and within in that part."

On Dec. 2, 1696, the choir was opened for divine service, the first held on the spot since the great fire of 1666. This was on the day appointed for thanksgiving for the Peace of Ryswick; and service has been continued without interruption to this day, or a period of nearly two hundred years. On Feb. 1, 1699, the morning-prayer chapel was opened for services with appropriate ceremony; and finally, in 1710, when Sir Christopher had attained the seventy-eighth year of his age, about thirteen years before his death, the highest stone of the cupola was laid by his only son, Mr. Christopher Wren, assisted by the venerable architect, Mr. Strong the master-mason, and the Lodge of Free and Accepted Masons, of which Sir Christopher was for many years the active and honored Master. Thus the cathedral was built under one architect, one master-mason, and one bishop, though a period of thirty-five years was employed in its erection. The cost was $3,739,770, including $53,000 for the stone wall, iron fence, and other accessories. We cannot refrain from quoting the copy of a document which Sir Christopher caused to be posted in various parts of the structure. It explains itself, and also redounds to the credit of the great architect.

SEPTEMBER 25,1695:—Whereas, among laborers &c., that ungodly custom of swearing is too frequently heard, to the dishonor of God and contempt of authority; and to the end, therefore, that such impiety may be utterly banished from these works, intended for the service of God and the honor of religion—it is ordered, that customary swearing shall be a sufficient crime to dismiss any laborer that comes to the call; and the clerk of the works, upon sufficient proof, shall dismiss them accordingly. And if any master working by task, shall not, upon admonition, reform this profanation among his apprentices, servants, and laborers, it shall be construed to his fault; and he shall be liable to be censured by the commissioners.

This is the only cathedral of England in the Roman or Italian style of architecture. On examining the structure we found that we had previously formed a just conception of it. It had a more modern and clean appearance on the exterior than we had expected; but, while it was grand and imposing, it did not impress us with the feeling of vastness. There being no points of view from which its great length can be seen to advantage, we have never yet obtained a right impression of it, and could not help smiling at what may be the obtuseness of our intellect, in being unable to get enthusiastic as Sir John Denham did, when in contemplation of it he wrote as follows:—

Crowned with that sacred pile, so vast, so high,
That whether 'tis a part of earth or sky,
Uncertain seems, and may be thought a proud
Aspiring mountain or descending cloud.

Its length is 500 feet; width at transepts 285 feet, and at the west front 180 feet. The campaniles are each 222 feet high. The dome is 145 feet in diameter, and 365 feet high from the grading. The Golden Gallery, as it is called, is a balustrade-enclosed walk, at the apex of the dome outside, and is reached by a circuitous walk and climb of 616 steps. From this, one can go up, through the lantern or cupola, into the great copper ball crowning the structure, and surmounted by a large gilded copper cross.

On another day we went into it. The last part of the passage is made by climbing through an opening inside of eight five-inch-thick iron scrolls that assist in supporting it, and are in part designed as decoration. These are about six feet high, with openings a few inches wide between them, through which the wind rushes, and through which views of the entire city may be obtained. Our hats left in the clock-room below, we passed up through this division and through an opening perhaps eighteen inches in diameter at the bottom of the ball; and there, a company of four, not uncomfortably crowded, we had a *high time*. Strong iron bracework was about on the inside, and an iron post or principal support, perhaps five inches square, was at the centre. There was a very slight vibration, but much less than we anticipated, and it gave us no impression of insecurity. The hum of great London was below. We could hear no distinct sound save the whistle of the wind around the cross, or through the iron scrollwork. The day was comparatively still, though some air was stirring.

We will not attempt to picture our feelings while here, at almost the highest point over London to which a mortal has ever climbed. Old St. Paul's had a spire that extended up 165 feet above this, and so men have climbed up 520 feet, to the top of the highest building ever erected in Great Britain. On this building they have been to the top of the cross, 20 feet higher than we were when in the ball; but this is exceptional, and we had done almost as well as the best. Here had sat the immortal Wren. Here had been kings and queens, the nobility of all lands, poets, philosophers, prelates, and many of no renown.

As we pass down we examine the Whispering Gallery, inside of the cathedral, in the drum of the dome. We look down as before from the top, or eye of the inner dome,—on pavement and pygmies below. How awe-inspiring and vast! From this height, as also from the more elevated position above, we were fully impressed with the immensity of the structure, and were able to realize something of the greatness of the architect who conceived it.

The attendant in the Whispering Gallery tells us to put our ears against the side wall, and he would whisper to us and exhibit this accidental wonder. He, being opposite, against the wall, says in a whisper: "This Cathedral was built by Sir Christopher Wren, and was finished in the year 1710. This dome is, &c., &c." All was as distinctly heard as if we were by his side. We had heard for ourselves the wonder. We had experienced all that any one can experience, so far as the material work is concerned. When we put our name on the visitors' book we felt that we did more than that, for we joined the company of those who for two and a half centuries have been doing as we did. As long as mind endures, as often as the hand of thought reaches out, it must gather whether it will or not.

It is not far from 6 P. M. of this Sunday. Service is being held, and the great nave is half filled. The audience are trying to hear, and a part of them are sincerely worshipping; the remainder, like ourselves, are "seeing the cathedral." The sounds were confused and the echo troublesome, though not so much so as at other places. We were favorably impressed with the great length of the cathedral, and with its general look of vastness,—not awe-stricken, but filled with delight at the privilege we were enjoying in being in great St. Paul's. The large piers and arches, and the arched ceiling (tunnel-like, but here and there pierced with small and too flat domes), all appeared heavy and substantial,—built to last. Elegant colored-glass windows are about the apse, or chancel end, but the others are of small square lights of clear glass. A common square black and white marble tiled floor; monuments and tablets here and there against the columns and walls; an elegant oak organ-case, in two parts, on the side walls of the choir, and just back of the high, iron screen-work that separates the choir from the nave; the rich oaken stalls,—these make up the interior of St. Paul's. The great central dome has dim paintings by Sir James Thornhill, done at the time the cathedral was built. Seen, as the inside of the great dome is, through smoke, which the rays of light from the large windows above penetrate and make visible (this effect is ever present during the light), the great dome awakens a feeling of solemnity. We felt something of what we were contemplating.

The shades of night were falling; the assembly had broken up, and here and there were solitary visitors, moving about weird-like in the dim light as if loth to leave. We at length passed out, and returned to our lodgings at West End.

What ground has been gone over between the hours of 4 and 8 P. M. Hyde Park, Westminster Abbey and Bridge, Parliament Houses, the almost classic river, a look at St. Paul's,—and we are at home and resting.

The comparatively recent construction of St. Paul's deprives it of such ancient monuments as may be found at the Abbey, and in other English cathedrals. Those here are of white marble; and, although some of them are nearly a century old, they yet have a newness of design akin to statuary. One to the memory of Lord Nelson is the most costly and attractive. It is in one of the alcoves, or small chapels, at the west end, and the entire room, some twenty feet square, is devoted to it. It is elaborate and highly decorated. There is another of some eminence at the left side of the choir. It is a life-size statue of Dr. Samuel Johnson, the great lexicographer. He is buried at the Abbey; but one so poor as to live in the obscurity of a garret, at length became so great as to win the second monument in this important church.

"There's a divinity that shapes our ends,
Rough-hew them how we will."

The monuments of this church are of consequence as regards their elegance of design. In no other English cathedral is there so large a percentage of works of this kind. Impediments to the introduction of monuments were offered; and it was not till 1791 that the opposition was overcome, when application was made to erect a stone to the memory of John Howard, the philanthropist, who died at Kherson, Russia, Jan. 26, 1790. The door thus being opened, under the supervision of the Royal Academy many others have been erected, among which those of men of military fame prevail. The first monument was set up in 1795. In the south aisle, against the wall, is a full-size statue of Bishop Reginald Heber. He is dressed in canonical robes, his right hand on his breast, his left resting on a Bible standing endwise. He died at Trichinopoly, India, April 3, 1826, at the age of 42, and is celebrated as being the author of the well-known hymn beginning, "From Greenland's icy mountains." The cathedral has a fine basement, hardly inferior in interest to the great room of the cathedral above it, and always visited by the tourist. Here, as at the Whispering Gallery, the fee of a shilling is charged. The room is fifteen feet high, and is clean and airy. The floor is paved with stone slabs, and a large number of windows thoroughly light it. Innumerable columns of stone, for the support of the arching overhead, and floor resting upon it, give the room a forest-like appearance; though by no means depriving it also of the look of a vast chapel, for at the proper place there is an altar and its appurtenances. In this vicinity are a few effigies and tablets from the first cathedral. Forming an architectural museum, are a lot of relics that were found in the ground at the building of this cathedral, and so are of Roman origin, or were used as parts of the old cathedral.

Under the centre of the great dome, in this crypt, stands the granite sarcophagus in which rests the dust of Arthur Wellesley, the Duke of Wellington, who died at Walmer Castle, near Deal, Sept. 14, 1852, at the age of eighty-three. This sarcophagus is grand. So justly great is the public esteem for the man, that monuments to his memory are almost as common in England as are tablets of "the Lion and the Unicorn fighting for the crown," or as Washington Streets and men named "George W." are in America. In the crypt is the gorgeous catafalque on which were borne the remains of Wellington at the funeral procession,—the elegant wheels made from cannon captured by him. For a small fee persons are admitted within the iron fence to make examinations,—always accompanied by a guide, whose duty is to see that visitors carry away nothing save the story he tells them.

To us the most interesting object in the entire cathedral is in this crypt. At the right hand, as one faces the rear end, and well along on the side, is the last resting-place of the architect of the building, Sir Christopher Wren. The spot was selected by himself, and is really, though unpretending, a choice place of sepulture. It is under one of the windows, and is very light; and, if we mistake not, rays of the sun at times fall on the tomb. There is no imposing monument,—only a level stone slab some three feet wide and six feet long, two feet from the floor, bearing this simple statement:—

HERE LYETH
SR. CHRISTOPHER WREN
THE BUILDER OF THIS CATHEDRAL
CHURCH OF ST. PAUL &C.
WHO DYED
IN THE YEAR OF OUR LORD
MDCCXXIII
AND OF HIS AGE XCI.

On the western jamb of the window is a marble tablet, six feet three inches long, and three feet high, sunk into a panel, finished with a well cut egg-and-tongue moulding, and inscribed as follows:—

LECTOR SI MONUMENTUM REQUIRIS
CIRCUMSPICE.

(Reader, if you seek his monument, look around you.)

He contracted a cold in coming from Hampton Court to London, which doubtless hastened his death, but he died as he had lived, in great serenity. In the last days of his life he was accustomed to take a nap after dinner. On the 25th of February, 1723, his constant servant, thinking he slept longer than usual, went into his room and found him dead in his chair.

Two events of special interest took place in this year. On the 16th of July was born Sir Joshua Reynolds, the eminent painter. Elmes says:—

The placid soul of Wren might, by a poetical license, be imagined to have informed the equally placid mind of Reynolds, for no two men could be found to form a more just parallel; equally distinguished for industry, love of art, placidity, modesty, communicativeness, and disinterestedness.... At the head of your respected arts, ye both lie in honor, and in possession of the love and reverence of your countrymen, beneath the same vast dome that honors both your memories. Goodness and ye fill up one monument.

In this year also, 1723, was erected our old Christ Church on Salem Street, Boston. The design of this has been attributed to Wren, and we are inclined to think that indirectly he aided its conception. As he died at the great age of ninety-one, and was very feeble before his death, it can hardly be presumed that he made the drawings; but he may have dictated them. More probably he may have made a design some years before, which, being at hand, found its way to Boston; or the plan may have been made by a former apprentice, who carried on his master's work. Again, this design may have been copied, almost without the change of a line, from St. Bartholomew's-by-the-Wardrobe; for that, so far as the interior is concerned, is its prototype, even to the painted cherub-heads in the spandrils of the arches over the galleries. St. Bartholomew's was built from Wren's designs in 1692, and so was 31 years old at the time of the erection of our Boston church. The London church is 79 feet long, 59 feet wide, and 38 feet high. The dimensions of Christ Church are 70 feet, 50 feet, and 35 feet. Aside from the likeness of their interiors, there is a singular agreement in the pillar-capitals and gallery fronts, and also in the mouldings, combinations, altar-work, and vases. Their exteriors have little in common. There are two ranges of windows in each; but those of the London church are circular-headed on the second range, and only segmental for the first, like those at Boston King's Chapel; while at our Christ Church all the windows have circular tops. The London church has a plain flat-roofed tower, 80 feet high, without a steeple, though it is quite possible there may at some time have been one. This tower is at the right-hand corner instead of at the centre of the front.

The steeple on our Christ Church was blown down in the great gale of 1815, and rebuilt by Bulfinch, it is said, according to the original design. In its important features, and even details, this steeple is much like Wren's. This is not the place to argue the case,—but we repeat, the probabilities are that Christ Church was indirectly designed by the distinguished architect of St. Paul's.

The National Gallery of Paintings is a building of large dimensions, situated on Trafalgar Square, one of the main business centres, which is not far from half a mile from the Thames, and about midway between Westminster and St. Paul's. It contains eleven rooms for the display of over six hundred pictures, all of them being choice works of the Masters. The building is open to the public daily.

The British Museum is an enormous building, light and airy. In it, free to the public, is an unsurpassed collection of preserved animals, which can better be imagined than described. How wide is the field to which one is introduced, in the works of art or places of entertainment, in this vast metropolis! Museums and galleries abound. Accessible to the public, they are practically free, and better than can be found elsewhere in the world.

How abundant are the means of travel. The cab system is here at its perfection. The low prices are regulated by law. It costs one passenger a shilling, and two passengers a shilling and sixpence, to go a reasonable distance,—farther than from the Boston North End depots to those at the other part of the city. Cabs are plenty and are to be found standing in the centre of all principal thoroughfares. It is the law also that a tariff-card, in readable type, shall be put up inside of every cab.

Omnibuses abound, always with seats on the top as well as inside. The horse-cars, or trams, are heavier than ours, and not so handsome, but they are clean and well managed. Like the omnibuses, they have seats on top, where the travellers sit back to back. Then there is the underground railway. This runs almost around the entire city, and has a double track. Steam trains, of many carriages, are constantly passing both ways. At convenient points are stations where passengers descend and return by wide stairways through well-lighted and spacious trainhouses. This road is in all respects a great success. Perhaps half of it is through tunnels, but much of it is open to the sky, and the cars are lighted artificially. So frequent are the trains that one goes to the station at random, as he would to an omnibus, sure of not having long to wait.

We have spoken of the oft-running and well-patronized boats on the river. London is perfectly supplied with facilities for transit. Not for a moment would the over-crowded horse-cars, often seen here in our Boston be tolerated. We do not remember once standing in any public conveyance in England or on the Continent.

The public parks of London are very numerous, and are admirably located for convenience. Their total extent is greater than in any other city of the world. Prominent among these are Hyde Park, containing 400 acres; St. James's and Regent's parks, containing 450 acres each; and Kensington Gardens with 290. All these are within the metropolitan district, and are as readily accessible to the public as Boston Common or the Public Garden. Besides these, London's suburban parks are of incredible number and extent. It is enough to name some of them, and say that all these, and many more, are within six or eight miles of the centre of the city and easily reached. Victoria Park has 300 acres, Finsbury 115, Hackney Downs 50, Woolwich

Common and Greenwich Park 174 each, Peckham, Rye, and Southwark 63 each, Wandworth Common 302, Wimbledon 628. A little farther off is Richmond Park with 2,253 acres, the largest park near London. Then comes Windsor with 3,800, and Hampton Court and Bushey Park 1,842 each, and finally Kew Park and Gardens (the finest botanic garden in England), containing 684 acres. Most of them date back for centuries. Kew Garden is remarkable for its neatness, and hundreds of thousands annually visit it. In the vicinity are refreshment houses, kept in good order, which make the gardens a favorite place of resort, on Sundays as well other days.

Volumes might be written in regard to these parks, and then only vague descriptions would be given. None of them are finished like Central Park, New York,—that is, as far as bridges and lodges are concerned,—but in all else the London parks are its equals, and the city has done nobly for the comfort and health of the public. The more one experiences of London life, the more he realizes its greatness. Everywhere he discovers what is well adapted to the wants and tastes of our century; the old appears new, and the new old. Within a few minutes' walk of each other are over forty churches built immediately after the fire of 1666, two hundred years ago. Some of them have fine interiors, as St. Bride's, St. Stephen's Walbrook, Bow Church, St. Martin's in the Fields, and St. Clement Danes. In beauty, save perhaps the pews, these excel the churches newly built, with the exception of a few modern Gothic structures. Few of the churches named have many worshippers; the population has removed, but veneration for the old spots, and an inherent disinclination to change, say "Stay!" and so the old churches stand forlorn.

So interesting are all the old churches of London, that it is with an effort we refrain from speaking of them in detail. One, however, we feel justified in naming, and in giving a few items of its history. St. Sepulchre's is near the Old Bailey prison. Here preached John Rogers, the first of the martyrs during the reign of Queen Mary. He was burned at the stake in Smithfield, Feb. 4, 1555. The place of his execution is now a small square near his church. He is the John Rogers of the New England Primer, wherein we are told that "his wife followed him to the place of execution, with nine small children, and one at the breast." The perplexing question of number has been solved, for other accounts say distinctly that there were ten children in all.

Of more than common interest to Americans is the fact that in St. Sepulchre's church are buried the remains of Capt. John Smith, who in 1606 made the settlement of Virginia at Jamestown, and whose life was saved by the intercession of Pocahontas. He was born at Willoughby, England, in 1579, and died in London, June 21, 1631. He made voyages of discovery along the coast of New England, landing at the Isles of Shoals. Just 250 years afterwards, in 1864, a stone monument was erected to his memory on Star

Island. There was formerly in this church a monument in remembrance of him, which has long been removed. We have been fortunate enough to obtain the poetical part of the inscription:—

Here lies one conquered, that hath conquered kings,
Subdued large territories, and done things
Which to the world impossible would seem,
But that the truth is held in more esteem.
Shall I report his former service done,
In honor of his God and Christendom?
How that he did divide, from pagans three,
Their heads and lives, types of his chivalry?—
For which great service, in that climate done,
Brave Sigismundus, King of Hungarion,
Did give him, as a coat of arms, to wear,
Three conquered heads, got by his sword and spear;
Or shall I tell of his adventures since,
Done in Virginia, that large continent?
How that he subdued kings unto his yoke,
And made those heathens flee, as wind doth smoke;
And made their land, being of so large a station
An habitation for our Christian nation;
Where God is glorified, their wants supplied;
Which else, for necessaries, must have died.
But what avails his conquests, now he lies
Interred in earth, a prey to worms and flies?
Oh! may his soul in sweet Elysium sleep,
Until the keeper, that all souls doth keep,
Return to judgment; and that after thence
With angels he may have his recompense.

By the will of Robert Dow, a London citizen and merchant-tailor, who died in 1612, the annual sum of 26s. 8d. was bequeathed for the delivery of a solemn exhortation to the condemned prisoners of Newgate near by, on the night previous to their execution. Says the historian Stow:—

It was provided that the clergyman of St. Sepulchre's should come in the night time, and likewise early in the morning, to the window of the prison where they lie, and there ringing certain tolls with a hand-bell appointed for the purpose, should put them in mind of their present condition and ensuing execution, desiring them to be prepared therefore as they ought to be. When they are in the cart, and brought before the wall of the church [on the way to Tyburn], there he shall stand ready with the same bell, and after certain tolls, rehearse the appointed prayer, desiring all the people there present to pray for them.

A work entitled "Annals of Newgate" says, it was for many years a custom for the bellman of St. Sepulchre's, on the eve of execution, to go under the walls of Newgate, and to repeat the following verses in the hearing of the criminals in the condemned cell:—

All you that in the condemn'd cell do lie,
Prepare you, for to-morrow you shall die.
Watch all and pray, the hour is drawing near,
When you before th' Almighty must appear.
Examine well yourselves, in time repent,
That you may not t' eternal flames be sent;
And when St. 'Pulchre's bell to-morrow tolls,
The Lord have mercy on your souls!

Past twelve o'clock!

We visited many of these venerable churches, generally always on week-days, and found female sextons in attendance,—sometimes almost ready to hang their harps on the willows, as they related the decline from days of old. Our Old South, on Washington Street, is not nearer to commercial activity, nor more removed from the resident population, than are a hundred churches in the world's metropolis.

On our visit to St. Clement Danes, in the Strand,—an elegant structure without and within, nearly 200 years old,—we inquired for Dr. Samuel Johnson's pew, for he there attended church; and we found it near the end of the left gallery, a front pew, No. 18. There are columns as in King's Chapel, Boston, and against one of these the old lexicographer sat for years, often with the smooth-thinking and easy-going Boswell beside him. Making mention of one of these occasions, Boswell says:—

On the 9th of April, 1773, being Good Friday, I breakfasted with him, on tea and cross-buns; Dr. Levet, as Frank called him, making tea. He carried me with him to the church of St. Clement Danes, where he had his seat; and his behavior was, as I had imagined to myself, solemnly devout. I shall never forget the tremulous earnestness with which he pronounced the awful petition of the Litany: "In the hour of death, and at the day of judgment, good Lord deliver us!" We went to church both in the morning and evening. In the interval between the services we did not dine; but he read the Greek Testament, and I turned over several of his books.

In memory of the former occupant, a brass plate, some six inches high and eight inches wide, is let into the back of the pew, and reads as follows:—

In this pew, and beside this pillar, for many years attended divine service the celebrated Dr. Samuel Johnson, the philosopher, the poet, the lexicographer, the profound moralist, and chief writer of his time. Born 1709, died 1784. In the remembrance and honor of noble faculties, nobly employed, some of the inhabitants of the parish of St. Clement Danes have placed this slight memorial, A. D. 1851.

The inscription is said to have been prepared by Dr. Croly, rector of St. Stephen's Walbrook. Each of us sat where the verger informed us Johnson used to sit. The pulpit is placed as it is in King's Chapel, and the Johnson pew is within easy reach of it. We thought of Dr. Taylor, the rector, who was called up at night, when Johnson's wife Tetty died, to go to Johnson's house, and attempt to soothe and assuage his grief. He had a great mind and, when stricken, great was his sorrow. The record is:—

The letter calling him was brought to Dr. Taylor at his house in the cloisters, Westminster, about three in the morning, and as it signified his earnest desire to see him, he got up and went to Johnson and found him in tears, and in extreme agitation. After a little while together Johnson requested him to join with him in prayer. He then prayed extempore, as did Dr. Taylor, and thus, by means of that piety which was ever his primary object, his troubled mind was in some degree soothed and composed.

Dr. Taylor once told Boswell that, on entering the room, Johnson expressed his grief in the strongest manner he had ever read, and that he much regretted his language was not preserved. It was doubtless in this house in Gough Square, that Johnson passed ten melancholy years. Sad indeed must have been his distress, when he was compelled to write the following to his friend Richardson, the novelist.

GOUGH SQUARE, 16th March, 1756.

SIR,—I am obliged to entreat your assistance. I am now under arrest for five pounds eighteen shillings. Mr. Strahan, from whom I would have received the necessary help in this case, is not at home, and I am afraid of not finding Mr. Miller. If you will be so good as to send me this sum, I will very gratefully repay you, and add to it all former obligations. I am, sir, your most obedient and most humble servant,

SAM. JOHNSON.

Sent Six Guineas.

Witness, WILLIAM RICHARDSON.

This reminds us of Will's Coffee House where Johnson, Addison, Goldsmith, and others of like spirit so often congregated. We found it an ordinary three-story brick building, at the corner of a street near Covent

Garden. There is a common liquor store in the first story, and a tenement above.

There are three particular things one who visits London should always see,— the Tower, Hampton Court, and the Bunhill Burial-ground.

The Tower, as it is familiarly called, is not a tower simply, nor any single building, but twelve acres of ground enclosed by a massive stone wall, one side of which borders the Thames. Inside the enclosure are stone buildings, the principal of which is the large one in the centre. It is several stories high, square in plan, measures about one hundred and fifty feet on each side, and has square towers at each angle. These are continued up some twenty feet above the main building, and each is crowned with a Moorish dome and a weather vane. The White Tower, as it is called, is another of the buildings, and was erected in 1078.

One finds a comfortable waiting-room just inside the grounds, and there is always a company of visitors in waiting. When twenty are present, one of the guards leads the way hurriedly through the portcullis, calling attention to the several parts of the edifices.

We go through the Museum of Armor. On each side are effigy horses, facing towards the passage-way, and on them are images of the kings dressed in the armor worn in life.

We go into the dungeon where for twelve years Sir Walter Raleigh was confined; the ancient chapel of St. John, five hundred years old; the modern armory; the dungeon-keep where are deposited the crown-jewels and other articles of royal value, all enclosed in glass, and protected by iron-work.

Hastily we see the Traitor's Gate, through which Raleigh, Sidney, and Russell were taken into the Tower; the room opposite, where the two sons of Edward IV. were murdered at the instigation of Richard III.; the Beauchamp Tower, where Anne Boleyn and Lady Jane Gray were detained; the old banquet-hall, in which are sixty thousand rifles. For particulars the reader is referred to "Historical Memorials of the Tower," by Lord de Ros, published at London in 1867.

Hampton Court is reached by steam railway, and is fifteen miles from London. This palace was founded by Cardinal Wolsey; and of his building, three large quadrangles, in the Tudor style, remain. Large additions were made by William III., from designs by Sir Christopher Wren. The state rooms contain a splendid collection of paintings by Holbein, Vandyke, Kneller, and West, and also the seven original cartoons of Raphael. Some of the rooms are still furnished as sleeping-rooms, as they were when occupied by kings and queens centuries ago. The public are freely admitted to the entire premises.

The extensive grounds are laid out in Dutch style, with fine avenues. In its greenhouse is the largest and the most productive grapevine in Europe. It was planted in 1767, and at the time of our visit it was said to have over three thousand bunches of Black Hamburg grapes upon it. The roots of the vine are in a garden, and the trunk, which is about six inches in diameter, extends three feet from the ground, along the wall of the house, which it then enters. Inside, the vine spreads over the entire top, which is built in the usual conservatory style, with a roof having but one slope. It is hardly needful to say that these grapes are raised solely for the royal family.

There are hundreds of acres in the grounds, and adjoining it is a park, the circumference of which is over five miles,—a delightful spot to visit. The trees, embowered avenues, terraces, gardens, and long vistas yet remain as they were centuries ago. The soil, once sacred to the tread of royalty, is now a republican delight to the multitude.

A remarkable depositary of the sainted dead is Bunhill Burial-ground, in one of the busiest parts of London, on a great thoroughfare, opposite the house in which John Wesley died on the 2d of March, 1791. Almost adjoining this is the church in which Wesley preached. The burial-ground was laid out for a sacred purpose; the burial of Non-conformists and their friends, who have made the ground classic. No cathedral cemetery, to which they could not be admitted, has an honor greater than this. Here rests the sacred poet, Isaac Watts, whose monument tells us that he died Nov. 25, 1748. There is a monument to the memory of Susannah Wesley, the mother of nineteen children, two of whom were John and Charles. Here is the grave of John Bunyan, who died Aug. 31, 1688; and that of Daniel Defoe, the author of "Robinson Crusoe." Could the doctrine of a literal resurrection be true, no grander company would assemble at one spot, or walk forth into glory clad in whiter robes than theirs. No pope or bishop, of Roman Church or English, could understand the plaudit, "Well done good and faithful servant, enter thou into the joy of thy Lord," better than would they. These came up out of great tribulation, and so would shine resplendent.

London is great. A volume appropriated to each of a thousand things would not tell the story. Her history has a vast reach and the records have been well kept. Her population is a round four and a half millions,—as much as New York, Philadelphia, Chicago, Cincinnati, Boston, and ten more of our largest New England cities combined. Her great Library at the Museum has as many books as Harvard and Yale colleges, and the Boston Public Library, all put together.

Our stay here was from Sunday, May 12, to Saturday the 25th, about two weeks, and no hour of time was unemployed. We were amid scenes of which history had made the letter somewhat familiar; and now personal observation made the spirit a living reality. No one can know London till he sojourns there for months, visiting its places of interest, and reading anew the history of each in the admirable works written for the purpose.

As regards the habits of daily life we find but little that is peculiar. The influence of the press and of travel have changed the system of domestic as well as political economy. Both nations, American and English, have given and received. It savors perhaps of egotism, but it is exceedingly easy to say that the influence of the daughter excels that of the mother. There are more traces of America in England, than of England in America. The modifications have been from our direction, for it is true now, as in Bishop Berkeley's day, that "Westward the star of empire takes its way." Liberalism in England is not Communism, and will never be. Liberty may be ill-used by fanatics, but the sound sense of England will take care of itself, and "out of the bitter will come forth sweet." There are some points of English polity to be spoken of, but not now.

On this Saturday, May 25, we take a train at 1 P. M. for Oxford.

CHAPTER IX.

OXFORD.

We now begin a tour through the central part of England, in a northerly direction towards Scotland, for we intend to see England with unusual thoroughness. Our first place of sojourn is Oxford, where we arrive at 3.30 P. M., Saturday, May 25, having had a two and half hours' ride from London. The place presents a rural appearance, trees and gardens being interspersed among the buildings. Nowhere is there a commercial look, for it is emphatically a university town, and dependent mainly for support on its colleges. It was made a seat of learning at an early day, and is thus referred to by Pope Martin II. A. D. 882. Situated between the rivers Cherwell and Isis, it has a population of 31,544, and is irregularly built, with many narrow and crooked streets. Many of the buildings are old, yet in good repair. Tradition says that this was a favorite resort of Alfred the Great.

In one of the public streets the martyrs Latimer, Ridley, and Cranmer were burned. The spot is opposite Balliol College, and marked by a very imposing brown sandstone Gothic monument about thirty feet high, erected in 1841, from designs by Gilbert Scott.

Latimer and Ridley were led to the stake Oct. 16, 1555. A bag of gunpowder was fastened about the body of the former,—probably as an act of charity, to hasten his death,—and so he died immediately. While being bound, he said to his companion: "Be of good comfort, Master Ridley, and play the man; we shall this day light such a candle, by God's grace, in England, as I trust shall never be put out." It never has been extinguished, and will continue to "shine brighter and brighter, to the perfect day."

Latimer and Ridley, John Rogers, who was burned at Smithfield, Feb. 4 of the same year, and Cranmer, burned in Oxford March 21, 1556, were graduates of Cambridge, the rival university of Oxford. These two distinguished seats of learning are to England what Harvard College and Yale are to New England. Cambridge has long been recognized as liberal and reformatory in tendency, while Oxford has prided herself on her conservatism. Dean Stanley, in a late speech, ventured the remark that Cambridge was celebrated for educating men to be martyrs, and Oxford for burning them. Cranmer was a fellow-laborer with Latimer and Ridley. He was arrested and cited to appear at Rome within eighty days, but could not do so, and was condemned as contumacious. He was at first firm, but the fear of death overcame him and he recanted, and repeated his recantation many times, but without avail. In his last effort he declared that he had been the greatest of persecutors, and comparing himself to the penitent thief, humbly begged for pardon; but in spite of all, on March 21, 1556, Queen

Mary—who had a bitter hatred towards him, as did the bishops, who were resolved not only on his degradation but his death—directed him to prepare for the stake. A recantation was given him, which he was ordered to read publicly to the spectators. He transcribed and signed it, and kept a copy, which he altered, making a disavowal of his recantations. After listening to a sermon, he finally avowed himself a Protestant, declaring that he would die in his old faith; that he believed neither in papal supremacy nor in transubstantiation, proclaiming that the hand which had signed his recantation should be the first to suffer from the fire. He was taken to the spot where Latimer and Ridley were burnt the October before, and died like them, his death adding light to the candle which could never be put out. As the flames rose about him he thrust in his right hand, and held it there till it was consumed, crying aloud, "This hand hath offended; this unworthy right hand." His last audible words were, "Lord Jesus, receive my spirit."

The city has been for centuries one of great respectability and repute, and Charles I. once made it his headquarters. The cathedral attached to Christ's College is on the site of a priory, founded in the eighth century. It is Gothic, of the style of the twelfth century, and has a spire 146 feet high. This is one of the five cathedrals of England having spires; but it is, however, only a remnant of a church which, probably, when entire, had little merit. St. Peter's is the oldest church in Oxford; but St. Mary's is also venerable, and has a steeple 180 feet high.

The Bodleian Library, opened in 1602, contains three hundred thousand volumes. There is connected with the library a museum containing many portraits of distinguished people. In this room, among other prominent objects of interest, is an oaken chair, once a part of the ship in which Sir Francis Drake made his celebrated voyage around the world. He set sail from Plymouth, England, Dec. 13, 1577, over three hundred years ago, and reached home again in November, 1580. He died and was buried at sea, near Puerto Bello, Dec. 27, 1595.

The poet Cowley, in 1662, composed the following verse, which is engraven on a silver plate and affixed to the chair:—

To this great ship, which round the Globe has run,
And matched in race the chariot of the sun,
This Pythagorian ship (for it may claim
Without presumption, so deserved a name)
By knowledge once, and transformation now,
In her new shape this sacred port allow.
Drake and his ship, could not have wished from Fate,
An happier station, or more blest estate;

For lo! a seat of endless rest is given,
To her in Oxford, and to him in Heaven.

Here is exhibited the lantern used by Guy Fawkes in the memorable plot to blow up the Houses of Parliament, Nov. 5, 1605. It is an ordinary lantern, with holes through the tin. In fact, it is precisely like those used in New England fifty years ago.

The college buildings are mostly built of yellowish sandstone, now bedimmed with age, and many of them are much decayed. They are unlike our college buildings, being constructed with an imposing façade, through whose centre is an arch, under the second story, opening into an enclosed quadrangle. These quadrangles vary in dimensions, from one hundred to one hundred and fifty feet square, and the students' rooms open into them. Out of the quadrangle nearest the street, similar arches may often lead into other quadrangles in the rear of the first, or at its sides; so that the establishment may be extended, in a series of buildings, without losing its primal characteristics.

These roofless squares have velvet grass, with wide walks around the outside, against the buildings, and cross-paths leading to the doorways and arches. Scrupulously clean is every inch of college ground in Oxford. Not a piece of paper litters the lawn; and many students have flower-pots at their windows. Fuschias, petunias, nasturtiums, and geraniums were abundant. The buildings vary in design, but are all three or four stories high. Some of them are built out flush; and others have corridors, cloister-like, under the second story, around their quadrangles.

Connected with many colleges are large parks, for centuries used as places of academic resort. They have avenues and trees like Boston Common, and the main avenue at Merton College has a circuit miles in length. Too much cannot be said in praise of those classic grounds. Flower-plats are cultivated, and fine shrubbery; and there are brooks, embankments, and bridges. In a word, if paradise ever was lost, much of it has here been regained. It is no stretch of the imagination to think that Milton, educated amidst similar grounds at Cambridge, was on their account more inclined to meditate on "Paradise Regained."

The antiquity of Oxford as a seat of learning is undisputed. It is so referred to by Giraldus Cambrensis, in 1180, more than seven hundred years ago. Vacarius, a Lombard, lectured here on civil law, about the year 1149. The first use of the word University (*universitas*), in this sense, appears in a statute of King John in 1201. It was applied to similar institutions in Paris, in an ordinance of Pope Innocent III., bearing date 1215. The place was so recognized as a desirable resort for persons of education, that Wood, its principal historian, says: "At one time there were within its precincts thirty thousand persons claiming to be scholars, though of course not all belonging to the university." Its first charter was granted by Henry III. in 1244.

On the 10th of February, 1355, a disturbance occurred,—or what in our day would be designated a rebellion,—which ended in an edict from the Bishop of Lincoln, whose diocese included Oxford, that thereafter there should be annually celebrated in St. Mary's Church a mass for the souls of those who were killed, and that the mayor, two bailiffs, and sixty of the principal citizens should be present and offer a penny each at the great altar, in default of which they were to pay one hundred marks yearly to the University. The penance was afterwards mitigated, but was not abolished till 1825; so that, in some form, it remained for nearly five hundred years.

Passing over many interesting facts, we name the colleges in the order of their foundation.

The University comprises twenty colleges: University, founded 1249; Balliol, 1263 to 1268; Merton, 1264 (removed from Malden in 1274); Exeter, 1314; Oriel, 1326; Queen's, 1340; New, 1386; Lincoln, 1427; All Souls, 1437; Magdalen, 1456; Brazenose, 1509; Corpus Christi, 1516; Christ Church, 1546-1547; Trinity, 1554; St. John's, 1555; Jesus, 1571; Wadham, 1613; Pembroke, 1620; Worcester, 1714; Keble (by subscription, as a memorial to Rev. John Keble), 1870. The number of undergraduates for the year 1873-4 was 2,392; the whole number of members on the books was 8,532. The college buildings are located near each other, though they extend over an area of at least a square mile. Three or four are sometimes on a single street, their grounds adjoining. The undergraduates in each college average one hundred and twenty—or if all the students and members be included, the average is four hundred and twelve: numbers, which are small when compared with those of our leading American colleges.

These colleges are in most respects as independent of each other as if they were in different towns. Each has its own Master, or, as we should say, President. It governs its own affairs to the minutest detail, but acts always in subordination to certain regulations made by the Council of Management, which is composed of all the Masters.

No institutions have exerted a greater influence on the world than this and its companion at Cambridge.

As we walked along the shadow of these venerable walls, beneath the shade of their old trees, or sat beside the gently flowing streams; as we went into the dining-halls and looked upon the portraits of renowned men and upon their heraldry; as we sat on the benches which had been occupied by eminent men; as in the chapels we were inspired with new reverence for things great and good; as we wandered at will—at this time of college vacation—from close to close, and remembered the name and fame of the ecclesiastics, poets, historians, philosophers, scientists,—new school and old, High Church, Low Church, and No Church,—and thought of the six hundred years of results since the charter and first foundation,—we felt that Oxford was inexpressibly great.

The fine weather—which, as we say at home, was apparently *settled*—enabled us, for the first time since our landing, to dispense with overcoats; but, as the sequel proved, only for an hour.

The new foliage, the odor of flowers, the birds, the familiar croak and incessant wheeling of the rooks, seemed part and parcel of the premises, as if, like the trees and buildings, they had been there for a century.

We attended worship at St. Peter's, heard the service read, not intoned, and listened to a matter-of-fact sermon, about as well delivered as the average of sermons at home; and at 5.30 P. M., of this same Sunday, were ready to move on to Stratford-upon-Avon, the home of Shakespeare. Our visit was in vacation time, but many students remained in the city, and we noted their fine physique. None of them were puny, and hardly one had the "student's look." They were good specimens of Young England, square-built, solid, healthy, and stocky. Uniformity of size, demeanor, and conversation prevailed. With the pleasantest memories of Oxford, so admirably adapted to its great purposes, we moved out of the station towards the home of one who did so much to make great thoughts the common property of literature and life.

CHAPTER X.

WARWICK—STRATFORD-ON-AVON—LEAMINGTON—
KENILWORTH—COVENTRY—BIRMINGHAM—LICHFIELD.

When we started Sunday for Stratford we only thought of briefly visiting Old Warwick on our way; but after a two hours' ride, arriving here, we were tempted to remain over night, and were soon at a comfortable hotel, a commercial-travellers' house, near the station. It being but eight o'clock, and not yet sunset, we walked out for a view of the historic place, which we soon decided was one of much interest. Half the houses were picturesque, many of them built in the timbered and plastered style. All sorts of thoroughfares were there, from broad and level, to narrow crooked and hilly. Evening service being just ended, an unusual number of well dressed people were in the streets, and the hour reminded us of a New England Sunday.

Warwick is situated on the right bank of the Avon, and has a population of 10,986.

The castle is one of the finest feudal structures in England. It is grandly situated, its colossal rear making a bank of the river, and there are meadows and groves near by. All is in most perfect repair, and on Monday it was our good privilege to visit it and its remarkable grounds. It is occupied by the Earl of Warwick, who kindly permits strangers to examine the premises at certain times. One passes through the arched gateway, on one side of which is a room containing a museum of antiquities. A prim young miss, daughter of the matronly gatekeeper, glibly but bashfully gives the history of an enormous punchbowl and other interesting things. An optional fee makes things agreeable, and we pass through the grand avenue, turning back now and then to look at the high solid walls of the ivy-covered tower.

We go through a remarkable lawn and gravelled avenues, and not far in the distance at our right, partially embowered in green,—at times on a level with us, at others on the little hillsides,—we see the ruins of monastic establishments. How scrupulously everything is cared for, bearing evidence of constant watchfulness of the servants, such as only the English aristocracy can secure.

Next we walk over the great lawn, to the greenhouse five hundred feet away. We are invited there by the venerable gardener, but not without hope of reward. Here is the celebrated Warwick Vase; and who, claiming knowledge of art, has not heard of it? It stands on a pedestal six feet high. It is of marble, now of yellowish tinge, but tolerably white. It is remarkably rich in carvings, and of great age, its early history being lost in antiquity. It appeared to be six feet in diameter, and the same in height. It was years ago found in a lake near

Tivoli, and presented to the Earl of Warwick. All over the civilized world may be seen copies of this vase, made by permission of the owner.

Standing at the door of this conservatory, and facing towards the castle, a scene of wonderful beauty is presented. The spot is somewhat elevated, and we look for miles over hills, velvet fields, and woodlands. Conspicuous among the trees, making our picture's foreground, are spreading cedars of Lebanon. The river meanders on its quiet way; and the winding road, half hidden, adds its charm. Bordering the lawn which makes our left foreground is the cheerful castle, in color a sort of buff-tinged granite. It is by no means ancient in appearance, but the reverse, except in its design. The main tower is 128 feet high, and dates back full five hundred years. There is another, 147 feet high, of uncertain date. Ivy has its way, and covers parts of the great structure. The castle is colossal, its outlines broken by octagonal and square towers. Let us visit the castle itself. An additional shilling is to be paid to the young woman who guides us, and who only commences her tour when the proper number of visitors has accumulated. We pass through four or five large rooms, of elegantly finished oak and pine, painted and gilded. The furniture and upholstery are rich in design,—some ancient, some modern, but all in keeping with the place. Pictures abound,—many of them are by the Masters. Bric-a-brac is in profusion, much of it hundreds of years old, presented to former earls by royalty. There is also a museum of armor. In one room is a chimney, or open fireplace, with its cheerful fire. It is some nine feet wide, projecting well into the room, and is high enough to walk into.

What fine views from the rear windows! Beyond are the meadows and the groves; and to the right, extending countryward, are the hills and scenery before described.

The town was formerly walled, and there yet remains a gateway, surmounted by a chapel. Half a mile up the main street is Leicester Hospital, endowed centuries ago by the Earl of Leicester, and charmingly described by Hawthorne. Here is the ancient chair, said to be a thousand years old, accurate copies of which are for sale.

Near by is the church, built in 1693, with its massive tower of delightful proportions. How charming are the old mansions with their profusion of trees, all combining to make Warwick a most inviting place.

In the twilight, at the late hour of 9.30, the worshippers were coming out of old St. Mary's Church, which is situated at the most public centre, in the midst of a venerable churchyard. It is an ancient Gothic edifice, having an end tower with a tall spire above it. The dim-lighted interior carried us back into a distant age.

What ground have we gone over in a few hours!—hours not over-crowded by any means.

Monday we are up early for a new ramble,—first to see the town anew; next to visit the castle already described; and then to go over the Old Hospital, and to hear its history from a guide-inmate. Built and endowed by one of the old earls hundreds of years ago, it has apartments of two or three rooms each, accomodating perhaps ten families. These are for old soldiers, who are past a given age and possess certain requisites. They must have wives, and on the death of one soldier his place passes to another. About $350 a year is given them for subsistence, out of an endowment fund, and of course the rent is free. On the death of the husband, $100 is given to the widow, who must vacate the premises. If the wife dies first, then the husband also gives up the apartment and endowment, and goes into the common home, in another part of the building. Great neatness prevails, and all is under supervision of the chaplain, or Master.

STRATFORD-ON-AVON.

We arrived here at 2 P. M., after a ride of an hour, and took coach to the famed Red Horse Hotel, made famous by Washington Irving's "Sketch Book." The parlor, a low room some twelve feet square on the first floor, fronting on the street, is used by visitors. This is the room occupied for months by Irving, and his armchair is still in use. The tongs and shovel, and the iron poker—Sir Geoffrey's Sceptre—are still there, though the latter, having become classic, is on exhibition and not for use.

The town is small, and is somewhat of a business place at the very centre; but it is mostly rural, though a few of the streets are paved and the buildings of some consequence. It is situated on the River Avon, a small stream, and has a population of 3,833. It was a place of some consequence as early as the eighth century.

It of course derives its principal interest from associations with the great poet, born here, probably, April 23, 1564, and who died here on his birthday in 1616. The house in which he died was torn down by its proprietor many years ago, much to the regret of the inhabitants, as well as the visitor; but that in which he was born, and lived for many years, still stands. It is situated on a principal street, though in a quiet locality, and stands close to the sidewalk, with no yard in front. It is two stories high, having a pitched roof, with some breaks in it for windows; and is now supposed to be as in Shakespeare's early days. It is a timbered building, with bricks filling the spaces, plastered over and painted a light-gray or steel color. Its extreme length on the street may be forty-five feet. Like our Mount Vernon, it is owned by an association, and kept for the inspection of those interested in places of the kind. Two matrons—some sixty-five years of age, genial in demeanor and at home in conversation, and having the whole story at their tongues' end—take turns with each other in doing the agreeable, which costs each visitor a modest shilling. We are shown the kitchen, or living-room, into which the street door opens. It has no furniture except a chair or two for the accomodation of visitors. The fireplace is still there,—the worn hearth and the oak floor. Next we see the dining-room, and the chamber in which tradition says Shakespeare was born. The low ceilings and the saggy condition of everything aid the imagination; it is easy to feel that probably he was born here. In an adjoining room are collected many things once owned by the great bard; letters written by him, and other writings with which he was associated; portraits of him by various artists. The number of daily visitors is large. After a walk of ten minutes we are at the Church of the Holy Trinity, a Gothic structure, large and in thorough repair. Situated in the centre of a burial-ground, and enclosed with trees, it is very long, and has a tower and lofty spire. A source of revenue to the parish are Shakespeare's remains. A shilling is paid, and we enter on the side, near the west end, pass down the nave, and come to the holy of holies. The chancel is perhaps thirty feet long and twenty feet deep, enclosed by a simple altar rail at the front. On its left end wall, some six feet up from the floor, is the celebrated bust of the poet. It is painted, as described by Briton, in 1816:—

The bust is the size of life; it is formed out of a block of soft stone, and was originally painted in imitation of nature. The hands and face were of flesh color, the eyes of a light hazel, and the hair and beard auburn; the doublet, or coat, was scarlet, and covered with a loose black gown, or tabard, without sleeves; the upper part of the cushion was green, the under half crimson, and the tassels gilt. After remaining in this state above one hundred and twenty years, Mr. John Ward, grandfather to Mrs. Siddons and Mr. Kemble, caused it to be repaired and the original colors preserved, in 1784, from the profits of the representation of "Othello."

In 1793 Malone foolishly caused it to be painted white. In his right hand he holds a pen, and appears to be in the act of writing on a sheet of paper lying on the cushion in front of him. Beneath is a tablet containing the following inscription. The first two lines in Latin are translated as follows:—

In judgment a Nestor, in genius a Socrates, in arts a Maro; The earth covers him, the people mourn for him, Olympus has him.

And next are those in English:—

STAY, PASSENGER, WHY GOEST THOU SO FAST?
READ, IF THOU CAN'ST, WHOM ENVIOUS DEATH HATH PLAST

WITHIN THIS MONUMENT,—SHAKESPEARE; WITH WHOME
QUICK NATVRE DIDE; WHOSE NAME DOTH DECK YS TOMBE
FAR MORE THAN COST; SIETH ALL YT HE HATH WRITT,
LEAVES LIVING ART, BUT PAGE TO SERVE HIS WITT

OBIIT ANO. DEI. 1616; ÆTATIS 53, DIE. 23 AP.

Near the monument, and in the chancel, is a plain stone, beneath which the body lies buried; and upon it is the following inscription said to have been written by the poet himself:—

GOOD FREND, FOR IESVS SAKE FORBEARE
TO DIGG THE DVST ENCLOASED HEARE;
BLESETE BE YE. MAN YT. SPARES THES STONES,
AND CVRST BE HE YT. MOVES MY BONES.

In the charnel house of this ancient church are many human bones. These Shakespeare had doubtless often seen, and he probably shuddered at the idea that his own might be added to this promiscuous heap. This thought seems to have been present when he makes Hamlet ask: "Did these bones cost no more i' the breeding, but to play at loggats with them? *Mine ache to think on't.*" This dislike perhaps influenced him to bestow a curse or a blessing, as future authorities might disturb or respect his remains. His wife lies beside him. On her gravestone is a brass plate, with the following inscription by an unknown author:—

HEERE LYETH INTERRED THE BODY OF ANNE, WIFE OF WILLIAM SHAKESPEARE, WHO DEPARTED THIS LIFE THE 6TH DAY OF AVGV: 1623, BEING OF THE AGE OF 67 YEARES.

There is also a Latin verse, written by her daughter, and rendered into English as follows:—

Thou, Mother, hast afforded me thy paps,—
Hast given me milk and life; alas! for gifts
So great, I give thee only stones. How would
I rather some good Angel should remove
This stone from hence; that, as Christ's body rose,
So should thy form! But wishes naught avail.
Com'st thou soon, O Christ! let my imprisoned
Mother, from this tomb soar to seek the star.

A brief outline of Shakespeare's[1] life is as follows:—

Tradition says that he was born April 23, 1564. The ancient parchment parish register—which we were permitted to see—shows that he was baptized three days after. At the age of nineteen, an unusual proceeding took place in the quiet old town, for the authorities were asked to permit the marriage of the young man to Anne Hathaway, and after but one publication of the banns, instead of three, as was both practice and law. A bond signed by Fulk Sandalls and John Rychardson, for indemnity to the officers of the Bishop of Worcester's ecclesiastical court,—for granting the questionable permission which they did, and issuing the document,—bears date Nov. 28, 1582. The marriage took place during the Christmas holidays, but the exact day is to this time shrouded in mystery.

On the 26th day of May, 1583, six months after the hastened marriage ceremony, the parish register has a record of the baptism of his first child Susanna, and on the 2d day of February, 1585, of his second daughter.

It is presumed that his first play, the "First Part of Henry VI." was brought out at Blackfriars Theatre, London, in 1590, while its author was at the age of twenty-seven; and it is reported that he produced a play once in every six months afterwards, till the completion of all attributed to him. On the burning of the Globe theatre of London, (Southwark), which was simply a summer theatre and without a roof, he removed back to the town of his nativity in 1613, where he died April 23, 1616, on his fifty-second birthday, and realizing his own lines,—

We are such stuff

As dreams are made of, and our little life
Is rounded with a sleep.

We have no reliable account of the cause of his comparatively early death; but the Rev. John Ward, vicar of Stratford-on-Avon, in 1662, forty-six years after his death, writes as follows:—

Shakspeare, Drayton, and Ben Jonson had a merie meeting, and drank too hard; for Shakspeare, it seems, died of a feavour there contracted.

The next object of interest is the spot where was born and resided Anne Hathaway, the wife of Shakespeare. This is in a cluster of farmhouses called Shottery, situated within the parish of Holy Trinity, and about a mile away from Shakespeare's birthplace. From a gateway on the common road, a circuitous lane continues half a mile through gates or bars, then resolves itself into a footpath, fenced in by light wirework. The houses are of the usual rural style. At last we are at the cottage where, three hundred years ago, the Shakesperian courting was done. It stands endwise to a beautiful road, but some fifty feet from it, and enclosed by a wall. No house in England is more picturesque, either in itself, or its surroundings. It looks ancient, though in good repair. It is not far from sixty feet long, a story and a half high, or fifteen feet, with a pitched roof covered with thatch. The small upper windows, cut into the eaves, show the thatch a foot and a half thick. The building is of stone, plastered and whitewashed. It is entered from the side, and occupied seemingly by two or three families. There are vines climbing over it, and flowers in the long yard by the entrance; and there is a museum in the Anne Hathaway part.

We have not ceased regretting that we did not go in there; let the reader be admonished not to go and do likewise.

Children were at play in the old road, as they were three centuries ago. We had come three thousand miles to look upon what they hardly think of; but without the right kind of eyes one is blind. Another says, and says well: "A dwarf, standing on a giant's shoulder, may see more than the giant himself." There may be an undeveloped—*unevolved*, perhaps we should say—Shakespeare among those boys. He was once thoughtless and playful as they. Here Shakespeare walked and thought. A good road extended from Shottery Village to his home, but the short-cut across the fields alone would satisfy his mind. Philosophy and poetry were at their best in the shorter footpath, away from the "busy haunts of men." He could go quicker to the house he *would* go to in the early eve, and quicker also to the one to which he *must* return at the early morn! So it continued, until about Christmas of 1582, when hope ended in fruition, and Richard Hathaway's daughter became Anne Shakespeare, so to remain for forty-one years till 1623,—seven after her William had been gathered to his fathers. It is a coincidence worthy of notice, that Shakespeare's mother also survived her husband, John Shakespeare, seven years.

The bond of indemnity—holding the magistrates safe from penalties that might be imposed by the Bishop of Worcester or his consistory court—was in the sum of $200. The signature of the bondsman bears the mark of R. H., the initials of Richard Hathaway, the bride's father; so he of course approved the proceeding.

At 8 P. M. we took cars for the beautiful town of

LEAMINGTON,

where we arrived after an hour's ride, and remained over night, much enjoying our accommodation at the Avenue Hotel. Next morning, after breakfast, took a stroll out over the town. It is a noted place of aristocratic resort for pleasure, and for its springs—a sort of cross between English Bath and American Saratoga. Everywhere were facilities for the enjoyment of pleasure or health-seeking tourists. It would seem as though one could hardly be sick here. It was in this place that Sir Walter Scott wrote "Kenilworth," and as one breathes the exhilarating air, he is inclined to reduce the honors usually accorded to the great writer, and imagine that it is nothing strange that, with such surroundings, he wrote as he did. A visit to Leamington, and one is in the secret of Sir Walter's power when he wrote that smoothest of romances.

Perhaps we ought to make a more economical use of adjectives in describing the neatness of streets and the beauty of public and private grounds, for this is the universal and not exceptional condition.

The pink hawthorn is in bloom, and such pansies as we never saw at home. Remember, this is May 28. We have not anywhere in our travels seen Indian corn growing, and think it is not raised. We have seen no fields of potatoes, only small patches for family use; and these are six inches out of the ground. Carrots and early cabbages are fully grown and exposed for sale. We visited one grapery, where the Black Hamburg vines were forty years old and in good bearing, the grapes being about the size of peas. The vines were set in the borders of the greenhouse, which were two and a half feet wide, and the vines were three and a half feet apart,—the stocks, or trunks, being not more than an inch and a half in diameter. On the outside of a small conservatory was a fine heliotrope, one and a half inches in diameter, nine years old, which had often been well pruned and was in profuse bloom.

The town has a population of 22,730, and is very pleasantly situated on the River Leam, a tributary of the Avon, and is one of the handsomest towns in England, and more American in appearance than any other place we saw on our journey. The spring waters are saline, sulphurous, and chalybeate. They came into use in 1797, and are visited constantly by the *élite* of the land.

KENILWORTH.

"Kenilworth Castle!" says the reader. That and more! The station is reached by a half-hour's ride from Leamington, being about five miles in a direct line from Stratford, Leamington, and Coventry. The country is hilly and abounds with fertile fields, on which are grazing sheep, cows, and horses in countless numbers. Everything has an inhabited look. Elms, oaks, horse-chestnuts, and poplars abound. There are fine groves that might be called woods. The town itself is a small one of 4,250 inhabitants. It has manufactures of ribbons, gauzes, combs, and chemicals, and is a market-town, to whose public square the farmers bring their produce, while traders, from temporary stands, offer for sale all kinds of wares. For centuries these market-days have been a part of the weekly life of the people.

There is a very ancient church, and the ruins of an abbey, founded in 1122; but the great object of interest is the ruins of its celebrated castle, made so familiar by Sir Walter Scott's romance. The spot was reached by a pleasant walk of about a mile from the station. When we had passed through a well shaded country road,—through the woods, as we should say in America,—

there was presented to view a most enchanting scene. Ahead of us, say five minutes' walk, our road seemed to terminate in a gently rising plain, a miniature common, on which were three or four stone residences, partly public and partly private in appearance. The scene reminded us of a New England common.

To the left, bounding the road, was a stone wall; from this, gently sloping, for perhaps two hundred feet, was a grazing pasture. At the upper end of this were the ruins, not of the castle proper, but of some of its outbuildings. These massive and ivy-dressed ruins alone would have satisfied us, and we mistook them for the castle itself, but we went up to the little plateau, and round to the left hand, to get admission to the grounds; for we were now somewhat educated on the ruins question, and believed there was more in waiting for us. Lads and lasses, and some very old women, offered their services and guide-books. They told their story well, but we told ours better. We found the gateway, paid our shillings, and decided to be our own guides.

First, there was a flower garden,—centuries ago cultivated as now, but then only for the inmates of the castle. Here was also a museum, containing many articles once used in the castle. We did not get up enthusiasm enough to go in; and now content ourselves by saying, "Where ignorance is bliss, 'tis folly to be wise." Beyond another gate, we find ourselves in a closely cropped sheep-pasture. No lawn in our Boston suburbs equals this carpet of green, acres in extent. To our left, five hundred feet away, were the ruins observed before. We don't discount this beauty even now, and we never will. Put those ruins in Brookline or Brighton, and we'd stand our ground even with Englishmen. But what shall we say about the ruins of the castle itself,—there on our right, two hundred feet away?

This is Cæsar's Tower. Square in plan, the surface is broken with piers and vertical projections of varying width; the top is perhaps sixty feet from the ground, and made irregular by its decay. It is roofless, of course, and has walls sixteen feet thick at the bottom; half the surface is covered with dark-leaved ivy, precisely such as is grown in our houses. We go nearer; now on our right, two hundred feet on our front, and left, leaving a half enclosed square, are other portions of this great castle. What variety of outline! What solidity! There are patches of ivy fifty feet square. Measuring a single trunk, conformed to the crevices of the wall, we found it to be 3 feet 10 inches wide, and 16 inches thick at the centre, decreasing to a thickness of 3 inches at the edges. We should have been unable to believe this story, had it been told by others, and will not find fault with any one who now doubts our accuracy.

The castle was founded by Geoffrey de Clinton, treasurer to Henry I.; and in 1286 it was the place of a great chivalric meeting, at which it is said, "silks were worn for the first time in England." The very gorgeous entertainment given here in 1575, to Queen Elizabeth, is immortalized by Scott in "Kenilworth." Of the original castle, all now remaining is the corner tower. All else, though to all appearances as old looking, is of later date. The hall erected by John of Gaunt, who died Feb. 3, 1399, is 86 feet long and 45 wide, having mullioned windows on each side, and large fireplaces at each end.

The domain passed to the crown, and was bestowed by Henry III., who died Nov. 16, 1272, on Simon de Montfort, Earl of Leicester. When he was defeated and killed, his adherents held it for six months, but at length made favorable terms of capitulation. Edward II., who was murdered Sept. 21, 1327, was a prisoner in it for some time. It next fell into the hands of Edward III., who died June 21, 1377. Then it fell to John of Gaunt, who died twenty-two years afterwards, when it passed to his son, Henry Bolingbroke (Henry IV.); and on his accession to the throne, Sept. 30, 1399, it became again vested in the crown, and so remained until Queen Elizabeth bestowed it on her favorite Dudley, Earl of Leicester. She visited it three times, the last visit being so graphically described by Sir Walter. It was dismantled and unroofed in the time of Cromwell, and has never been repaired. At the Restoration it fell to the Clarenden family, and is now the property of the family of Eardley-Wilmot.

The ruin is more stately than most others, and was built on a grander scale. There is no particle of wood about it; all is enduring masonry. The floors are like its lawns, overgrown with beautiful grass, interspersed with wild flowers. Birds build their nests in the crevices; ivy hangs over it like a careless mantle.

The residence of kings and queens, of the bluest blood of the land, and for a period of four hundred years,—could the old walls speak, what tales would they tell! Intrigues, amours, sorrows, intenser than the peasant ever dreamed of. The rise and fall of dynasties, the advancing and receding of the waves of national life, were felt most definitely here, and full four centuries were employed in the record.

A home, a prison, the Elizabethan house of love,—it is to-day a marvellous curiosity-shop for the civilized world. Where young royalty prattled and crept, the speckled reptile, with "a precious jewel in its head," leaps and the snail crawls. The curtain of two centuries drops its thick folds between our age and Kenilworth's royal activity.

COVENTRY.

We arrived here at 2.45 P. M. May 28, after a short ride from Kenilworth. Few places in England are better known in history than this quaint old town. It is situated on the River Sherbourne, and has a population of 39,470. The town derives its name from a Benedictine Priory, founded in 1044 by Leofric, Lord of Mercia, and his Lady Godiva. The cellar of the old institution still exists, 115 feet long and 15 feet wide. No place affords a better example of an old English town than Coventry. In one section little if any change has been made, and here are timber-and-plaster houses, in streets so narrow that the projecting upper stories are but a few feet apart.

There are three churches, all with high towers and spires; and they are so located as to form an apparent triangle when seen from almost any point of view, and are seemingly an eighth of a mile apart. The steeple of St. Michael's is 363 feet high, and Trinity is 237 feet. They are of Gothic architecture, and two of them elaborately finished. There is a free school, founded in the time of Henry VIII.; and St. Mary's Hall was built in the fifteenth century. It is 60 feet long, 30 feet wide, and 34 feet high, with a curiously carved oak ceiling, and has a splendid colored window. It was built by Trinity Guild, and is now used for public meetings. As long ago as the fifteenth century an active trade was carried on in caps, bonnets, and camlet-cloth. These have given place to silks, fringes, and watches, more of the latter being made here than in London. Coventry was anciently defended by walls and towers; but only a small portion of the former and three of the latter remain, the others having been destroyed by Charles II., on account of the favors shown by the citizens to his enemies. Twelve parliaments were held here, which shows the ancient repute of the place. The people were noted for their love of shows and processions. Religious dramas, called mysteries, were performed here as early as 1416, and often in the presence of royalty. Until the present century, an annual pageant honored the memory of Lady Godiva, and is even now occasionally revived. The story is, that she obtained from her husband, Leofric, the remission of certain heavy taxes, of which the citizens complained, on condition that she should ride naked through the streets at noonday. She ordered the people to keep within doors, and to close their shutters; and then, veiled by her long flowing hair, she mounted her palfrey, and rode through the town unseen,—except by an inquisitive tailor. He has been immortalized under the sobriquet of Peeping Tom, and it is said that he was punished by instant blindness. This is the story on which Tennyson founded his poem. It was first recorded by Matthew of Westminster, in 1307, two hundred and fifty years after its supposed occurrence. When the pageant takes place now, a strikingly clad female is the leading character. There is a bust of Peeping Tom at the junction of two streets, the angle of which is rounded, three stories high, and painted drab. From an upper-story window, without a sash, the figure of Tom leans out in an inquisitive attitude. He is painted in the various colors of flesh and clothes, appears to be about forty years old, and wears a sort of military cap and coat. He has peeped out on the main street for centuries, the observed of all observers. The spot is said to be the one from which the original Tom was so rash as to look. We believe he is yet a source of revenue to the stores in the neighborhood, for there are often groups of strangers in the vicinity. To catch a share of the traffic, there are other Peeping Toms. In the venturesome spirit of the veritable Tom, some of these imitations are proclaimed, in painted placards, to be the great *original*,—"original in that place!" somebody said!

At 9 A. M. of Wednesday we left for

BIRMINGHAM,

where we arrived at 11 o'clock, and found the place, as we had anticipated, very smoky in atmosphere, and largely inhabited by poor working-people. High taxes, lack of education, and hard usage keep the people down. The public buildings and stores are spacious, but our surroundings were uncomfortable and we made but a three hours' stay.

Birmingham is a city of immense manufactures, and may well be considered the great workshop of England. Here John Bull everywhere has on his workshop paper cap, and shows the brawniest of brawny arms, and the smuttiest of smutty faces. A Birmingham dry-goods clerk, by reason of the smoky atmosphere, is about as untidy as an average American mechanic.

The city lies on ground sloping to the River Rhea, and canals radiate to several railroads. It has three parks: Adderly, triangular in shape, opened in 1856; Calthorpe, near the river, in 1857; and Ashton, in 1858. The older portions are on low grounds. The Town Hall is of Anglesea marble, 160 feet long, 100 feet wide, and 83 feet high, and is of Corinthian architecture, in imitation of the temple of Jupiter Stator at Rome. The public hall is 145 feet long, 65 feet wide, and 65 feet high,—that is, 30 feet longer than Boston Music Hall, 15 feet narrower, and of the same height. The organ is one of the most powerful in Europe, and has 78 stops.

The old church of St. Martin has a massive tower, and a spire 210 feet high. This church contains monuments of the De Berminghams, the ancient lords of the place. It has 343,696 inhabitants, is first mentioned in Doomsday Book under the name of Bermingeham, and remained an obscure village for centuries.

Its first impetus towards manufactures was given at the close of the last century, by the introduction of the steam-engine,—especially by the demand for muskets created by the American Revolution and the French wars. There are many large factories, but more than elsewhere is it customary for persons of limited means to carry on manufactures on a small scale. They generally employ men to work by the piece and at home; or, where steam is required, they hire rooms furnished with the requisite power.

In 1865 there were 724 steam-engines in the place, with 9,910 horse-power. There were 1,013 smelting and casting furnaces, and 20,000 families were engaged in manufactures. The value of hardware and cutlery exported in 1864 was $20,000,000. There were also exports of firearms, glass, leather, machinery, iron and steel wire, plate, copper, brass, zinc, tin, and coal, to the amount of $185,000,000. History says that 5,000,000 firearms were furnished during the Napoleonic wars; and during the first two years of the Civil War in America, 1,027,336 were exported to the United States. 30,000 wedding rings have in a single year passed through the assay office. This city is noted for its steel pens. At the Gillott establishment 500 workmen are employed, and 1,000,000 gross are produced annually. The whole number of pens made in the city is 9,000,000 annually, and 500 tons of steel are consumed in their manufacture. Every kind of manufacture in metals is carried on here, and to name the items would bewilder us. Birmingham is the workshop of Great Britain, and we may say of the world, for no other place approaches it in the extent and variety of metallic work. Our next move was for

LICHFIELD.

We reached it after an hour's ride from Birmingham, arriving at 3 P. M. Valises deposited at a very homelike chateau, not far from the station, we were out for sights. Through a couple of short and narrow streets, where the brick buildings were painted in light colors, we passed into an opening dignified by the name of Square, measuring perhaps a hundred feet on each side. On the right-hand corner is an ancient Gothic church. On our left, making another corner, is the house in which, on the 18th of September, 1709, was born Samuel Johnson, the great lexicographer, son of "Michael Johnson, bookseller and stationer, sometime magistrate of Lichfield," and who died, leaving his family in poverty. The house is three stories in height, with a hipped roof. It has nothing striking about it, and is forty feet or so square, of stone or brick, plastered on the outside, and painted cream-color. In the youth of Johnson, it contained a store, but has long since been remodelled, and the store is now the common room of the dwelling-house. The houses about it are closely built; no yard, garden, or tree is in sight.

In front, in the centre of the square, is a statue of Johnson, on a pedestal much too high. The statue is in a sitting posture, and looks too young for a man who did not come into public notoriety until much beyond the age represented by this sculpture. The unpretentious birthplace is more interesting than the monument. These streets, through which he so many times walked,—the church in which he so many times attended worship, and in which he was baptized,—these were too real not to make their impression. We could see the scrofulous boy of ten years, with his disfigured face and injured sight and hearing, his education already begun, and he a student of Latin at the Lichfield free school. He was five years there, then one at Stourbridge; and at the age of sixteen desired to enter Oxford, but was prevented by poverty. Going as assistant to one more fortunate in worldly affairs than himself, at length, in 1728, he was admitted to Pembroke, where, the record says, "he was disorderly, but not vicious." He died in London, Dec. 13, 1784. What incidents and great events go to make up his history for those intervening years! Wherever the English language is spoken it is influenced by his labors.

Not much antiquity is anywhere apparent in Lichfield. Take Johnson and the cathedral away, and there would be nothing of moment, for it has little business.

We soon arrive in the vicinity of the cathedral, and the scene changes as by magic.

The cathedral, with its centre and two western towers and spires, is of vast length and good height, built of a very red sandstone. It is about an eighth of a mile off, and well embowered with trees, with the river between us and them. The lower portions of the cathedral are hid from view. To the left, and not as far up, is another group of buildings, among them the Lichfield Museum.

On the second floor we find the place in charge of a matronly lady, who is at home in her work, and admirably fitted for the position. We look at old armor, at pictures, and relics "brought over the sea and from foreign parts," but better remains behind. In a glass case are exhibited things once owned and handled by the great writer who, next to the cathedral, gives Lichfield its interest and renown. Here are his silver shoe-buckles, the blue and white pint-mug from which he drank, the favorite saucer on which his wife Tetty used to put his morning breakfast biscuit; and here also are letters written by him. This was one of the especial treats of our tour.

We found the great cathedral in perfect repair. A small close surrounds it, with lawns, trees, and rooks. After a general look at it we take a turn along the river, and off to the rear and right of the cathedral, to walk around the promenade enclosing, like Chestnut Hill, the city reservoir.

Encircling the water, we come upon an exquisite little Gothic church and burial-ground. The area of the reservoir and its avenues is perhaps fifty acres,—the size of Boston Common,—and as one stands on the rear avenue, facing the town, the scene is most enchanting. The place is surrounded by a mixed landscape, in which fine trees abound; at the extreme left is the village, seen partially through the trees. On the right is the cathedral, nearly hid by the trees. Along the entire line are fields, gardens, and mansion-houses; and, behind all, are high lands, extending towards us, and around back of the little gem of a church. Behind us are aristocratic residences with intensely rural surroundings. On to our left, and behind, is the venerable St. John's Church, whose bell is plaintively tolling for evening prayers. From this to the town are brick buildings, and homes with their little gardens. When other scenes are forgotten, this evening in Lichfield will be as charming as now. Johnson would have been even more uncouth, but for the good influence of scenes like this; and his early removal hence deprived him of visions of daily and educating beauty.

In these churches—in St. Michael's near his home—he worshipped, and seeds were planted which in after life bore their pious fruit. He was not wholly rough in nature, nor entirely given to a love of literary gossip and coffee-house ease. Not solely inclined to entertainment by Garrick or Boswell, he loved the clergy as well, for he was a deeply religious man in his own way.

The cathedral is 400 feet long, 187 feet wide at the transepts, and has three spires,—the central 353 feet high, and the others, at the west end, 183 feet each. The western front is the best in England. No cathedral suffered more, in the destruction of its monuments at the time of the Reformation, than this. With the exception of the stone effigies of two prelates, and a few others of less importance, all were destroyed. There are, however, monuments of later date. One of the most noted is that to Lady Mary Wortley Montague,—a figure in marble, with an inscription recording her agency in introducing into England inoculation for smallpox. She was a native of Lichfield, and Dr. Smollett says: "Her letters will be an important monument to her memory, and will show, as long as the English language endures, the sprightliness of her wit, the solidity of her judgment, and the excellence of her real character."

The bust of Dr. Johnson was placed in the cathedral, as the inscription states, as "a tribute of respect to the memory of a man of extensive learning, a distinguished moral writer, and a sincere Christian." Near by is a cenotaph erected by Mrs. Garrick to the memory of her husband, the eminent dramatist and actor, who was the pupil and friend of Johnson, and died at London, Jan. 20, 1779.

The bishops of this cathedral have been men of especial note. Among them may be named Bishop Schrope, who was translated from this See to that of York, and was celebrated for his resistance to the usurpations of Henry IV., in consequence of which he was beheaded in 1405, and was long revered as a martyr.

Rowland Lee was appointed bishop of Lichfield in 1534. He solemnized the marriage of Henry VIII. with Anne Boleyn, in the nunnery of Sopewell, near St. Alban's. During the establishment of the reformed religion he was mortified to see his cathedral at Coventry entirely destroyed, notwithstanding his earnest endeavors to save it.

Ralph Bayne was one of the foremost persecutors of Queen Mary's reign, and caused women to be burnt at the stake. On the accession of Elizabeth to the throne, he refused to administer the sacrament to her, for which refusal an act of parliament deprived him of his See.

William Lloyd was one of the seven bishops committed to the Tower by James II., for refusing to read the Declaration of Liberty of Conscience, as it was called; although the real intention of it was to undermine the Protestant religion, and to set up popery again in its place.

John Hough, who was made bishop of this See in 1699, was, at the time of the Reformation, Master of Magdalen College at Oxford, and in like manner resisted the royal order. He was elected head of the college against the king's will, and so was forcibly ejected by the commissioners; but he was restored the next year.

One of the most memorable of all the bishops is Hackett, who came here in 1661. It was he who did so much in the way of restorations, after the destructive work of Cromwell, who dealt roughly with the Lichfield Cathedral. All churches, as well as abbeys, monasteries, and priories, were Roman Catholic institutions, and they suffered greatly in the suppression of papal worship. Statuary was destroyed, no matter what its value. Pictures and frescoes were defaced, altars torn down, and everything reduced to Cromwell's ideas of a Protestant level. This involved the destruction of a vast number of shrines and monuments, those of bishops and prelates suffering especial desecration. The iconoclasm was thorough. Roofs were taken off, buildings dismantled, and their rebuilding or occupancy prohibited under severe penalties. This accounts for the many fine ruins in Great Britain; Melrose Abbey, Furness Abbey, and a thousand others, are now in decay in consequence of these desecrations.

We deplore the loss of works of art and antiquity, but we must not judge from a nineteenth-century and American standpoint. Had papist institutions been left where for centuries they had been entrenched, Protestantism could have made little headway. People of low intellect, with its accompanying ignorance and superstition, are best reached through the senses. Pageants, images, pictures, devout genuflections, were powerful then as now. The authorities of the Roman Church knew this as they now know it. The new Protestant government of England realized that these religious emblems were great obstacles in its way, and was uncompromising in their extermination. The next generation, coming up under a new administration, was more tractable. This was unavoidable, if the rulers would prevent friction in the new machinery. Let us not speak ill of the bridge that carried freedom and toleration safely over.

This cathedral was for various causes an object of hostility. The adjacent green was fortified, and was alternately in possession of each party; and of course the cathedral suffered the injuries of a constant siege. History has it that two thousand cannon-shot and fifteen hundred hand-grenades were discharged against it. The central spire was battered down, and the others shared nearly the same fate. The statuary of the west front, around these towers, was shattered; the painted windows were broken; the monuments were mutilated; and the mural stones were stripped of their brasses. Dugdale says:—

It was greatly profaned by Cromwell's soldiers, who hunted a cat every day in it with hounds, and delighted themselves with the echo of their sport along the vaulted roofs. Nor was this all; they profaned it still further by bringing a calf into it, wrapt in linen, which they carried to the font, and there sprinkled it with water, and gave it a name in scorn and derision of the holy sacrament.

When Bishop Hackett was appointed to the See in 1661 he found the cathedral in this hopeless confusion; but, in spite of such discouraging conditions, on the very morning after his arrival he prepared for improvements. With laudable zeal he aroused his servants early, set his coach-horses, with teams and laborers, to removing the rubbish, and himself laid the first hand to the work. A subscription soon amounted to $45,000, of which the bishop contributed $10,000. The dean and chapter contributed a like sum; and the remainder was raised by the bishop, who solicited aid from every nobleman and gentleman in the diocese, and of almost every stranger who visited the cathedral. He obtained from Charles II. a grant of one hundred timber-trees out of Needwood Forest, and in eight years saw his cathedral perfectly restored. With joy and great solemnity it was re-consecrated Dec. 24, 1669.

The next year Bishop Hackett contracted for six bells, only one of which was hung in his lifetime. His biographer Plume says:—

During his last illness he went out of his bed-chamber into the next room to hear it; seemed well pleased with the sound, blessed God who had favored him in life to hear it, and observed at the same time that it was his "own passing-bell." He then retired to his chamber, and never left it again till he was carried to his grave.

That bell still sounds from the tower. The same decorations present themselves, and by these the good bishop yet speaketh. Unfortunate are the visitors who, amid scenes and sounds like these, having eyes, see not, and having ears, do not hear.

The war history of one cathedral is the history of all, for each was desecrated, and each has had some Bishop Hackett; though not every restorer was as capable as he in purse and brain. Restorations were everywhere begun, and in many instances the new work exceeded the old; but superstition and ignorance were common even among the high clergy, and oppression accompanied their daily life, as it did that of our New England ancestry.

At 10.20 A. M. of Thursday, May 30, we left for that peculiarly named town, Stoke-upon-Trent.

CHAPTER XI.

STOKE-UPON-TRENT—STAFFORDSHIRE—MANCHESTER—LEEDS—CARLISLE.

We arrived at Stoke-upon-Trent at noon. Our valises deposited at the coat-room of the station, we sallied out for a restaurant dinner and a visit to the pottery of the Mintons. There are many places of crockery manufacture here, all having a dingy look; most of them are of brick or stone, and two or three stories high. The buildings are not large, but each establishment has several, with chimneys forty to sixty feet high, tapering largely as they rise. The greatest facilities are furnished for visiting the works. We greatly enjoyed our visit, and theoretically know just how it is done; yet we couldn't excel practically the youngest apprentice. It is hardly in order to give lessons, but some information may be worth a passing word.

The clay is uncommon and found in but few places. It has also to be peculiarly prepared. When ready to be moulded it looks very much like putty or wheaten dough. The dish is made in the usual manner, on the potter's wheel, or on a mould. It is partially dried and then baked in a great oven, from which it comes out white as chalk. If it is to be white and undecorated, it is then dipped into a tank of liquid sizing, in appearance like dirty milk. It drips off, and is then put again into an oven and subjected to intense heat. The sizing melts or vitrifies, and turns into glazing. The oven cools off slowly, and the ware is taken out glossy and ready for sale.

If the dish is to be ornamented, the figures are put on with a stencil-plate, or printed on the white ware after the first baking and before the glazing. Of course any desired color can be rubbed over the stencil. If the ware is to be printed, this is done with a soft roller, which takes its tint and impression from a stamp. This roller is passed over the stamp as a similar article is rolled over printer's type; only the figure is imprinted on the pottery, not with the stamp or type itself, but with the roller, from whose soft surface the figure is readily absorbed by the moist clay. After this the ware is dipped into sizing and finished as before described. If the ware is to be rudely ornamented with flowers, these are often painted on it by hand, after the first baking, women and girls being employed for the purpose. Of course glazing and burning must always follow the decoration. If colored stripes are desired, these also are put on by hand. If ware is to be elegantly adorned, with pictures of flowers, animals, or landscapes,—in a word, Sèvres or Worcester ware,—this also is done by the patient hand-labor at the benches. A hundred women are sometimes at work in a single room, as if they were making water-color drawings. If gold lines are to be put on, this is done with gold paint. It is black when it comes from the furnace, but is then rubbed down with cornelian burnishers and the gold color restored. China is no more nor less than thin ware made of a peculiar clay. Of the secrets of coloring we know nothing. Hundreds of years have been employed in experimenting on the minor details; and with all their generous entertainment of strangers, and perhaps of angels unawares,—not being sure the visitor is not a fallen one, and so inclined to abuse the information,—the artisans are not free to impart information which seems small, but is really of the utmost importance.

The town is situated on the River Trent, as its name implies, and the entire parish, including Stanley and many other suburbs, has a population of 89,262. It has numerous wharves and warehouses, and is intersected by the great Trent canal and the Staffordshire railway. It has the honor of being the birthplace of Rev. John Lightfoot, the celebrated ecclesiastical writer and Hebrew scholar. He was born here March 29, 1602, and died at Ely, where he was prebend at the cathedral, Dec. 6, 1675. The town receives its notoriety solely from its potteries.

Our second visit was to the warerooms of Minturn & Hollins, who are celebrated, as are the original Minturns, for the elegance of their work, which is well known in America as well as Europe. Their display was wonderful for fineness of execution and exquisite coloring.

Our notebook, as well as our vivid recollection, defines it as "an inexpressibly smoky place, with hundred of chimneys, in groups of from ten to twenty, belching forth thick and black smoke."

At 4 P. M. we took a train for another great workshop, and on our way must needs go through, not Samaria, but Staffordshire, which is one of the best examples of a *smoke district*; and—like Niagara in this—that one is enough for a world.

STAFFORDSHIRE.

In this region the smelting and manufacture of iron abounds. Hundreds of chimneys, large and small, single and in groups, begin to meet the view as soon as we are fairly out of Stoke Village. Everywhere the air is permeated with dense though by no means very disagreeable smoke; that is, it did not produce half the ill effect on the eyes or the body that it did on the shirt bosoms and the mind.

The vast extent of the domain astonished us. As we merged into the thicker part, the sun was entirely obscured, the people were weird-like, and all things wore a smoky aspect. Condensed masses of smoke hung like thunder-clouds, and they were lighted up by the glare that issued Pandemonium-like from a hundred chimney-tops. In the dimness below, the men at the blastfurnaces, handling red-hot rods, or pouring molten iron into moulds, seemed like so many imps, and we had a vivid representation of the *other place*, that was talked of a hundred years ago. We were glad of the experience, for it was unlike anything seen before, or likely to be seen again; but how we enjoyed a change to clear atmosphere and a blue sky, and how increased was our ability to enjoy the

"Sweet fields of living green,
And rivers of delight,"

by which the swift train presently hustled us!

We need not say that bituminous and not anthracite coal is used in England. It burns with a brilliant red flame, and its smoke is either black, gray, or white. It is found in great profusion (as hard coal is in our Pennsylvania) in the same regions with iron ore.

It is as common to see coal-mine openings—their cheap houses over them, and their railways,—as to see iron mines. No manufacturing region would seem complete without them. It is providential that these two useful minerals, coal and iron, are found together, and so conveniently near the geographical centre of Great Britain as to make them accessible to each section of the island.

We are at our journey's end, in

MANCHESTER,

after the ride of less than two hours. It was not our intention to remain here long, and our first view of the place confirmed the wisdom of our decision. It is a large city, smoky from the thousands of manufactories, with nothing antique to be seen. Our older western cities, like Cincinnati, much resemble Manchester. Our stay was occupied principally with an observant walk of some miles through the principal avenues and among the manufactories. There are grand buildings, but the general smoky outlook prevails. Manchester is situated on both sides of the River Irwell, and has a suburb called Salford. The city proper has a population of 351,189, and the latter 124,801,—475,990 in all. There are two municipal governments, but the two cities are practically one, being united by eight bridges.

This spot was a chief station of the Druids, who here had an altar called Meyne. In A. D. 500 it was an unfrequented woodland. In 620 it was taken by Edwin, king of Northumbria, and soon after was occupied by a company of Angles. It next passed to the Danes, who were expelled about 920, by the king of Mercia. A charter, giving it the privilege of a borough, was granted in 1301.

The first mention of Manchester cotton was in 1352, and designated coarse woollen cloth, made from unprepared fleece. At the time of the Civil Wars it had become a place of active industry, and suffered much from both parties. In 1650 its manufactures had wonderfully increased, and ranked among the first in extent and importance; and its people were described as the most industrious in the northern part of the kingdom.

The value of cotton exports, as early as 1780, was $1,775,300; in 1856 it was $190,000,000; and in 1862 more than one half the operatives were thrown out of employment in consequence of the American Civil War, which deprived Manchester of the raw material. In 1871 there were connected with the cotton and woollen manufactures 322 factories, employing 33,671 persons, and using 21,000 horse-power of steam. In the manufacture of metal goods, glass, chemicals, and leather, there were 467 manufactories, 14,895 work-people, and 3,996 horse-power. The mechanical list, including builders, and cabinet-makers, involved 2,783 shops and 73,235 employees, using 28,515 horse-power.

The Royal Exchange, commenced in 1868 and just completed, is one of the finest structures in Great Britain, costing $1,250,000. Hospitals and charitable institutions are plentiful. The schools are of a high grade, and the city is one of the most enterprising in England.

At 10.20 A. M., Friday, we left for Leeds. These three places, Birmingham, Manchester, and Leeds, are an epitome of English manufactures, and we can hardly pass without examining them, though we confess to a daintiness obtained from the beauties amidst which we had been passing the weeks; and we feel that we shall be glad when our tour through the manufacturing districts ends, for we are impressed anew with the proverb, "God made the country, but man made the town."

LEEDS

is situated on both sides, but chiefly on the left side, of the River Aire, and has a population of 259,212. The site was once a Roman station, and the mediæval name was Loidis. As a manufacturing town it dates back to the sixteenth century. The larger part of the city has an old look. The streets generally are narrow and crooked, but well kept. The new streets are wide and contain many fine buildings; and the tramways and omnibuses give it a Bostonian appearance. The spacious town-hall was completed in 1858. Like all the principal English cities, it has its share of statues, and a fine one of Robert Peel is in front of the court-house. It is said to have 225 places of public worship. In woollen manufactures and leather-tanning Leeds surpasses all other places in the kingdom. 12,000 persons are employed in manufacturing woollen goods alone. The city is a railroad centre. There are 200 collieries in the surrounding district. It is reported that one quarter of the inhabitants are engaged in manufactures of some kind, and yet pauperism flourishes fearfully. There is a library founded in 1768, by the renowned Dr. Priestley, of scientific as well as theologic fame. He was pastor of a church in Leeds, and gave much attention to religious subjects. After an industrious life of some years here,—a large portion of which was employed in scientific pursuits and authorship,—he removed to Birmingham, and was pastor of a church there. At length he went to America, arriving in New York, June 4, 1794, and dying at Northumberland, Pa., Feb. 6, 1804. A celebration, in honor of his discovery of oxygen, was inaugurated by American chemists at the place of his death, Aug. 1, 1874, and on the same day his statue was unveiled in Birmingham, England. In 1860 another statue was placed in the museum of Oxford University. A catalogue of his publications, prepared for the library of Congress, for the Centennial of 1876, comprises more than three hundred works on chemistry, history, theology, metaphysics, politics, and other subjects.

The markets of Leeds are large. New potatoes, May 31, were for sale, smaller than English walnuts. The fish markets are supplied with more varieties than we have seen anywhere else. The flower marts have great displays of perfect plants, especially pelargoniums and geraniums.

Kirkstall Abbey is about three miles away, on the edge of the city. Nothing can excel the beauty of this ancient place. It is situated near a country road, and slopes to the river a distance of perhaps a thousand feet. The walls are varied in outlines and heights. The tower and walls are quite complete, and the adjoining ruins are as fine as any in England. They comprise many rooms, roofless for centuries. The low-cropped grass, with its thick math, fills them, and there are ten or twelve elm-trees, full two feet in diameter, growing in the deserted apartments. In one part is the small enclosed garden, perfect as at the first. In the walls are places of burial of the pietists who once dwelt here; and on one side are rooms, opening into the garden, that once were monks' cells and their later place of sepulture. There are many stone coffins; and the apartments and the close, with the ivy-mantled walls, are of extreme beauty. The position is remarkably fine. Removed from other habitations; quietly situated at the side of the great road, and on this meadow-like lawn; the river running leisurely by, washing the borders; the old trees; its ingenuity of arrangement,—this gem is a connecting link between the old dispensation and the new. We could but wish we might do as Scott advises of Melrose Abbey, "visit it by the pale moonlight;" but we did not have that privilege. We could only see it at the close of this fine day, when the low sun sent its rays aslant the openings, and gave an indescribable tranquillity to the place.

This is one of the few spots we would again make an effort to see. As the lamented Bayard Taylor was lured from his course of travel by Longfellow's "Belfry of Bruges," and could not rest till he had been there, so this Kirkstall

Abbey influences us, and will till the end of earthly journeys. Built in 1157, in the Reformation it was abandoned and unroofed, its relics destroyed, its tombs rifled, and ruin begun; and now for more than three hundred years, as if subservient to the will of Cromwell, and mute with alarm and solitary in its shame, it has stood beautiful and enduring, though dying atom by atom in its own loneliness.

On Saturday, June 1, a pleasant day, though so cool that overcoats were still comfortable, we took train for

CARLISLE.

This is another cathedral town, and the last in England we are to visit till we have passed through Scotland. We have journeyed from London northerly to Oxford; then, northwesterly to the manufacturing towns; and now we are to go from Carlisle to Glasgow, and we expect to see London again in a couple of weeks after. The places are most of them but a few hours' ride apart. The trip is quite like one from Boston, through Worcester, Springfield, Albany, to our western cities, and then southerly, via Washington and Philadelphia and New York, to Boston, and as easily performed. We arrived at 2 P. M., and were fortunate in making our visit on a market-day, when the place was full of people; for here was an opportunity to see an English market-day at its best. On hundreds of tables, and in stalls and booths, every conceivable kind of domestic article was displayed for sale,—crockery, tinware, dry-goods (such as White or Jordan & Marsh never have for sale), new and second-hand clothing, hardware, provisions of all kinds; and a happier set of people we had not seen. Both buyer and seller were in fine mood, and good cheer prevailed. These market-days are a part of the common life of the people, and to abolish them would be taken as one more sign of the near approach of the final consummation of all things.

The city is situated on the River Eden, and is a grand old place with good buildings and streets, all replete with fine specimens of English people and life. It is one of the very oldest in England and was a Roman station. Its proximity to the border made it an important place at the time of the wars between the English and the Scotch.

The cathedral is situated not far from the centre of business, and the iron fence on one side of its grounds marks the bounds of an important thoroughfare. The ground is not large—perhaps an acre in extent—and is well kept. The cathedral itself was originally an important building, but is not now remarkable for size or beauty. Cromwell destroyed the greater part of the nave. The building is only 137 feet long, but it is 124 feet wide at the transepts, and the height is 75 feet from floor to vaultings. The parapet of the tower is 127 feet from the ground. The cathedral was nearly destroyed by fire in 1292, and the present choir was completed 1350. This fire is said to have consumed thirteen hundred houses. The tower was built in 1401. The edifice was originally dedicated to the Virgin Mary, but Henry VIII., after he had suppressed the priory connected with it, named it the Church of the Holy and Undivided Trinity. Up to that time it had been under the administration of twenty-nine different bishops,—many of them men of note, of whom it would be pleasant to speak did our limits not forbid. Owen Oglethorpe, the thirtieth bishop, was noted as the only one who could be prevailed upon to crown Queen Elizabeth, all others having refused to do so. History says that "during the performance of the ceremony he was commanded by the queen not to elevate the host; to prevent the idolatry of the people, and to omit it because she liked it not." It is a question whether he obeyed. Wood says: "He sore repented him of crowning the queen all the days of his life, which were for that special cause both short and wearisome." He was fined $1,250 by the council for not appearing at a public disputation, and was soon afterwards deprived of his office.

A worthy and well-known bishop of this cathedral was James Usher, who was appointed in 1642. He was an Irishman by birth, and had since 1625 been Archbishop of Armagh in Ireland. He died March 21, 1655, at the age of seventy-five, and Cromwell ordered him a magnificent funeral, which took place at Westminster Abbey, and the great Protector signed a warrant to the Lords of the Treasury, to pay Dr. Bernard $1,000 to defray the expenses of it. Bishop Usher was a theological writer, noted as the author of the system of chronology which is frequently printed in the margin of the Bible. On the restoration of the church, Richard Sterne was elected bishop. He is celebrated as having been domestic chaplain to the notorious Archbishop Laud, and attending him on the scaffold. He was also a prisoner in the Tower, with several others, on complaint made by Cromwell, that they had used the Cambridge College plate for the king's relief at York; but in 1664 he was translated to York Minster, and died there in 1683.

One of the honors of this cathedral is that, in 1782, William Paley, the writer on Political Economy, Natural Theology, and Evidences of Christianity, was its archdeacon, and it was here that these works were written. His burial-place and monument are both in the cathedral.

Near the market-place are the remains of a castle, built by the Normans in 1092. It is much dilapidated, but prominent portions are in excellent preservation. A race of people at the zenith of power erected and used this castle. This race declined, and a new one came out of its decay. Kingdoms have since risen and gone into oblivion. The march of humanity has for eight centuries been going on its way, but the castle remains,—changed only as time has disintegrated the stone, and so gradually that no one generation has realized the transformation. More substantial material for thought may be obtained from these old English places, than from almost any other spots in Europe.

At 6 P. M. this Saturday night we took train for Glasgow, and so are for a short time to be among the stalwart Caledonians.

SCOTLAND.

CHAPTER XII.

GLASGOW—THE ROB-ROY COUNTRY—THE LAKES—CALLENDER—STIRLING.

On their own soil, or anywhere in the world, the record of the Scotch is good. Those hard-working and reflective qualities, nurtured by John Knox, have borne fruit. Not dependent on priest or bishop for rule or thought, the people have long felt their individual responsibility. Industry, frugality, integrity, have been nursed by the child with its mother's milk. A hard theology cramped the mind in exploring fields of philosophy, and the range of thought has been limited. The people employed so much time in preparing for another life, that they had but little to devote to making themselves comfortable in this world. Indeed, comfort was considered suspicious; but these conditions were preparing them to contend with German Rationalism, and the blending of the two will make a good harvest. While the Scotch element has been eminently conservative, and so a brake on the wheels of a hurried advance, the German element has been doing its work of lifting thought to a higher plane. Each has given and received, and American thought, engendered three thousand miles away, is a golden mean between the two. Calvinism in America has been at its best, and also, we trust, at its worst. The German mind has also influenced America. The flint and the steel strike fire, and it is consuming the superstitions of one system, and purifying the rationalism of the other.

At 6.30 P. M. we ride out of the Carlisle station. The sun is yet high, and the fine scenery of Northern England meets our view. It is more hilly than it is farther south, and better wooded. Everything looks more like New England. Gardens prevail, and many things to remind us of home. Nothing struck us more strangely than the length of the days, and, to use an Irishman's expression, "the evening end of them." At 9 o'clock P. M. we can see to read and write; and at Paris a month later, July 4, we could see to write distinctly at 9.30 P. M., and could see the time by the watch at 9.50. After a ride of three hours, we glide into the station at

GLASGOW.

This chief commercial and manufacturing city of Scotland is situated on the River Clyde, twenty-one miles from its mouth, and forty-one miles southwest of Edinburgh, and has a population of 477,141, or, including the suburbs, 547,538. The level city is three miles long, and lies on both sides of the river, which is five hundred feet wide, crossed by two suspension and three stone bridges, and has several ferries.

It became a *burgh*, or town, as early as 1190, and was then granted the privilege of holding an annual fair. In 1556 it ranked the eleventh among the towns of Scotland. It is the fourth town in Great Britain in its exports, and the second in wealth and population. The Romans had a station on the Clyde at the location of the present city. In 1300 a battle was fought in what is now High Street, between the English and Wallace, and in it the noted Percy was slain. In 1650 Reformed Superintendents superseded Catholic Bishops; and in 1638 the famous Assembly of the Presbyterian church was held here, and Episcopacy was abjured. For several years after, the city was a prey to both parties in the civil wars, and fire, plague, plunder, and famine desolated the place. June 4, 1690, the charter of William and Mary conferred on the townsmen the right of electing their own magistrates.

Glasgow is well laid out; the streets are wide and clean, and there is little to be seen that is peculiar. The aspect is commercial. Stores and warehouses prevail, and the question often arises, "Where do the people live?" The centres of population are around outside the business portion, and the mansions exhibit more thoroughness of construction than fancy in decoration. We are in one of the great places of Scotland, not in one of France or Germany; this fact is everywhere apparent. Liverpool represents it, not Paris. The city has four parks. The Green has 140 acres, on the north bank of the river, and near the east end of the city. Kelvingrove Park has 40 acres at the west end; Queen's Park, 100 acres. Alexandra Park has 85 acres, on elevated ground, portions of it commanding views of the entire city. A stream runs through it, and primeval groves, grand avenues, lawns, and flower-plots make the place one of great attraction. On Sunday, at the time of our visit, tens of thousands were enjoying it. Adjoining this are the grounds of Glasgow University, yet more elevated. The grand edifice is of a domesticated Gothic architecture, built of gray limestone, and stands on the highest ground. It was finished in 1870, and cost $1,650,000. This college was founded in 1443 by James II., but it had only a feeble existence till 1560, when Queen Mary bestowed upon it one half of all the confiscated church property of the city. The library was founded in 1473, and contains 105,000 volumes. It has an observatory and a good cabinet, and the grounds contain 22 acres. The city is supplied with water from the celebrated Loch Katrine, by an aqueduct 26 miles long, and it sustains two theatres, two museums, and as many public libraries. It has 175 churches and chapels, and a very fine botanic garden of 40 acres, which is kept in perfect condition and open free to visitors.

The cathedral is of all edifices of the kind the most ancient looking. It is on the border of the city, and enclosed with a high iron fence, being surrounded by a small burial-ground. A peculiarity is that many tombs and monuments are entirely encaged, the top included. The iron-work, generally about four feet wide, seven feet long, and seven feet high, is rusty and produces a disagreeable effect. We were disgusted with the appearance of the grounds of this metropolitan church, really the finest old Gothic building in Scotland. It is not large but is on a site that overlooks most of the city. It was begun in 1192, and was ready for consecration in 1197. It enjoyed an unmolested use for the papal worship during four hundred years; but, notwithstanding this long service, it was not finished till the present century. Its noteworthy features are the crypt and a profusion of brilliant stained glass. Near the cathedral is a cemetery called the Necropolis, situated on very elevated ground, and highly attractive. The place is approached from the cathedral by a grand stone bridge, and has a park-like entrance and inside avenues at the base of the hill. This burial-place, built for all time, was provided by private munificence, and makes the cage-work and ill-managed grounds of the cathedral look all the more heathenish. The cemetery is not large but may comprise three or four acres. It is on high land, that, but for the terraces and inclined avenues traversing the hillside, would be very difficult of ascent; but good engineering makes it most inviting. The views from this spot of the city and suburbs are very grand, and it is constantly resorted to as a park. One peculiarity of the place is the number of neat monuments, and a general absence of ordinary gravestones. The monuments are nearly all of white marble, and set in close rows. There are more beautiful designs than we have seen before or since. The taste manifested is exquisite, and would do honor to Paris,—instead of dishonor, as do the monuments of the noted Père La Chaise, the Mount Auburn of France.

In this ground is an imposing monument, erected to martyrs, whose blood is "the seed of the church." The statements on this monument interest not only the people of Glasgow but Americans; and so, although the cold and intense wind makes it a work of difficulty, we copy them. They have been read by thousands and will be read by thousands more; they inspire fortitude, and will thus be a perpetual honor to the noble ones whom they commemorate. On the west side is the following:—

TO TESTIFY GRATITUDE FOR INESTIMABLE SERVICES
IN THE CAUSE OF RELIGION, EDUCATION, AND CIVIL
LIBERTY;
TO AWAKEN ADMIRATION
OF THAT INTEGRITY, DISINTERESTEDNESS, AND COURAGE
WHICH STOOD UNSHAKEN IN THE MIDST OF TRIALS,
AND IN THE MAINTENANCE OF THE HIGHEST OBJECTS;
FINALLY,
TO CHERISH UNCEASING REVERENCE FOR THE PRINCIPLES
AND
BLESSINGS OF THAT GREAT REFORMATION

BY THE INFLUENCE OF WHICH OUR COUNTRY THROUGH THE
MIDST OF DIFFICULTIES
HAS RISEN TO HONOR, PROSPERITY, AND HAPPINESS,
THIS MONUMENT IS ERECTED BY VOLUNTARY CONTRIBUTION
TO THE MEMORY OF JOHN KNOX;
THE CHIEF INSTRUMENT UNDER GOD OF THE REFORMATION
IN SCOTLAND, ON THE 22ND DAY OF SEPTEMBER 1825.
HE DIED—REJOICING IN THE FAITH OF THE GOSPEL—
AT EDINBURGH—
ON THE 24TH OF NOVEMBER A.D. 1572, IN THE
67TH YEAR OF HIS AGE.

On the north side is the following:—

PATRICK HAMILTON, A YOUTH OF HIGH RANK
AND DISTINGUISHED ATTAINMENTS,
WAS THE FIRST MARTYR IN SCOTLAND FOR THE CAUSE OF
THE REFORMATION.
HE WAS CONDEMNED TO THE FLAMES AT ST. ANDREWS IN
1528 IN THE
TWENTY-FOURTH YEAR OF HIS AGE.
FROM 1530 TO 1540 PERSECUTION RAGED IN EVERY
QUARTER; MANY SUFFERED
THE MOST CRUEL DEATHS; AND MANY FLED TO ENGLAND
AND THE CONTINENT.
AMONG THESE EARLY MARTYRS WERE JEROME RUSSELL
AND ALEXANDER KENNEDY
TWO YOUNG MEN OF GREAT PIETY AND TALENTS WHO
SUFFERED AT GLASGOW
IN 1538. IN 1544 GEORGE WISHART RETURNED TO
SCOTLAND FROM WHICH HE HAD
BEEN BANISHED, AND PREACHED THE GOSPEL IN
VARIOUS QUARTERS. IN 1546
THIS HEAVENLY MINDED MAN, THE FRIEND AND
INSTRUCTOR OF KNOX, WAS ALSO
COMMITTED TO THE FLAMES AT ST. ANDREWS.

The south side has the following:—

THE REFORMATION PRODUCED A REVOLUTION IN THE
SENTIMENTS OF MANKIND
THE GREATEST AS WELL AS THE MOST BENEFICENT THAT
HAS HAPPENED SINCE THE
PUBLICATION OF CHRISTIANITY.
IN 1547, AND IN THE CITY WHERE HIS FRIEND GEORGE

Wishart had suffered, John Knox, surrounded with dangers, first preached the doctrine of the Reformation. In 1559 on the 24th of August, the Parliament of Scotland adopted the Confession of Faith presented by the Reformed Minister, and declared Popery to be no longer the religion of this kingdom. John Knox became the minister of Edinburgh, where he continued to his death the incorruptible guardian of our best interests.

"I can take God to witness," he declared, "that I never preached contempt of any man and wise men will consider that a true friend cannot flatter; especially in a case that involves the salvation of the bodies and souls, not of a few persons, but of a whole Realm." When laid in the Grave the Regent said, "There lieth He who never feared the face of man, who was often threatened with the dag and dagger, yet hath ended his days in peace and honor."

On the east side we have the following:—

Among the early and distinguished friends of the Reformation, should be especially remembered Sir James Sandilands, of Calder, Alexander Earl of Glencairn, Archibald, Earl of Argyll, and Lord James Stewart, afterwards known by the name of "the good Regent:" John Erskine of Dun, and John Row, who were distinguished among the Reformed Ministers for their cultivation of ancient and modern literature. Christopher Goodman and John Willock, who came from England

TO PREACH THE GOSPEL IN SCOTLAND; JOHN WINRAM,
JOHN SPOTTISWOOD, AND JOHN DOUGLASS, WHO WITH
JOHN ROW AND JOHN KNOX COMPILED THE FIRST
CONFESSION OF FAITH
WHICH WAS PRESENTED TO THE PARLIAMENT OF SCOTLAND,
AND ALSO THE
FIRST BOOK OF DISCIPLINE.

The monument is composed of a plinth, some six feet square, upon which is another of less dimensions, with the sides somewhat inclined inward, bearing the inscriptions; then, two low plinths smaller yet; and resting on these is a Grecian Doric column some two feet or more in diameter; and on the abacus, or cap, at its corners, are ornaments above it. Next there is a low pedestal, or corniced plinth, and the whole is surmounted by a life-size statue of John Knox. The whole may be about thirty-five feet high.

The city, though largely given to traffic, has extensive manufactures. Among these are the St. Rollox chemical works, the largest in the world, covering sixteen acres, and employing a thousand men. The chimney is 450 feet high, 220 feet higher than the large one at East Cambridge, Mass.; or, to make it more definite, it is exactly the height of the East Cambridge chimney with Bunker Hill Monument on top of it, for they are respectively 230 and 220 feet high. There is one in Glasgow ten feet higher than this,—that belonging to the artificial manure works, which measures 460 feet.

At 11.30 on this Sunday we attended service at one of the Presbyterian churches. As an act of charity let the church be nameless, for we must add that the services were very tedious. The prayer was extraordinarily long and prosy; six verses were sung in each psalm; the explanatory remarks on the Scripture readings were long and tame; and the sermon, of a full hour's length, while well written and delivered, was a rehash of the commonest platitudes. While the theologic world moves, this parish was too near an ancient theologic centre to derive much advantage from the motion. It is yet a philosophic question whether the exact axis of a revolving shaft moves at all, and we can but think that a part of the Presbyterian Church of Scotland is near such a fixed centre. But we went to hear some actual Scotch Presbyterianism, and were not sorry that we did so; though conscious that we could have displayed fortitude under our disappointment, had we found the stanch Knoxites discussing the signs of the times.

We love this old church for the vast good it has done. As our ships need anchors, so the Church Universal needs conservatives; and, in spite of our liberalism, she will have them as long as they are needed.

There was more order in Glasgow, more of the Puritan's quiet Sunday, than we ever saw before, at home or abroad. There are no horse-cars or omnibuses visible, and few teams of any kind. No shops were open, though there were many drunken people. Sunday drinking is prohibited; though the sale is licensed on other days, as in Boston. It is said to be "under wholesome management." Transpose the syllables, and instead of *wholesome* say *somewhole*, and you have the truth. At the Albion Hotel we had thought ourselves in a temperance house, at least for Sunday; but all day long groups of all ages and conditions and both sexes were at the bar; and so large was the number that a sentinel only let in new customers when others went out. Till ten at night the rum-mill was in operation. License men to do wrong, and you throw the reins on the back of your horse. Spend less time in the church, and devote more to enforcing the law, and God's kingdom will sooner come.

June 1 is as cold and damp as a Boston day in March or April. Great coats are near us, as good friends ought to be.

At 10 P. M. to bed,—not to sleep, nor, as Shakespeare has it, to dream, but to hear the incessant tramp of the tipplers; "aye, *there's* the rub;" but we drop a veil over the theme. We arose at dawn, breakfasted by-and-by, and at 7 P. M. continued our tour towards Edinburgh, sorry for some things that must be said, if we would fully describe the Glasgow that now *is*,—not the Glasgow that is to be.

The passage to Edinburgh may be made in a few hours, but we are to go the way of all tourists who can afford a day or two for the journey.

We follow down the Clyde for some miles, amid pleasing, though not very interesting scenery. There on our left are the ruins of Dumbarton Castle, situated on a cliff, and picturesque amidst their solitary beauty. This was once a fortress, and is the place from which Mary, Queen of Scots, took passage for France when a child.

A few miles more, and we arrive at Balloch. This is a little hamlet at the south end of Loch Lomond. This lake covers forty-five square miles, and is one of the Scottish lake-group, corresponding to the Killarney lakes in Ireland. We here embark in a fine little steamer. The lake is not large in appearance, as its small bays occupy much of its area; and in most respects it resembles the upper lake of Killarney, or our lakes George and Winnipiseogee. The water is clear, and the margin prettily wooded; and this end is well studded with islands. There is a grandeur about the highlands of Scotland not to be seen on the Irish lakes. Prominent among the mountains is Ben Lomond, standing out in sublime greatness. It is 3,192 feet high; but, while really lower than some hills at Killarney, its contour intensifies its impression. We appreciate its companionship, and, as we sail on, are constantly introduced to Ben Lomond's companions. Ben Dhu, as it is familiarly called, though the real name is Ben MacDhui, is 4,296 feet high. These highlands are rugged in their outline, and present vast glens, crags, ravines, and broken peaks, being unlike those of southern Ireland, which are generally smooth and rounded. The mountain haze is seen in great perfection, and the hills are well wooded, and exhibit a splendid verdure. There is a peculiar moisture and softness in the air, with a fragrant and stimulating quality. In contradistinction to the Irish lakes, these of Scotland have a bold and masculine appearance. We speak of elegance and nicety at Ireland's lakes, but here we have, added to those qualities, vastness and power reflected from their mountains.

We admire Glen Luss, Bannochar, and Glen Fruin, as well as other objects of interest touched upon in the "Lady of the Lake," especially in the rower's song, "Hail to the Chief," for we are at the very scene of the poem. It adds a charm to recall the fact that many a time Sir Walter Scott here sailed and admired; and afterwards recalled his thought,—intensifying it and materializing all, till his verse became a thing of life. Our steamer touches at Landing Luss, on the left, and at Rowardennan on the right; then we cross to Tarbet on the left, and after an inspiring sail of two hours we are at Inversnaid. This is an old fort and a landing. It is of no importance as a fort, but was built in 1713, as a defence against the Macgregors, led by the celebrated Rob Roy.

The principal interest in the place lies in the fact of its having been the *lairdship* of Rob Roy before he became an outlaw and a freebooter. Lower down, at the foot of Ben Lomond, we are shown the prison, a rocky fastness at the edge of the water, where it is said he confined his captives. Every nook of these Highlands is full of romance. The writings of Sir Walter have surcharged the very atmosphere with it; and people who are ever so matter-of-fact at home, here become permeated with the etherialistic influence. Ideality has free play. At home they say, "I don't believe a word of it." Here they are different people, and say, "It may have been so." Rob Roy, whose history has been immortalized by Scott in his novel of that name, was largely connected with this neighborhood. A few words concerning him may be of service to the reader who has not the history at hand. He was born about 1660, the exact time and place not being known. He died, it is said, at Aberfoyle in 1738, at about the age of seventy-seven. His true name was Robert Macgregor, which, when the clan Macgregor was outlawed by the Parliament of Scotland in 1693, he changed for that of his mother, and was afterward known as Robert Campbell. Prior to the Great Rebellion of 1715 he was a cattle-dealer. He was very artful and intriguing, and gave the Duke of Montrose an excuse for seizing his lands, and then retaliated by reprisals on the Duke; and for many years he continued his double-facedness, levying blackmail on his dupes and enemies, in spite of a garrison of English soldiers stationed near his residence.

We now leave our steamer and take open teams, with four fine horses to each, for a ride of eight miles to Loch Katrine. Never a finer ride than this, over the beautiful heaths of Scotland. The mountain scenery is exquisite in all directions. At times we ride along precipitous paths, where we can look down from "awfully giddy heights to valleys low," the road winding amid the hills and constantly changing beauties. A heavily wooded country and splendid vegetation prevail, and there is no trace of barrenness, as in the Gap of Dunloe.

We go along the shore of the meandering river and Lake Arklett, and now the driver tells us that here was the cottage of Helen Macgregor. Mountains are about us, and here is an enclosed plain, perhaps half a mile wide and a mile long, level as our house floors, and nearly covered with heather,—which is a sort of heath, quite like that grown by us as a house-plant, and, being of a dark tint, gives a purplish hue to the moor. The space we are now going over, all between the two lakes, is the country referred to in the novel. Over these very roads that singular fellow rode and walked. The air here was remarkably exhilarating. It seemed new, as if it was for the first time breathed. The ride was much too short. There were millions of reasons for wishing it longer, so many things were waiting to entertain us on the right hand and on the left, before and behind us, under foot and overhead. It was good for us to be there, and the inclination was strong upon us to build tabernacles. At length Loch Katrine was reached. It contains an area of only five square miles, and is the one, though twenty-seven miles away, from which water is taken for the city of Glasgow. It is claimed that it is one of the finest lakes in the world, and it is certain that no one can imagine its superior. The teams leave us at a very comfortable two-story hotel, at the head of the lake, and here we are to dine; which service over, we walk out for a ramble, as an hour is to elapse before the steamer arrives from the other end of the lake. A wide road separates the hotel from the latter; a wharf extends from it, and to the left is a sea-wall, perhaps a hundred feet long, with a protective rail along the top. To the left of that, and in the corner, on the border of the lake, is a fine grove belonging to the hotel, with swings and other entertainments for tourists. In the rear of the house are the stables; and back of these, and around and back of the grove, is a hill which anywhere but in Scotland would be called a mountain. To the right of the hotel, and bordering the lake, were a grove and field, with here and there a cottage. The mountains in the distance loomed up grandly; and the borders of the lake, while more or less irregular and indented, had a very clean-cut look. The lake was not very wide here,—perhaps a fourth of a mile,—and it stretched on, without much change.

We take the little steamer here at Stronaclacher,—we had almost forgotten to tell the name,—and as we look down into the crystal water, it seems too pure for a steamer to sail in, for it is quite equal in clearness to Seneca Lake, New York, and reminds one of it. Remove the town of Geneva from its cosy situation at the end of the lake; put there a long wooden hotel; border the shores with a heavily wooded country to the water's edge; add some mountains off in the distance to the right and the left, at Ovid, Lodi, and Hector; put some more opposite on the other side of the lake, and a large lot of them at Watkins; then condense all to one quarter the size, and you have the size and shape of Loch Katrine.

We have now left the Rob-Roy Country, and are in that of the "Lady of the Lake," for this Lake Katrine is the one Sir Walter had in mind when he penned that fairy-like romance. We come first to a little island, well covered with trees and thick shrubbery, where the meeting of Fitzjames and Douglas is assumed to have taken place, and where the charming heroine was seen in her boat. Ragged Ben Venu appears; and ahead of that are the sharp peaks of Ben A'an, the whole surrounded by heavy woodlands, here and there extending well up the mountains, and marked by great glens and gorges. After the sail of an hour, much too soon we change our vehicle; and here, at the little wharf, carriages are ready to take us to Callender. Our party numbers about thirty, and we are to go through the Trosachs, which comprise some of the finest scenery in Scotland. We soon arrived at Ardcheanocrohan, a fifteen-lettered place, whose name we were shy in pronouncing; and we confess it takes some courage to write it, but we presume it's good Scotch.

As we stand at the door of the tavern,—that's just what it is,—or rather as we sit on our coach-seat in front of the building and look across the lake, there, in superb repose, three or four miles away, is the Clachan of Aberfoyle, well remembered by the readers of "Rob Roy." We ride through mountain scenery, equalling if not excelling any at the White Mountains of New Hampshire, and strongly reminding one of the Notch. Our road winds to the right, and Loch Achry comes to view,—a lovely gem we would fain transport to America.

In due time we arrive at the Turk Water, and the place celebrated in the "Lady of the Lake," where, as Sir Walter says,—

When the Brigg of Turk was won,
The foremost horseman rode alone.

This is a single-arched stone bridge, which crosses this stream. We are now introduced to the great pine-lands of the Glenfinlas. The trees are very tall, and the scenery is wild and unusual. In front is the heathery Craig Moor, Glenfinlas Hills, with their winding valleys, and Loch Vennachar with its clear water and bordering shrubs. We pass a waterfall, which runs out of

Loch Katrine, and helps to supply Glasgow with its water. This used to be known by the uneuphonious name of Coilantogle Ford, and is the spot where Fitzjames and Roderick Dhu had their conflict. Now appears the stately Ben Ledi, one of the tallest giants. We pass on, over the Callender bridge, and are at the town of

CALLENDER,

an old settlement of small account. It has a main street bordered by stone and brick houses with pleasant grounds.

We take the train for Stirling, and lose sight of the hill-country which for hours has enraptured us. It was the treat of a lifetime, and as such to be appreciated and enjoyed. We pass the town of Dumblane, to which allusion is made in the song of "Jessie, the Flower of Dunblane," and then over the famed Bridge of Allan, familiar by the ballad of "Allan Water."

After a ride of an hour, at 5 P. M. we approach

STIRLING.

This is a place of special note. It is situated on the River Forth, thirty-one miles from Edinburgh, and has a population of 14,279. In beauty of situation it rivals the capital. The buildings present an appearance of modernized antiquity, being interspersed with mansions of the Scottish Nobles. The society here is highly aristocratic. Stirling was a favorite place of residence for James V., who died at Falkland, Dec. 13, 1542. He was one of the kings of Scotland, born at Linlithgow Palace, April 13, 1512. The old House of Parliament, built by him, is still standing, and now used as barracks. The ancient Gothic church is the one in which James VI. was crowned, and there are the remains of an unfinished palace, begun in 1570, by the Regent, the Earl of Mar. Near the town are the ruins of the famed Cambuskenneth Abbey; and not far from the town, perhaps three miles away, is the celebrated field of Bannockburn, on which the battle was fought June 24, 1314. War had raged between England and Scotland for many years under Edward II., who, in contentions with his parliament, had neglected Scotland. Robert Bruce III. recovered all of Scotland with the exception of the fortress in Stirling, which alone held out for the English; and even that, the governor, Mowbray, had agreed to surrender, if it was not relieved before the feast of John the Baptist. Edward was aroused by this report, and he encamped near it at the head of a large army. He was met by Bruce with 30,000 picked men, on the eve before the day fixed for surrender. The battle of Bannockburn was the result, and ended in the utter defeat of the English. Bruce was now able to dictate terms, and he exchanged prisoners for his wife, sister, and other relatives, who had long been in captivity to the English. This success being attained, the Scotch assumed the offensive, and invaded Ireland; and, meeting with success there, Edward Bruce, brother of Robert, was crowned king of that country, May 2, 1316.

As one stands at the castle, 220 feet above the surrounding land, two miles away lies Bannockburn; a few stone walls and a grove designate the famed spot. The eye takes in a wide scene of unparalleled beauty. Cows and sheep graze peacefully there, with no one to disturb or molest. The air is free from suggestions of smoke of powder or boom of cannon.

CHAPTER XIII.

STIRLING CASTLE—EDINBURGH.

Grand old Stirling Castle! It is situated on high ground. On one side the land is very precipitous; in fact the walls are on the actual verge of the high bluff, and there is an almost vertical fall of more than two hundred feet. In all directions is a view never excelled. There lie the quiet fields, extending from the base of the hill, while the river, like a serpent of gigantic but graceful proportions, curves across them. Here and there are charming groves and solid woodlands, and on, in the distant west, are the famed Highlands. To the north and east are the Ochil Hills, with their companions, the Campsie Hills, on the south; and on the rear lies Stirling town, naïvely antique.

How natural is it to look farther over the great landscape. As we face the town, off at our right, on a great hill,—almost a crag,—is the Wallace Monument, of which we will speak by and by. In the distance are the bewitching ruins of Cambuskenneth Abbey and the Abbey Craig, the Bridge and the Water of Allan, the Great Carse, the Valley of the Forth, the Field of Bannockburn, and a thousand points of beauty.

It is no wonder that here kings and queens have delighted to stay. The building is open to visitors, and for the small fee of a shilling one may take his fill of delight. The edifice is a thorough castle. Built of brownish stone, it has a subdued look; but its low towers and battlements, its varied outline and its great extent, all impress the beholder with reverence. It would be a work of many chapters to describe in detail the various articles on exhibition,—reminders of remarkable events. Here is the Douglas Room, where James II. assassinated the powerful and aggravating Earl of Douglas in 1440. The windows are shown from which these men leaned and conversed before the bloody work; for they remain precisely as they were more than four hundred years ago. There resided all the king Jameses, from the First to the Sixth inclusive, as did Mary Queen of Scots. The castle is used as barracks for English soldiers, though a portion of the building is fearfully vacant, and one prominent quarter is a museum of antiquities. We return through the large courtyards by which we entered, and through the great arched opening, in which is run up the ponderous portcullis, or strong lattice gateway, whose

"Massive bar had oft rolled back the tide of war."

The home of kings and of the most noted persons of the civilized world! Soil made sacred by the tread of nobility. But we were free men, unhindered observers, at liberty to examine and criticise, in unqualified republican American fashion, things once too sacred for common people to look upon. How changed! What has done this but popular education, and the growth of religious liberty,—elements underlying the Magna Charta, which has discounted royalty, and opened the great doors of civilization? Where are now the kings, the queens? Their places of habitation are our intellectual banquet-hall; their household goods form a museum of curiosities for all who are disposed to visit it.

Our next visit was to Gray Friars Church, founded by James IV. in 1594, and here a strange thing met our view. The edifice is in the usual form of a Latin cross. A large door has been made in the centre of each transept, which are used as large vestibules for the two auditoriums into which the choir and nave of the edifice have been converted. The choir, which is the oldest part and of Norman architecture, is used as a chapel for the soldiers, and the nave as one of the parish churches of the city. Both are in use, and services are held in them at the same hours. The military church is under the English government, and of course the service is Episcopalian; while the other is Scotch Presbyterian. Of course the church was originally Roman Catholic, but in the old times John Knox often preached there. How little endures! One set of people exist and build and occupy. Here their saints are made, die, and are buried, and the stones become sacred to their memory. But by-and-by other people come into possession. In a day the accumulated sanctities are despoiled, and, as it were, evaporate. Nothing but the soil stands secure from mutation and danger. In a place like this we realize the force of the statement: "One generation goeth and another cometh, but the earth abideth forever."

Near by is Guildhall. At the house adjoining we make our desires known, and the young lady attendant, key in hand, accompanies us to the old room, which is perhaps thirty feet wide, fifty feet long, and twenty feet high. The quintessence of antiquity is here. Imagination in full play could conceive nothing more fascinatingly mediæval. Dimly lighted, the heavy oak finish looked the more quaint and feudalistic. What things of interest we behold! Here are pictures which centuries have mellowed, and here, in the middle of the room, is the pulpit in which John Knox preached a memorable sermon at the coronation of the infant king, James VI., Aug. 29, 1567. It is octagonal, and made of oak; and only the upper part, or that in which the preacher stood, is left, its floor resting upon the floor of the hall. We stood in it, and, like John Knox on a certain occasion, pronounced the text, "Put not your trust in princes, nor in the son of man in whom there is no help."

Here was an old Crusader's hat, which we tried on. It is large, not much decayed, has a broad brim, and is made of soft felt; in fact it is what is now called a slouched hat. Near by is a burial-ground, unlike anything we had ever seen. It contains some two or three acres, has through the central part a romantic ravine, and in it are monuments and old statues embowered in trees. Adjoining it is a lofty elevation of natural stone, from which are charming views. There are monuments devoted to the martyrs who died in defence of principle. The gravestones are thick, and the place contains but few things that can be paralleled elsewhere. There are fine trees, thick shrubbery, and an atmosphere of romance.

Off at a distance of a mile or so, accessible by horse-cars, is the Wallace Monument, standing on Moncrief, like a lone sentinel. Moncrief is a piece of ground quite park-like in its aspect; a good avenue is graded for a quarter-mile through the woods, winding so as to make an easy ascent to the summit, which is a very small level table-land. The entire city is visible, with the castle as a background; and off to the right, in the distance, are the famed Highlands. In the near foreground is the river, with a background of woods. Here and there are villages and hamlets, and Bannockburn is seen to best advantage, and places where battles were fought by Wallace and Bruce. The monument stands at the centre of the table-land, which is 226 feet above the streets of the city. The monument is square in plan, about 40 feet on each side, and 200 feet high. It is built of brown stone, with trimmings that resemble granite. It is of a castellated design, and in appearance is hundreds of years old, though in reality it has been finished but six years. The keeper's house adjoins it, and is incorporated into the structure. Either the castle, the Wallace Monument, the old church, the Guildhall, or near burial-ground amply repay the effort required to make a visit to Stirling. The monument was erected to the memory of Wallace, as its name implies, and a few words concerning him may be of interest.

William Wallace was born in 1276. He had a fierce and warlike disposition, and, while at the high-school at Dundee, he stabbed the son of the English governor of Dundee Castle, and fled. For a long time he was an outlaw and dwelt in the fastnesses of Scotland. He had great personal accomplishments, and many persons became his followers. He organized an army, and held it in readiness for invasions. An insurrection having broken out in 1297, when he was but twenty-one years old, he attacked an English Count at Scone, took many prisoners, and killed many more. Under his direction, Sir William Douglas surprised and compelled the English garrisons of Durisdeer and Sanquhar, which were holding the castles, to surrender. So great was his intrepidity and daring, and so formidable had his army become, that Edward I.—the sovereign against whom he was fighting, and to whom the people of Scotland were opposed—sent 40,000 men and cavalry, under command of Sir Henry Percy and Sir Robert Clifford, to oppose him. Wallace made an attack on them when they arrived, but was repulsed and fell back to Irvine in Ayrshire. Soon after this, however, disputes arose among the Scottish leaders, which resulted in an agreement which Wallace and Murray did not approve; so they retired into the northern countries, quickly recruited a formidable army, and surprised and captured the English garrisons at Aberdeen,

Dunnottar, Forfar, and Montrose. Wallace had also begun a siege at Dundee; but being informed of the advance of a large English force in the direction of Stirling, he abandoned the siege, and, gathering adherents as he went, reached Stirling with 40,000 foot and 180 horse. The English mustered 50,000 foot and 1,000 horse, under the Earl of Surrey. Messengers, deserters from the Scottish army, were sent to persuade Wallace to capitulate, and a free pardon was unconditionally offered, but the overtures were rejected. The English crossed the river, and the noted battle of Cambuskenneth was fought near Stirling Bridge, Sept. 10, 1297. The result was that the English were driven to Berwick, almost completely cut to pieces. Inflated by success, Wallace, by general consent,—in the absence of the lawful monarch, King John, who was then confined in the Tower of London,—was declared guardian of Scotland. A severe famine followed, and Wallace, to obtain supplies, invaded the northern counties of England. He laid waste the country, returned with his spoils, and began to reorganize Scotland. Edward, smarting under the terrible defeat, and realizing the insecurity of his possessions near the border, raised an army of 80,000 infantry and 7,000 horse. A portion of the force landed by sea on the northeast coast, and there suffered a reverse; but the main body advanced by land northward, and on July 22, 1298, met the Scottish forces at Falkirk, where a decisive battle was fought, and Wallace's army was defeated with a loss of 15,000. This was really the fall of his remarkable power. He was only 22 years old, and from this time carried on a guerilla warfare for several years, until at length he went to Paris to seek French intervention. In 1304 he was declared an outlaw, large rewards were offered by King Edward for his arrest, and he was immediately betrayed by Sir John Menteith. The day after his arrival in London, the form of a trial was gone through with at Westminster, and in derision of his pretensions he was decorated with a crown of laurel. He was condemned to death, and the same day, Aug. 23, 1305, at the age of thirty-five, he was dragged at the tails of horses to Smithfield, and there hung, drawn, and quartered; his head being sent to London bridge, where it was perched on the top of the Southwark Tower, while his other limbs were exposed to the anathemas of the populace at Newcastle, Berwick, Perth, and at Stirling, the seat of his daring deeds. It is for this patriot that this lofty monument was erected, 570 years after the close of his eventful life, which also gives a basis for Burns's "Scots wha hae wi' Wallace bled!"

The castle is now used for barracks; and at the time of our visit some hundreds of men were here stationed,—all of that robust nature for which English soldiers are celebrated. A sad waste of the flower of Great Britain, and the day is not far distant when the mistake will be seen. The ambition for increased territory is one of England's elements of weakness. Too much distant territory is breaking her down. Soldiers are everywhere required to maintain possession. This takes her picked men, and the people must be taxed to feed an army of drones.

We were especially interested in one thing here. The ground, within the castle walls, is paved with small cobble-stones, like our gutters. Springing up among them were knot-grass and small weeds. Three or four soldiers, with sharp-pointed case-knives, were digging up this grass, scrupulously removing every trace of it. We asked why this was being done, and were informed that it was a punishment. For infraction of some rule soldiers were sentenced to this menial work—in the presence of comrades and visitors—for a day, or perhaps a week; and some were also deprived of dinner. The misdemeanor might have been not returning at the proper time when off by permission, being drunk while away, insubordination, deceiving officers, uncleanliness, or neglect of accoutrements.

We have devoted much attention to Stirling, for it is connected with events not only in the history of Scotland, but of England as well.

At 12.30 P. M. the day after arrival, Tuesday, June 4, we took train for Edinburgh, the chief city of Scotland, and in many respects one of the finest cities in the world. The ride from Stirling is through a pleasant country, much like that between Worcester and Springfield. It is but an hour and a half before we see the spreading smoke-cloud, and we know from experience that there is the city. The suburbs remind one of an approach to Baltimore, Washington, and other Southern cities. Most of the houses are brick, and two stories high. All are dingy, though not very ancient or peculiar in design. We are at a central point in Scotland, but we see nothing intensely *outlandish*.

American tourists mistake in supposing everything to be unlike home. Most things are such as are familiar, or not sufficiently eccentric to arouse astonishment. The press, pictures, and travel compel interchange of ideas and methods. They are common levellers, producing wonderful uniformity in buildings, dress, and habits. All these tend to oneness, and help to make "the whole world kin." Strange objects are exceptional. They belong to other days, and are interesting to their possessors and the present generation—as they are to us, who have come from a longer distance to see them—as curiosities. History is common property. Bunker Hill has an interest to the intelligent Scotchman, that Bannockburn has to us.

But we are at Edinburgh, and ready to say, as was said of Jerusalem of old: "Beautiful for situation is Mount Zion, the joy of the whole earth."

EDINBURGH.

The name was probably given to it by Edwin, king of Northumbria, about the year 449, and for more than four hundred years afterwards it remained little better than a village of mud-and-fagot houses, collected on Castle Hill. In 854, more than a thousand years ago, Simon of Durham speaks of it as a village of importance. In the beginning of the thirteenth century Alexander II. held a parliament here, and this fact gave the place so much importance in the reign of David II. that it was the chief place in Scotland. In 1384, Froissart, a French historian, visited it, and speaks of it as the Paris of Scotland. The assassination of James I. (of Scotland) at Perth, in 1437, led to the selection of Edinburgh as the capital of the kingdom. James II. caused it to be walled in.

The place now has a population of 196,600. It comprises two distinct parts, the old and the new, and these are separated, a half-mile or more, by a deep ravine which, however, is under the highest state of cultivation, and used as a park. As one stands at a central point on the elegant avenue of the new portion, in front of him is this ravine; and beyond this is the Old City with its dark-colored, quaint, ten-storied buildings pierced with many windows. Innumerable gables present themselves, the stories often jutting out over each other; and the compact buildings rise in the rear, generally conforming to the slope of the land. On the extreme right on the further side is the castle, at a very rocky elevation, and forms a fit termination to the aggregation of sombre houses.

At the extreme left of the Old City, and terminating it, are the lofty elevations known as Salisbury Crags and Arthur's Seat. These seem to be veritable mountains, and their blue haze adds a charm nowhere else to be seen near a great city. At the lower end, in front of the crags, the land is level, and the city extends around to Calton Hill, another grand eminence. The old part of the city and the new are well matched. This new part is covered with important buildings and grand avenues. Among the former are structures of Grecian architecture, for museums and art-galleries. The thoroughfare on which we stand, Princes Street, is one of the finest in the world. It is wide and level, and has fine buildings along its whole length on the side opposite the park, and so facing the old city. At its centre, near the park fence, is the noted monument to Sir Walter Scott.

Throughout the New City many of the brown stone houses are of classic architecture; and while there is an absence of the light effect, in color and design, of the buildings in Paris, yet there is an air of comfort that well compensates for this lack, and speaks distinctly of those traits for which the reliable and thoughtful Scotch are celebrated. The world furnishes no better counterpart to Paris than Edinburgh. The ravine was for centuries a lake; but it was drained in 1788, and afterwards turned into gardens. The foundation of the first house in the New City was laid Oct. 26, 1767, just 106 years ago, by Mr. Craig, who was the general engineer of the New Town. He was a nephew of Thomson the poet, author of "The Seasons." From that time to the present the city has been extending in all directions. We can name but few of its interesting points, for Edinburgh is not only a place of deposit for objects of interest, but is a museum of itself.

Calton Hill is at the lower end of the New Town. There a road winds to the top, a sort of pasture, from which a comprehensive view of Edinburgh is to be had, as well as an extensive view of the country outside. From this eminence is seen the Frith of Forth, an arm of the sea two miles away. The island of Inchkeith nestles cosily in it, and the long pier of Leith, a city of 56,000 inhabitants, stretches itself out into its waters. The imposing Ochil Hills form the background, and in a clear day Ben Lomond and Ben Ledi loom up majestically. The city extends well up and around the base of Calton Hill. At one part of the grounds is an amphitheatre-like spot, given to the citizens by James II. as an arena for tournaments. The sides are called Caltoun Craigs and Greenside. According to the marvel-loving Pennant, it was here that the Earl of Bothwell made his first impression on Queen Mary, by the daring feat of galloping his horse down the precipitous face of the hill. The most prominent objects are Nelson's Monument and the National Monument. The former is on a rocky elevation, 350 feet above the sea. It is a square structure with embattled bastions at the corners, the whole of castellated design; and from the centre rises a round tower, crowned by a circular lantern of less diameter, the whole 100 feet high. At the top is a flagstaff, from which a large ball drops at one o'clock, Greenwich time, moved by mechanism in the Royal Observatory. The time-gun is fired from the castle at the same moment, so that all within seeing or hearing distance are apprised of the hour.

The National Monument was begun in 1816, the proposition being to erect a structure in imitation of the Parthenon at Athens, as a memorial of soldiers who fell at Waterloo. Thirty thousand dollars were subscribed at the first public meeting. An attempt was made to place the affair under the patronage of George IV., and the interest declined. The foundation was laid in 1822, and remained untouched till 1824,—when, with $67,500 on hand, work was resumed. All the money was expended, as was the case with the New York Court-house in the structure of white marble, the three colossal steps, and the ten columns in front, with the two flanking pillars on each side, together with the architrave, or horizontal stones, upon them. To this day it remains in this condition. The general sentiment seems to be that this unfinished building, mute in its solitary grandeur, is a more appropriate memorial than a completed building could be.

There is a monument to Dugald Stewart, the distinguished professor of mathematics, and afterwards of moral philosophy, in Edinburgh University; and another to John Playfair, also a professor of mathematics, well known the civilized world over.

The Burns Monument at the base of the hill is a stone structure some forty feet square, surmounted by a circular section surrounded by Corinthian columns, on which is a pedestal, crowned by a low dome and terminated by four griffins. For a small admission fee we were admitted, and were charmed by the relics exposed to view, once the property of the Scottish Bard. It is useless to attempt to name them, but many were linked with a melancholy interest to a poet, whose life, like that of Keats, "was writ in water."

Sir Walter Scott's Monument is doubtless the finest in the world. It is built of brown sandstone, in elaborate Gothic architecture, and is two hundred feet high. It was erected in 1844, at an expense of $80,500, from a competitive design furnished by George Meikle Kemp, a young self-taught architect of great promise, who died before the monument's completion, he having been drowned in the Union Canal, when going home one dark night. Beneath the open Gothic rotunda, with its groined arches, is the colossal marble statue of Sir Walter, in a sitting posture, by John Steell. Many of the niches on the exterior are occupied by statues of characters in Scott's romances. At the centre of the great monument, and up 100 feet from the base, is a room in which are relics of the great bard; and near the top, at the height of 175 feet, is a gallery on the outside of the monument, from which are fine views of the city. As one looks down on the busy mass below; when he sees the ruins of this animated map spread out beneath him,—hills, ravine, parks, monuments, princely edifices, as the busy hum of life surges up to him,—he loses sight of "the good time coming," and is satisfied with that which has come already.

Holyrood Palace is situated on the level ground between Calton Hill and Salisbury Crags, the portion connecting the old and new parts of the city. The edifice is built of a brown freestone, and the palace is open to visitors for a small fee. The only portion of great antiquity is the northwest tower, in which are the original Queen Mary apartments, erected by James V., who died in 1542. Long ago abandoned as a place of royal residence, this palace, when it is now used at all, is occupied by the clergy of the Presbyterian, or the established Church of Scotland, at the time of their annual convocation, which lasts about two weeks. Here the ministers are entertained during their stay. How passing strange! The home of rulers distinguished for hostility to anything but a ceremonial religion is now used as the house of convocation for strong Dissenters! Much of it is vacant. We go first into the picture-gallery, which was the banquet-hall. It was in this room that Charles I., when but a prince, held grand levees. The room is 150 feet long and 27 feet wide, elegantly finished in oak. Here are pictures of 106 Scottish sovereigns, from Fergus to James VII. They are mostly fancy portraits, and painted by order of Charles II. to flatter the vanity of the pleasure-seeking king. Their merits are delicately hinted in the wonderment of Christopher Croftangier, that each and all of the Scottish kings should have "a nose like the knocker of a door." The paintings more recently added are genuine. There are rooms which remain furnished as they were centuries ago. Among them is Lord Darnley's Chamber, and here are many relics of Queen Mary, and a portrait of Darnley when a youth. From this room is the private staircase by which Rizzio's assassins ascended to Mary's apartments above. The murder of Rizzio is conspicuous in the annals of Scotland.

Henry Stuart Darnley was the second husband of Mary, Queen of Scots. When it became known that the queen proposed to marry again, Darnley, who was possessed of a very handsome person and accomplished in many of the fine arts of the day, proceeded to Scotland, urged his suit, and was accepted. The marriage took place in the chapel of Holyrood, adjoining the palace, July 29, 1565. "He was," says Randolph, "conceited, arrogant, and an intolerable fool." He was overbearing, and towards Mary was petulant and insolent. He repaid her kindness by profligacy and infidelity, and finally alienated her affections by participating in the murder of her secretary, the Italian Rizzio, March 9, 1566, within a year after marriage.

While she and Rizzio were together in the Queen's apartment, Darnley rushed in, and held the Queen while Ruthven, George Douglas, and other conspirators stabbed Rizzio. Mary pleaded with loud cries for the life of her favorite secretary; but, hearing that he was dead, she dried her tears and said: "I will now have revenge. I will never rest till I give you as sorrowful a heart as I have at this present." Darnley afterwards repented, and aided Mary in driving his confederates from the kingdom; but his vices and follies were deep-seated, and the breach widened. On the 19th of June of this same year their son James (afterwards James I. of England) was born. In the next January, Darnley was taken with the smallpox, and removed to a house which stood by itself at a place called the Kirk of Field, near Edinburgh, it being feared that if he remained at Holyrood Palace he might communicate the disease to the young prince. The Queen visited him a few times during his sickness, and manifested apparent sympathy. On the night of February 9 the house was blown up with gunpowder, and the dead bodies of Darnley and his servant were found in a mangled condition not far from the ruins. Bothwell, already the Queen's lover, was the chief actor in this tragedy, and in three months they were married. The room of most interest is the apartment of Queen Mary. This, like some of the other rooms, is finished with a heavy-panelled oak ceiling, and has an uncarpeted oak floor. There is also rich panel-work about the deeply recessed windows and doors. The room is not large,—about 18 feet by 20 feet square, and 12 feet high. It contains a few chairs, a table, and bed,—the latter with high corner posts, square framework at the top, and a canopy of red tapestry silk. Though three hundred years have passed since their owner died, the furniture, together with the mattress and richly embroidered quilts, are still in a fair state of preservation, and the bed appears ready for instant use. It was in this room that the Queen held many angry disputations with her hated opponent, John Knox. She is reported at one time to have demanded of the reformer, "Think you that subjects, having the power, may resist their princes?" and to have received the bold reply, intrepid as the heart of him whose brain conceived it, "If princes exceed their bounds, madam, no doubt they may be resisted with power."

At another interview the Queen turned her back in derision of her faithful attendants. Knox, who never let slip a chance to fight the "beasts at Ephesus," addressed himself to the maids of honor and remarked: "O fair ladies, how pleasing were this lyfe of yours if it would always abyde, and then in the end we might pass to heaven with all this gay gear. But fye upon that knave Death, that will come, wheddir we will or not."

On the adjoining premises are ruins replete with interest. Both Holyrood palace and chapel are thought-inducing. Beneath this roof, within these walls, have been concocted schemes which have influenced the destinies of the world. That chapel, now a glorious ruin, was consecrated a thousand years ago by the prayers and resolves and sacrifices of pious monks, and later by deposits of dust, which once made the world tremble. There is an impassable gulf between that day and this. Scarcely more appreciative than the mantling ivy or the crumbling stones, or the inanimate dust of regal sleepers, are we concerning past realities. At best we but "see through a glass darkly."

The abbey ruins at Holyrood, and almost adjoining the palace, are enchanting. The walls of the building are nearly whole, and reasonably free from decay, and have been in their present condition for centuries. Ivy clambers over large portions of it. The rich door-work is almost entire, and many windows, save the glass, are perfect, and the carpet is of thick grass.

Here Charles I. was crowned king of Scotland, and also James II. and James III. Mary and Darnley were married here; and within these walls the Papal Legate presented to James IV., from Pope Julius II., the sword of state, which is preserved among the regalia of Scotland.

The last time the chapel was used for worship was in the reign of James VII., who had Mass celebrated in it,—which excited the populace to its destruction at the Revolution. Several of the kings of Scotland were buried in the monastery, but the remains were desecrated by the mob of 1688; and it is doubtful whether the bones of David II., who died Feb. 22, 1370, James II., who died in 1460, James V., who died Dec. 13, 1542, Darnley, who died Feb. 9, 1567, are now in the royal vault. Rizzio, by command of Queen Mary, was at first interred in this tomb, but, to prevent scandal, he was afterwards removed to that part of the chapel nearest the palace.

In the centre of the square in front of the palace is a large and elaborate fountain, a copy of one that stood in the court of Linlithgow Palace. The spot was once occupied by a statue of the Queen, which is said to have been so ugly that, at her majesty's request, it was buried six feet deep in the courtyard of the royal stables. Perhaps it will some day be exhumed, and become a puzzle to the archæologists of distant centuries. In the garden is a curious sun-dial, described as Queen Mary's, but really of later date, for it was constructed in the reign of Charles I. The apex of the pedestal has twenty sides, on each of which is a dial. Outside the palace gate is a circular building known as Queen Mary's Bath, where she is reported to have enhanced her charms by bathing in white wine. It was by this lodge that Rizzio's assassins made their escape. During some repairs in 1789 a richly inlaid dagger was found sticking in a part of the roof. It was of very antique form, and corroded with rust. The presumption is that it was concealed there by the conspirators.

Next demanding attention are the highlands near the lower end of the city, and back of the older part. These are within a few minutes' walk of the main streets, and make a lofty background called Salisbury Crags. They are very bluff-like on the side towards the town; but the top and rear are more level, and covered with grass, and a grand avenue is graded circuitously to the table-land, from which there are remarkable views of the entire city, for this point is 576 feet above the level of the sea. As one looks at this elevation from the city, it has a dark appearance, and is enveloped in that blue haze, or atmosphere, so peculiar to our Blue Hills at Milton. In the rear of this table-land, perhaps an eighth of a mile away, is Arthur's Seat, 822 feet above the sea-level,—247 feet higher than the table-land of the Crags. The macadamized avenue continues as far as this, and from the summit are visible twelve counties and innumerable mountain peaks, and among them the Grampian Hills.

The Old City lies stretched out from the highlands, and it is entertaining to the most ardent antiquary, although great changes have taken place. Here are buildings varying from four to ten stories in height, with gables to the street, and over-jutting stories in abundance. We think of this main street as it must have been in the days of the Stuarts, when these projecting gables, over-jutting windows, and hanging stairs were gayly decorated with flags and streamers, and the roadway was thronged with spectators as some royal pageant passed along.

Peculiar to this street are its *closes*, or *wynds*. These are spaces in the rear of the front buildings, surrounded by tenements, and having a contracted opening from the main street. They are occupied by a low class of people, but were formerly the residences of distinguished persons.

Riddle's Close is one, in which David Hume began his History of England, though he finished it in another part of the city, Jack's Land, in the Canongate. At the end of the place is a house once belonging to Bailie MacMoran, who was shot dead by the high-school boys in 1598, when he was attempting to restore subordination during a barring-out.

Farther down is Brodie's Close, named for Deacon Brodie, who was executed for a daring burglary in 1788. Till the very eve of his trial he was a citizen of renown, considered exemplary and pious; but it was proved beyond question that for years he had been concerned in extensive robberies.

Lady Stair's Close is near by, and is named for Lady Elizabeth Stair. While her first husband, Viscount Primrose was abroad, that singular event happened which is so well described in Sir Walter Scott's story, "My Aunt Margaret's Mirror." She occupied the house in the close where the date, 1622, is over the doorway.

Baxter's Close contains the first lodging occupied by Robert Burns, in 1786. He stayed with his friend John Richmond, who was a law student and clerk, and they two were the only persons in the house. On the opposite side is a house, bearing on its front, in Gothic letters, one of those legends that the custom of those days sanctioned:

BLISST—BE—THE—LORD—IN—HIS—GIFTIS—FOR—NOV—AND—EVIR.

Near this spot is the chapel called the Maison Dieu. It was in this that the General Assembly met in 1578, when perpetual banishment was given to high ecclesiastical titles. The act was as follows:—

It is here concludid that Bischopes sould be callit be thair awin names, or be the names of Breither in all tyme coming, and that lordlie name and authoritie be banissed from the kirk of God, quhilk hes bot ae Lord Chryst Jesus.

In this chapel, in 1661, the martyred Marquis of Argyle lay in state for some days, till at length his body was buried at Kilmun and his head affixed to a gable of the Tolbooth, an old building, once the Parliament House, but then a prison.

The church of all churches in Edinburgh is St. Giles's. Many repairs and restorations have been made upon it, so that only a portion of the tower retains its original design. The first mention of the venerable edifice is in the charter of David II., in 1359. The structure was large and cruciform, and after the Reformation the four parts were appropriated to various uses. One was devoted to religious services, and it was here that the Solemn League and Covenant of the Scotch Covenanters was sworn to and subscribed by the Parliament, the General Assembly, and the Commissioners, in 1643. Another part was used as a prison. The town council used to meet in it; the town clerk held his office here, and a transept was used for the police. A writer says of it:—

The city corporation treated it like a carpet-bag, which could never be crammed so full but that room might be made for something more, which could not be put elsewhere.

So earnest were they to utilize—we may say secularize—the old structure, that even the spaces on the outside, between the butresses, were from A. D. 1555 down to 1817, a period of 262 years, filled in with small shops, whose chimneys belched smoke against the old edifice.

This was the parish church of Edinburgh at the Reformation, and is celebrated as the place where John Knox made his appeals to the piety and patriotism of the metropolis,—appeals which, more than all other means, established the Reformation not only in this country, but the civilized world over. An exciting scene took place here in 1637. Archbishop Laud had arranged for the introduction of the liturgy, to establish by authority the service of the Church of England. As the custom was, Jenny Geddes brought a stool with her to church, and when the obnoxious prayers were begun, and the Bishop of Edinburgh had just requested the Dean to read the Collect for the day, Jenny arose and exclaimed: "*Colic*, said ye; the Devil colic the wame o' ye; wud ye say Mass at my lug?" and she sent her stool flying at the Dean's head. The famous stool is still preserved in the Antiquarian Museum.

The ancient cemetery of the church is now covered by the second House of Parliament, and used as a court-house. John Knox died Nov. 24, 1572. He was buried in the burial-ground not far from the church. This large area is now the approach to the court-house, and is paved with large flagstones. As nearly as can be ascertained, this burial-place is designated by the letters J. K., cut in one of these stones; and this is the only monument that Edinburgh can show for one of her greatest citizens. Over the grave of Knox was once a stone with that celebrated epitaph by Regent Morton:—

HERE LIES HE WHO NEVER FEARED THE FACE OF MAN.

On the outer walls of St. Giles's is a monument to John Napier, who died here April 4, 1617, and was celebrated as the inventor of logarithms.

The Tolbooth was originally a parliament house, and at last a prison. It is referred to in Sir Walter Scott's "Heart of Midlothian," and is marked as the northwest corner of St. Giles's by the figure of a heart cut in the pavement.

The house in which Knox resided is one of the quaintest imaginable. It is not far from St. Giles's, and is very irregular in outline, of a dark brown color, three and a half projecting stories in height. He occupied it from 1560 to 1572, when he died in the 67th year of his age. Over the door is the inscription:—

Lufe God abuf all., and ye nychtbour as yiself.

One can imagine some of the remarkable questions here considered, for matters pregnant with great issues were held in this building. At one time the care of all the Scotch churches, and even of the nation itself, rested heavily on the spirit of John Knox; but he was not often the morose fanatic he is sometimes represented. Few men enjoyed social intercourse more than he, or more readily availed themselves of an opportunity for its enjoyment. A few days before his death he desired his servant to tap a cask of wine that had been presented to him, that he might share it with friends who were paying him a visit, remarking that he was "not likely to tarry till it be finished." We must content ourselves with an extract from the Diary of James Melville, in which he gives a graphic description of his preaching, and more especially that of his last days:—

In the opening of his text he was moderat the space of an halff houre: but when he enterit to application, he made me sa to grew and tremble, that I could nocht hald a pen to wryt. Mr. Knox wald sumtyme come in and repose him in our college-yard, and call us scholars to him, and bless us, and exort us to know God and His wark in our country, and to stand by the guid caus. I saw him every day in his doctrine [preaching] go hulie and fear [cautiously] with a furring of martriks about his neck, a staff in the ane hand, and guid godlie Richart Ballenden, his servand, holdin up the other oxtar, from the abbey to the paroche kirk, and by the said Richart and another servand, lifted up to the pulpit, where he behovdit to lean at his first entrie, but or he had done with his sermon, he was sa active and vigorous that he was like to ding that pulpit in blads and flee out of it.

As early as 1746 a theatre was established in Edinburgh, and the church of those days, intensely conservative though it was, rather encouraged than opposed it, for Dr. Carlyle says:—

When Mrs. Siddons first appeared in Edinburgh during the sitting of the General Assembly, the court was obliged to fix all its important business for the alternate days when she did not act, as the younger members of the clergy, as well as the laity, took their stations in the theatre on those days by three in the afternoon.

On St. John Street near by, Smollett, the historian and novelist for a time resided with his sister, Mrs. Telfer. The next building to this was the Canongate Kilwinning Lodge, where Robert Burns, poet-laureate to the lodge, was made a Royal Arch Mason. At No. 13 lived Lord Monboddo and his beautiful daughter, Miss Burnet, whose death Burns so touchingly commemorated. Lord Monboddo anticipated Darwin, for he propounded the theory that the human family had ascended from the monkey. His contemporaries were not disposed to favor his opinions, which exposed the noble lord to the jocular request, "Show us your tail, Monboddo." At No. 10 was the residence of James Ballantine, the printer of the first editions of the Waverley Novels, whose commercial failure involved Sir Walter Scott, as a partner, in the anxieties which beclouded the best years of his life, and compelled him to overtask his strength in the honorable ambition to "owe no man anything." Ballantine was in the habit of giving a great dinner at this house on the occasion of every new publication by Sir Walter, and therefore it is linked with the memory of most of Scott's literary contemporaries, who, with the Duke of Buccleuch, were usually invited to the feast. At Panmure Close the celebrated Adam Smith lived for twelve years, and died July 8, 1790.

Before closing this account of places of especial interest—and we have spoken of but one of a thousand—we must name what is called the Abbey Sanctuary, the only one remaining in Scotland. This is a large territory, in the vicinity of Holyrood Palace, and includes the whole range of Arthur's Seat, Salisbury Crags, and the Queen's Park. It was set apart centuries ago, as a district into which poor but honest debtors might flee for safety from imprisonment. So long as they could prove that they were not fraudulent bankrupts, they were safe in this land of refuge, and on the Sabbath they could go over the city, wherever they pleased, until sunset. This freedom naturally tempted some of them to transgress the hour, and they were then in peril of the bumbailiffs; but history says that "as the bailiffs would no more dare to cross the sacred strand than a witch can pursue its victim over a running stream, there were often tremendous *treats* at the foot of Canongate." On one such occasion the fugitive fell just as he was at the strand, or boundary line. His body was on the safe side, but his legs were captured, and held by the bailiffs till an arrangement was made for his temporary relief. The question of jurisdiction came up in Parliament, and after much grave discussion it was decided and resolved that, "as the bailiff could do nothing with a man's legs unless he had the body they belonged to, the debtor must be allowed to take his legs along with him."

Sir Walter Scott's residence for some years was No. 39 Castle Street, and a literary Frenchman has remarked that "it was a right number for Sir Walter, as it was fitting that the Three Graces and Nine Muses should take their station there." It was in this house that occurred the ludicrous incident which Sir Walter utilizes in the "Bride of Lammermoor," when he represents the faithful Caleb Balderstone as excusing the non-appearance of dinner by the fact of a fall of soot down the chimney. Sir Walter had invited numerous guests to dinner. As they were chatting together the butler entered with a face like that of him "who drew Priam's curtain in the dead of night." Beckoning to his master he informed him of the catastrophe which had taken place. Sir Walter carried his guests to Oman's Hotel in Charlotte Square, where the mishap added zest to the banquet thus speedily prepared.

The castle is not only interesting to Scotland, but to the civilized world. Burns says of it:—

"There, watching high the least alarms,
Thy rough, rude fortress gleams afar;

Like some rude veteran, gray in arms,
And marked with many a seamy scar;

The ponderous wall and massy bar,
Grim-rising o'er the rugged rock,

Have oft withstood assailing war,
And oft repelled the invader's shock."

Castle Rock, on which it is built, is a very high elevation at the upper end of the Old City, and has the almost undisputed honor of having been occupied by a native tribe long before the Roman Conquest. St. Margaret's Chapel is older than 1373, in which year Sir William Kirkcaldy, who held the fortress for Queen Mary, was compelled by his garrison to surrender to the combined forces of the Scotch and English, but not till after the fortress was laid in ruins. The barracks adjoining the castle—now a portion of the structure, an ugly pile, half house and half factory in appearance—was erected in 1796. This structure being one of the four fortresses of Scotland which, by the Treaty of Union, were to be kept fortified, is always occupied by a regiment of the line. There is but one approach to it, and that is by the main avenue up from the old part of the city, which ends in a square called the Half Moon Battery. This is a level plain of the form indicated by its name, and contains an acre graded with clean gravel. Salutes are fired on public occasions, and a daily gun, at 1 P. M., marks the Greenwich time. This is fired by means of a wire stretching over the city from the Royal Observatory at Calton Hill. The sound can be so distinctly heard on a calm day that it is the regulator of time for a circle of forty miles' diameter. Admittance is gained by passing over a drawbridge across the moat, once filled with water, but now used as a playground by the soldiers. The castle is open to the public on payment of a shilling. The old dark stone walls tower up, castle-like, before us,—sombre, massive, aged, and varied in outline. The structural assemblage is what we had imagined a large castellated fortress to be. We walk over the bridge, and through the Portcullis Arch, above which is the old State Prison, where the Marquis of Argyle and other illustrious captives were confined previous to their execution. The last state prisoners lodged here were Watt and Downie, accused of high treason in 1794, the former being executed. The gate passed, we are met by one of the guides, who leads us through the contracted grounds and into the building. First comes the Crown Room, where the regalia are kept. These consist of a crown, a sceptre, a sword of state, and a silver rod-of-office, supposed to be that of the Lord Treasurer. They were long thought to be lost; but, after lying in an oak chest from the date of the union with England in 1707, they were restored to the light in 1818, chiefly through the instrumentality of Sir Walter Scott, the Prince Regent having granted a commission for a search of the Crown Room. The Scotch people are justly proud of these symbols of their independence, these relics of a long line of monarchs, beginning with the hero of Bannockburn. A part of the crown, at least, was worn by Robert Bruce; and, not to mention other sovereigns, it encircled the brows of Queen Mary, her son James VI., and her grandson Charles I. The sword was a gift from Pope Julius II. to James IV.

In Queen Mary's Room that lady was delivered, June 19, 1566, of her son James VI. of Scotland, afterward James I. of England. This part of the castle was built by the Queen the year preceding, for her palace, and so is 317 years old. There is a vaulted dungeon below this room, partly excavated in the solid rock; and at the south side of the castle there are other dungeons, in which were confined prisoners taken in the wars of the First Napoleon.

The miniature chapel of Queen Margaret stands on the highest part of the castle rock. The pious queen of Malcolm Canmore probably erected the chapel, and she certainly worshipped there till her death, Nov. 17, 1093, almost eight hundred years ago. It is a complete church, but measures only $16\frac{1}{2}$ feet long, and $10\frac{1}{2}$ feet wide within the nave. It looks inexpressibly ancient, but is in excellent preservation.

The old cannon, Mons Meg, stands on the battery. It is large and peculiarly formed, with a heavy wooden carriage, considerably decorated with carvings. It is commonly reported to have been made at Mons, France, in 1476; but several authorities in archæology, including Sir Walter Scott, maintain that there is good evidence of its having been made in Scotland, and that it was forged at Castle Douglas for James II. by McKim, a local blacksmith, when the king was besieging the Castle of Thrieve. The maker called the cannon

Mollance Meg, the first word being the name of the estate given him by the grateful monarch because of its manufacture, and Meg being the name of his wife. It was injured when firing a salute in honor of the Duke of York's visit in 1682. In 1684 it was removed to the Tower of London, but it was restored to the castle in 1829, by order of George IV.

As may readily be imagined, there are good views of the entire city and its surroundings. The Castle Esplanade was for centuries the promenade of the citizens of Old Edinburgh; and as such it is referred to, with King's Park and Leith Pier, in various acts for the better observance of the Lord's Day. It has often been the scene of public executions. Foret, the vicar of Dollar, and others of the early Reformers were here burnt at the stake during the persecution raised by Mary of Guise and the Romish hierarchy. Language does not suffice to express our regret as we think of what we have *not* spoken of, as the suburbs also are full of charms; but we must forego all, and take the train for Melrose, where we arrived at 12 o'clock Thursday, June 6, after a ride of an hour and a half. We are now on our way back to London by a somewhat circuitous route, and mainly in a southerly direction, on the east side of England.

CHAPTER XIV.

MELROSE—ABBOTSFORD.

The ride from Edinburgh is through a farming district, and strongly reminds one of southern New England. As the reader anticipates, we are to stop at Melrose for two purposes; to visit the ruins of its abbey, and to make the short tour of five miles to Abbotsford. The town of Melrose is intensely rural and charming. In 1851 it had a population of 7,487. It has a number of small and comfortable hotels, and carriages are on hire at reasonable prices. There are avenues for rambling; and at the border-line is a grand hill, which stretches along the entire length of the village. The road winds along the hill at a good elevation, and displays to advantage the valley of the Tweed and the hills on the opposite side, from three to five miles away. In the level parts of the great valley the land is under excellent cultivation, though largely devoted to grazing. The groves, the heavy woodlands, and the single trees which remain from the primeval forest are arranged with scrupulous care and a view to the picturesque. It would seem that one like Scott could not help being inspired by scenes like these. As one considers beautiful Edinburgh, he gets the impression that *there* is the more befitting residence for the great romancer; but once in Melrose, and on the top of these lovely hills, he feels that here Scott was in his element.

Our first step was to go to a hotel, dine, and determine the proper course for sight-seeing. Talking the matter over with our hostess we were advised to join a party of two or three others, take a team, and go first to Abbotsford, and stop on our way back at the abbey, which was in fact but a few minutes' walk from the hotel. The advice was accepted, and we were soon on the way to Abbotsford.

We passed through several streets, and into the suburbs; then, over pleasant roads, by beautiful farms, the lovely Tweed more or less of the time in view; and next, through narrow lanes, till we came in sight of Abbotsford. The place has a low look, for it is on the slightly elevated part of the meadow, in a northern parish of Melrose. Sir Walter bought the estate in 1811, being then at the age of forty. He soon after rebuilt the mansion, enlarging it as his fortunes permitted. He named it from an adjoining ford, called the Abbot's Ford, on the River Tweed, which here is a small stream that runs through the estate. It is quite sluggish in summer, about thirty feet wide, but greatly swollen by freshets. The house is large, and low in general appearance. It is built of gray limestone, is very irregular in castellated outline, with numerous small towers and gables. It is so low that we can look down upon it from the travelled road. The estate is approached by a lane from the main road. The garden is walled in, and the meadow-land outside reaches to the river. The external walls of the house and garden have built into them relics of ancient abbeys and carvings from old castles. At the decease of Sir Walter, Sept. 21, 1832, the building was occupied by James Hope Scott, Esq.; and his wife, the sole surviving daughter of Sir Walter, lived there until her death, Oct. 26, 1858. It then went by inheritance to their daughter, but during her minority it was let for the use of a Roman Catholic seminary. On the day of our visit we found her in possession; but during the larger part of the day visitors are admitted to the principal rooms of the first story.

The business affairs appear to be managed by a matron who, after taking our shillings, explains, systematically and hurriedly, the various objects of interest for about half an hour,—all the time she can afford, and as much perhaps as we should give if standing in her place. The house is a source of great revenue, for no pleasant day passes without visitors. In the reception-room we await the return of the maiden, who is just then guiding another party. They come into the room wearing an expression that says they *have seen*, if they have not conquered. They wend their way slowly out of the grounds, up the narrow lane, to their carriages, and then, though breathing freer, they continue so absorbed in admiration that they have no energy to expend in regrets over the shortness of their stay. The experience of one party is that of all who have brains to comprehend the facts. A visit to Abbotsford is like a flash of lightning, which, for the moment, lights up miles of landscape, and then leaves the beholder to mentally repicture what is still there, but veiled from his view. An experience like this was ours at Strasburg, where a momentary light from our high hotel window exhibited the cathedral, the lofty roofs of the houses, and the storks standing on one leg on the chimney-tops. Brief was our half-hour at Abbotsford, but it was enough to write the spot indelibly upon memory's tablets.

But we now follow our guide, and are ushered first into the study. This is a room not far from twenty feet square and fifteen feet high. It is finished in oak, and has a heavy wrought ceiling of the same material. On one side is a coal grate, surrounded by a red marble mantel, with a lamp upon it, and a small marble obelisk monument. The grate, fire-screen, and poker remain as they were fifty-one years ago. At the centre of the room is the mahogany desk at which he sat,—plain and flat-topped. It has five drawers on each side, with an opening for the sitter's feet between the rows. The armchair is near it,—a good-sized comfortable chair, and covered with light-brown leather. The wall-spaces are filled with books, and a light cast-iron gallery extends partly around the room. Above this gallery are other reference books. On the side opposite the chimney, in front of a window, is a sort of casket, having a plate-glass top. It needs not that the maid should tell us that here are the last clothes worn by the poet. A well written paper so states, but the pictures of him have long before given the information. For their description we appeal to our note-books. At the left are the shoes,—large, thick, and made of coarse leather. They are moderately low-cut, much strained by his high instep, well blacked, and considerably worn. They have no binding or lining, and are tied with leather strings laced through four or five holes. In the centre is a well ironed and carefully folded pair of pants, once black and white, but now yellowish plaid,—the plaids a scant quarter-inch square; and there is the large waistcoat with alternating brown and white stripes, perhaps a sixteenth of an inch wide, and running lengthwise. Next there is a large white and wide-brimmed stove-pipe fur hat, with rather a short nap. It shows hard usage, for there are a number of dents in it. Finally, there is a dark-blue frock-coat,—said to have gilt buttons, but they are folded out of sight.

How pleasing it would be to pass into a reverie in this great presence! We pass into the splendid and unusual library. The ceiling has oak mouldings and deep panels, said to be copies from an ancient castle. The sides are covered with books from floor nearly to ceiling. The furniture is rich and various, much of it presented by distinguished men. In a square showcase on a table are exposed for exhibition small articles that were given to Sir Walter by kings, queens, and other persons of noble blood. Among them are snuff-boxes,—gold, silver, ivory, pearl, shell, and papier-maché. The floor is of polished oak, and without carpets. The library is not far from twenty-five feet wide, forty-five long, and fifteen feet high.

We next pass into the dining-room, which is about twenty feet wide and thirty feet long, and is the one in which the great owner breathed his last. It also has an oak floor, and is without furniture, save a few chairs for the use of visitors. At one end is a large bay-window, looking out on the great lawn, extending from the house to the Tweed. It adds a peculiar interest to know that Sir Walter so loved nature that, when he saw the great consummation approaching, he desired to be removed from his chamber to this room, where he might once more gaze upon this scene and his favorite river, which was flowing away like his own life. A couch was brought, and placed against the side wall, with its foot towards the window, and there the silver cord was loosed, the golden bowl broken, the pitcher shattered at the fountain, the wheel broken at the cistern, and the poet was no more a mortal.

The temptation is resistless to say a few words about Scott's previous life. He had become worn down with his attempts to earn enough to meet the claims made against him, $400,000, in consequence of the failure of his publisher, Ballantine. At first he left Abbotsford and went to London to do this work. Becoming a mere wreck of his former self, he went to the shores of the Mediterranean; but at last, when hope deferred had made the heart sick, he returned to London, went to a small hotel, the St. James, at 76 Jermyn Street, and there passed three melancholy weeks before going to his home on the

Tweed. Mr. Lockhart, who was with him, gives the following graphic account:

When we reached the hotel, he recognized us with many marks of tenderness, but signified that he was totally exhausted; so no attempt was made to remove him farther, and he was put to bed immediately. To his children, all assembled once more about him, he repeatedly gave his blessing in a very solemn manner, as if expecting immediate death; but he was never in a condition for conversation, and sank either into sleep or delirious stupor upon the slightest effort.

Mr. Ferguson, who was seldom absent from his pillow, says:—

When I first saw Sir Walter, he was lying on the second-floor-back room of the St. James Hotel in Jermyn Street, in a state of stupor, from which, however, he would be roused for a moment by being addressed; and then he recognized those about him, but immediately relapsed. I think I never saw anything more magnificent than the symmetry of his colossal bust, as he lay on the pillow with his chest and neck exposed. During the time he was in Jermyn Street he was calm but never collected, and in general was either in absolute stupor or in a waking dream. He never seemed to know where he was, but imagined himself to be still in the steamboat. The rattling of carriages and the noises of the street sometimes disturbed this illusion, and then he fancied himself at the polling of Jedburgh, where he had been insulted and stoned.... At length his constant yearnings to return to Abbotsford induced his physicians to consent to his removal,—a consent which, the moment it was notified to him, seemed to infuse new vigor into his frame. It was on a calm, clear afternoon of the 7th of July [1832] that every preparation was made for his embarkation on board the steamboat. He was placed on a chair by his faithful servant, Nicholson, half-dressed, and loosely wrapped in a quilted dressing-gown. He requested Lockhart and myself to wheel him towards the light of the open window, and we both remarked the vigorous lustre of his eye. He sat there silently gazing on space for more than half an hour, apparently wholly occupied with his own thoughts, and having no distinct perception of where he was, or how he came there. He suffered himself to be lifted into his carriage, which was surrounded by a crowd, among whom were many gentlemen on horseback, who loitered about to gaze on the scene. His children were deeply affected, and Mrs. Lockhart trembled from head to foot and wept bitterly. Thus surrounded by those nearest to him, he alone was unconscious of the cause or the depth of their grief, and while yet alive seemed to be carried to his grave.

He embarked on the steamer, and after a four days' sail, on the 11th of July his eye once more brightened as he caught sight of the familiar waters of the

Tweed, and when at length he recognized the towers of his own Abbotsford, he sprang up in the carriage with delight. He was carried to his chamber, where he remained till his death on the 21st of September.

We have no apology to make for this digression, for Scott has given to Scotland and English literature a new glory.

We now resume our walk over the house, and pass through the museum, which is some twelve feet wide and forty feet long. Various kinds of armor prevail, and many interesting things that were presented to the "Lord of the domain." Fifty-one years are gone since the great poet was here, but all else remains as it was. We sit down in his study, as if waiting for him to come; and so real is everything that, should the sound of his heavy feet be heard in the hall, should he enter in person, the gulf of years would as by magic be bridged over and forgotten. He arranged this house only for his home; but he unwittingly made it a Jerusalem for countless pilgrims.

We passed meditatingly up the lane, mounted the team, and in spite of the clack of the driver, of hills and dales,—in spite of anything material,—those unmaterial memories held sway. We had been to Abbotsford, and its inspiration would evermore be *ours*.

An odor or a sunset was never fully described, though some can tell the story better than others. A lamp lighted from another does not reduce the original flame, and so it is with visits to any shrine. A million may go to Abbotsford, but it loses nothing by these draughts of pleasure.

Our carriage ride ended, we are at Melrose Abbey. How many times Sir Walter stood on this spot. His advice was:—

If thou would'st view fair Melrose aright,
Go visit it by the pale moonlight,
For the gay beams of lightsome day
Gild but to flout the ruins gray.

This we could not do, but we saw the abbey at the close of a fine day, as the sun threw its rays aslant in long lines across the grand ruins. We are met by a young maiden whose father has charge of the premises. We pay our shilling to enter, and first of all are impressed with the great *beauty* of the place. It is a large church, once belonging to the abbey, the latter having long since been destroyed. The nave, aisles, and transepts are roofless. Here and there, neatly piled against the walls, are fallen stones that once were part of the edifice. The floor is covered with that velvety grass which delights to take possession of places like this; and it is not to be blamed, for the grass is emblematic of mortals who would do the same if they could. The walls are solid and lofty, and a part of the groined ceiling of the choir remains. The windows are perfect in their stone tracery of mullions and transoms. Instinctively we look for the great chancel with its east window,—and adore, and see the force of Scott's description:—

The moon on the east oriel shone
Through slender shafts of shapely stone,
By foliaged tracery combined.
Thou wouldst have thought some fairy hand
'Twixt poplars straight the osier wand,
In many a freakish knot had twined;
Then framed a spell when work was done
And changed the willow wreaths to stone.

In this wall, under this window, was buried the heart of Robert Bruce.

Here are tombs of men too great to have their dust mingle with common soil. We are delighted with the ivy, climbing at random,—sometimes very thick and grand in its mantling power. We pass out of the side door, and are in the burial-ground of two or three acres. Not cared for by mortals, Nature—in great unison with her possessions and conscious of her sacred trust—prohibits the intrusion of rambling vine or unsightly weed. How varied are the views of tower and gable, of buttress unbroken or in partial ruin! Remove a stone, or repair one, and you do injury. Here repose the ashes of monk and nun, who centuries ago entered their free immortality.

The abbey was founded by David I. in 1136, and dedicated to the Virgin Mary ten years after. It was occupied first by monks of the Cistercian order, who had come from Yorkshire. In 1322, after a peaceable occupancy of 176 years, its quiet was disturbed by the invasion of an army under the authority of Edward II., and the building was greatly injured. Robert Bruce soon after commenced its rebuilding, after the present design. It was not favored, however, with long repose, for in 1385 it suffered again; but it was again repaired, and then enjoyed a rest of 160 years. In 1545 it once more suffered severely from English invaders. Again repaired, it remained quiet for a time, but during the Reformation, under Cromwell, its choicest sculptures were mutilated. To the shame of human nature be it said, in later times many of its stones have been carried away for the erection of other buildings; but yet, after full five centuries have flown, it remains one of the few grand and satisfying examples of Gothic architecture in the world.

We leave the ruins for a ramble over the town. In the business parts there is neatness and a limited commercial life. Then we go to the rear, through one of the most romantic roads imaginable, and up the hillside for the views already described. We had arranged to leave town that night, but the entire hill seemed to beseech us to "Come up hither." We halted "between two opinions." One of the hard questions was to decide whether to go or to stay. Body and spirit were in antagonism; but remembering a long line of good places ahead, we urged our unwilling feet to descend this hill of Zion, which yielded "a thousand sacred sweets." If anything makes travelling companions mute, it is such a condition. No jokes, no attempts to say smart things, no more eulogistic talk about fine scenery are in order; the effort is to try and forget we are losing it. The walk to a station is not a Galop, but is rather a Dead March in such a mood.

At 5 P. M. we take cars for Newcastle-on-Tyne, and so in a few hours shall be out of Scotland, for we are on the border. Dundee, Dunfermline, Aberdeen, are unvisited,—and Dryburgh Abbey, where Scott's ashes repose, though it is but five miles away. Jedburgh Abbey also is unseen; but we trust the reader will some day go over this ground, and then he can really sympathize with our loss.

ENGLAND.

CHAPTER XV.

NEWCASTLE-ON-TYNE—DURHAM.

We arrived in Newcastle at 10 P. M., after a five hours' ride from Melrose. The city has quite a history, and as we desired to break the long ride to Durham, we were ready to stop here over night, for we made it a rule to refrain from night travel.

This is the chief town of old Northumberland, on the right bank of the River Tyne, eight miles from its mouth, and has a population of 128,443. It is built on three steep hills, although between them are the business portions on level ground. It extends two miles along the river, and is connected with Gateshead, on the opposite side of the river, by a handsome stone bridge. There are remains of ancient fortifications. The streets are spacious, and there are many elegant buildings, but there is that smoky condition characteristic of large manufacturing places. There are here fine buildings for public baths and wash-houses, built in 1859. The High Level Bridge across the Tyne was built by Robert Stevenson. It is supported by six massive piers 124 feet apart, and has a carriage-way 90 feet above the river; and 28 feet over that is the viaduct, 118 feet above the water. The cost was $1,172,250. There is an antiquarian museum in the old castle tower, containing the largest collection of lapidary inscriptions and sculptures in England. The castle was built in 1080, by Robert, eldest son of William the Conqueror. It has been restored in many parts. Though very small, being scarcely more than a low tower some 75 feet in diameter, it is one of the finest specimens of Norman architecture in the kingdom. Situated at the junction of the principal streets, and being readily seen from the station, the contrast between the ancient and modern is impressive.

The harbor, now greatly improved, has a quay 1550 feet long. The traffic is principally in bituminous coal, for which the city is the greatest mart in the world; hence the adage about the impropriety of carrying coals to Newcastle. This trade has been important from ancient time, for the burgesses obtained from Henry III. in 1239—more than 644 years ago—"a license to dig coal," and by the time of Edward I. the business had so increased that Newcastle paid a tax of £200. In 1615 the trade had so advanced as to employ 400 ships, and the traffic extended into France and the Netherlands. 200,000 tons of coke are sent out annually. Lead is also shipped in large quantities. The ore is brought from Cumberland, and the northwestern Northumberland Hills, and also from Durham, and is here worked into piglead, and manufactured into sheets and pipes. This trade is even more ancient than the coal traffic.

About a mile from the place is the holy well of Jesus Mound, now called Jesmond, which was formerly a favorite pilgrim resort. During the reign of

Charles I. the city was taken by the Scottish army in 1640, and again in 1644. The Church of St. Nicholas is an ancient but spacious structure of decorated English style, having a tower and spire 193 feet high, of elegant and graceful proportions. St. Andrew's Church is an ancient Norman edifice with a large, low, embattled tower. There are other churches of considerable renown,—such as All Saints, with a circular interior, and Grecian steeple 202 feet high; and last but by no means least, the Roman Catholic Church of St. Mary, of magnificent early English architecture.

At 9.30 A. M. of the next day, Friday, we left for

DURHAM,

where we arrived in an hour. In all England no more picturesquely situated place exists, for it is embowered in trees, and stands on a rocky hill, rising from the River Wear. On the summit is the cathedral built of yellow stone. It has three towers without spires, which, together with the roof and a part of the church walls, rise imposingly out of the surrounding foliage. The place has a population of 14,406. The river banks are skirted by overhanging gardens with fine walks, beyond which the houses rise above each other, till all are crowned by the cathedral itself. To add an intensity of beauty, on the summit of a rocky eminence near by are the remains of a Norman castle. The division north of the castle contains most of the stores, and has one of those English commercial conveniences, a market-place.

Among the public buildings are a town-hall in the Tudor baronial style, a theatre, seven parish churches, a school of art, and a university. The old Church of St. Nicholas, now in thorough repair, is one of the finest specimens of church architecture in the North of England. The old castle is opposite the cathedral. It was founded by William the Conqueror, who died Sept. 9, 1087, so that the structure is eight hundred years old; and was built for the purpose of maintaining the royal authority in the adjacent district, especially by resisting the inroads of the Scots. Many additions have been made to it, so that it is now difficult to say which parts are old and which new; but no question exists in relation to the great antiquity of the foundations and lower portions, and of the very ancient date of some of the higher parts of much above them. For many years it was the residence of the bishops of Durham, but of late has been given up to the use of the university.

The See of Durham is the richest in England. The revenues are very great, and one bishop left $1,000,000 at his decease a few years ago. Collieries and railroads have given a powerful impetus to this aristocratic place, which has now considerable trade and large carpet manufactures. It has long been noted for Durham Mustard, a commodity to be found in the best groceries of America.

In the vicinity of Durham is Neville's Cross, erected by Lord Neville, in commemoration of the defeat of David II. of Scotland, in 1346. There is also a Roman fortress, called the Maiden Castle.

Durham is permeated and enveloped not only with a pleasure-inspiring element, but with those æsthetic conditions which, although obscured, here and there crop out in cathedral towns. These latter words contain the secret of all this interest—*cathedral towns*. Once England was absolutely controlled by the Church.

There is a vast deal more in the expression Church and State, than is generally understood by a young American. The Church, both temporally and spiritually, was above king, prince, potentate, or judge. This was distinctly claimed by a bull of Pope Urban, and was acknowledged till the time of Henry VIII., who struck it a death-blow by proclaiming *himself* Head of the Church. How far this was in advance of the act of Richard Coeur de Lion,— "the lion-hearted," who died April 6, 1199,—who, when he left for the Holy Land, placed his realm definitely in the hands of the Bishop of Durham, where it had practically been for a long time before.

Of course the all-absorbing object of interest is the cathedral itself. As much soil is not covered by any other building in all England of more historic renown. It is indeed a feast of intellectual "wine on the lees, and well refined." It was founded in 1093, and so was four hundred years old when the realm was being disturbed by reports that Columbus was seeking aid for the exploration of a new continent of doubtful existence. It is 507 feet long, and 200 feet wide at the transepts. It has a central tower 214 feet high, and two others that are alike, at the west end, facing down to the river, almost on the verge of the cliff-like embankments. On account of its great height it is commanding in appearance. These west towers are 143 feet high, with a lofty gable between them. The whole west front is elaborately finished, though not bold in detail. There is great boldness of outline, though no deep and very distinct ornamentation. The material is yellowish sandstone, somewhat dingy, but plainly betraying its original tint. The edifice is mainly of Norman architecture, but repairs and restorations have been made; and, according to usage, each new part was in the style of architecture presented at the period of restoration,—which was not *restoration* but *alteration*; for there was really no restoration of *design*, and sometimes not even a reproduction of *form*. All styles of ecclesiastical architecture are to be found in one building,—from the Norman, down through the Early English, to the latest or Perpendicular Gothic. This is illustrated in Durham Cathedral, for here are examples of each style, though the Norman prevails; especially in the never overpraised interior, where the ponderous round columns, with their diagonal and lozenge decorations, and the huge round arches, with splendid chevron mouldings, intersecting arches,—and every contour and combination peculiar to the best of the old Norman works,—exist in their perfection.

While the beautiful work at Winchester and York Minster, and at Salisbury and Lincoln—in their soaring columns and lofty arches, their rich traceries and decorations, their long lines of groined ceilings, and (as at Salisbury and Lichfield) their grand heavenward-pointing spires—suggest the Resurrection, and the aspiration of humanity, and so do honor to Christianity as distinguished from the low and grovelling tendency of Egyptian or Grecian temple, or even Roman,—while Gothic architecture is suggestive of these higher qualities, the solid columns and arches of Norman Durham speak of eternity, and suggest that nothing good dies. These two were the great steps taken by humanity as it became Christianized. First came a consciousness of existing good, and an accompanying desire to perpetuate it. Next came aspiration,—a reaching out and up, after still better life.

The Egyptian or Grecian mind was satisfied with things as they were, and found consequent satisfaction in the low temple of Edfu or the unpinnacled Parthenon. It was for the Christian aspiration to demand and only be partially satisfied with—tall columns and lofty arches, high towers and spires, reaching sometimes, like that at Salisbury, more than four hundred feet toward

"The third heaven where God resides,
That holy happy place."

The ponderous pyramids of Egypt, the fantastic temples of India, had height and breadth, but not a suggestion of anything above and beyond themselves. They were, after all, only heaps of material, plain like the pyramids,—or gorgeous and uncouth Indian piles, having in view the honor of some earthly king or some imaginary god, one among many. There was no attempt to do honor to the "King of kings, and Lord of lords." Nowhere were the contributions of the people concentrated for their own good, and for the blessing of generations to come. A cathedral embodies this idea. It is a connecting link between the old dispensation and the new; and, unlike our Bible, it has no blank leaves between the Old and New Testaments.

Two things in Durham Cathedral demand our particular attention. One is the Sanctuary Ground, and the other is Galilee Chapel at the west end.

Outside the cathedral, at the great northern side door, there is a large and grotesque brass knocker,—a head with staring, hollow eyes, and a ring in its mouth. In olden time a criminal, fleeing from justice, who was able to reach and lift this knocker, was safe from arrest. A monk was all the time stationed inside to open the door to every applicant. The ground-floor of the northwestern tower was the sanctuary ground. A work on the "Antiquities of Durham Cathedral" gives the following statement:—

The culprit upon knocking at the ring affixed to the north door was admitted without delay, and after confessing his crime, with every minute circumstance connected with it, the whole of which was committed to writing in the presence of witnesses, a bell in the Galilee tower ringing all the while, to give notice to the town that some one had taken refuge in the church, there was put upon him a black gown with a yellow cross upon its left shoulder, as a badge of Cuthbert, whose *girth*, or peace, he had claimed. When thirty-seven days had elapsed, if no pardon could be obtained, the malefactor, after certain ceremonies before the shrine, solemnly abjured his native land forever, and was straightway, by the agency of the intervening parish constables, conveyed to the coast, bearing in his hand a white wooden cross, and was sent out of the kingdom by the first ship which sailed after his arrival.

The old knocker remains at its post, though centuries have passed since it last rendered its sacred service, and was tremblingly grasped by a panting fugitive. We assumed this role, but, fortunately or unfortunately, could not knock as a genuine culprit could.

The Old Galilee is a room perhaps 55 feet by 75, divided by columns and arches into five sections. The architecture is decorated Norman, finely mixed with Early English, the Norman, or circular arches resting on rather slender columns. It was built by Bishop Pudsey in the twelfth century. In this chapel are the remains of the Venerable Bede, and more venerated dust reposes not in any cathedral. He was probably born in Monkton in Durham, in 672, and died at Girvy, May 26, 735. He was educated in a monastery, and his learning and ability as a scholar and writer were remarkable. He was ordained a priest at the age of thirty. His "Ecclesiastical History of the English Nation" was a work of great labor, and is still the most reliable authority on the early period of which it treats. He compiled it from chronicles and traditions handed down in the convents, and from miscellaneous testimony; and it is remarkably free from those exaggerations and contortions which fill many books of later monkish historians. His other literary labors were extraordinary, and his devotion to such work was singularly enthusiastic. It is stated that during his final illness, he continued to dictate to an amanuensis the conclusion of a translation of St. John's Gospel into Anglo Saxon; and that as soon as he had completed the last sentence he requested the assistant to place him on the floor of his cell, where he said a short prayer, and expired as the last words passed his lips. In the cathedral are copies of his "Historia Ecclesiastica," as first printed in German in 1475; others are in the British Museum and in Paris. They were translated from the Latin into Anglo Saxon by King Alfred in 1644, and into English in 1722,—and many times since, the latest translation having been made in 1871.

It should be stated that pretended bones of Bede are scattered throughout the world; and though his monument is here, but little if any of his mortal remains are beneath it. Large volumes of manuscripts in his handwriting are in the library of the cathedral, and they are of inexpressible interest. It is related in the old chronicles that, being blind during the latter days of his life, he was led one day by a dissembling guide to a pile of rough stones, and told that there was present a company of persons desiring to hear him preach. Inclined to gratify their request he preached to them, and when he finished, the stones, animated by divine power, ejaculated, like an assembled multitude, "Deo gracias, Amen."

In this Galilee room are also the remains of St. Cuthbert, the patron saint of the church, who died in 687. He was, in 644, prior at Melrose Abbey. His austerity and fondness for monastic life were remarkable, and in order to gratify his feelings he retired to the Island of Farne. It was a very barren place, and destitute of wood or water, but he dug wells and cultivated grain. The fame of his holiness brought many visitors, among them Elfleda, daughter of King Osway the Northumbrian, with whom he condescended to converse through a window; but for more effectual seclusion from the self-invited crowd, he dug a trench around his cabin and filled it with water. In 684 he was induced to yield to the prayer of King Egfrid and accept the bishopric of Hexam, and from this he removed to Lindisfarne. After two years he resigned this office, so uncongenial to his taste, and retired to end his life in his former hut on the Isle of Farne. He died in it, and when the Danes invaded the ecclesiastical domain of Lindisfarne, the fleeing monks carried his remains with them from place to place, till at last they were deposited on the banks of River Wear, where a shrined convent arose, then a church, and finally this cathedral at Durham.

The legends concerning him are among the literary treasures of the cathedral, and by reason of the traditions as well as history are not unworthily appreciated. No one dead has spoken more effectually to the living than he. His name and fame, as a great intercessor with the Almighty, were for centuries a household word. He was considered by the northern peasantry as the saint of saints, and constant, tedious, and sacrificing pilgrimages were made to his shrine. Bede says that his body was found incorrupt eleven years after burial, and that it so continued. The coffin was opened in 1827, and the corpse found to be enveloped in five silken robes. The eyes were of glass, movable by the least jar, and the hair was of a fine gold wire. These things were done by deceptive priests, who annually pretended to take or cut hair from his head, which they said grew immediately. This is not the St. Cuthbert who was a Benedictine monk, a pupil of Bede, and who attended him in his last hours, and finally wrote the memoir of his life. There was yet another Cuthbert who was Bishop of Canterbury from 740 to 758.

The cathedral has but few monuments, and these are not of great interest. It is somewhat remarkable that monuments seem to prevail in some cathedrals, and that there is an absence of them in the others. Some communities then, as in our own day, appeared to consider the commemoration of the dead as a religious duty, and others to neglect the practice, or consider it hardly worthy of their attention. The places of New England burial in their respective variety of care or neglect attest this.

"For thus our fathers testified,—
That he might read who ran,—
The emptiness of human pride,
The nothingness of man."

This cathedral has had a long list of bishops, and among them very distinguished men. The name Durham has an ecclesiastical charm to a churchman, and to him the phrase, "Bishop of Durham," suggests honor, dignity, and renown.

Here once presided Bishop Poore, the famous architect of the cathedral of Salisbury. He was translated from that See to this, and was bishop here from 1228 to 1237, when he died; and then, in 1311, Richard Kellow was elected bishop. He brought with him an inflexible piety, but colored with the extremest humility of the cloister. He was celebrated for a steady and unflinching sense of duty. The meanest vassal shared his protection, and neither wealth nor rank could with him screen a criminal from punishment; and the proudest baron within his bishopric was once obliged to submit to the public penance imposed by a humble ecclesiastic, who, without forgetting his duties, made the imposition, and was sustained by Kellow.

Richard Fox, the founder of Corpus Christi College at Oxford, was bishop here from 1494 to 1501, when he was translated to Winchester. He was afflicted with blindness for many years before his death, but under the pressure of age and infirmity, yet doing his work well, his spirit of integrity was yet unbroken; and when Cardinal Wolsey, desiring his place, wished him to resign his bishopric, he replied that he could no longer distinguish black from white, yet he could discriminate right from wrong, truth from falsehood, and could well discern the malice of an ungrateful man. He then warned the proud favorite of the king to beware, lest ambition should render him blind to his surely approaching ruin; and he bade him attend closer to the king's legitimate business, and leave Winchester to her bishop. The aged prelate died in 1528, and was buried in his own chapel in Winchester Cathedral, where his tomb and its monument exist as fine specimens of the latest style of Gothic architecture.

The cardinal was himself Bishop of Durham for six years, and by reason of his grasping spirit and hold on the king, he was at the same time Archbishop of York; but at the death of Fox, the longed-for chair was vacant; he at once resigned York, and was made Bishop of Winchester. He continued to hold the See of Durham, but was never afterwards known to visit it.

It would be pleasant as well as instructing to review the life of this remarkable man, but limits forbid. Other bishops could with advantage be spoken of,—and they are many, and the record is interesting,—but we must forbear.

We only say in closing, that very eminent and conspicuous among them is the name of Joseph Butler, who was made Bishop of Durham in 1750, having been translated from the See of Bristol. He was born in Wantage, May 18, 1692, and died at Bath, while there on a visit in hope of recovering his health, June 16, 1752. No man has possessed more strength of mind, or better acuteness and clearness of reasoning than he, and of this his well known "Analogy of Religion" is ample proof. Nor have any excelled him in goodness of heart. He held the See but eighteen months; and, although in advanced years, he is spoken of to this day as a person of genuine modesty and a natural sweetness of disposition. It is said that when engaged in the more immediate work of his office,—preaching,—that a divine illumination seemed to pervade his entire being, and to fill the whole atmosphere. His pale and wan countenance was lighted up by a transfiguring light, as though the Holy Ghost were indeed speaking through him.

We must refrain from a long description of relics and especial things of interest seen here, but will name a small box in which are three gold seal-rings, not long ago removed from the coffins of bishops; one from the finger of Flumbard, who died in 1128; one from William of St. Barbery, 1153; and the other from Galfred Rufus, 1140. Next, are rings and other iron-work from St. Cuthbert's coffin; also, gold hair-wire, and parts of his robe. Books written by monks, and other things of moment and interest, are in profusion.

We would speak of the remarkable marble pulpit just put in, which cost $25,000,—of the elegant stained windows, of the grand old carved reredos, with the great number of statuettes; but we must forbear, and now take leave of the grand old place and of Durham itself. We have named but a few of the many things of great interest and moment. As each of these chapters terminates, there is painfully apparent a consciousness of what has *not* been described or even named, as well as regrets at the fact of a mere skeleton of description when the best thing has been done. If, however, enough has been said, and left unsaid, to create a taste for further reading, pursuit of information, consultation of histories, cyclopædias, and repositories of information relating to these things, then our best work is done, and our highest anticipations realized. And now at 3.45 P. M., this same day of arrival, we leave for York, the seat of the celebrated York Minster, of not only English celebrity but of world-wide renown.

CHAPTER XVI.

YORKSHIRE—YORK—SHEFFIELD—LINCOLN.

We are now leaving Durham for a ride of sixty-seven miles to the city of York, the other fashionable metropolis of England. The passage is through the county of Yorkshire, which, for the combination of good agriculture, population, manufactures, beauty of scenery, and historical renown, is not excelled if equalled by any other county of Great Britain. The people are peculiar, and have a dialect of their own; they are tall in stature, shrewd at bargains, and are tenacious of their own manners and customs. Here abound grand mansions, and large tracts of land laid down as parks, and so we find less uncared land than in any other part of England.

One cannot travel over this country and not think of the time when William the Conqueror, by his hostility to the inhabiting Saxons, caused destruction and ruin to prevail. History says:—

He wasted the land between York and Durham, so that for threescore miles there was left in manner, no habitation for the people, by reason whereof it laid waste and desert for nine or ten years. The goodlie cities, with the towers and steeples set upon a statelie height, and reaching as it were into the air; the beautiful fields and pastures watered with the course of sweet and pleasant rivers; if a stranger should then have beheld, and also knowne what they were before, he would have lamented.

We do not stop here, but can hardly fail to think of the Conquerer himself. As he lay in the agonies of death he cried out:—

Laden with many and grievous sins, O Christ, I tremble, and being ready to be taken by Thy will into the terrible presence of God, I am ignorant what I should do, for I have been brought up in feats of arms even from a child. I am greatly polluted with the effect of much blood. A royal diadem that never any of my predecessors did bear I have gotten; and although manly greediness on my triumph doth rejoice, yet inwardly a careful fear pricketh and biteth me when I consider that in all these cruel rashness hath raged.

But we must leave these intervening lands and speak of the famed city itself.

YORK.

This is *Old* York, while our New Amsterdam that was, Manhattan Island, is the *New* one. It is the capital of Yorkshire, and situated on both sides of the River Ouse, at its junction with the River Foss, and is 175 miles from London. Its population is 43,709. The river is crossed by a fine stone bridge, while there are also several others of less repute. The city is very compactly built. It is but three miles in circuit, and was once entirely, and is now partly, surrounded by walls originally erected by the Romans. It was entered by gates, four of which remain as they were centuries ago. The streets are not very wide, but are well paved and very neat, and the city presents a solid and substantial appearance. It has a good commercial or trade aspect in the market parts, and in the other portions has a homelike atmosphere, and a very large number of hotels, for the place is one of resort for fashionable winter life. It is the emporium of style for the northern part of England, and in this respect is hardly inferior to London. The buildings are mainly of brick, three or four stories high.

Its history reaches far back into antiquity. During the Roman dominion, York was the seat of the general government, and was important while London was yet rude and semi-barbaric. Are we fully prepared to realize that the Roman Emperor Septimus Severus lived here, and here died in the year 212, or but 179 years after the death of Christ? Here also died in 306, Constantius Cholorus, the father of Constantine the Great. 1577 years are gone since the death of the distinguished individual named! In the war with William the Conqueror, the citizens joined with the Scots and Danes for his repulsion, but on their defeat they razed their homes and city to the ground. It was rebuilt, and was destroyed by fire in 1137. During the great massacre of the Jews, which took place in England after the coronation of Richard I., several hundred Jewish inhabitants of York, having in vain attempted to defend themselves in the castle, slew their wives and children, set fire to their houses, and themselves perished in the flames. Lord Fairfax captured the place from the Royalists in 1644, and in 1688 James II., for its arbitrary measures in opposition to the crown, took away its charter, and its fortunes and conditions then varied for more than two thousand years. Indeed, its soil is classic ground. Here the Emperor Hadrian, one of imperial Rome's distinguished ones, dwelt, more kingly and regal than has since lived any king. Over these roads Severus, the great Emperor, has passed, and on Stiver's Hill, west of the city, the funeral obsequies over his mortal remains took place. Here Constantine, the first great Christian of many who came out of paganism, also dwelt. Everywhere there is a classic renown. Do we, as we are walking here on this fine summer day, comprehend the scheme? The birds in these trees sing as sweetly as in olden time; the sheep graze quietly on the outlying plains as they did a thousand years ago. The shadows, made by passing clouds, chase each other across our path as others did over theirs. Here are the same sun and similar clouds, and birds and trees, but the seasons of a thousand and a half of years intervene. Millions of beings have lived and died. Their dust has mingled with parent soil; it has been caught up, and transformed into plant and flower and tree; and, passing through fruit, or flesh of animal, into humanity, has gone back again and become mingled, and out into life yet again, and its history has been repeated in new organizations and bodies and forms.

We talk not of transmigration of soul, but we may say that the process has developed a better phase of humanity; and these last productions are more imperial and royal than Hadrian, Septimus, or Constantine; than William the Conqueror, Edward the Confessor, than Cromwell, Jeffries, or Laud. Upward and onward has been the march. The millennium has come in this way, and humanity has marched with steady tread towards it. Queen Victoria and Dean Stanley and John Bright and Gladstone are the blossoms, or a flowering-out,—a grand fruitage. In them, also, are the seed and germs of a yet greater progress, and another day is to gather fruit from these later trees, the leaves of which "are for the healing of the nations."

York gave birth, May 8, 1731, to Beilby Porteus, a distinguished prelate, who was chaplain to Secker, the Archbishop of Canterbury, in 1762, chaplain to George III. in 1769, Bishop of Chester in 1776, and Bishop of London, 1787, where he presided till his death, May 14, 1808. And she is also honored as being the birthplace of John Flaxman, the renowned sculptor, who was born July 6, 1755, and died at London, Dec. 9, 1826. Among his well-known productions are the monuments of the poet Collins at Winchester Cathedral, of Lord Nelson and of Howe, of Sir Joshua Reynolds, of Mansfield, and of Kemble. In early days he supported himself by making designs for the Wedgewoods, manufacturers of celebrated pottery and works of ceramic art; and by-and-by he astonished the world by his artistic illustration of Homer and Æschylus, and afterwards of Dante. He was also the author of Scriptural compositions,—excelling in fine diction as well as in deep religious fervor and pathos.

Here, A. D. 735, more than 1100 years ago, was born Flaccus Albinus Alcuin, even for that early day an eminent scholar and churchman, and a pupil of the Venerable Bede. He was a schoolmaster and librarian at the cathedral; and later, by invitation of Emperor Charlemagne, in 780, he went to France, probably to Aix la Chapelle, and opened a school, where his instructions were attended by the Emperor and his court; and this school is presumed to be the germ of the present University of Paris. He was the intimate friend and confidential adviser of the Emperor, and so even the destinies of nations are traced directly to him. Although he was the most learned man of his age, eloquent, pious, and renowned, yet his extreme modesty and fineness of temperament and nature caused him to shrink from the responsibilites of a bishop; and, though repeatedly urged to permit his ordination as such, he peremptorily refused, and would accept no higher office than that of deacon. He died lamented as few ever can be, May 19, 804, 1079 years ago.

Here was born in 1606, and died in 1682, Sir Thomas Herbert, the renowned traveller. Anticipating Stanley two and a half centuries, he published in 1634 his celebrated work, "Some Years' Travels into Africa, and the Great Asia, especially the Territories of the Persian Monarchy." He was made a baron by Charles II. Though a stanch and avowed Presbyterian, so kind was he, and so courteous in disposition and manner, that Charles I. retained him as one of his attendants to the last, long after all the others had been dismissed. We close the list of notable men by naming but one more of a vast number,— William Etty, the painter, born here March 10, 1787. He was a pupil of Sir Thomas Lawrence, and for a time unsuccessful; but in 1831 one of his pictures was admitted to the exhibition given by the Royal Academy, and this brought him before the public as an artist of ability. It was his "Cleopatra's Arrival at Celicia," in which the nude female form was depicted with remarkable correctness and voluptuous glow of color. He is now considered to have been one of the chief artists of the English school. He wrote his own biography, which was published in the London Art Journal in 1849. He died at York, Nov. 13, of the same year, at the age of sixty-two. The temptation is irresistible to add that in Keighly, a near town, on the 8th of December, 1823, was born that distinguished preacher and eminent lecturer, Rev. Robert Collyer, late of Unity Church, Chicago, now of the Church of the Messiah, New York; so that, by *personal* ties, *Old* and *New* York are worthily connected. Of the noble record of men of Yorkshire, there is none of which she may entertain a juster pride, than that of our great American divine.

We now leave York as a city, and her especial celebrities, to speak of two things of great interest to all tourists, viz: the remains of the abbey, and the famed York Minster. The Abbey of St. Mary, now a mass of elegant ruins, is not far from the Minster. It was founded by William Rufus, who was slain in the New Forest, Aug. 2, 1100. The college connected with the abbey was founded by Henry VI., who is believed to have been killed in the Tower of London in May, 1471. The grounds are acres in extent, and are well kept as a choice park, with great neatness and care. We enter them through a gate, at the side of which is a lodge, where tickets are procured, and guide-books, containing engravings, and an account of the premises from their first use for the abbey and its collegiate purposes. Elegant lawns and undulatory lands are here; grand old trees, large and vigorous; finely graded avenues and paths; clumps of flowering shrubs, among them the best of rhododendrons, which on the day of our visit were in fine bloom; and to add to the beauty of the scenery, sheep, such as England, and perhaps only Yorkshire, can boast; Jersey and Alderney cows quietly grazing,—neither sheep nor cows noticing the visitors, the best possible specimens of mind-their-own business-individuals seen on our whole journey. These all combine to give a tranquillity and finish to the landscape, such as befit the place now in use for centuries,—glorious in age, and charming in its loveliness.

The ruins are of the choicest and most enchanting kind, with high walls, columns, arches, mouldings, buttresses, and every detail in full, of window and door; and such a carpet of nice low-cropped but thick grass as is seldom seen. What finish everywhere! How little to touch in the way of repair or amendment! Here, as on all ruins, is the companion-like ivy, doing its good work. These ruins seem to be at home. The others we have seen appeared to have a solitary beauty; but here, so in the city, and surrounded by every-day life, finish, care, and animation, they are not companionless.

There is a sweet and indescribably good influence about a place like this. How one enjoys the odor of these flowers, the shade of these venerable trees, and of the walls themselves. How easy it is to commune in the extemporized reverie,—and it's no hard task here to extemporize one; how easy it is to "call up spirits from the vasty deep."

We examine the great things, and then sit down and admire; next we walk around and get new views. We think of novitiate, of nun, of monk, of collegian, dead and gone five hundred years. Next we go to the museum, a building on the grounds and part of the good premises. Between the main ruins and this building are small ruins, or evidences of things that were, but are not. We go in, and, as at the gate-lodge, a woman is in attendance, and desires a shilling, and we are willing, for the treat, to each give her one. We go in, and what interests are awakened! Old Rome herself can do no better. Not works of Englishmen are now to be examined, or of Briton even,—of Scot or of Celt, but of them of the Eternal City bred and born.

A new station for the railway was built a few years ago, and in digging for the foundation a large lot of things of Roman manufacture were found, which, with others once belonging to the venerable abbey, are now deposited here. Among the more noted objects of interest are stone coffins, in which are bodies, covered by a coarse cloth, and as they are imbedded in lime, it would appear that it must have been put about them in a liquid form. Some of these date back fifteen hundred years. Next are pieces of Roman pavement, into which are wrought various devices; and there are also many common, red-clay, earthen pots and jars, or vases of different sizes; a majority of them would hold about three gallons each. These were filled with ashes and burnt bones. They were nearly full, and the materials had either been forced in quite compactly or this solidity came by reason of age. In a glass case, some sixteen inches square and six inches deep, is the scalp of a Roman lady, almost entire, showing the brown hair very perfect, and arranged as it was at the time of her death. This was taken from a leaden coffin in which were found the remains, the date showing that they were buried full sixteen hundred years ago. There is also a display of pottery and household implements, old Roman statuary and utensils; and monumental stones and things of the kind are here in abundance.

Aside from these, and in addition, are many things once belonging to the abbey,—the whole a befitting appendage to these ancient grounds. It would seem that there is, in this famed enclosure alone, enough to amply repay one for a journey from America to York. If these ancient things could speak, they would want no more potent words put into their mouths than those of Burns, when he says

O wad some pow'r the giftie gie us,
To see, oursels, as others see us.

We are depending a bit on punctuation to aid the thought and application. Not so much as having heard of these ruins beforehand, we were the more surprised; in plastic condition of mind the impression was made, and it is indelible. "Forget what we may, let what will of our thought become bedimmed,—let memories of St. Mary's remain and be good and fresh as now," said we then, and repeat ever. Our first visit to York Minster was made soon after our arrival. At 6 P. M. the doors are closed, and as it was near or quite that hour, we were content with the good and great privilege of examining the elegant grounds and magnificent exterior. The former are quite large and properly enclosed. The same carpet-like lawn-grass abounds, with a few grand avenues and paths over it, and trees of good age. All was cathedral-precinct-like, tranquil and sanctified; but even here sin and its consequences were present in material form, and the manifestation was quite what happens in Boston, where we have no venerable cathedral nor such grounds.

Off a hundred or more feet from the building, reclining on the grass and asleep, was a man beastly drunk. Two policemen came and aroused him and led him away. As at home, boys and women were interested and followed. To the credit of the policemen they did their work well, and in a way befitting the place, they could not well use less force, and they needed to use no more. As we saw the old, old sight, we thought of the terse and comprehensive verdict of Boston's once famous coroner, Pratt, who had held an inquest on one found not only dead drunk, as this man was, but *drunk dead*; and the simple verdict was, "Rum did it." Many instances occur where we have to repeat the old verdict. It's a good safety-valve to our feelings, and having said a true, a comprehensive, an all-the-ground-covering thing, we "rest the case." Rum does it there and here and everywhere, the world over.

The great edifice is built of a yellowish and perishable sandstone; parts of it are now in much decay, and the dust or sand lay in small heaps, even about the threshold of the main entrance doors. It reminded us of the yellow dirt we call powder-post, from a dry-rot decaying pine timber. For the most part, however, the structure is in good repair, and in a short time this great west front will be attended to. The decorations of this part are very rich and elaborate. The whole is of exquisite proportions and design, even to minute details. This is the most highly wrought of all the cathedral churches of England. It is the largest so far as extent of ground covered, though not the longest, as it is excelled in length by Winchester, and perhaps by one or two others. The history of the establishment begins in the seventh century; but the present edifice was not begun till after 1150, and it was not completed till 1472, and had been twenty years finished when Columbus discovered America. It is in the form of a cross, with a magnificent square central tower at the intersection, 213 feet high, or only seven feet lower than Bunker Hill monument, though it has not that effect of height. There are two other towers flanking the west front. These are each 196 feet high. They end with an elegant light parapet, and turrets at the four corners and centres. The extreme length is 524 feet. The breadth at transepts is 247 feet. The great east window is 78 feet high and 32 feet wide, filled with elegant stained glass representing about 200 historic events. The tower has a peal of 12 bells, one of which weighs 11½ tons, and is with the exception of that on the great clock tower at the Houses of Parliament, and the new one just placed on the tower of St. Paul's at London, the largest bell in the kingdom.

We have spoken especially of its exterior, and are to speak of its interior and its bishops; but before we do so, we are inclined to think we shall once for all render a good service if we devote part of our space to saying a few words in defining or explaining these terms, *minster* and *cathedral*, for as a general thing they are not well understood. We have previously said something on the point, but at the risk of being accused of repetition, will more definitely state the case.

Till the time of Constantine no houses for Christian worship existed. After his conversion to Christianity, or as soon as A. D. 325, they were not only tolerated but encouraged. Soon some of them came to be large and imposing, and the assemblies were composed of rich and influential persons. These congregations being able to well support and appreciate preachers of ability and renown, such divines were established at important stations. By and by assistants were demanded; next, canons or special preachers; and yet again others, as assistants in parish work. A place like this was called a cathedral, and all such churches were known by that name. In process of time the term came to denote only the one church in a diocese at which the bishop presided, or was identified with, and is so used to this day. There were of course other large churches or edifices quite equalling in financial standing, or in social and general dignity and influence, the cathedral itself, and these were not inclined to pay obedience to the bishop, and they simply remained as they were,—in fellowship, if we may use the expression, with the whole Church, but yet independent of it so far as the bishop's, or any outside authority, was concerned; so it is seen that Independency did not originate with the Puritans or Dissenters. Westminster Abbey is of this class, and this accounts for the independent condition of Dean Stanley, who from his office of Dean of Westminster, owed no allegiance to the Bishop of London, although the abbey is but a mile from, and in sight of, St. Paul's Cathedral. An abbey like Westminster is, if we may so say, the church of an abbey once at Westminster; while the abbey itself was destroyed, the church has remained. A *minster* like this at York, or that at Beverly, is the church edifice, or place of religious worship, of a former monastery, and so is called York minster.

Next a word in regard to the Archbishopric of York. An archbishop is the head bishop, to preside at meetings of the house of bishops, and to exercise some especial functions, like the president of an association, but subject to rules and regulations in the performance of his work as set forth by ecclesiastical laws made by the convocation of bishops. Canterbury has from the first been the seat of the archbishop, and of course great importance and dignity attach to the place where the archbishop's seat is. York having for centuries been very important in wealth and social standing, and possessing the grand old minster, disputed this claim, and at times was influential enough to seriously interfere with the ancient arrangement; and, as a sort of compromise, York was advanced to a position second only to that of Canterbury. Its bishop, or head official, is dignified with the title of Archbishop of York, and is therefore the second primate of England; or, as we may better express it, he is the vice-bishop of the entire English Church. The principal seat of the Archbishop of Canterbury, and of the whole Church, is at Lambeth Palace, on the Thames below Southwark, and opposite the Houses of Parliament. Here are held all great convocations of bishops, and the business of the Church is done here; but by ancient usage Canterbury Cathedral is the seat of the archbishop, or, as he is termed, the Primate of all England. Some years ago an arrangement was made whereby some few places, or Sees, hereafter named, were given into the charge of the Archbishop of York, so that he is an archbishop by virtue of his office, though yet inferior to his lordship of Canterbury. We next proceed, after the long digression, to speak of the interior of the cathedral, or minster.

It is grand and imposing, and its great width and height impress the beholder with a feeling of reverence and awe. The windows are of painted glass. Most of them are ancient and dim-appearing, and probably were never of rich design or very brilliant color. Every part of this vast interior is in the best possible repair, and the utmost neatness prevails. The cathedral has a crypt, or basement, and centuries ago it was customary to hold services in it. By the payment of a sixpence each, persons are permitted to visit it in company with the verger; and at all cathedrals, and in waiting, are these guides. It should be understood that visitors are freely and gratuitously admitted at any time from sunrise to sunset to all the cathedrals, but for visiting especial parts, such as the top of the tower, the crypt, if there is one, or places where valuable relics are kept, this small fee named is taken, first, as payment of salary for the guides, who are in constant attendance, and next, the surplus goes for repairs of the cathedral; and we may add that we visited none where workmen were not making repairs.

We cheerfully paid our fee and went down into the grand old crypt, now full one thousand years old. Indescribable are the sensations experienced and the emotions awakened as one is here. The place is but dimly lighted, and there are antique and grotesque columns and arches, solid, prison-like masonry, and groined ceilings of stone. It is not hard to imagine the former sound of sandal-footed monks or nuns, of subdued voices engaged in prayer,—to know of the odor of incense, wandering about the columns and arches as it did of old. All is solid, fortress-like, and secure; but in spite of solidity and thick stone walls, the aspirations of monks and nuns went out through them, for their prayers were not confined. Centuries now are gone since their spirits went out of their bodies, and the custom even of their service here came to an end. The new dispensation has come, "a better covenant, established on better promises." The race has advanced; and now, nought but the grand and vast light room above, the incense of an intelligent devotion, and the music of the great organ can render the desired aids to devotion. We find here a superb reminder of a vast antiquity, in a piece of Saxon work in stone, of the *herring-bone* pattern. This was part of an ancient Saxon church, built before the visit of the Normans. Do we comprehend the fact? No. We believe the story, and admire the place; and next, as best we can, we try and know the thing as no one can know it for us, but with only partial success.

At the rear of the altar is the tomb and monument of Tobias Matthew, one of the early translators of the Bible into the English language, who was the author of the address, or preface, to the King James translation in present use. The chapter-house is entered from the north transept, and is a room of remarkable elegance. All is of course built of stone. The ceiling is strangely elaborate, and there is a wainscot around the room, at the top of which is elegant flower and leaf work, and vines, with a profusion of grotesque figures of nondescript animals.

At the right side of the choir is a chapel, in which are kept a few things of unusual interest. Here is a Bible and Prayer Book, presented by Charles I. to the cathedral; also a copy of the Bible, in two large folio volumes, given by Charles II. Next, we have a fine old chair in which sat at their coronation all the Saxon kings. There is also a silver crozier of seven pounds' weight, and 200 years old. As at Durham, here also are exhibited gold seal-rings once worn by bishops, and each is nearly or quite seven hundred years old.

What as a whole was most entertaining was a drinking-vessel, in the shape of a buffalo horn. It is over one thousand years old. The grant of land on which this cathedral stands was made by Prince Ulpus, and, according to the usage of the time, wine was put into this horn, and in presence of the cathedral authorities was drank by the Prince, or donor; and the horn was then presented, to be forever kept as evidence of the grant. The last royal marriage solemnized in the minster was of Edward III., of the Norman line, to Philippa, daughter of the Count of Hainault, Jan. 24, 1328.

The elaborate choir-screen is of a light-tinted stone, and in niches contains statuettes of all the kings of England from William the Conqueror, who died at Rouen, Sept. 9, 1087, to Henry VI., who died in 1471 in the Tower of London. The structure was injured by fire in the roof in 1829, and again in 1840. The archbishop's palace is on the north side of the cathedral. It was built near the close of the twelfth century, and is used as the library of the dean and chapter. The archbishop's present residence is at Bishopthorpe, a short distance from the city. His ecclesiastical province includes the dioceses of Carlisle, Chester, Durham, Manchester, Ripon, Sodor and Man, York, and Newcastle-on-Tyne.

At 2 P. M. of this Saturday, June 8, we took train for

SHEFFIELD,

where we arrived at 5.30, after a ride of 3½ hours. It was our anticipation of remaining here till dark, about 9 P. M.; but, owing to an earlier departure of the train than we anticipated, we were compelled to be satisfied with a stay of but one hour. Not entertaining a desire for long tarries in these great manufacturing centres, we found this visit answered our purpose well enough. The city is situated at the junction of the River Sheaf, and three smaller streams uniting with the River Don. These streams together form a grand water-power, which is used in this great seat of manufactures. The city is very compactly built on the side of a hill in amphitheatre form, and open to the northeast. It has a dingy look, and is much smoked. The streets are well paved, of good width, and are quite inviting. It has a population of 261,019. Sheffield was one of the Saxon towns, and received its charter as a market-town from Edward I. in 1296. Early in the fifteenth century it was under control of the earls of Shrewsbury, who had a castle here, and a manorhouse in a park a mile east. It was in one of these that the greater part of the captivity of Mary Queen of Scots was passed. The castle was demolished by order of Parliament in 1648; and in 1707 the park of the manor was divided into farms. The place is celebrated for its manufacture of cutlery, as well as for a vast amount of other metallic goods, as steel wire, Britannia, and German silver-work. The cutlery business was of very early date, and a Cutler's Company was incorporated by statute of James I. in the sixteenth century. It had a large monopoly, which, interfering with the business of the place, was somewhat restricted in 1801, and wholly abolished in 1814, after a use and authority of nearly 300 years. In 1864 the breaking away of the Bradfield reservoir in the hills above the city, like the disaster at our Mill River, Massachusetts, destroyed $5,000,000 worth of property, and caused the loss of 300 lives.

The town, by reason of neglect of proper drainage, is very unhealthy; and in addition is the unhealthfulness of some of the occupations, so that the bills of mortality are greater here than in any other place of England. The railway stations being about a mile apart, we went on foot, and so were able, aided by the amphitheatre-like form of the place, to obtain a pretty correct judgment in regard to it; and then our remaining ride out through it, and the view from the suburbs, confirmed all; and so we felt that it was enough to say we had seen the famed Sheffield,—a place where from time out of mind have been made knives, bearing the stamp of Rogers & Sons. We had hoped to catch a view of their famed manufactory, but did not. This name, and that of Day & Martin, High Holborn, London, are familiar to every American schoolboy. What civilized community has not at some time used things from both places?

At 6.30 P. M. this Saturday night, when, as in any of our great New England manufacturing places, thousands were released from their week's labors, and were out on the streets for their Saturday night purchases, and a great crowd of people were at the station, bound somewhere,—amid this scene, and making two of the crowd, we took our seats in the car for

LINCOLN,

and in two hours arrived there. Another cathedral town, and a grand one, the capital of Lincolnshire and a county in itself. It is situated on the River Witham, and has a population of 26,762. It has grand elements of antiquity flavoring its history. It abounds with ancient remains, including the castle of William the Conqueror, and traces of town walls, a gateway of which, still standing, is one of the most perfect relics of Roman architecture to be found in the country. It has a fine old conduit; also the palace of King John of Gaunt, and many antique houses. There is no single place of England where there is a better blending of the very old and the very new than is to be found here. After the departure of the Romans, Lincoln became the capital of the Saxon kingdom of Mercia, and suffered much during the struggles of the Saxons and Danes. It was at the time of the Conquest, and long after, one of the richest places in England. It suffered greatly during the baronial wars, and also in the civil ones, when its grand cathedral was used for barracks. The city is well built. It has an old and substantial look, though not one of antiquity like parts of Chester and Shrewsbury. These two are the ones of all England that carry us—by many of their houses, stores, public buildings, and entire streets—far back into an exquisitely interesting antiquity. Here we have all the marks of age, of good old-fashioned domestic life and comfort,—whole streets of stores of a fair average grade, and a busy population; and so it is a good place of residence, and a very desirable spot to visit. The principal buildings are the county-hall and jail, within the old castle walls; the ancient guildhall; a session-house; city jail, and house of correction; and a grammar school founded in 1583. There is a very old Roman canal called Fossdike, connecting the city with the River Trent. The place is distinguished for having given birth to the renowned King John of Gaunt, or Ghent, the fourth son of Edward III., born in 1340, and died 1399.

The principal industries are breweries, tanneries, iron-foundries, grist-mills, boat-yards, and rope-walks, and in the vicinity are good nurseries, lime-kilns, and brick-yards. It may be said that this, as well as most English cities, is built mainly of brick. The land is level at the railroad station, and in a part of the business portions, and then rises very abruptly and at an inclination quite hard to climb. Full two thirds of the place are on this hill. The streets here are much steeper than any in our Boston, at the West End, and a few of the thoroughfares are so conditioned as to make it necessary to put iron handrails on the sides of buildings, and even at the edgestones of sidewalks. All is very clean, well paved and lighted, and thoroughly supplied with water. At the top of the hill and surrounded by houses, mansions, and stores, are the grounds of its grand and indescribably fine cathedral.

As we have before said, when we approach one of these structures, so imposing and wonder-inspiring,—so out of proportion with everything else to be seen or imagined in the region,—when we suddenly come upon one of these, we are inclined to consider this to be *the* cathedral, and as though there was, or could be, but one in all England, and this enough for all, and that the remainder were simply parish churches. We wonder every time anew, how they could have come into existence; where the means for their erection came from, and what influence could possibly have been brought to bear on any lot of mortals to induce the required interest.

The later thought is that it was done centuries ago, when monastery and abbey and priory and convent were in full action, church and state one, Papacy powerful in the extreme, this life nothing, and the other everything. A superstitious reverence was superior to an intelligent Christian faith; and so time, labor, money, all were free to erect these great centres of religion and faith.

Next, the country was divided into communities with interests of their own, and composed, as it were, of tribes, often hostile to each other, though entertaining a common superstition and reverence for what they thought to be truth and divine things. There were few roads across the country, and so comparatively little intercommunication or exchange of thought. With no books and no newspapers, the people were shut in and ignorant; and only was the condition disturbed and the lines removed when by some invasion,—as of Saxons or Normans, of Danes or of Scots,—or the result of civil war, the kingdom of Mercia or of Northumbria became weakened and was absorbed by a stronger power. These cathedral towns or provinces were then realms with an identity of their own; and so cathedrals were not only possible, but necessities, and were begun, and continued, and used for centuries, till by-and-by, isolation being unnatural, the great laws of association acting,—for "He made of one blood all nations of men, to dwell on all the face of the earth,"—as enlightenment came, advancement came also; a union of interest followed, which meant a division for use of the best things; and then cathedrals became in a sense common property, not only to people of England, but by-and-by to those of America as well.

Protestantism has not thus far been favorable to the production of cathedrals equalling those of old; but it has of late begotten a new spirit and desire for restorations and repairs, and is to-day, and for a half-century has been, conscious of its responsibilities to care for and preserve these great achievements of genius and taste; and so this seed sown will germinate and bear its fruit, which will be in the "good time coming." Those of that day, greatly advanced and advancing, will build new ones outglorying even the old. This is sure to come. The race does not recede. At times the work goes slowly, and seems to be retarded. The march is yet on and up, despite appearances to the contrary. As one in looking at a company of persons passing up the inclined road of the tower of Pisa, when the company are in particular positions would consider them at a standstill, so to observers of humanity, inaction appears sometimes to be the condition; but it is on and up, and when farther around on the great road, the whole is seen at a flank view, and the entire procession is found to be grandly advancing.

We are now back from a long detour, and speak of this elegant cathedral. It is built of a drab-colored stone, and is in fine repair. We pass through a large arched gateway, with keeper's lodge at the left hand, and into the cathedral precincts. Not now have we a great lawn or close, but nicely macadamized streets and roads in front of the great structure, and along the right side and back around the rear. On these borders are buildings belonging to the corporation,—schools, canons' residences, and those of curates. On the other side of the building, and at part of the rear end, is a fine old burial-ground, of some two acres, and charming in the extreme. All is on a grand scale—cathedral, streets, and grounds.

The great front has a peculiar construction, with two elegant towers just back of it, each 180 feet high, of very elaborate finish. There is another grand tower, at centre of building, 53 feet square, and 300 feet high, equalling Bunker Hill Monument in height, with a third of another like it on its top! In this is the famous bell, Tom of Lincoln. Cathedral bells have often had names,—that is, the large ones,—as Big Ben at Westminster, Great Peter, Large David, and others. The cathedral is 524 feet long, and 250 feet wide at the transepts. It is in all respects one of the finest in the kingdom. The interior is very light, having large windows; many of them are of elegant colored glass, and superior to those at York Minster.

This cathedral, like the others, has a good history. In 1075 Remigius removed the Episcopal see from Dorchester to Lincoln, and was the first bishop. Immediately after his arrival he began to build this church. It is known to have been nearly finished, or at all events ready for use, in 1092. Remigius, feeling his end to be near, being then very aged, invited all the prelates of the realm to be present at its consecration, which was to take place on the 9th of May. Robert, Bishop of Hereford, was the only one who refused the invitation, and his excuse was that he foresaw that the cathedral could not be dedicated in the lifetime of Bishop Remigius. In those days astrology was much believed in, and its predictions were relied on as prophetic truth; and strange to say, the Bishop of Hereford's casting was right, for Remigius died May 8, 1092, the day before that set for the consecration.

Robert Bloet was the second bishop, and he completed the work and dedicated it in 1124, which was not till thirty-two years after the time originally set. Of course great repairs and restorations have from time to time been made, and there have been large extensions and additions. The interior has an unusual number of old and new monuments. We are hoping that the few hints we throw out will induce readers to investigate the cathedral question, and an abundance of good information can be found in Winkle's "Cathedral Churches of England and Wales."

It was indeed a hard blow to the Romish Church to lose these fine buildings. There was, however, an advance made, but "the end is not yet." The intelligence of this nineteenth century will not long be satisfied with present conditions. Another and fresh Reformation is sure to come. As in John Wesley's day, the great Church needs new life infused into it. Rather than ask Methodists to come and be absorbed by herself, as has of late been suggested, better that the venerable Mother Church go and dwell with the Daughter; but neither will be done. The grand old historic Church will in good time come into the ranks of a more every-day and less formal life; and the Methodist, while retaining a good per-cent of her activity, and the element that reaches the common people, will drop some of her peculiarities; and as humanity advances, both will move toward each other, and, acting in unison, hasten the time when there will be but "one fold, and one shepherd."

At noon of this day we left for Boston; and, as ever, the step was somewhat reluctantly taken, because we were in love with Lincoln; but Boston also had charms, and so we wended our way there on this fine Whitsunday. This is the paradise of the year for travel in England, and this is an Eden-like portion of the old kingdom to go over. How hallowed the hour is; what better one in which to go from this cathedral town, almost celebrated for its hostility to all that savored of non-conformity, to the one where New England Boston's John Cotton, her early minister,—here not vicar nor even curate,—left, because of his non-conformity, 243 years ago.

CHAPTER XVII.

BOSTON—PETERBORO—LYNN.

Arrived at 2 P. M. on Whitsunday, June 9. What a charm has this word Boston. It is to us of greater interest than any spot in Old England. Now the anticipations of years were about to be realized. This, our mother city, is a seaport of Lincolnshire, situated on both sides of the River Witham, and six miles from the sea. It is on the Great Western Railway, 107 miles northeast of London, and has a population of 15,576, which was the number of our Boston's population in 1765, more than a century ago. The two divisions of the town are connected by an iron bridge of 86½ feet span, so it will be seen the river is quite narrow at this part, which is about the centre of its population and business. The place may be said to be noted for the neatness of its streets. It is well lighted, and supplied with water from a distance of 14 miles. There is a grammar school, established in 1554, and founded by William and Mary. It has a court-house and a market-house, and there are commodious salt-water baths, established in 1830 for the use of the public. Its principal manufactures are sail-cloth, cordage, leather, and brass and iron work. A monastery was established here in 654, by the Saxon St. Botolph, and was destroyed by the Danes in 870. Hence, as Lombard says, "the name of Botolph's town, commonly and corruptly called Boston." During the civil wars Boston was for a time the headquarters of Cromwell's army. Its decline subsequent to the sixteenth century was caused by the prevalence of the plague, and also by the increasing difficulty of the river's navigation. The healthfulness of the place has been greatly improved by drainage of the surrounding fens, and commercial prosperity has been somewhat restored by the improvements of the river. Vessels of 300 tons may now unlade in the heart of the city.

The city is celebrated as the birthplace of John Fox, the martyrologist, in 1517. His "Book of Martyrs" first appeared in London in 1563. In his introduction he says that it details "the great persecutions and horrible troubles that have been wrought and practised by Romishe prelates, especially in this realme of England and Scotlande, from the yeare of our Lorde a thousande, unto the tyme now present." The work met with great success, though its truthfulness has always been denied by the Catholics. He died in London in 1587, at the age of seventy.

The building of most interest of course to us Americans is the grand old church of St. Botolph, for it was in this church that John Cotton was vicar, and going as he did from there to our Boston, and being minister of its first church, our city was named Boston in honor of him. The edifice is built with its west end, at the centre of which is the elegant tower, with only a narrow road in front, facing the river, the rear end extending well up into the fine square, or most business-like part of the city. It is of a brown sandstone, 291 feet long, 99 feet wide; and the grand west-end tower, with its fine lantern, but with no spire above it, is 291 feet high, or just the length of the entire church. There is a good burial-ground around it, kept with remarkable neatness.

The interior is very grand and imposing, having the usual range of columns and Gothic arches, and all is in color a very light cream-tint, or almost white. The great east window of the chancel was paid for by the subscriptions of American Bostonians, and is a worthy and elegant testimonial. This is the largest church without transepts in the kingdom. It was built in 1309, and so is now 574 years old, but in most perfect repair. All the surroundings are very neat, and the parish is one of great influence and importance.

Rev. John Cotton, who connects our Boston so intimately with it, was born at Derby, England, Dec. 4, 1585. He was educated at Trinity College, Cambridge, where he was entered in his thirteenth year. In 1612, or at the age of 27, he became vicar of St. Botolph's, where he remained for 20 years, and was noted for fine elocutionary power, and as a controversialist. He inclined toward the doctrines and worship of the Puritans, and was so influential that he carried a large part of his people with him; and great danger was threatened to the parish in denominational points of view. He would not kneel at the sacrament, and his non-conformism at length became so apparent, and was pronounced so odious, that he was ordered to appear before Archbishop Laud's high-commission court. He was too confirmed in his opinions to recant; and for safety fled to London, where he remained for some time, and then left for America, arriving in our Boston, Sept. 4, 1633.

In October he was installed as colleague with Mr. John Wilson, pastor of the church. He was for a long time the leading spirit and mind in the New England Church. His death was occasioned by a severe cold, taken by exposure while crossing the ferry to Cambridge, where he went to preach, his death occurring Dec. 23, 1652, the length of his ministry in each of the two churches, here and in old Boston, being alike. He was very learned, and was a fine Greek critic; he is said to have written Latin with great elegance, and it is stated that he could discourse freely in Hebrew. He was a strong Calvinist, often spending twelve hours a day in reading Calvin's works.

He was very strict in his observance of the Sabbath, and in accordance with his interpretation, and from the authoritative nature of the statement that "the evening and the morning were the first day," he argued for the keeping, as holy time, from Saturday evening at sunset, till sunset of Sunday; and so influential was he that he stamped the impress of his belief and custom on all New England, and thousands yet living remember well the practice. In fact it would not be difficult to find individuals, if not families, who yet observe the custom. He was zealous for the interests of both civil and religious matters, as he understood them, and was rigid and intolerant of those who differed from him in opinion, however honest their convictions.

He was a great foe of Roger Williams, and did much towards making him odious, and caused him at length to be banished from Boston in 1635, when he went to what is now Providence, R. I. As he says: "Having a sense of God's merciful providence unto me in my distress, I called the place Providence, and desired it might be for a shelter for persons distressed for conscience."

Mr. Cotton wrote and published some works, among them one called "Milk for Babes," designed for children, but containing what would in our time be considered strong and indigestible theological meat, and so it is very properly withheld. His daughter was wife of the celebrated Dr. Increase Mather, pastor of the Second Church in our Boston, who was president of Harvard College in 1681. Their son, the renowned Dr. Cotton Mather, who was born in Boston, Feb. 12, 1663, and died Feb. 13, 1728, was named for his grandfather, John Cotton.

Our time of arrival was too late for attending service as we thought to do, and so we enjoyed a walk over the city, and much to our pleasure. As before named, the river runs through the centre of the place; and at the principal parts a wall is built along its banks, with good cut stone for a half-mile or more, with the proper stairways down to the water. The remainder of the way, and at the outskirts, the banks are very muddy and irregular, with deep gorges or indentations. They were, as we saw them at low water, full twenty feet deep, and struck us very unpleasantly. One sight impressed us rather strangely—a series of sheep, swine (perhaps), and cattle pens, with low fences for divisions, along the centre of the main street or thoroughfare, but having a good wide avenue on each side.

Hotels, or taverns, seemed to abound, and, as in all England, they have peculiar names. So interesting was this idea to us, while the theme was new, that at one time we began to note them down, but soon found the work so increasing on our hands as to compel us to desist. A few of them—though of course not all in Boston—are as follows, Old Hen and Chickens, Ring O' Bells, Little Nag's Head, Raven and Bell, Dog and Partridge, Grapes and Bell, Five Ways Inn, Packhorse Tap, Hop-pole Inn, Leather Bottle, The Old Fox Inn, The Three Cups, Haunch of Venison, Running Horse, Fighting Cocks. These are but examples of what may be seen in almost any English town. We are sorry to have to add that in old Boston, as in the new one, rum-holes and drinking places abound. In this, the mother emulates the daughter.

There are very pleasant walks out from the place, and we much enjoyed those near the suburbs, they were so much unlike anything to be seen here at home. Some of the streets of this Old Boston are very narrow and crooked, though not especially antique, nor very ancient in appearance; yet these low two-story buildings had an entire absence of so much as an intimation of anything new, though all was very clean and tidy. The walk around to the left, at the edge of the river in this district, is very charming, for from here St. Botolph's great tower is seen to fine advantage, and we shall never forget the sweet sound of the bells at sunset.

We continued our walk back into the square at the rear of the church, and now met a very large crowd of people. No homeward-bound Catholic audience in our Boston outnumbers them. It seems a service had been held at 6.30 P. M., of which unfortunately we were not aware. We availed ourselves of the opportunity of the open house, and so had a good visit to the church itself. In one of the walls was a marble tablet set up to the memory of John Cotton. It was put there by American subscriptions, through the labors and efforts of Hon. Edward Everett. The tablet, and the great east window; this old tiled floor, on which we stood, so many times walked over by Boston's great minister; these walls and columns and arches, which for twenty years resounded with his voice,—how befitting were the influences to make holy to us the Sabbath.

We had walked in the morning about the great cathedral at Lincoln, to which See this St. Botolph's pays allegiance and tribute, and where Cotton himself had many times worshipped, and had doubtless preached. We had perchance kept the early part of the day in a manner he would not approve; but now sunset had come, and freedom of action, according to his law of interpretation.

Boston has yet remaining a few of the antique buildings, and they are prized highly. We saw one, a good specimen of the kind. It was of the timber-and-plaster construction, two stories high, with three gables; and all was recently put in perfect repair, and it is said to be 600 years old. Near the venerable church is the workingmen's reading-room, in which there is a case of books donated by our city of Boston, or, it may be, by some of her citizens. We were happy to be able to make a small contribution in the shape of half a dozen of our city newspapers—Heralds, Travellers, and Journals. We had taken a room at a quiet, comfortable, little commercial-travellers' house,— and most of England's towns have them,—and so now, at 10 P. M., after a good inspiring ramble along the other side of the river, among nice little two-story brick houses with their pretty gardens, we ended the day. Monday A. M., up early for a new ramble over the place. It appeared charmingly homelike. The good market-square was just being used, and stores, or shops, were opening. We must and did pass up once more into the burial-ground, or churchyard, of St. Botolph's. We admired over again the lofty tower and belfry, which is a landmark forty miles at sea.

We tried to think of it, and see it as it is, hundreds after hundreds of years old. As the strong breeze of that clear morning blew over it, and whistled about its turrets, we saw its great power of resistance to storms, but the results of them were apparent. Time-worn, weather-beaten, and old it looked to be; and by-and-by came the thoughts that never do come early,—that all is ancient, and was very old before our country was thought of.

We walked along the farther side, to the great east division,—for there are two distinct parts to the fine old edifice,—and then, as we looked critically at the large windows, unusual in dimensions, and filled to repletion with most elegant stone tracery, we left, admiring St. Botolph's. Next we passed over the bridge, passing by the nice cream-colored hotel, and through the long and not over-wide streets, with two-story-high brick houses on either side, and here and there, on side streets, a few gardens, all not much like things American, though not peculiar enough to give them great interest; and so we passed on to the station, and had *been* to Boston,—a treat to us then, and ever since, and the time cannot be so extended as to injure the charm. We love *new* Boston now all the better since we have seen the *old*, and know it had an honorable parentage.

We now, at 8.30 A. M. on this fine Whit-Monday, June 10, leave Boston for Peterboro', another of the good cathedral towns. We have only just begun our seventh week of travel. As we here remember all we have thus far written, and think that only six weeks have been employed in making this grand tour, we are bewildered, and inclined to ask: Did we ever employ, or shall we ever use, another six weeks to so good advantage? We ride on among the hills and over fertile fields, amidst fine vegetation—fresh from some showers of yesterday, which we didn't name, they were so little disturbing. We are charmed on this tour, and admire the industry everywhere manifest; as out of our Boston, good cultivation of the land is a rule, and no exception. Here are elegant landscapes, fine trees, single and in groups, and woods, or what the English Bostonians call *forests*. We had wondered how these things were,—whether all the trees had not been cut off. We were prepared to see miles of territory treeless. But no! trees abound, and over pretty much all the territory we have been through.

Except for long lines or masses of woods, or timber-lands, such as we see at home, the aspect varies little from that of the average of New England. All that strikes one forcibly is an absence of ruggedness, and such rocky or barren conditions as we often find in New Hampshire or Connecticut, or along the Maine shore. Take the good, fertile, undulating part of New England; remove fences and stone walls, and, instead, put about a tenth as many divisions, made by hedges; reduce the number of apple orchards,—and you have the English landscape. As you near the seaboard of England from any side, you get the rocks, and more of the seaboard look. This is strikingly so at the south part of the kingdom, towards Canterbury and Brighton. Very New Englandish, even like Essex County from Salem to Newburyport, does all appear. But now at 10.30 A. M. on this Monday, after a beautiful and refreshing ride of 2¾ hours, we are at the famed cathedral city of

PETERBORO'.

Who that in other days saw the old, entertaining, and good Penny Magazine doesn't know something of this grand old place, and the cathedral with its three great west arches, and its central tower without a spire? This was a semi-holiday; it so seemed, for most of the inhabitants were in the streets, and at liberty. A pleasant day; but, though the 10th of June, it was cool enough to make our overcoats comfortable, and we wore them till noon. Valises deposited, this time at the station, we went direct to the cathedral.

It was a way we had. These great objects of interest are centres from which all other good things appear to radiate. Make for one of them and you make no mistake, for entertainment is at hand. You are well pleased; all thoughts are occupied; other persons are there before you, and are like-conditioned. Never one cathedral yet visited when we were first of the lot, or alone. The doors are always ajar and the verger in readiness, as though stationed there and in waiting for us in particular, even as though we had telegraphed that we were to come. Not at all officious are they, or over-inclined to get in our way. Never are they troublesome or interfering with even our thoughts, or quiet examination alone,—but tractable and ready, at the first overture on our part, to civilly answer any question, to explain, to tell us what we want to know. They are masters of the art of judiciously informing us that there are yet things hid from view that we can see if we wish, and how gently they name the small fee required. If there had been normal schools, or rather one, in all England, and it had been a requisite before employment in these cathedrals that they should attend the school, graduate, and then pass examination in the way of doing these things,—had this been done, no more propriety and judiciousness could be manifested.

We were surprised with the building. We admired it. We had been so highly fed on food of the kind we were getting dainty, but this was taken in with a relish. What a fine close around the old structure! How quiet! How varied its landscape! Well, the whole this time was enchanting, for it was unlike others. So many nooks and corners for pretty rambles; so many old walls and ruins about the premises; for very extended was the thing here in the centuries gone. We were in admiration with the grounds in their many departments;

for once the cathedral itself was second; but soon we turned to the thing that makes the grounds what they are, and were at first sight struck with the good repair of the entire structure, and with its clean and solid appearance. The architecture is Norman and Early English.

It is very old, for the See was established, or rather the cathedral was founded, by Peada, one of the kings of Mercia, which was one of the ancient divisions of England. It was destroyed by the Danes, and afterwards rebuilt as it is. It is 476 feet long, with transepts 203 wide, and has a central tower 150 feet high, ending with lofty turrets at the four corners. There are also two small spires at the ends of the great west front. This part forms a section 150 feet in height and breadth, and consists of three magnificent arches 80 feet high, surmounted by pediments and pinnacles, flanked by the small towers before named; and in this front the cathedral is peculiar. It was begun in 906, and at the time of the Reformation was considered one of the most splendid religious edifices in the kingdom.

The interior is very grand and imposing. It is light-colored, almost white, having been restored, as it is called; which means that repairs have been thoroughly made in every part, and all washes, or tinted coatings, have been cleaned off, and as near as possible the work left in its original or natural color. There was a time, however, when all cathedrals had more or less of gorgeous decorations in fresco and high positive colors; next a white or tinted preparation covered all; and now, as that has been removed, more or less of the old frescoes show, but of course in a badly disfigured condition, and are only interesting as relics of another age. The probabilities are, the time will come when all will be re-frescoed in the gay colors of old.

At the Reformation everything savoring of art, in the way of painting in churches, was condemned. A great reaction seems to be taking place, and the church has discovered that it is quite possible to use and not abuse these things; and in some instances artists were at work in cathedrals, painting small portions as specimens for re-decorating the entire work. Some examples of frescoed ceilings are already complete. Peterboro' is now very white and clean, and the effect of its great interior is most pleasing.

It abounds in monuments, and many of them are of great antiquity and interest. Our statement must be so meagre that we dislike at all to enter the field of description, but will venture a little.

Catherine of Aragon, first wife of Henry VIII., is buried here; and it is said that on account of the fact of this being her place of burial, the king was pleased to give orders that the cathedral be mildly dealt with, and so it escaped that destructive action that so much injured all the others.

Mary, Queen of Scots, was also buried here, but when her son James I. came to the throne, her remains were removed to Westminster Abbey, where they now repose. The graves of these two eminent women were together, and now the verger tells us: "There lies Catherine of Aragon, and there next to her, and for years was buried, Queen Mary, but by reason of that letter," pointing to a letter, glass and framed, hanging near by, "her remains were removed to Westminster." We peruse the letter in the king's handwriting, and muse on the fact with a melancholy interest, and pass on. So much was this cathedral admired by King Edgar, that he bestowed such valuable gifts upon it that he caused the name of the city to be changed to Goldenburg, the Golden Town, which title at length gave place to its present name, derived from St. Peter, to whom the cathedral was dedicated.

The dean and chapter, by virtue of their office, exercise so much authority in the civil government of the city as to make it practically under their jurisdiction.

This being Whit-Monday, and a holiday, the cathedral was open free in all parts to the public, and hundreds were going and coming all the time we were in it,—a large part of them doubtless from out of town. We were thus favored with a view of an English town on a holiday, and traces were present of what gave the country the title of Merrie Englande. All the people were well dressed, sober, courteous, and full of enjoyment. Band-concerts and horse-trots were in order, and a balloon ascension in a park. The eating-houses were full, and from our experience of the results of the practice "first come, first served," it practically meant, that he that did not first come, was likely to be served poorly, or perhaps, what was better, not served at all.

Peterboro' has the honor of being the birthplace of the renowned Dr. William Paley, who was born in July, 1743, and died May 25, 1805. He was graduated at Christ College, Cambridge, in 1763; in 1782 was made Archdeacon of Carlisle. In 1785 appeared his celebrated work, "Principles of Moral and Political Economy," the copyright of which brought him $5,000. In 1794 was published his "View of the Evidences of Christianity," and in 1802 his great work, "Natural Theology." These works were long used as text-books in theological studies, and mark their author as one of superior intellect and of profound reasoning powers. While the deductions of his reasoning and arguments from given data are freely admitted, yet later thought—and the breaking forth of that light from the Scriptures, which the Pilgrims' minister, John Robinson of Leyden, expected would come—has destroyed some of his data, or premises from which he argued, and of course the results are anything but such as in his day, and as seen from his standpoint, appeared reasonable or right.

In the vicinity of Peterboro' is Milton Park, the seat of Earl Fitzwilliam. The estate is said to be a most elegant one, and freely open to the public at certain hours of the day. This custom is one that strikes the tourist very favorably, and always awakens a sense of gratitude. No cathedral or building of importance is ever closed from, say, 9 A. M. to 6 P. M., and facilities are furnished the visitor to examine all parts. Much of it is entirely free, and when a fee is charged it is a reasonable one, and only such as will prevent a rush of loafers to the premises; and the fee goes to pay the salary of the attendant, or for repairs of the structure. And now at 3 P. M. came another time for "moving on," so we took train for

LYNN.

As will be observed, we are at times in places of very familiar names, and to us this is one, and a place also we much desired to see; for from this, our Lynn in New England took its name. It was arrived at after an hour's ride, and is a beautiful place, in certain respects reminding one of our Lynn, for, although the houses are mostly of two or of three stories in height, and of brick or stone, yet they have so many gardens intervening, and a general freedom from compactness for a majority of the place, as to give it a somewhat rural character; though in the more immediate business part it has an old, perhaps aged look, and is compact and very business-like. The streets are well paved and lighted; there are many fine stores, and the old market-square is surrounded by very substantial stone buildings.

The city is situated on the River Ouse, nine miles from the North Sea; so that, as at our Lynn, the salt water flows by its few wharves, and tides rise and fall regularly. There are here also salt marshes, and, while we were there, the tide being out, the banks of the river showed to worst, or, as we should say for our purpose, to best advantage, for we would see them at their worst, and, from the "lay of the land," could imagine them at their best. The water was, at this time of tide, down some 20 feet from the surface of land, and was perhaps 800 feet wide. The banks were quite irregular and very muddy from their top down to the water, and the river, while running in one general direction, was rather crooked. From the opposite bank was a grand sort of upland meadow, of perhaps a quarter of a mile width, and beyond this, slightly higher land, stretching well to the right and left; and of a most pleasing nature was this landscape, for there were fine mansions embowered in fine groups of trees, splendid lawns, and every evidence of a good civilization. Taken as a whole, this peculiar river, with schooners, yachts, scows and fishing-boats; a general lack of finish to anything about the river except the grand meadow and fine domain bordering it; the, to us, very natural and pleasing odor of the salt water,—even New-England-Lynn-like, as it was on this fine warm summer afternoon,—these combined to make us definite in our praise of this Lynn Harbor.

At our back was the city, and along at the edge of the river were just such old, and, if not dilapidated, certainly not lately built or repaired wharves; and on them were just such things, for fishermen's use, as are required to make a place of the kind in harmony with itself and complete. There were old warehouses, three and four stories high, quite thickly bordering on the wharf-street, or narrow roadway. Not a thing that was new any time during this half-century, and most of it was old on the other side of 1800; but the aggregate was complete, for this, like our Lynn, is a semi-commercial place. Back of these storehouses were the town streets, and the good business portion; and here in the midst was one of the best possible examples of a very large, almost cathedralish, ancient, stone, Gothic church, St. Margaret's, founded in the twelfth century. It was enclosed in part by a high but open iron fence, and the usual ancient burial-ground was about it.

Another church of antiquity and note is St. Nicholas. It was erected in the fourteenth century, and is, for a thing of the kind, one of the finest in the kingdom. It is in the Gothic style, 200 feet long, and 78 feet wide. The city has a population of 17,266, which was the population of our Lynn sometime between the years 1850 and 1860. It has been said that the place is situated on the River Ouse, that stream being the principal river, but there are four other small streams, or navigable rivers, running into the city, and these are crossed by more than a dozen bridges. Anciently the place was defended on the land side by a fosse, which is a ditch or moat, with here and there strong bastions, or battery structures; and there are the remains of an ancient embattled wall and of one gateway. The city has a free grammar school, founded in the fifteenth century. To give it character as a place of antiquity, it has the ruins of a convent and an octagonal Ladye Tower. It has several ancient hospitals for the poor, an ancient guildhall, a jail, theatre, library, mechanics' institution, a large market-house, and a fort. Up to fifty years ago the trade of Lynn took rank as the fifth in England. A bar of shifting sand at the mouth of the river seriously troubled it, and a decline came, but its good prospects are now on the increase. It has quite large exports of corn and wool, and it has shipyards, breweries, iron-foundries, cork-works, and rope and tobacco manufactories; and steamers ply between this place and Hull. Lynn was remarkable for its fidelity to the royal cause in the time of King John, who died Oct. 19, 1216; and, as a reward for its fidelity, the king presented the place with a silver cup and sword. The people were also very loyal, and espoused the cause of Charles I., who was beheaded in London, Jan. 30, 1649.

Our rambles along the river and through the streets of this place were very entertaining; a rural atmosphere prevailed, as before named, through a large part of it, and a good, healthy, substantial, business-like air through the remainder. At 4.30 P. M. we took cars for Wells.

CHAPTER XVIII.

WELLS—NORWICH—ELY.

We arrived at 6 o'clock. The ride from Peterboro', through Lynn, and to Wells, was a pleasing one, for the land in the entire region was different from any we had seen. There were but few elevations, and, instead, meadows and fens abounded. Dikes and ditches were frequent. Windmills, as in Holland, were common, and in many respects we were riding over veritable Lynn Marshes, as we had done a thousand times, at home.

At length, arriving here, we anticipated seeing the cathedral, but alas for human endeavors and calculations! this was to be *the* place of our entire journey mistake. Wells proper, that of cathedral renown, was hundreds of miles away. This is a little, east-side-of-England seaport town of 3,760 inhabitants. Many of the houses are one-story, stone, plastered, and whitewashed. We felt in one quarter very at-homeish, for the street alongshore was much like one at Gloucester or Rockport, or in Joppa at Newburyport, Mass. There was an intense odor of fish, and the fishermen themselves were Joppa-fishermen-like, and not simply sailors. Heavy clothing was theirs, and of a cut and style not like Boston or Paris. Their boots were innocent of a waste of blacking, *souwesters* for hats, and Guernsey frocks. We didn't have very hard work to be reconciled, and "making the best of it" wasn't enough in the nature of a sacrifice to transform it into a virtue. We were seeing a fine old English seaboard town, and now we have an unexpected source of thought to draw from. We have it sure, and ever shall.

The mistaken detour was a blessing in disguise, a cloud with a silver lining. Next A. M., after a fine night's rest in that invigorating atmosphere, at 7 o'clock took train, and rode along landscapes not much like the other before passed over, for we were soon out into higher land, with some fields, and amid many fine gardens, groves, and woods,—in fact, in a quite New-England-appearing territory; and at 9 A. M., on this June 11, arrived at

NORWICH.

No doubt this time in the minds of either of us whether or not this was *the* Norwich, for in grand relief, off a quarter of a mile, was the cathedral, with its centre tower and spire, 315 feet high, which is one of the five spired-cathedrals of England. The city is well situated on the River Wensum, and has a population of 80,390, and is the capital of the county of Norfolk. It is a very ancient place, for there are good evidences that it was founded A. D. 446, or more than 1400 years ago. On the departure of the Romans, who settled it, it was taken by the Saxons, and in 575 it had improved and become the capital of Anglia. In 1002 it was attacked by a Danish fleet under command of Sweyn their king, and was captured and burnt to ashes. In 1328 the foundation of its permanent prosperity was laid by Edward III., who made it the staple town of Suffolk and Norfolk; and, conferring important privileges thereby, induced large numbers of Flemings to settle in it. A larger number yet arrived during the reign of Queen Elizabeth; and so great was the industry and ingenuity of the people, that their manufactures soon became famed throughout the world. The city has given birth to many distinguished men. Among these may be named the following: Matthew Parker, a distinguished Archbishop of Canterbury, and so, Primate of all England. He was the second Protestant Bishop of Canterbury, and died at London, May 17, 1575. A more extended notice of him will be given in the description of the cathedral of Canterbury.

Next is Dr. Samuel Clark, born Oct. 11, 1675, and died May 17, 1729. He graduated at Cambridge, and was of a very philosophical turn of mind. Having mastered the system of Philosophy of Descartes and Newton in his 22d year, he published a work on physics, which became popular and a textbook in the university. He next turned his attention to theology, and became chaplain to Dr. More, Bishop of Norwich. In 1706 he translated into English "Newton's Optics," which so pleased the great mathematician that he presented him with £500, and Queen Anne made him one of her chaplains and rector of St. James Westminster, and this was when he was less than 31 years old. He was a very scholarly and voluminous writer, and all his works are marked by erudition and are on important themes. He was a philosopher, and a scientific thinker, as well as an historical, or theological one; and on the death of Sir Isaac Newton, he was offered the place of Master of the Mint, but strongly attached to his profession as a Christian teacher, he declined the office, as being unsuitable to his ecclesiastical character. His death occurred at the age of fifty-three, and few have died more worthily or universally lamented.

Here also was born, May 21, 1780, Elizabeth Fry, the celebrated Quakeress and philanthropist, who was, in 1798, converted to pure Quakerism through the instrumentality of William Savary, the American Quaker, then on a visit to England. She died at Ramsgate, Oct. 12, 1845, greatly lamented the Christian World over.

Here also was born, Nov. 12, 1769, Mrs. Amelia Opie, the well known poetess and prose writer, who died here Dec. 2, 1853.

And here was born, June 12, 1802, that remarkable writer, Harriet Martineau; and, in 1805, her hardly less celebrated brother Rev. James Martineau, the distinguished Unitarian divine; and thus we find the list of notables increasing to a degree that demands a refrain of enumeration even. The old city is hardly less celebrated as having been the seat of very marked and interesting historical events.

In 1381 Bishop Spencer led an army, and successfully repulsed an attack made on it by 80,000 insurgents, led by Sitester, a dyer, in the Wat Tyler Rebellion. Muscular Christianity was at a premium, sure, in those days, and a political sermon was then looked upon as a mild offence. In 1531 Bilney and Lews and Ket were burned at the stake for their religious opinions. In the reign of Elizabeth 4,000 Flemings fled from the cruelties of the Duke of Alva, and established in this place the manufacture of bombazines, which work is carried on to the present day. In 1695 a mint was established here. In the years 1407-1483 was built, of curiously arranged cobble, or round flintstones, the present guildhall, with panels in the front, ornamented with armorial shields of the time of Henry VIII. In one of the rooms is the sword of Admiral Winthuysen, taken at the battle of St. Vincent, Feb. 14, 1797. In Pottergate Street is the old Bridewell, built in 1380, of flintstone, and once the home of Appleyard, the first mayor of Norwich.

A recital of interesting facts and description of relics could be made which alone would require chapters of the length we are using. The temptation is very great, when we are saying anything of these grand old historic and antique centres, to enlarge, and give a greater amount of those interesting old facts; but a moment's reflection calls attention to the impropriety of making an encyclopædia, and we forbear, and turn to the more modern ideas.

The manufactures of the place are at the present time, as they always have been, very varied; and prominent among them is that of woollen goods, which are of a great and ancient celebrity, for the Flemings obtained long wool, spun in the village of Worsted, nine miles away, and of this made that peculiar cloth. This kind of yarn thus took the name of *worsted*, and is so known to this day. It is said that there are 1400 looms working in this city and the neighborhood. The city has a business-like appearance, and a commanding look in its main thoroughfares. It is well built of brick and stone, and everywhere, at intervals, there are the evidences of age, in the old stone churches, of which there are more than forty in the city,—some of them very venerable, and built of split cobble-flintstone, and many of them of great antiquity.

The city has a noble feudal relic in the shape of a castle founded by Uffa in 575. It was extended and improved by Anna in 642, and again in 872 by Alfred the Great, or more than 1,000 years ago; and now still stands, grand and imposing, at the centre of the city, on a quite lofty eminence with precipitous sides, and is surrounded by its massive wall and donjon tower, but has been in modern times altered on the interior, to fit it for its present use as a jail. Another part is remodelled for use as the shire hall. The bishop's palace and the deanery are imposing structures, old and interesting, and approached, as the cathedral itself is, through what is called the Eppingham Gate, a remarkable structure consisting of a lofty pointed arch, flanked with semi-octagonal buttresses, and enriched with columns, mouldings, and 38 male and female statues in canopied niches. The market-place is large, and ranks as one of the finest in the world. The city was formerly surrounded by walls; fragments of them still remain, but most have been removed and the material used for more useful purposes. It was provided with numerous watch-towers, and was entered by 12 gates.

Owing to the quantity of ground used, just out of the centre of the city, for gardens and orchards, as the place is approached by rail it presents a very rural appearance; and being built mostly on a hillside, and quite steep in parts, it strongly resembles its namesake in our Connecticut, and it covers a much larger space, or territory, than any other English place of a like population. Not a few of the streets are narrow and winding, and many of the houses that line such are antique with overhanging stories, and presenting long rows of gables; they are, however, generally of brick, and more interesting for their antiquity than for any merits of architecture.

Great improvements have been made in the suburbs, and even in the city proper; new streets have been opened, old ones widened, and many modern and tasteful buildings erected. Hospitals and charity schools and institutions abound. The literary and scientific institutions have a library of 18,000 volumes, and the mechanics' and young men's institutes have 11,000. There are numerous public parks or gardens, bowling-greens, and great facilities for the amusement and pleasure of its inhabitants.

A grand and venerable old place is this of Norwich,—full of inducements for a visit, or even a permanent stay. It should have been named that the suburbans, and those living on the outskirts, give much attention to farming, and that Norwich is in some respects like our Brighton, for it has weekly market-days for the sale of cattle, and has the largest market in the kingdom, with the single exception of those near London. The stores, many in number, and a large portion of them of high grade, present for sale every conceivable article, and argue of a high civilization.

"The cathedral,—what of that?" says the reader. Well, it is by no means forgotten, and we next tell of that. It is situated on low and level land, and is from a distance looked down upon, or over to, rather than up to, as is the case at Durham, Lincoln, and in fact in many other places. It is built of a dark-gray sandstone, and has a rather sombre look, and is located in the midst of grounds, about in which are walls and ruins of the old monastery, and the original garden walls yet remain; so that while the cathedral is not out among buildings of ordinary character, but has ample grounds and shrubbery around it, yet it has no grand close, or park, as at Salisbury, Hereford, and many others; but all is complete within these precincts, and charming in the extreme. A charming quiet pervades these ancient-appearing and large premises, and all is befitting the venerable structure.

Like all cathedrals, this boasts of a good antiquity. The See was removed from Thetford to Norwich in 1096. The first establishment consisted of sixty monks; they took possession of the premises in 1106, and Bishop Herbert laid the cathedral foundation in 1115. The work advanced, so that on Advent Sunday, 1278,—or 163 years after the laying of the corner-stone,—it was consecrated by Bishop Middleton, in presence of King Edward I. and Queen Eleanor. In 1272 the tower was badly injured by lightning; and this was but the precursor of a greater evil, for on the 18th of September of that year a riot occurred among the populace, and they turned their attention to the edifice. Most of the court buildings were destroyed, the cathedral itself much injured, several of the sub-deacons and lay-servants killed in the cloisters, the treasury ransacked, and all the monks but two driven away. In 1289 Bishop Walpole began a spire of wood, covered with lead, completed in 1295, which remained some years, when it was blown down, and much injury was done to the roofs. Bishop Percy erected the present stone spire in the years 1364-1369, so that as we now see it, it is 536 years old.

The building is 416 feet long, transepts, 185 feet wide; and the tower, which is 45½ feet square, is 140 feet high, with a stone spire, 169½ feet above this, or an aggregate 309½, exclusive of iron-work, above it. The cloisters are 150 feet square, and the open close about them is one of the finest in England. The interior is very solid in appearance, yet as well decorated as any in the kingdom. Indescribable is the solemnity of grand effect. How complete all is; and how of eternity itself do the great Norman columns speak! Had we not already employed so much eulogy in praise of other cathedrals, we now could use adjectives to advantage; but language has never yet adequately described a cathedral's interior. There is more to the thing than matters of curiosity and a tame entertainment. We first are interested, next admire; soon a feeling of awe and solemnity is inspired, and the strong sensations tone down, and one feels to be in the presence of men of other generations. Bishops of distinguished renown have here held sway more than half a thousand years ago. Here have kings and queens worshipped. These arches through the centuries have echoed back a million songs and psalms and prayers; about, amid this lofty vaulting, have the odors and smoke of Roman Catholic incense wandered on; and here at the foot of these ponderous columns, and at these shrines, have thousands, yea millions, of pious devotees tried to do honor to the King of kings and the Lord of lords; and here also by-and-by, in aid of reformation, was ruthless work done, and images of saints and grand sculptures, made by monks and pious ones, were hurled from their quiet resting-places, to be broken and to be cast out, after centuries of service,—to be as common things, ground to powder and trodden under foot of men. The good Scripture statement is that there is joy among the redeemed over repenting mortals. If joy, then knowledge and observation of what mortals do. Is it too much to think that, with extended vision and enlightened conditions, seeing truth clearly, and rid of its dress and habiliments of superstition and enslaving penance and wordy ritual, that even the seeming desecration, speaking of advancing conditions and better ones for after worshippers,—that listening to this, they too rejoiced in the work, and that always after they have been interested here at these great shrines, and are present and communing? Is there not now, as of old, a great cloud of witnesses? When one walks through the vast cathedral nave, and the sound of his feet makes echoes that pass from one to another of their lofty arches, is it too much to think that these are not all the sounds awakened or elements set in motion? "Things are not what they seem," for the poet has well said:—

As the temple waxes,

The inward service of the mind and soul
Grows wide withal.

This place so sacred, and now in grand repose, has been desecrated to an incredible degree. The world's people and the monks have at times come to blows. In recounting the desecrations which took place during one of the civil wars, Sir Thomas Browne says, that "more than one hundred monumental brasses were taken from the mural slabs in this cathedral, and were carried away and destroyed." Bishop Hall says:—

The rebel musketeers committed abominable excesses in this cathedral church, which they converted into an ale-house. They sallied out habited in the surplices and vestments, sounding on the organ pipes, and grossly parodying the litany, and burned the service-books, six copies, and records in the market-place.

No cathedral makes a greater show of monuments, in wider variety of design, or commemorative of more influential and distinguished men; and first may be named the elegant memorial window at the west end of the nave, to the memory of Bishop Edward Stanley, who was father of the celebrated and now worthily lamented Dean of Westminster at London. The bishop was born in 1779, and died at Norwich in 1849, having been made bishop of this cathedral in 1837. In the presbytery is a table-tomb to the memory of Sir W. Boleyn, who died in 1505. He was the great-grandfather of Queen Elizabeth.

Near by is a wall tablet commemorating Bishop George Horne, who died Jan. 17, 1792. He was distinguished as a preacher, and became President of Magdalen College, Oxford, in 1768, Chaplain to the King in 1771, Dean of Canterbury in 1781, and Bishop of Norwich, 1790. He was a very voluminous writer; his chief work is his "Commentary on the Psalms," on which he labored for twenty years, and published it in 1776. As one lingers among these remains he is forcibly struck with the antiquity of the monuments, and finds himself counting their age by hundreds of years; and among them are the following bishops with the year of their death. They will be given in the order in which they are met with, not regarding priority of dates: Bishop Nix, 1536; Parkhurst, 1575; Dean Gardner, 1589; Bishop Herbert, 1682; Goldwell, 1499; Wakering, 1425; Overell, 1619; Bathurst, 1837; Prior N. de Brampton, 1268; Prior Bonoun, 1480; Reynolds, 1676; R. Pulvertoft, 1494; and so might the list be continued. Here are bishops, deans, curates, priors, sir-knights-templars, members of parliament; and distinguished women also, for not unfrequently appears the title of Dame, as Dame Calthorp, who died in 1582. As we think of these for whom monumental stones have been raised, and the hundreds in the old grounds, who are "unknelled, uncoffined, and unknown;" of monk, nun, abbot, and abbess; Catholic and Protestant; of them of ancient dispensation, as well as of them of the new; the whole a great company, more in the aggregate than all they who in the city entire are yet in the flesh,—as we loiter here and think of these things, we see the force of the remark, "One generation cometh and another goeth, but the earth abideth forever." We have said, after all, comparatively nothing concerning this place of so much interest and renown, but time with us moves as it did with those who a thousand years ago labored and died here. The great bell in the tower solemnly counts off the hour of 3 o'clock, and we wend our way from these sacred precincts, and drop the curtain, but not without the promise that whenever again at London, we will come over to Norwich; and now at 3.30 of the same Tuesday, we take cars for the next cathedral town, which is famous old

ELY.

We are at the seat of another of the famed cathedrals, having arrived in just an hour's ride from Norwich; so on this remarkably fine day as it is proving to be,—at home in Boston, America, we should call it a first-class middle-of-May one,—valises deposited at the railroad station, our stay not to be long, we are soon walking about the city. This is a small rural place, situated on the River Ouse, and with a population of 8,000. It is exceedingly rural in aspect, and has but little look of business or manufactures. Half embowered with trees, the octagonal tower of the cathedral is looming up in the distance, a half-mile away. The place has one principal street, and but few others of more than ordinary importance, and while clean to a fault, it has many old buildings, and little that is new; and, as before intimated, gardens and lawns are common, and the entire place has a charmingly rural character. The churches of St. Mary and of Holy Trinity are remarkable for their age and an ancient splendor. There was a convent founded here about 673, by Etheldreda, wife of Egfrid, King of Northumberland, and she was its first abbess. It was destroyed by the Danes in 870, and one hundred years later was rebuilt by Ethelwold, Bishop of Winchester, who placed in it monks instead of nuns. The city is on an island, and is said to have received its name from the great quantity of eels that used to be taken here. It has some manufactures of earthen-ware, and tobacco-pipes, and there are also flax and hemp-seed oil-mills, and lime-kilns; but the principal source of income for the laboring people is agriculture, and it has very extensive gardens for the cultivation of market vegetables, the produce of which is mainly sent to Cambridge, sixteen miles away, for use at the colleges.

The monastery and former abbey being established here, made it at an early day one of the celebrated religious centres of England; and, as often the case, the church of the institution was important, and in time became a cathedral. The See was established in 1107. In 1066 Thurston was abbot, and he defended the Isle of Ely seven years against William the Conqueror. In 1081 Simeon, a prior of Winchester, was abbot, and laid the foundation of the present cathedral.

In 1107, as before stated, the See was established, and Hervey, who had been Bishop of Bangor,—and, it is said for good reasons, had been driven away,—was elected Abbot of Ely; that is, he was head of the monastery. He made an effort to have this a seat of the bishop, and, succeeding, was himself made its first bishop. Simeon, who laid the cathedral foundation, lived only long enough to finish the choir and one transept, and of his work this transept only now remains.

The nave, the great western tower as high as the first battlements, and the south transept were finished, the former in 1174, and the latter in 1189. The great western portico was begun in 1200, and finished in 1215. In 1552 extensions were made, and in 1322 the octagonal lantern of the tower was begun, and it was finished in 1328. A spire of wood was built on this in 1342, which was afterwards removed. Various repairs and restorations have been from then till now going on, and we have it at present in fine condition of repair. It is built of a grayish, or dark soapstone-colored stone, resembling the cathedral at Salisbury; and on the stone is a large lot of lichens,—a species of fungus or moss, such as is often seen on our common stones of field walls, though so very thin and close to the stone as at times to appear simply like a stain on the material. The building is 517 feet long, 179 feet wide at the transepts, and the nave and aisles are respectively 78 feet wide and 70 feet high.

A marked and important feature of this cathedral is the great west tower, on the four corners of which are large octagonal buttress piers, ending in very lofty turrets, crowned with battlements; and inside of these, but somewhat lower, is an octagonal lantern section, also crowned with an embattled parapet. The tower is very elaborate and elegant in its finish and proportions, and is in all 306 feet high. Another peculiarity of the cathedral is that at the intersection of the nave, transepts, and choir, are four subordinate sides in which are elegant windows, and the whole great octagon, ending at the outside lines with groined work; and the centre part is a lantern which is open well up into the great tower over it.

The interior of this cathedral is elegant and wonderfully elaborate, and is excelled by no cathedral in the kingdom. Here, if anywhere, may it be said that rich Gothic architecture is "frozen music." Speak as favorably as one will of other cathedrals, they may yet be lavish in praise of Ely; and it may be added that the painted glass windows are incredibly fine and in keeping with the grand building they illuminate. Of one thing we repeatedly speak, and it is that we are glad that we did not see the interior of a cathedral like this first; else many of the others would have appeared tame and weak. All, however, have their own peculiar glories, and, as productions of art, do their own respective work.

There are but few monuments of note in the cathedral. There were once, however, many of bishops, priors, and deans, but all have been destroyed or removed but two; they are of Bishop Gray and of Lewis de Luxemburg, who was made bishop in 1438, and who held the bishopric by special dispensation of the Pope, being at the same time Archbishop of Rouen, France, and also a cardinal.

Among the eminent men who have been bishops of this cathedral is Matthew Wren, who was elected bishop in 1638. He was uncle of the distinguished architect of St. Paul's at London, Sir Christopher Wren, and he held the following offices at different periods: Master of St. Peter's College, Cambridge; Dean of Windsor; and Bishop of Hereford, and also of Norwich. He was a great sufferer during the Usurpation and the Rebellion, but outlived both, and before his death saw peace and tranquility restored. In looking over the list of Ely's bishops, one is astonished to observe how eminent they must have been, if we may judge from their having previously been bishops in other cathedrals. Simon Langham, elected here in 1332, was a cardinal, and, after being here, was bishop at Canterbury. Thomas de Armdel, of 1374, was translated to York, and then to Canterbury. John Morton, of 1478, was afterwards Archbishop of Canterbury. Thomas Goodrich, of 1534, was once Bishop of Westminster, and also of Norwich. Simon Patrick, of 1691, was at Chichester as bishop, and was dean at Peterboro'. Remarkable confidence seems to have been reposed in the bishops of Ely for uprightness and integrity, and a business talent as well; for as many as twelve of them were chancellors of England, and four of them founded colleges or were masters at Cambridge.

As we try to select a few items of especial interest from the vast amount before us, the task is bewildering, and when a final work has been done, it is so meagre and paltry as to cause uncomfortable thoughts, and put to flight all anticipations of even a reasonable satisfaction.

These vast buildings, so elegant in decoration, so aged, so satisfying to the beholder, as remarkable works of skill in decorative and constructive points of view, are great museums and libraries of themselves; and to the reflective observer there *are* "sermons in stones." When here and at like places, we are amid the results of the anticipations and prayers and labors of centuries. We go back to the day when a lot of mortals, full of a pious aspiration for the good and the true,—yet superstitious,—were travelling over these spots in quest of a best place for study and repose; and they at last here rested, and founded an abbey or monastery, a priory it may be, or a simple nunnery. By-and-by the foundation of a great church was to be laid, but with no hope or expectation of ever seeing those foundation walls of an entire cathedral reach even the earth's surface: comprehending the scheme, they plied themselves to the task, and labored and died; others came, the walls arose, and centuries passed. Tower, battlement, and roof climbed heavenward, and then came consecration and worship, but never rest. Death of prelate, then monuments were in order; repairs of cathedral; civil wars, rebellions, destruction of the art-work of centuries; overturnings of doctrines, disputes, and surrender of cathedral, and all its sacred belongings come; new doctrines are inaugurated, and become the law of the land. Generations after generations are born and die. The cathedral grows old, aged; the grounds only remain as they were; and *not* as they were, for the soil is raised by the dust of the thousands that are buried and moulder in it, and so, in transfigured glory, even the old trees that throw their grateful shadows have in their fibre earth that was once the royal bone and flesh and sinew of bishop, cardinal, or king. At places in cathedral premises are charnel houses, or rooms where are deposited bones and remains exhumed, or taken from tombs, and these are thrown into promiscuous heaps to moulder on a little longer, and, having become resolved back to mother earth, to be quietly shovelled out as food for grass and flowers on the great lawns. These are the seen, the temporal; but the unseen, the eternal, is no less fact, nor less real, for the influence these men exerted lives and acts. The mortal is greater than any material thing he builds. That decays, and as an organized thing ceases to be, but the influence of thought dies never. We know not into whose little mass of earth, whose narrow house, the rootlets of the tree whose branches shade us have gone, and taken up their infinitesimal particles of human earth, and carried it on to make leaf and blossom, or fibre of wood or bark. We know it has been done, and is yet doing, and has been so for centuries; for, as Shakespeare has it:—

Imperious Cæsar, dead and turned to clay,
Might stop a hole to keep the wind away;
Oh that the earth, which kept the world in awe,
Should patch a wall to expel the winter's flaw!

Not seen as fact, with material eyes, but known beyond peradventure by the less material thought; so it is of the deeds done,—living and acting, when the authors are dead, as the world judges and declares. But are not the great arch and pillar of nave influential now? Is not the elegant decoration of cut stone refining to those of this day? Does not the largeness even of the cathedral inspire us now to do large things? Does not the patience of monk, of old bishop, of the master mind of those back ages,—content to but lay a foundation and then resignedly die,—does not that beget the like, even in this hurrying nineteenth-century time? And the determination of Cromwell or of Henry VIII., even though destructionists,—iconoclasts not only of stone, but unwittingly of superstitions and religious tyranny,—though in a sense tyrants themselves, does not their work make it comfortable for free conscientious worship now? Does not the work of such ones and their sustaining bishops,—of martyrs, by their faithfulness and sacrifices even of life itself,—do not these make our good conditions possible, which but for them would never have been? Cathedral *is* museum and library; it is shrine,—inspiring thought and evolving new good, and in no way inferior to picture-gallery or depository of mechanical production or of curious art.

A long digression this, and but for the license we at the start reserved, apology would be due. We greatly enjoyed Ely and all things in it. A fine long walk came next, from the cathedral off half a mile into a back road, where, amid the good suburban shade of overhanging garden trees, and enveloped in the nice odor of flowers, we took our last view of the old structure, and turned our feet to the station. Dreamish was the whole thing. A few hours ago we were not in sight of the famed place, where has crystallized the greatness engendered by centuries. A choice bit of earth, covered over and enveloped in extraordinary history and momentous events, the site of any cathedral is. A few hours only there at the shrine, and the material curtain for us two drops, and never perhaps to be raised while we are in the flesh. It was another scene of lightning-like presentation, but the photograph was taken. The impression is clear, clean-cut of detail and outline; and though it may be dimmed it will never be effaced, nor beyond recall. We leave the famed place, and, entering the station, sit mute in our car. The common things of every-day life take us in charge. Engine, embankments, bridges, tunnels, fields, every-day things, terribly modern, come up in front, and gently absorb attention. The mind quietly and imperceptibly yields. We are kindly let down, and the spell is broken.

We are on our way to Cambridge. It's 6.30 P. M. only, and that's early for these long English June days. Classic and worthily renowned Cambridge! Our thoughts go *on* and not *back* now. When one has been thinking of a great thing, it's a comfort, when ruthlessly removing from it, to be permitted to think of another as great or greater.

CHAPTER XIX.

CAMBRIDGE.

Our arrival here was at 7.30 P. M. on Thursday, June 11, with but an hour's ride from Ely. This city, as is well known, is the other great university place of England, with its sister Oxford, and is in many respects like that; for aside from its being a great seat of learning, the general look and surroundings are much the same. Fine meadows surround the city, and the River Cam runs through it, as does the Cherwell at Oxford. The place is one of great antiquity, for in Doomsday-book it is described as an important place, and is there called Grente-bridge, from one of the then names of the river. Its present name is derived from the more modern name, Cam, which is nearer correct. The pronunciation by the inhabitants was Cambridge, giving *a* its sound as in *can*, instead of its long sound as in *came*, by our usage. In 871 it was burnt by the Danes; rebuilt; and burnt in 1010. Subsequent to this it has been the scene, at various periods, of great historical events, but we will leave its ancient history and speak of it as it now is.

The present population, including about 8,500 students, is 35,372. What makes it of peculiar interest to people of Massachusetts is, that from it is taken the name of our Cambridge, which was done in honor of some of the early settlers, who were graduates here, and also of Rev. John Harvard, who removed from here to America, and died at our Charlestown, Sept. 24, 1638. At his death he made a donation to our college of money and his library of 300 books.

No more beautiful place of sojourn in the kingdom of Great Britain exists than this. There is at one of the principal business sections quite a commercial aspect, there being good stores for the sale of goods of all kinds, and the bookstores are exquisitely tempting. Here and there are fine old mansions elegantly embowered in trees; and winding about among them, and for long distances, are the most rural of roads imaginable for quiet rambles, strongly reminding one of the more retired parts of our Roxbury, most of them being shaded by venerable trees. There are examples of churches, with their surrounding graveyards, which boast of very great antiquity, and they also greet us with a *look* of centuries. The people are blest with a becoming and good reverence for these time-honored enclosures and venerable buildings, and they religiously repair them when needed, but refrain from amending.

Happily for them, public sentiment is such that no Old South campaigns, such as balls, fairs, and "Carnivals of Authors," are required before they will refrain from putting them out of existence. An atmosphere of learning, and suggestions of high cultivation, and that of centuries' duration and exercise, prevails and is everywhere apparent. Even the business portion seems to be subdued, refined, and classic. After making due allowance for the fact of knowledge of the nature of the place and interest in it exciting, perhaps, a too intense admiration, one gets the impression that the children are more refined, and that even the street horses are better behaved than elsewhere; he all the time feels as though he was enveloped in an atmosphere of unusual propriety, for there's a sort of Sunday-air about everything.

As at Oxford, the colleges are many in number, and the buildings are of peculiar construction, entirely unlike ours in America. We have given a full description of those at Oxford, and remarks concerning them apply alike to these, for in most respects they do not vary much from each other. It may be said that, take at random one half of those at Oxford, and exchange buildings and grounds with an equal number from Cambridge,—take them promiscuously, and put each respectively in the place of the other,—and you would in no way attract especial attention so far as style, size, or kind of architecture is concerned. Of course all vary from each other, but part of those in one place do not vary from part of those of another, any more than each varies from its neighbor.

Here are the same courts, or closes, called *courts* at Cambridge, and *quads* at Oxford. They are always entered by a principal arch or gateway from a main street, and there enclosed is the elegant lawn of that indescribably velvet-like grass, for which such places are celebrated, and which the mild and moist climate so well takes care of and favors. Then there is a grand and scrupulously clean gravel-walk around it, and up against the buildings; and it may be there are good paths across it, leading to other openings, through under the first story to another court of like nature, and yet again to others,—for some colleges have four or more of these.

Everywhere exists a neatness that is remarkable,—no particle of paper nor bit of anything to mar the nicety. Windows innumerable are filled on their outside sills with pots of flowers. We often say, as we pass through the courts and observe the perfect repair every building is in,—the cleanliness, the comfortable quiet,—"How perfect, and what a good public sentiment among the students there must be to make the condition possible."

Aside from these courts, some, and perhaps most of the colleges, have very large and great park-like grounds and of many acres in extent, with walks ancient and shaded with venerable trees. The lazy River Cam moves leisurely through them, as if loath to leave, and as though admiring its visit and stay. As we stood on one of the grand old bridges crossing it,—and there are quite a number on the grounds leading from one division of the park to another, and sometimes, as at St. John's College, connecting two buildings,—as we stood looking down into the water we almost felt that it, as we did, realized that the visit was one of a lifetime, and not to be hurried over.

How inducive of thought are these old classic grounds, centuries in use? Poets, philosophers, and martyrs, the most renowned men of the world, have here walked as we are walking. Oxford has had her great men, and we bow reverently at the thought or even mention of their names. How the destinies of the kingdom and those of the world have been influenced by men to whom Oxford was *alma mater*, but an intense conservatism has always nestled in her bosom and been suckled at her breasts. For centuries it was Oxford's conscientious duty and work to be conservator of religion and philosophy, and, as she understood it, to see that the ship did not drag anchor, drift, nor move a particle from her ancient moorings of received doctrines and principles; and so, if burning of martyrs would aid the cause, martyrs must be burned, and Hooper and Latimer and Ridley and Cranmer, *Cambridge* men, must be ensamples and victims. As a result the flame of poetry burned low in that university, and if the world was to have a Milton and a Spenser, a Gray and a Byron, Christ's, Pembroke, and Trinity of Cambridge must furnish them. So of great philosophers! Cambridge's Trinity must furnish Newton and Bacon; and, as named, the great martyrs Cranmer, Latimer, and Ridley must go from Jesus, Clare, and Pembroke of this university; and what vast influence in our New England was exerted by the labors of John Robinson, the Pilgrims' minister and spiritual adviser, who although he died before he was permitted to look on this promised land, yet was to the moment of his death their best earthly friend; and so we may speak of Elder Brewster and of John Cotton; of Shepard of Lynn, and Parker and Noyes of Newbury, and all their fellow-contemporaries in the work of the ministry,—hardly one, save the two last named, who did not graduate at Cambridge! Archbishop Laud declared Sidney, Sussex, and Immanuel Colleges here to be "the nurseries of Puritanism." To use the thought of Dean Stanley: "It seems to have been the mission of Cambridge to *make* martyrs, and the work of Oxford to *burn* them."

But we pass on and notice the colleges themselves. From their great number and the long history each has, it will be impossible to give even a respectable synopsis of their history, and we can do but little more than name them, as was done for Oxford, in the order of their founding, with the date, and give a sample only of names of the eminent men who have been educated at each; and first in the list is St. Peter's, founded 1284, by Hugh de Balsham, Bishop of Ely. The library contains 6,000 volumes, and has fine old antique portraits of some of the masters and fellows, dating from 1418 to 1578. Among its eminent men were the famous Cardinal Beaufort, Bishop of Winchester, who died 1447. Thomas Gray, author of the renowned "Elegy in a Country Churchyard," died in 1771, and Lord Chief Justice Ellenboro', 1818.

The second in antiquity is Clare College, founded by Dr. Richard Badew, Chancellor of the University, in 1326. Elizabeth Clare, the third sister and co-heiress of Gilbert de Clare, Earl of Gloucester and Hertford, of her bounty built the college buildings, and in 1347 endowed it with land; and from thence it obtained the name which it has held for over five centuries. The grounds named are inconceivably elegant, and a graceful poet of Oxford, in speaking of them, remarks as follows:—

Ah me! were ever river-banks so fair,
Gardens so fit for nightingales as these?
Were ever haunts so meet for summer breeze,
Or pensive walk in evening's golden air?
Was ever town so rich in court and tower,
To woo and win stray moonlight every hour?

Some of her eminent men are, beside the martyr Latimer: John Tillotson, Archbishop of Canterbury, died in 1594; Ralph Cudworth, D. D., the celebrated writer, 1688; and Rev. James Hervey, author of the Meditations, 1758. The next is Pembroke, founded in 1347, by Mary de St. Paul, second wife of Aymer de Valence, Earl of Pembroke. She obtained her charter from Edward III. Her husband had died suddenly in France in 1324. The venerable appearance of the buildings caused Queen Elizabeth, when she visited it for the first time, to salute it in a Latin exclamation, a translation of which is, "O house antique and religious." The thought may have been suggested by a remembrance of John Rogers, and of Bradford and Ridley, who suffered martyrdom in the preceding reign, and who were all of this college, the last named having been its master, or, as we say, its president.

The chapel was built in 1665, from designs by Sir Christopher Wren, architect of St. Paul's London. The library contains 10,000 volumes. This college has been called Collegium Episcopale, from the great number of bishops who were here educated. Among her eminent men was the martyr Ridley, who was burned at the stake in 1555; Edmund Spenser the poet, 1599; and William Pitt, 1806.

Gonville and Caius College (Caius is called *Keys* by the students) is next. It was founded by Edmund de Gonville in 1348. He proceeded to erect buildings, but did not live to carry his design into full execution; he, however, left money for their completion. In 1557 John Caius, M. D., physician to Queen Mary, endowed the college largely, and, having procured a charter of incorporation, it took his name. Dr. Caius was master of his college from 1559 till within a few weeks of his death in 1573.

There are in the college grounds three gates, which lead to as many of the courts. One, erected by the Doctor in 1565, has the Latin inscription over it, HUMILITATIS, meaning, this is the gate of Humility. The second was built in

1567. This has two inscriptions, one on each side. One is VIRTUTIS, the gate of Virtue. On the other side is JO CAIUS POSSUIT SAPIENTIÆ, "John Caius built this in honor of Wisdom." The third is inscribed HONORIS, the gate of Honor, and was built in 1574. On the north wall of the chapel is an inscription to the founder of the college. It is in Latin, a free translation of which is as follows: "Virtue our Death survives. I was Caius, aged 63, Died July 29, Anno Domini 1573." Dr. Caius gave to the college a beautiful Caduceus, or silver mace, ornamented with four twining serpents; it is two feet and a half long, and, by his direction, is borne before the master at the principal college festivities.

This has been marked as the Medical College of Cambridge, and has produced a long roll of eminent physicians, among whom is William Harvey, the discoverer of the circulation of blood, in 1657. It has also produced several antiquarians, who were distinguished for their valuable researches. Among her eminent men may be named Sir Thomas Gresham, founder of the Royal Exchange, London,—died 1579; also the distinguished Bishop Jeremy Taylor, 1667.

The next in order, the fifth, is Trinity Hall. This is the only college which retains its original designation of *hall*. A few years ago there were three others so called, Pembroke, Clare, and St. Catherine's. The first of these changed appellation about thirty years ago; the two latter quite recently, to avoid being confounded with the *private halls* contemplated in the University act, but afterwards changed to *hostels*. This college was one of the hostels for the accommodation of students, but was purchased by John de Cranden, Prior of Ely, for the monks to study in; and in the year 1350 it was obtained of the prior and convent of Ely by William Bateman, Bishop of Norwich, with the lands thereto appertaining, who constituted it a "perpetual college of scholars of canon and civil law in the University of Cambridge;" and, in accordance with the founder's intentions, it is particularly appropriated to the study of civil law.

It is situated on the banks of the river, and has three courts. The eminent men are Stephen Gardiner, a distinguished Bishop of Winchester, died 1555; Lord Howard of Effingham, commander against the renowned Spanish Armada, 1573; Thomas Tusser the poet, and author of the somewhat celebrated "One Hundred Points of Good Husbandry," 1580; and, above all, the distinguished Earl of Chesterfield, Philip Dormer Stanhope, 1773. Among the bright lights of modern times may be named the late Lord Lytton, the novelist, poet, and statesman; and also Sir Alexander Cockburn, Lord Chief Justice of England, who took so conspicuous a part in the controversy between England and America concerning the Alabama Claims.

The sixth is Corpus Christi. Two ancient Saxon guilds were united to form it, and in 1352 King Edward II. granted a license for its founding. This college has one modern and elegant building, the corner-stone of which was laid July 3, 1823. All its appointments are grand. It has in its museum some plate that is very old and curious; an antique drinking-horn, presented to the guild of Corpus Christi, in 1347, by John Goldcorne; the cup of the Three Kings,—a small bowl of dark wood mounted with silver; thirteen silver-gilt spoons, terminated by figures of Christ and the apostles; an elegant salt-cellar nearly a foot high; a magnificent ewer and basin; and a cup with a cover weighing 53 ounces.

Among her eminent men are the justly renowned Mathew Parker, Archbishop of Canterbury, died 1575; Christopher Marlowe the dramatist, 1593; John Fletcher, the dramatist, and colleague with Beaumont, 1625; and Archbishop Tennison of Canterbury, 1715.

The seventh is King's. This royal and very magnificent institution arose from the munificence of the meek but unfortunate King Henry VI., who endowed it in 1443. His misfortunes prevented him from carrying out designs which would have made it greatly excel any other college. It was aided, however, by Edward IV. and Richard III., but it was reserved for his thrifty nephew, Henry VII., by devotions in his lifetime and by his will, to provide funds for the completion of the noble edifice.

However pressed for space, we must employ enough to speak of the remarkable chapel, which is one of the great objects of attraction at Cambridge, and one of the most interesting buildings in Christendom. It is of what is known as the perpendicular Gothic architecture. Its length is 316 feet. The corner-stone was laid by Henry VI., July 25, 1446. The work progressed till 1484, when it came to a standstill for want of funds; but in 1508 Henry VII. took it in hand, contributing £5,000, and his executors bestowed £5,000 more in 1513. It was not till July 29, 1515, in the seventh year of Henry VIII., that the exterior was finished. This was just 69 years from its commencement. Nothing more was done till 1526, when arrangements were made for the fine painted glass windows. The elegant screen-work and elaborate oak stalls were put up in 1534. All this work is very curiously carved, and was done when Anne Boleyn was queen; the west side is ornamented with several lover's knots, and the arms of Queen Anne impaled with those of the king. On this screen, in the old cathedral style, is the organ, which is of very large capacity, and in 1860 £2,000 was expended on it.

It would be next to an impossibility to adequately describe this magnificent interior. It is of very great height, and the ceiling is of fan-tracery of the most elaborate design of open-work cut in stone. Arms of all the kings of England, from Henry V. to James I., are here. The painted glass windows, twenty-five in number, are remarkably large, and for brilliancy of color and artistic design are surpassed by none in the world. They represent Old and New Testament scenes. The designs are entirely English, and the date of their manufacture ranges from 1516 to 1532, so that the very latest is more than 346 years old, or 88 years before the Pilgrims set sail for America. Choral service is performed in the chapel every afternoon. The grounds are very grand, and too much cannot be thought or said of this institution.

Among her eminent men were Robert Woodlark, founder of St. Catherine College; Sir Francis Walsingham, secretary of state to Queen Elizabeth; Bishop Pearson, author of the celebrated "Exposition of the Creed;" and Sir Robert Walpole, the renowned and royal minister of state.

We cannot leave these grounds without asking the reader to go with us to the great and single-arch stone bridge,—King's Bridge,—and for a moment enjoy the grand views to be had from it. To the right is to be seen the front of the Fellows' Building and the west end of the great chapel. Immediately in front is Clare College, with its picturesque bridge. The bridges and avenues make a grand view, bounded in the distance by the grounds of Trinity College. On the other side the view is of a more retired character. In the distance to the left are the spires and turrets of Queen's College, and extending along the side of the river is the terraced walk and quiet shady grove of the same institution. The venerable avenue at right-angles with this, tradition has long pointed out as the favorite walk of Erasmus; and in deference to this tradition the University purchased it of the town, by whom it was doomed at one time to destruction.

Queen's College is the eighth in order. This, in its architecture, history, and plan, is one of the most picturesque and interesting of all the colleges. It was founded in 1448 by Margaret of Anjou, consort of Henry VI., who, amidst a career perhaps one of the most troubled and chequered on record, found time and means to emulate the example of her royal husband, and, while he was erecting King's College, became the foundress of this. The civil wars interrupted the work, but Andrew Doket, the first master, by good management secured the patronage of Elizabeth Woodville, consort of Edward IV., who set apart a portion of her income for its endowment, and she has since been annually celebrated as a co-foundress.

Among the things of especial interest is a sun-dial, said to have been made by Sir Isaac Newton; and next is the Erasmus Court and tower. When the erudite and ingenious Erasmus visited England, at the invitation of his friend Bishop Fisher, then Chancellor of the University, he chose this college as his place of residence, "having his study," says Fuller, "at the top of the southwest tower of the court now called by his name." This college, like many others, has gardens and fine grounds on both sides of the river. They are connected by a wooden bridge of one span,—an ingenious piece of carpentry, and frequently called the Mathematical Bridge. To the right of this is the Grove, a most inviting place for quiet meditation. The terraced walk on the banks of the river is a delightful spot, shaded by lofty overhanging elms, at the end of which a striking view is obtained beneath the great stone arch of King's Bridge.

The eminent members here, or a few of the vast lot, were John Fisher, the master of the college and Bishop of Rochester, who was beheaded 1535; Thomas Fuller, D. D., the great Church historian, 1561; Dr. Isaac Milner, master, and Bishop of Carlisle, 1820; and Samuel Lee, the eminent linguist, 1852.

On the opposite side of the street is the ninth college, St. Catharine's, founded in 1475, by Robert Woodlark, D. D. The chapel was consecrated 1704, by Simon Patrick, Bishop of Ely. The especially eminent men here are John Bradford, martyred 1555; John Strype, the learned ecclesiastical historian, 1737; and Benjamin Hoadley, Bishop of Winchester. It was he who gave rise to what is known as the celebrated Bangorian Controversy, in 1761.

The next college in order of date, the tenth, is Jesus. It has a most rural situation and pleasing aspect, for it is located back some distance from the road, and is charmingly surrounded with gardens, which give it a very domestic character.

As a general thing, the main college buildings at Cambridge are out, bounding the street or road; but this one is beautifully situated as named, and its retired position is said to have called forth the remark of James I., that if he lived at the University he would pray at King's, eat at Trinity, and study and sleep at Jesus. It occupies the site of an old Benedictine nunnery, dedicated to St. Rhadegund, founded in the reign of Henry II. Towards the close of the fifteenth century the nuns became notorious for their dissolute lives and extravagance; and in a few years the buildings fell into decay, and their remains were so wasted that only two nuns were left. At this period John Alcock, Bishop of Ely, determined to convert it into a college; and in 1497 he obtained letters-patent to put the college into possession of the property belonging to the nunnery, and the latter institution was dissolved.

The college has four courts, and its chapel is second only to that at King's College. Among its ancient men were Cranmer the martyr, burnt at Oxford 1556; Lawrence Sterne, the author of "Tristram Shandy," 1768; and Samuel Taylor Coleridge, 1835.

The next, and the eleventh, is Christ's. This was founded 1456, by Margaret Beaufort, Countess of Richmond, and mother of Henry VII. It arose out of a hostel called God's House, which had been endowed by Rev. William Byngham of London in 1442. In 1505, Lady Margaret obtained a license from her own son, Henry VII., to change its name to Christ's College, and endow it. The library contains 9,000 books, among which are many that are ancient and very valuable; there are also a great number of manuscripts and curious old works, particularly a splendid copy of the Nuremburg Chronicle in Latin, printed in 1494. The college also possesses some beautiful old plate, which belonged to the foundress, especially two exquisite saltcellars, engraved with Beaufort badges, and a set of Apostle spoons. The garden is very tastefully laid out, and contains a bowling-green, a summer-house, and a bath; but the great attraction of all others to visitors is the celebrated mulberry-tree planted by John Milton when he was a student. The trunk is much decayed, but the damaged parts are covered with sheet lead. It is banked up with earth covered with grass, being also carefully propped up, and every means used for its preservation; though so aged, it is still vigorous, and produces excellent fruit. From the southeast of this garden most charming views are had through the foliage, of King's College Chapel and other buildings. Among the eminent men were Latimer the martyr, 1557; John Milton, 1674; Archdeacon Paley, author of the Evidences, 1805; and Francis Quarles, author of the Emblems, 1644.

Our next, and twelfth, is St. John's, and derives its name from a hospital dedicated to St. John the Evangelist, founded in the reign of Henry II., which occupied the site of the present college. It was founded, like the one last named, by Countess Richmond, mother of Henry VII. After having founded Christ College, she was induced by Bishop Fisher of Rochester to found this. In 1505 she took measures for converting St. John's Hospital into a college, but various causes prevented its being done in her lifetime; but she added a codicil to her will empowering her executors to carry out her design. She died June 29, 1509, and the college was opened July 29, 1516. Rich endowments, made since, have raised it considerably above the original design, and it now ranks as second college of the University.

The new chapel is one of the most elegant structures in the kingdom. The corner-stone was laid in 1864. It was from designs by Scott, and cost £53,000. It is 193 feet long, and 52 feet wide, divided into chapel proper and ante-chapel. The tower is 163 feet high including the pinnacles. It is very massive, and is open on the inside to a height of 84 feet. As at King's College, attempts at full description must not be made. It is enough to say that the finish of the interior is extravagantly elegant, and that the windows are remarkable for their wealth of imagery, and brilliant color. We will venture to say that the ceiling of the great chapel is vaulted in oak, in nineteen bays, decorated by a continuous line of full-length figures, and by scrollwork in polychrome. In the central bay at the east end is a representation of Our Lord in Majesty. The other eighteen bays contain figures illustrating the eighteen Christian centuries after the first one, and are indescribably grand in design and execution. They are mainly devoted to representation of the bishops, college-founders, or of her most eminent men, and we give the ninth century panel as an illustration. It portrays Henry Martyn, missionary of India, William Wilberforce, statesman, William Wordsworth, poet, Thomas Whytehead, missionary to New Zealand, Dr. Wood, Master of St. John's College and Dean of Ely.

Passing out of the third court by an archway on the south side, a picturesque old bridge of three arches leads us to the college walks and gardens, which are more pleasantly laid out and more diversified than any others of the University; from them a fine view is obtained of the library and bridge of Trinity College. These walks consist of a series of terraces, and retired paths encompassing meadows, which are planted with fine trees, among which are some stately elms. Beyond these is the Fellows' Garden, or Wilderness, a large piece of ground containing a bowling-green; and the trees are planted in such order as to resemble, when in leaf, the interior of a church. These grounds are said to have been laid out by Matthew Prior, the poet. Of her eminent ones may be named the famous Ben Jonson, 1637; Thomas Wentworth, Earl of Strafford, beheaded 1641; Mark Akenside and Henry Kirk White, poets, who died 1770 and 1806.

The thirteenth is Magdalen, which occupies a portion of the site of a Benedictine priory, established about 1430. On the suppression of monasteries by Henry VIII. this college would soon have become extinct, had not Lord Audley of Walden procured in 1542 a grant of it, and a charter to establish on its site a college to be named St. Mary Magdalen College. It has but two courts, and the first is next the street.

Among the matters of especial interest is the library of Samuel Pepys, Esq., who died in 1703, and left his whole collection of books and manuscripts to this college. In the library is that curious and inexpressibly interesting manuscript, the original of the celebrated Diary of Mr. Pepys. We confess that nothing in any of the college libraries was of so much interest as were these works of the gossipy Pepys, and so while at this college it was our good fortune to examine the original manuscripts of the remarkable Diary in six volumes, about eight inches or so square, and two inches thick. If we say that the short-hand resembles almost strictly any of our present styles of phonography, with here and there a word fully written out, we give the best possible idea of it. All is exceedingly clean and free from any blot or blemish, and just such as may be imagined would have been prepared by the nice

Pepys. The Diary was to us, before, one of a few choice books; and now since we have seen his work, and his portrait by Sir G. Kneller, we are more than ever if possible in mood to think well of him who has written as none but he could or would write.

The distinguished personages of this college, besides Pepys, are Bryan Walton, Bishop of Chester and editor of the Polyglot Bible, who died in 1661; Dr. James Dupont, the celebrated Greek Professor, and master of the college, 1679; and that other learned divine and college master, Dr. Daniel Wheatland, 1740.

The fourteenth is Trinity, and without question this is the noblest collegiate institution of the kingdom, whether we regard the number of its members, or the extent and value of its buildings, or the illustrious men who have been educated within its walls. A large volume might be written in relation to these, and then but a synopsis be given. It is composed, or rather was organized, of others,—St. Michael's House, founded in 1324, King's Hall, in 1337, and Physwick's Hostel, the most important institution of that kind in Cambridge, and with this was included, six other minor hostels. These, in 1546, were surrendered to Henry VIII. as a preparatory step to the founding of one magnificent college, and he by letters-patent, Dec. 19, 1546, founded this in honor of the Holy and Undivided Trinity, and endowed it with very considerable possessions; but his death in a few weeks after stopped whatever further he may have contemplated. His son and successor Edward VI. issued the statutes of the college, and his daughter, Queen Mary, considerably augmented its endowments.

The courts, five in number, are very elegant and full of interest, but we must pass all by, simply stating that what is called the Old Court is said to be the most spacious quadrangle in the world and is in dimensions as follows, for the four sides respectively, omitting inches, 287 feet, 344 feet, 256 feet, and 325 feet, giving an area of 79,059 square feet.

There is nothing done in the preparation of this series of articles that demands a greater sacrifice of inclination to the contrary than does this abrupt termination of what would be a long and interesting statement, but limited space forbids even the record of full regrets. Of thousands of eminent men here educated may be named the illustrious philosophers Bacon and Newton, who died in 1626, 1727; also Crowley, Dryden, Byron, and Crabbe, poets; Dr. Isaac Barrow, the learned divine; Richard Porson, the eminent Greek critic and scholar; and Lord Macaulay, the historian and essayist; and we cannot well refrain from adding that there also was educated England's greatest modern poet, Alfred Tennyson.

Having begun a somewhat extended description of the colleges composing this famed university, we are devoting more space to them than at first anticipated, but feel justified, as the subject is one of great interest to us all, our own University City being most intimately related to it; and so we speak of the remaining of the seventeen colleges before we proceed to speak of other items of interest.

The next in order, the fifteenth, is one of very great moment to us of New England, for our interests are so closely connected with it; and that is Emanuel, which occupies the site of a dissolved monastery of Dominicans, or Black Friars. On the dissolution of monasteries this site was granted to Edward Ebrington and Humphrey Metcalf, of whose heirs it was purchased by Sir Walter Mildmay. This distinguished statesman was one of the most eminent adherents of what were termed Puritanical principles; and, with possibly the idea of establishing a nursery of those doctrines, in the year 1584 he obtained from Queen Elizabeth a charter for the incorporation of this college.

No college of the University has done so much toward deciding the fortunes, and it may be said the existence of New England, as has this. Established in 1584, which was but 29 years after the burning of the martyrs at Smithfield and Oxford, and coming into existence as it were in spite of those deeds of darkness, it became the one of all others to which those stanch men and advancing ones would send their sons, and a grand and mighty power was wielded, and strength and even respectability were given to the movement. This college is intimately connected with our history; and New England will not have done her duty, nor availed herself of a good privilege that is hers, till in these college-grounds she has erected a memorial to those determined and worthy men who did so much for New England.

John Robinson, the Pilgrims' minister, who was to have come to America the next spring but who died before his eyes could be gladdened by the sight, was educated at Emanuel. To our disgrace be it said, his dust to-day moulders in the soil of Holland, without so much as a plain slab to tell of his resting-place; and only as the guide in the church informs one, in reply to a request to be pointed to the spot, is the resting-place of the great departed ever seen.

Thomas Shepard and Henry Dunster, the latter our Harvard's second president,—these also to-day in their death, as they did in life, honor this as their Alma Mater.

The library contains 20,000 volumes, and some very rare and valuable manuscripts. The building itself was for nearly a century the college chapel; but so much of the Puritan element was here, that the chapel proper was never consecrated. Little however, did this trouble the worshippers, but the contrary was the case. By-and-by the church was in the ascendant, and then, in 1677, a new chapel had been built from designs by the celebrated Wren, "built due east and west," and all the appliances came of a non-dissenting church, consecrated by Bishop, and from then till now in good established use.

Here were educated William Sancroft, the renowned Bishop of London at the time of building St. Paul's Cathedral, and afterwards Archbishop of Canterbury, in 1693; Sir William Temple, statesman and essayist, 1700; and Dr. Parr, 1825. This, with the next college to be described, was considered by Archbishop Laud, as a very dangerous institution, and he designated the two as nurseries of Puritanism.

That sister college—the sixteenth, Sidney Sussex—was built on the site of a monastery of Gray Friars. On the subjugation of their institution it was granted by Henry VIII. to Trinity College, of whom it was purchased by the executors of Frances, daughter of Sir William Sidney, and widow of Thomas Radcliffe, third Earl of Sussex; who, by will dated Dec. 6, 1588, bequeathed £5,000 and some other property to found this college, and the corner-stone was laid May 20, 1590. The building was completed in three years, and the college at once took a high rank and good standing. It will always be celebrated for its connection with Oliver Cromwell, who entered here as a student April 26, 1616, at the age of seventeen, and on the college books is the following record:—

Oliverus Cromwell Huntingdoniensis admissus ad commeatum siciorum Aprilis vicesimo sexto, tutore mag Ricardo Howlet.

An amusing interpolation in a different and later handwriting appears, and speaks of him as:—

Grandis impostor; carnifax perditissimus, etc.

His father dying the next year, and leaving no property, the son was obliged to leave college; but, as Bishop Burnett was pleased to say, "some Latin stuck to him." His room was one in which is an Oriel window, on Bridge Street. There is in the master's lodge a fine portrait of the great Protector, made near the close of his life, and it is said to be remarkably faithful to the original. The long coarse gray hair is parted in the middle and reaches venerably to the shoulders. The forehead is high, majestic, and bold, and has a deeply marked line between the eyes, which are gray, and suggesting the repose of a vast power. The complexion is high-colored, mottled, and the features are large and rugged like the nature of the man himself; but it has—now that the feverish dream of his eventful life has declined—come to appear to have, by new interpretations and as seen through new mediums, a calm, dignified, and, some would say, a benevolent look. It is enough for one college that for a year Cromwell was her foster-child.

And now, for centuries, founding at Cambridge ends. Puritanism has set the world astir. The church, reformed as she prided herself to be, had her hands full to look after the already educated ones, and so no more founding of colleges for a long time was to be done; and we bridge over the chasm of 121 years, till, in 1717, Sir George Downing qualifiedly devised several valuable estates for the founding of a college within the precincts of the University; and so this is the seventeenth, and the last in order.

He died in 1749. The sole inheritor of the property died in 1764, and left the estates to his lady; but the terms of Sir George's will being that if his heirs died without issue the property was to go to the founding of a college as named, the estate was claimed by the University; and after years of litigation the validity of the will was established, and the seal was affixed to the charter of the new college, Sept. 22, 1800.

The corner-stone was laid with great ceremony, May 18, 1807, and it was opened in May, 1821, or more than 225 years from the date of the opening of the next one preceding it. The date of the founding of the first one, St. Peter's, being 1257, a period of 564 years intervened between the establishment of that first and this last one; and in all, from then till now, 626 years have passed, or more than a third of all the time since the birth of Christ.

However pleasant it would be to pass in review a few of the thoughts that come as it were demanding attention, we must pass all. Replete with interest are these two great centres of learning, Cambridge and Oxford, England's Yale and Harvard. How the destinies of men and nations, the civilized world over, have been not only influenced, but made and controlled by their influence! What hallowed grounds are these classic walks amid these trees, by the River Cam! How interesting are these venerable weather-worn walls, these courts, these half-destroyed stairs of stone, rasped away, and deep into, by feet of men distinguished and great in all the departments of intellectual life!

It was our intention to have spoken extendedly of the government of these institutions, and of many things pertaining to them, but we must refer the reader to the more appropriate sources of information for that. We would have spoken also of those grand old dining-halls, of which every college has one. Some of them are many centuries old, with quaint rich finish of old English oak, high open-timber roofs, fine windows, and grand old portraits adorning their walls. These halls are museums of interest inexpressible. Here are the very benches on which the boys sat, the greatest men of earth in embryo. The libraries, with their mementoes, their curious and rare old articles and books and paintings! How well we know that not one of our readers, who has not seen these things, can even approximately comprehend what we write. The old and new chapels! What repositories of greatness, and what charms inhere!

We would have spoken of great things outside the University, for there are many that are indeed great, and they crowd themselves up now, if for nothing more, for an honorable mention. The Fitzwilliam Museum has grand picture-galleries, and works of art and antiquity incredible; the building itself is a marvel of good architecture. Old St. Benedict's Church, one of the most perfect examples of Saxon architecture in England, is a thousand years old, with an extremely ancient burial-ground surrounding it. Old and grand St. Edward's was erected in 1350,—533 years ago. Here Latimer preached. How venerable and calm, interesting to admiration, is its little cemetery, 500 years old. The Church of St. Mary the Great, begun in 1478, completed in 1519, was towerless till 1608; and in the 130th year later arose the grand and imposing tower we now behold. That classical structure, the University Library, has 230,000 printed books and 3,000 manuscripts, of every language and tongue,—all this in addition to the 17 other libraries of the respective colleges! The great Geological Museum is excelled by none in the world; St. Michael's Church, built in 1324, is elegant now and in grand repair; as one has expressed it, "the old structure is to-day the most seemly and creditable in the town." The ancient Round Church consecrated in 1101, and afterwards restored, in a sense is itself a worshipper, as well as a place of worship for humanity.

We must speak of that curious fragment of architecture of the twelfth century, the School of Pythagoras. How quaint, how more than ancient! And we can only speak of—and, as it were, by the act slight that other antiquity—Barnwell Priory, founded in 1112, by old Payne Peverd, for Augustine canons. Once a place of magnificence, it declined, with none to care for it. At length a single department remained, and now that has come to the ignominious use of a common private stable. The Anatomical Museum, and the fine Botanical Gardens of thirty-eight acres, deserve mention. They shall have that much; they deserve volumes in their praise.

In closing a list of these objects of interest we name only one more, the Hobson Conduit. This is one of the things of general interest, for the students of the University for 200 years have looked upon it time-and-time-again. It is an octagonal structure, monumental in design, crowned with a cyma-recta dome, and having niches in each of the principal sides. Below these is a moulded octagonal section, resting on a square plain base. It was built in 1610, and stands at the city end of an artificial water-course leading from a place called the Nine Wells, three miles distant, and supplies the city with water. From the Hobson Conduit pipes distribute it over the place. Hobson's name is closely connected with Cambridge. He was born here in 1544, and is said to have been the first person in the kingdom who adopted the system of letting out horses for hire, and history says he did a flourishing business with the University students. He made it an unalterable rule that every horse should have an equal portion of rest as well as labor, and would never let one go out except in its turn; hence the celebrated saying often heard nowadays, when more than two hundred years old, repeated in America, "Hobson's choice,—this or none." He died Jan. 1, 1631, and though he had attained the patriarchal age of eighty-six, his death is attributed to his being obliged to discontinue his journey to London, while the plague was raging in Cambridge, and to this fact Milton alludes in the two humorous epitaphs he wrote on him.

There is one matter of interest yet remaining to be spoken of, and that relates to the government of the University. As before named, there are in all seventeen colleges. Each is an independent body, but is subject to the code of laws of the University, and in their administration all bear their share. The principal officer of the University is the Chancellor. His power is, strange to say, only nominal, and is, at that, delegated to a Vice-Chancellor elected annually from one of the heads of colleges. He is considered for the year the governor of this literary commonwealth. On all official occasions he is preceded by three Esquire Bedells, each bearing a large silver mace. There are next, elected annually, two Proctors, to attend to the discipline of the students of all the colleges, and assist in the general management of the University. Next is the Public Orator, who acts as the mouthpiece on all public occasions. We next have what are called Syndices, who are members of committees chosen to transact all special University business. There are many other minor officers, but those are the more important. The members of the University are, like our own, divided into two great orders, graduates and undergraduates, or those who have taken their degrees, and those who are yet students, and not graduated.

Each college also has its head, or, as we term it, President. At this University they are termed Masters, or sometimes, though less generally, Heads. Then, each has more or less members who are called Fellows. These are such as are maintained by the college revenues. Next are Pensioners; these are the ordinary students, who simply pay their own expenses, receiving no pecuniary advantage from the college. What are termed Scholars are students who, having displayed superior attainments, are elected by examination to have rooms rent free, payments of money, and other advantages, as a good and honorable residence and welcome at their Alma Mater. Finally are the Sizars. These are students of limited means, who have their commons free, and receive other emoluments. It may be well to mention that each college has its own peculiar undergraduate's gown, and that most of the degrees and faculties are distinguished by different costumes. The total number of members of the University is about 8,000. The University sends to the House of Commons two members, who are chosen by the collective body of the senate.

The revenues of the separate colleges are large, and derived from endowments and fees; but those of the University are small and rarely exceed £5,500 a year. The students are divided into four classes: Noblemen, who pay £50 caution money; Fellow-Commoners, who pay £25, and who receive their name from their privilege of dining,—having their commons at the table of their fellows; Pensioners, who pay £15, and form the great body of the students not on the foundation; and Sizars, who pay £10 and are students whose poverty prevents their taking advantage of many of the privileges of the University, though they are not shut out from any of its educational facilities. Sizars were once obliged to perform the most menial offices, but for many years this custom has been abolished. The matriculation fees for these classes of students are respectively as follows, £16, £11, £5. 10s., and £5. 5s.

There are various degrees of payment for tuition, according to the degree and condition of the members, and slightly varying in the several colleges. The annual, unavoidable average expenses of an undergraduate or student are about £70, or $350. There are in the University 430 fellowships tenable for life, but in most cases conditioned upon taking holy orders within a given period, and their value varies from £100 to £300 per annum. Since the days of Newton, Cambridge has been the chosen seat of mathematical science, but the tendency to make it a stronghold of learning in all the various branches has been increasing of late years.

It would be a pleasing work to follow on and give more extended notes of this great seat of learning. One while here is conscious that he is in no common place, for on this spot many of the mighty and really influential of earth began their great careers. No equal quantity of the earth's surface has been trodden by greater men than have walked here, and reverently we take our leave of the famed place, well conscious of what we have *not* spoken of.

The returns of 1880 gave the number in college as 1,399; 1,409 in lodgings; total, 2,808.

The following returns, compiled by the University Marshals, show the present number of residents at the various colleges, and also the number of unattached students. In the returns, graduates as well as undergraduates are included.

	In college.	In lodgings.	Total resident.
Trinity	335	340	675
St. John's	215	195	410
Jesus	74	147	221

Caius	100	98	198
Trinity-Hall	53	105	158
Christ's	70	80	150
Pembroke	49	87	136
Corpus Christi	79	45	124
Clare	56	68	124
King's	68	30	98
Emanuel	66	27	93
Magdalen	47	16	63
Queen's	41	19	60
St. Catharine's	39	21	60
St. Peter's	55	3	58
Downing	30	26	56
Sidney	41	12	53
Non-Ascripti	0	162	162
	1,418	1,481	2,899

We now take our departure for London, completing the round trip which has employed twenty days inclusive. No like number can ever be filled with more satisfaction, or be replete with a greater interest. The route gone over is in all respects one that the experience has proved admirable and to be relied upon, as giving a sample of the best things that England and Scotland have to exhibit.

CHAPTER XX.

LONDON—WINDSOR—STOKE POGES.

We are now, at 10.30 A. M., back in London, after a ride of two hours from Cambridge. The old charm of London still remains. It never would grow old. We have two days left, before we start for the continent, and employ them to the best advantage we can. The first, and a very natural act, is to go to our banker's in Philpot Lane, for letters and papers from home, and also to obtain some of that, the love of which one of old thought the root of all evil. Next, home to our old lodgings at No. 46 Woburn Place, for reading documents and writing replies. Next we take an omnibus ride down through High Holborn to Newgate Street, and alight near St. Paul's. It's full time that we go there again, and to worship in our own way. Delighted even more than at first, we find ourselves unable to comprehend it. First views are never as comprehensive as later ones.

A feast of contemplation here, and then a walk through Cheapside, to view once more the Fire Monument. It stands in Fish Street and was built to commemorate the great fire of 1666. In design it is first a platform, on which is a pedestal 21 feet square, with a moulded base 28 feet square. It has a bold cornice, and all, to the top of this, is 40 feet high. On the top of this pedestal is a Roman Doric column, and above all is a vase, or urn, with what was designed to represent a flame issuing out of its top. The flame is gilded, and the entire monument is 215 feet high, or but five feet less than ours at Bunker Hill. It is so located that, should it be laid down lengthwise in a certain direction, extending from its present location, it would exactly reach the spot at which the fire originated in Pudding Lane.

Here we stop by the way to remark that in London the idea—and no bad one—prevails of retaining old familiar names. Philpot Lane is yet the cognomen for the place of eminent bankers. Mincing Lane is the seat for certain kinds of merchandise traffic. Fish Street retains its name as at the time of the fire; and Piccadilly, Cheapside, Paternoster Row, High Holborn, and Crutched Friars are, to most Americans, even as common as household words.

The monument is built of the white Portland sandstone; and inside, Bunker Hill Monument like, are circular stairs, 345 in number, leading to the iron gallery around on top of the capital of the great column. This gallery was inclosed some years ago with iron-work from the top of the rail, up some 8 feet, and covered at the top, forming an iron cage to prevent people from throwing themselves off with suicidal intentions, as was at times done. The great pedestal at the base contains in its four panels bas-reliefs, commemorative of the fire and events connected with the structure's erection. The monument is open daily, and for a small fee visitors are admitted to the gallery cage, from which very commanding views are had of the larger part of Old London, as well as the River Thames, and many outlying places in all directions. As from the top of the cathedral, the prospect is charming, and one is delighted as he views and contemplates this largest city of the world, more than two thousand years old, spread out below him; and how as by magic comes the thought that, from this elevated position, kings, queens, the most renowned ones of the old world and the new, have, as we are doing, looked out upon and been lost in contemplation of the scene!

The monument was built from designs furnished by Sir Christopher Wren. It was begun in 1671, and finished in 1677. It is justly esteemed as the noblest column in the world, being 24 feet higher than the Trajan Column at Rome. Next a walk to London Bridge, where, as Pepys would have said, "by boat to Westminster." As stated in our other remarks on London, this is an exceedingly pleasant way to travel from one part of London to the other; the boats ply often and thousands thus travel. And next, another tour through the grand old Abbey, and about the vicinity of Parliament House and Westminster Bridge; and so the day was well filled up. As at first, very interesting are these London rambles.

Friday, we are ready to take steam-cars for the famed city of

WINDSOR,

for which we start at 9 A. M. The ride of 23 miles is through well cultivated lands. The best of England are these fine suburbs. For 2,000 years have these same fields been cultivated, but they seem new and as virgin soil to-day. They are not povertized by continual takings-off and no returns, but manures are applied, constant attention is paid, and grand results come.

At length arrived, we find ourselves in the pretty rural city, with a population of 11,769. It is situated on the right bank of the Thames, and presents a very neat appearance, with a smart enterprising condition everywhere apparent. The streets are well paved and lighted, and while there is little that is antique to be seen, yet it is interesting from its look of substantial and finished appearance. Here, at the seeming centre of the place, or at least in the midst of a solid population, is the famed Windsor Castle, and of course this is what we have especially come to see. It is the occasional residence of the Queen, and the buildings cover twelve acres of ground, being surrounded by a terrace on three sides, which is 2,500 feet in length. They stand in an enclosure called the Little Park, which is four miles in circumference, and connected on the south by a long and remarkably fine avenue of trees with the Great Park, which is 18 miles in outline; and then again west of this is the Windsor Forest, having a circuit of 56 miles. Windsor has long been a seat of residence for royal blood, for here resided the Saxon kings before the Norman Conquest. The present castle however is less ancient, as it was founded by William the Conqueror, who died Sept. 9, 1087. It was, however, largely rebuilt by order of Edward III., under the supervision of William of Wykeham, the celebrated Bishop of Winchester, who was architect of the remarkably elegant nave of his cathedral, and died Sept. 24, 1404. The antiquity of the castle is from these dates readily seen; and we may add that one of the reasons which induced us so often in these articles to give dates of the death of important individuals, was to enable the reader to have data as regards the age of buildings, or of the time of occurrence of events narrated. Various repairs were made after that; but, so far as general arrangement and design are concerned, no changes were made for centuries, and they so continued till 1824-8, when new work was done and all put in complete condition under the superintendence of Sir Jeffrey Wyatville.

Visitors are freely admitted to the grounds and the castle, and a company is always present, thousands availing themselves of the privilege. We enter through the gateway from the city thoroughfare, which, as stated, is here very populous, and is even a commercial part of the place.

Not far inside the grounds, which here are simply macadamized, with no tree or shrub or grass lawn present, we first visit the grand St. George's Chapel, strongly reminding one of the chapel of King's College at Cambridge. The interior is magnificent, with lofty columns and arches, splendid traceried-stone, vaulted ceiling, a rich altar-screen, and stall-work of oak. It has no transepts, but, like the prototype named, is one long, high, and not over-wide room.

Beneath the chancel is what is called the Royal Vault, in which are the remains of Henry VI., died 1471; Edward IV., 1483; his queen, Margaret of Anjou, 1481; Henry VIII., 1547; Jane Seymour, his wife, 1537; Charles I., 1649; George III., 1820; his wife, Charlotte Sophia, 1817; George IV., 1830; his daughter, the Princess Charlotte; and later, the Duke of Kent, the Duke of York, William IV. and his queen, and other members of the royal family.

"Very royal dust this, and in great quantity," says an intense and high civilization; but, stript of its outward insignia, the royalty has gone, for no more is their dust respected by the great laws of nature, than is that of the beggar who sues for an humble pittance at the church door. The great destroyer makes all equal. Death is indeed a great leveller. The king in his marble sarcophagus is a beggar; and the beggar, uncoffined, it may be, in his common earth-grave, is a king. Harriet Martineau has well said:—

All men are equal in their birth,
Heirs of the earth and skies;

All men are equal when that earth
Fades from their dying eyes.

At the rear of St. George's is an ancient chapel, but of late refitted on the interior as a mausoleum, or place of burial, of the late Prince Albert, and in a style of magnificence rarely seen and never excelled. This was done at the expense and order of Queen Victoria. The finish around the room, for a quarter of its great height, is of very elaborate workmanship of marbles of various colors; and above this are beautiful Gothic windows of painted glass, the most brilliant and costly in the kingdom. The room may be 40 feet wide, 75 feet long, and 40 feet high; and at one end is the altar, and a most elegant cenotaph to the especial memory of the worthy Prince. Astonishingly magnificent is all.

We pass from the chapel to the great Central Tower. This is on a mound of earth, and may be fifty feet in diameter and as many feet high. From the top may be seen miles of the surrounding country, and all is indescribably grand. Off some miles, and quietly nestling, embowered in trees, is Newstead Abbey, where Byron received his rudimentary education; and in another direction, five miles away, are two objects of remarkable interest. One is the famous Eton School, one of the celebrated academical institutions of England. The other, to us Americans, if the statement is true, is a place yet more interesting,—the mansion-house, with its ample grounds, once occupied by William Penn, the founder of Pennsylvania. Yet a mile beyond is another spot of great fame and renown, the burial-place of the poet Thomas Gray; and so in sight is the identical old church, to which he refers in his Elegy:—

Save that from yonder ivy-mantled tower,
The moping Owl does to the Moon complain

Of such as, wandering near her secret bower,
Molest her ancient solitary reign.

A guide, stationed on the flattish roof of the great tower, is glib of tongue, telling of this and that thing to be seen. As he goes around with his company the entire circuit of the parapet, a part of the statement is that he has been stationed here now for eleven years. He likes Americans, he says, and can tell them the moment they appear in view. He thinks them very intelligent; but is amused, he adds, when he asks them where William Penn was buried, for not a man or a woman of them knows. We of course were a source of amusement to him, and were pleased to be the innocent cause of his mirth. Anything, consolingly we thought to ourselves, to break the monotony of his life; and so we were happy in the thought of the contribution we had made, and so unwittingly.

Down from this, and a walk about the premises, to here and there look over the walls, on the scenes outside and below. A guide came up, and, informing us that he was one of the appointed ones, we submitted; and so he became the fifth wheel to our coach. We were, however, *taken in*,—the first time and the last in our journey. When we went to the door of the castle proper we found *he* must remain outside, or we must pay for his admission. We thought we could find our way to the gate without him, and so we were rid of our encumbrance, though not without a tilt of large words in strong Saxon.

That door passed, we were in the waiting-room; and soon our turn came, and that of about a dozen others, to make a tour of the place. Certain rooms only are open to visitors. A portion of the structure is devoted to the private uses of the Queen and the royal family; but the reception-room, banquet-hall, and many semi-private rooms, most elegantly furnished, are open to visitors, and the articles exhibited are many of them of great value, having belonged to former kings and queens. The guide passes through these rooms with his company, explaining, as he passes, that this room is used for such a purpose, or was occupied as a sleeping-room by King So-and-So, or his queen, and that the furniture is now precisely as it was at the time of their death.

All is very interesting. But never is the situation or fact fully comprehended. To enjoy the sights and be entertained in these royal apartments, once so very private, and into which no common visitor was permitted to enter, is one thing; but to realize the great fact is another. How strange that these domicils of kings, and of the high blue-blood of the great realm of England, should come to be museums, gratifying the curiosity of American republicans, the very antipodes of all that is royal or monarchical.

After a very pleasant stay inside the buildings, we take a look at the exterior and the grounds. The latter, so far as seen by the visit we made, were simply bare, macadamized squares, but just outside the walls, on the other sides, are the great and elegant park-grounds, arenas, gardens, ponds, waterfalls, fountains, fine old tree-shaded walks; and every production that brain can devise or wealth procure has been lavished on these acres. The building called Windsor Castle is a vast deal more than a single edifice; and so, in considering it, let not that mistake be made. It is composed of many parts, or portions, with large open courts, or squares, wholly or partially surrounded by the buildings. The latter are quite irregular in outline, and none of them are very high; but there are a plenty of square and round towers of different sizes, with battlements around their tops, of castle-like finish, and a variety of windows, to give it the castle look. If any mistake was made by us in advance, it was to anticipate too compact a building, and not enough of great extent,— one too old and ancient in appearance, and of too high an elevation. From the rise of ground on which the castle stands, the whole is conspicuous from many points on the railway, for miles distant; and the view of the granite-like colored structure—clean, large in extent, very irregular in outline of upper part as seen from these points, the whole beautifully embosomed in thick foliage of trees—presents a charming effect. When the Queen is present, which is for a few weeks at a time at intervals, a large flag floats from the top of the great tower, and that is evidence of her royal presence.

We pass out of the great gate and are again in a seemingly republican street, and things resume an American aspect and appearance. Another dreamish condition we have been in, and now seem back on the substantial ground of common humanity and, we may add, common sense. We breathe freer, *and* as we think the whole scheme over, of the work doing by John Bright, by Gladstone, and a host of others,—when we remember that now for the first time in English history all of the people, *think*, *talk*, and *act*,—we know the outcome will be good and an advance be made.

Having been alternately filled with admiration and disgust,—with indescribable charm and wonder, and with grand anticipations of the good time coming,—we say "Another dream-day has come and is passing," and we reluctantly move on and ruthlessly tear ourselves away from these bewitching conditions and contemplations; and now at 3 P. M. are ready for a visit to the famed Stoke Poges. Ever memorable, and to all coming time it will be, as the spot made classic by Gray's "Elegy in a Country Churchyard."

At 3.30 P. M. we leave the castle gate, and negotiate for our team to Stoke Poges, a place of very uneuphonious name, but classic and known the civilized world over. Teams for hire are in abundance, and are with their drivers in waiting for employment. The appearance of a stranger, especially if an American, is a signal for an attack. We had long since learned the art of management of a case of the kind at Montreal and Quebec in our own country, and the flank movement is to appear to be in want of anything *but* a team. One must work up alongside the boundary line of fact and truth; and the tendency is to at times cross it and get over on the other side. When taking most notice, and doing best work of selecting, the Yankee, to appearance, never did hire a team, and never will. To make the story short we will say that without a beating down as regards price, but to accommodate the driver, who was spoiling to carry us for $3.00,—when at first he, with all his fellows, made a mistake, and asked $5.00,—we were at length seated in his team; and, while the army of other drivers were retiring crestfallen, were being trundled in the heavy English top-buggy, top turned back, and were being grandly transported through the pretty streets of Windsor, out among the fine gardens, and half-metropolitan, half-suburban scenery, on our way to Stoke.

Never will be forgotten that inspiring ride, for all the way it was through charming scenery. At times over broad thoroughfares, in which the refinement of a high civilization had for 500 years concentrated; then into narrow lanes finely hedged on their sides, shaded by grand old elms and ever-fragrant lindens, sweet in their good foliage and new blossoms; and so on and on—new scenes charming, the clear air invigorating, thoughts of Old England inspiring—we, after the ride of three miles, are at one of the great seats of academical education—the famed Eton School, as well known, and for centuries it has been, as any college at Cambridge or Oxford. This, and that at Newstead Abbey, the old London St. Paul's, the Blue-Coat School, and the Westminster one, are a part of England's history and are as renowned as the soil itself. What a charm there is to the story of Eton and Rugby! The grounds are ample, well laid out, and contain fine old trees and shrubbery,—few or no houses encroaching, or in the neighborhood; the whole territory has a very retired and rural appearance. There is nothing however of the very antique or ancient look such as we anticipated. As a whole, all was to us, with our pre-conceived idea, too modern and new. The buildings are of brick. They are somewhat broken in outline and design, but suggested a factory-like appearance. How many poets, philosophers, and men in all the learned walks of life here fitted for the great universities! How very renowned and sacredly classic are these grounds! We would stop by the way and enumerate, but must forbear and pass on to the more immediate object of our tour; for off in the distance, charmingly embowered in trees, is the sharp-pointed spire of the poetically immortalized church, resting on its "ivy-mantled tower." The spire is built of a whitish stone and is very sharply pointed. How alluring and attractive it is, how entrancing is the thought that about it, and so near us, is the "yew tree's shade," of which the pensive poet speaks!

We ride on, and pass down into the old lane leading to Lord Taunton's park; we go into his carriage-path, and how charming the finish of everything, and what sublime repose! We pass along and arrive on our left at a pleasant, homelike cottage, with a neatly kept yard in front. How familiar the scene! Honest old hollyhocks, delicate petunias, gorgeous marigolds, sweet mignonette, and such things as are intensely American, and countryish at that, are in profusion. The arrival of a team—and many come every day—is the signal for a buxom, rosy-cheeked damsel to come out of the cottage and open the gate. No remarks by her. She does not comprehend the scheme. All is mechanically done, and is a result of usage and every-day life. If she thinks at all, it is to wonder why the visitors come. A lesser thing never comprehends a greater. To her, as to any one without a proper standard, as Wordsworth said,—

A primrose by a river's brim,
A yellow primrose was to him,
And it was nothing more.

The fence across our road, of which she opens the gate, is of open-work, iron, plain paling, and encloses one side of the churchyard of which Gray wrote:—

Where heaves the turf in many a mouldering heap,

Each in his narrow cell forever laid,
The rude forefathers of the hamlet sleep.

It is an enclosure of perhaps two acres, and simply fenced in from a large grazing-field. The place is by no means solitary in appearance, though no house save the cottage is near it, or in near view, for it is out in the full sunlight, and has for company and suburbs, fine groves, lawns, distant hills, and every accompaniment of good rural character. As Whittier says of our New England burial-grounds,—

With flowers or snowflakes for its sod,
Around the seasons ran,

And evermore the love of God
Rebuked the fear of man.

The ground inside has a very clean and well-kept, though not especially ancient look. There are many gravestones, and but few monuments. A wide modern path, or carriage-way, leads from the gate to the church itself. The latter, which is perhaps 500 feet from the gate, has a very ancient look. It is low, and built of small flintstones. The roof is very high and presents two gable-ends, with a large Gothic window in each; at the other end two gables are also shown, with one some higher than the other. The tower is at the extreme right of the building, up at the farther end, and outside of and against the high part before named. It is square, quite large for its height, having a battlement around the top, and every part of it is so covered with ivy as to expose no portion of the stonework to view. The spire above this is very clean, and of a whitish stone. A large portion of the church itself is covered, or mantled, as Gray expressed it, with ivy; and it may here be added that the ivy is of the common, dark, substantial-leaved kind that we so commonly cultivate in pots, or, in the warmer parts of our country, on the outside of buildings. Who can stand in this place, gazing on this ancient church as the poet Gray many a time did, and not think of that terse and expressive line of the great poem, where he speaks of the quietness of the evening:—

And all the air a solemn stillness holds.

The famed "yew-tree's shade" is here, for at our left, as we pass up the great path, or driveway, and near the end of the church which is on our right, with little more than the path named between it and the great tree, the latter stands sentinel-like, as it has stood for a century,—its dark, sombre, fanlike horizontal branches reaching almost to the ground, and throwing pall-like shadows over our way. The side walls of the enclosure on two sides, and near the church, are of brick, and their tops and parts of their sides are grandly covered with ivy; and to the right, in the adjoining lot, are trees and thick shrubbery; and we are again reminded of Whittier, where he says of one of our country burial-grounds:—

Without the wall a birch-tree shows
Its drooped and tasseled head;

Within, a stag-horned sumach grows,
Fern-leaved, with spikes of red.

Under the large window of the left gable-end, the one nearest the road, and up five or more feet from the ground, is a marble slab, some fifteen inches high and two feet long, which bears the following inscription:—

OPPOSITE TO THIS STONE, IN THE SAME TOMB UPON WHICH HE HAS SO FEELINGLY RECORDED HIS GRIEF AT THE LOSS OF A BELOVED PARENT, ARE DEPOSITED THE REMAINS OF THOMAS GRAY, THE AUTHOR OF THE ELEGY WRITTEN IN A COUNTRY CHURCHYARD. HE WAS BURIED AUGUST 6, 1771.

The mother was memorable for her sorrows and her devotion to her family. Her husband was selfish, morose, passionate, and tyrannical. The mother kept a little china-shop to help educate her son. He wrote, for her tombstone in this burial-ground, as follows:—

HERE SLEEP THE REMAINS OF DOROTHY GRAY, WIDOW: THE CAREFUL, TENDER MOTHER OF MANY CHILDREN, ONE OF WHOM ALONE HAD THE MISFORTUNE TO SURVIVE HER.

Beautiful in all its conditions was this churchyard; and while we were here the birds sang merrily, and the sounds of summer and the odor of a new fresh vegetation made it a paradise complete. That quiet and repose, usual to a spot so removed from the "busy haunts of men," this hamlet of the dead, seemed to underlie all, and the "calm retreat" was all we had anticipated.

As we pass out of the gate and into the outlying field, to the left is a stately stone monument, not long ago built to the poet's memory. It is of good design, and on it are befitting quotations from his poetry; but after all we were sorry to see it. The churchyard, the church itself, the ivy-mantled tower, the Elegy, these are his better monument. He needs no other. It were foolish to "gild refinèd gold or paint the lily." It is well to say of these, as was said for the great architect of St. Paul's, Sir Christopher Wren, "If you seek his monument, look around you."

It should be stated, in passing, that another spot claims, and with some little show of reason, that it, and not this, is the famous "country churchyard;" but, after giving thought to the matter, it appears that till new evidence to the contrary is produced, this spot will have the honors.

As the Elegy has made this place celebrated, and immortalized its name as well as that of its composer, it may be well to say that when Gray had completed it, he handed his manuscript to friends, but he himself doubted its merits, and conscientiously thought it weak and too sentimental. Others, however, saw its value, and, to the author's astonishment, so great was its fame, that on being published, it was soon translated into Greek, Latin, Italian, Portuguese, French, German, and even into Hebrew.

He was born in Cornhill, London, Dec. 26, 1716. On the 30th of July, 1771, while at dinner, he was attacked with convulsions, and died a few days after, in his 55th year.

Of his memorable prose remarks we give but one selection, which shows the industrious habits and inside life of the man. He said:—

I am persuaded the best way of living is always to have something going forward. Happy are they who, if they cannot do anything greater, can create a rosebush or erect a honeysuckle.

As we think of this we are reminded of the like opinion held by the great Daniel Webster, who entertained so much regard for the Elegy that he had portions of it read to him but a few hours before his departure. When the statesman was once asked what was in his opinion the best way to enable one to be comfortable during the heat of summer, he replied: "Always have something to do. Keep busy, and you'll have no time to think of the heat."

It is said of General Wolf, that while he was floating on the River St. Lawrence, on the evening of Sept. 12, 1759,—the night before his memorable attack on Quebec, in which on the next day he lost his life,—he was beguiling an hour in reading Gray's poems, and closing the book, said: "I had rather be the author of that poem, the Elegy, than to be the captor of Quebec."

We now turn our feet homeward, and as our carriage passes, we take a distant look, perhaps half a mile away, of the old mansion and grounds once occupied by William Penn, or at least in which he is said to have resided. Of the proof of this we may say that we have none, aside from the assertion of the guide stationed on the tower at the castle and of people who reside in the region. Our history of the great man is somewhat meagre concerning his last days. One of his last official public acts in America was to aid in making our Philadelphia a city, the charter of which was signed Oct. 28, 1701. He soon after returned to England, and was for the next succeeding years involved in much trouble on account of his business matters in Pennsylvania, by reason of the vicious conduct of his son, to whom he had intrusted his affairs, and commissioned to act as his representative. And then as now, troubles never come singly; for after his already eventful life, at the age of 64 a new and grievous trouble was in store for him. At this time died his trusted friend and agent in London, a Quaker by the name of Ford, who left to his executors false claims against Penn to a very large amount. Conscious of his integrity, and to avoid the extortion, he suffered himself to be committed to the Fleet Prison in London. This was in 1708, and he remained there a long time, till finally released by his friends, who, as best they could, compounded with the creditors. In 1712 he made arrangements with the crown for a transfer of his rights in Pennsylvania, receiving from it $60,000. He soon after was afflicted with paralysis; and though living yet six more years, and experiencing other shocks which greatly impaired his vigor and faculties, especially his memory and power of motion, he finally died at Ruscombe, Berkshire, July 30, 1718, at the age of 74, and was buried in Jordan, a Quaker burial-ground, near the village of Chalfont, in Buckinghamshire.

In passing we remark that, during the plague at London in 1665, Milton made Ruscombe his residence, and that here he finished his great poem, "Paradise Lost." And who can say how much of the coloring of the celebrated poem is not to be attributed to the trouble the people of London, as well as the great bard, were, in consequence of the plague, experiencing? This parish is about twenty miles north of Stoke Pogis, in the county of Buckingham, as before named.

We took our team back for Windsor, and train from there to London, arriving at 8.30 P. M.,—well repaid for our labors of the eventful day, if labor which was a perpetual pleasure can be so called. For the first time in one's life, being at and seeing Windsor Castle and the seat of the great Elegy! A great thing doing and done! A long breath, and no befitting remark; only silence, thankfulness, and contemplation avail.

CHAPTER XXI.

LONDON—HAMPTON COURT—ROCHESTER—CHATHAM—CANTERBURY.

Saturday, this 15th day of June, back in London, we employ the day most pleasantly in visiting the London Docks, Hyde Park, some of the public gardens, and in taking general rambles about the city. One is seldom at a loss in a great city like this, with thousands of facilities everywhere for entertainment, how to employ time. Old but ever-new are these thoroughfares, the river, museums, and galleries.

Sunday A. M. visited several of the old churches, and made it a special business to take a look at as many as possible of those erected by Sir Christopher Wren immediately after the great fire of 1666. They are found in great number in the vicinity of Bow Church and St. Paul's, and some of these interiors are very elegant. St. Stephen's Walbrook is, next after the cathedral, a work of much ingenuity and merit. The building is small, and the exterior ordinary; but the splendid interior is a marvel of beauty and elegance, though more than 200 years old.

Arriving at Westminster Abbey, we found the great church filled to repletion, and hardly standing-room inside the door; but with the push peculiar to Americans we got in, and saw, but could scarcely hear, the distinguished Dean Stanley. Although we could not hear, yet we had unbounded satisfaction in the thought that even in the land of cathedrals, and where a deal of dull and prosy preaching is done, the Dean with his broad views, was here preaching Sunday after Sunday, and being listened to by so vast an assembly. Next we took a walk over Westminster Bridge to Southwark, and into a church there, and listened to a twenty-minute sermon from a young man of good talent and preaching abilities. The discourse took the negative form, the subject being, What we have *not* done for the Lord. It was a labored statement, enumerating sins of omission in great detail, was very evangelical, and perhaps did a good work.

Dined at a restaurant in Southwark, and at 2 P. M. took steam-cars for

HAMPTON COURT,

and our notebook says, "We were not only delighted, but astonished at the place." As we have said something of the place before, we now simply add that we found hundreds of people in the palace, and thousands in the fine grounds. The establishment is open Sundays as well as week-days, and it is a great place of resort. 1,100 oil-paintings are in the picture-galleries; and they are of all subjects, and most of them from the Masters. Another part of the palace of note and interest is the grand Hall of Henry VIII. The ceiling is of oak, very rich and heavy in design and ornamentation.

Tradition has it that Shakespeare's plays were first acted in this old hall. Portraits of Cardinal Wolsey, and of Henry VIII. and each of his six wives are on the walls. It is said, and is probably a fact, that in this room James I. held that memorable conference with the disputants of the Established Church and the Puritans, when he made the celebrated remark, "No bishop, no king." History has it that he afterwards wrote to a friend:—

I kept up such a revel with the Puritans these two days as was never heard the like; where I have peppered them as roundly as ye have done the Papists. They fled me from argument to argument, without ever answering me directly, as I was forced to say to them.

Remained here in this Eden till night, and back to London. Monday A. M. began our last day of tramping over this old metropolis, here and there attending to little matters till now neglected, now and then happening in, just for a few moments, to look at some grand old church,—as St. Bride's, and that marvel of good taste and construction, St. Martin-in-the-Fields, London; and so with visits and letter-writing the day was filled up, and all preparations made to leave London for France, but to stop by the way at Rochester, Canterbury, and finally at that "jumping-off place," Dover.

Tuesday, at 9 A. M., we took train for good old

ROCHESTER,

where we arrived at 11 o'clock, after a fine journey of two hours in this extreme southern part of England. This is a cathedral town, and quite old in look, but clean to a fault and very interesting. It has a population of 18,352, and is situated on the River Medway, crossed by a long, ancient, stone bridge of 11 arches, erected in the reign of King John, who died 1216. On an abrupt eminence near the river, and on the edge of the place, are the remains of old fortifications, and at a short distance from these is the grand old castle with its monstrous square tower, and a beautiful mantling of ivy. The castle was quite large, and is a most pleasing structure. These grounds are some acres in extent. They are laid out in grand taste as pleasure-grounds or parks, with avenues, lawns, fine trees, retreats, flower-beds; and every element required for the pleasure-seeker is here. The high ground gave elegant views of the surrounding country, and the pure, free, and invigorating air was most charming. The place has no manufactures of importance, but considerable trade, for it supports a large number of shops and small stores; one of the very best specimens of an old English market-town is Rochester. There is some commerce, as it is a port of entry, and considerable shipbuilding is carried on. On the other side of the river, and connected by the bridge, is

Chatham, concerning which we will give a few facts later. The long, narrow, winding main street of Rochester contains many antique buildings, which well remind one of old Shrewsbury. For a visit of a few hours, this one to Rochester amply repays.

What is of most interest here is the cathedral. It has no close, or grounds, but is strangely jammed in among buildings, in behind those on the main street, and fronts on a street which is hardly better than a lane; and many of the buildings on this lane, and in fact up against as it were the cathedral itself, are houses of great antiquity. Everything here is England as it *was*, but is very clean and tidy. Nowhere on an equal territory have we seen more antique charms than in the door-neighborhood of this cathedral. The edifice was originally a priory, founded in 604, and rebuilt about 1076. It has recently been restored, and is in good condition. It is in two very distinct parts; one is Norman, and is a fine example, and the remainder is Early English. It was originally built by Gundulph, its first bishop, soon after the Norman Conquest. Its length is 383 feet and it has a low tower but no spire.

There are many old and antique monuments, and but for an act of Dean Stanley of Westminster Abbey, and a few others, it would have been the last resting-place of the remains of Charles Dickens. In speaking of the monuments, the verger pointed to a stone in the pavement,—about three feet wide and five feet or so long, as now remembered,—which was up some few inches from its resting-place, and so left. "There," said he, "is the spot in which Dickens would have been buried. The stone was pried up and an excavation being made for building the brick grave, when information came that personal friends of Mr. Dickens had received notice of the desire of Dean Stanley, and other eminent men, that he should be buried in Westminster Abbey." The work of tomb-making ceased, and so Rochester was deprived of the honor of being custodian of his remains. Mr. Dickens's place of residence was at Gad's Hill, about three miles from Rochester, and he attended worship in this cathedral. His death occurred at that place, June 9, 1870. The cathedral is small compared to others, but it is very interesting and has an antiquity of look not found in any other cathedral.

The bishopric here is, next after Canterbury, which is not far away, the most ancient in England. There is connected with the institution a cathedral grammar school, founded by Henry VIII. in 1542; also what is called the Poor Traveller's House, founded by Richard Watts, in the reign of Queen Elizabeth, "for the nightly entertainment of six poor travellers." The old church of St. Nicholas is a grand old structure, built in 1420, and put in good repair and restoration in 1624. There are also several ancient walls, gateways, and ruins of monastic institutions.

CHATHAM,

as before spoken of, is on the east bank of the River Medway, at its confluence with the Thames, and is a large place, having a population of 44,135, including 8,000 dockyard men and soldiers. It includes the village of Brompton, just below it. It is a rather dirty and poorly built town, and, for a thing unusual, it has many old wooden buildings. On one side all the works are shut in by strong fortifications. Forts Pitt and Clarence are on the Brompton side, and on the Rochester side are Fort Gillingham and Upnor Castle, which is now used as a menagerie. The walk on the Rochester side and along the river, and used as an approach to the park at the base of the rock, is a very fine one, and has on it an ancient stone balustrade, perhaps once used as a parapet for the bridge. At 1.40 P. M. took train for

CANTERBURY.

We have remarked one thing especially in relation to the cultivation of land, and the agricultural habits of the people; and it is that as we approach the seabord from any part of England, and now particularly in the southern part, more attention is paid to the cultivation of garden vegetables and fruit, than is the case in the interior. Soon after leaving London and going southerly, as we did towards Rochester, we began to meet with fine gardens and fruit-raising, strongly reminding us of the eastern shore of Massachusetts. Cherries are raised in great quantities for London market, and now, June 18, while they are not ripe, are at that state of maturity at which they are in Boston forced upon the market. Black Tartarian and the common Ox Heart, and perhaps the Eltons, seem to prevail. We have seen some strawberries in the London markets, but none that were ripe, or, at all events, high-colored. They had a whitish look; and at the time of writing, after the experience in other countries, occupying the entire fruit season, we are sure that in fruit-raising of all kinds, New England is never excelled, unless we possibly except some portions of the Rhine Valley, where plums abound; but even there, no advantage is had over many places in New York State, as for instance on Seneca Lake. Roses are just now at their best. So far as date or time in the season is concerned, they have no advantage over the neighborhood of Boston, or any part of southern New England. Some green peas are in the market, but are really now only just at their best time of blossom. At times, as we pass on the railroad, we see acres of them; also other vegetables for the supply of markets. It has quite an Arlington or North Cambridge look, and we are much at home in the neighborhood of this fine agricultural district; and we cannot but be delighted with the industry of the people here, and the manner in which they manage their farms. We are at a loss to know why the idea is not more contagious than it appears to be. "Alas for poor Ireland," we feel and say,—that garden of the kingdom, as it might and should be. New-Englandize it, and the Irish millennium would come.

After our pleasant ride of about two hours, at 3.30 P. M. we arrive at the famed seat of all the Church of England, the great See of the Archbishop of Canterbury, and our first impression is a delight on landing in this quiet, ancient, neat, grandpaved, and in all respects well-cared-for, aristocratic town. How quaint are many of these venerable houses, Chester-like, with projecting stories,—all in fine repair and good preservation!

The place is pleasantly situated on the River Stow, 56 miles from London, and has a population of 16,508. It has no commercial importance, but is one of the principal markets of a rich agricultural district; and its pretty and inviting location has made it a favorite place of residence, as is evident from the many fine villas and mansion-seats in the vicinity. It has an ancient guildhall, a corn and hop exchange, and a Philosophical Museum. The town existed in the time of the Romans, and many of their coins and remains have been found in and near the city. It was the capital of the Saxon Kingdom of Kent; and it was here that Augustine baptized Ethelbert and 10,000 Saxons in 597, or nearly 1,300 years ago. Augustine was the first Archbishop of England, and died here sometime between 604 and 614.

Aside from the cathedral there are several grand old churches in the city. One of the most interesting is St. Martin's, very old and antique, and full of interest. In St. Dunstan's the head of Sir Thomas More—who was executed July 6, 1535, and buried here by his daughter—was found in 1835, or just 300 years after. He was disloyal to the throne and refused to acknowledge the royal supremacy. On the 1st of July he was brought to the bar of the Court of High Commission, charged with traitorously attempting to deprive the king of his title as Supreme Head of the Church. He was condemned and returned to the Tower. On the morning of his execution he was dressed in his most elaborate costume, preserved his composure to the last, and, as the fatal stroke was about to fall, signed for a moment's delay while he moved aside his beard, murmuring: "Pity that should be cut; that has not committed treason."

There are in Canterbury various relics of past ages. One of the most interesting of these is the great St. Augustine Monastery, once long used as a brewery, but which was at length redeemed from its ignominious use by the munificence of Mr. Beresford Hope, who purchased it, and presented it to the Church as a missionary college, himself also defraying all expenses of the restorations and enlargements.

By the liberality of Alderman Simonds a field called Dane John, containing a high conical mound, was laid out as a public park, and pleasant promenades have been built for the public. On the top of this fine hill has been built a rural structure, of an observatory nature, and from it most commanding and splendid views are had of the surrounding country.

What of course attracts the attention of visitors most, and holds it, is the famed cathedral,—at once the most interesting, all things considered, of any like structure in the kingdom; for it boasts of not only a vast antiquity, but of having been at an early day a church of so much wealth and importance, as to make it *the* seat of the Church, and of her Archbishop, "the primate of all England." The chapter consists of the archbishop, a dean, six canons, two archdeacons, six preachers, and five minor canons, besides the twelve choristers. The annual income of the archbishop is $75,000.

The foundation of the institution goes back far into antiquity; and we leave the minor items relating to its early history, and simply say that the cathedral had so far advanced, as to be ready for consecration in 1130. It, as all other cathedrals did, met with reverses and ill-conditions innumerable. Indeed, so varied is its history, and so full of great events, that we are discouraged at the thought of attempting the task of making a selection. It has been wonderful in its power and influence, and has in turn had in its embrace men of master minds, whose power has been of most decided character for good or ill; and we are sorry to have to say, that often the latter has transcended the former. A bishop of especial ability and power, if but loyal to the Church and its doctrines, as for the time understood and interpreted, was sure to be sooner or later installed here. "Translated to the See of Canterbury" is a familiar expression, and has been for centuries. How have the fortunes and condition of the entire kingdom, and the whole English-speaking world, been influenced by things said and done here! No spot beneath the broad canopy of the sky is so marked as this. Here Puritanism found its great foes and untiring enemies; and when we speak of this fact, or name the word *Puritan*, how much is involved! Non-conformist, Pilgrim New England, what she at first was and now is,—all that is involved and comprehended! *Archbishop of Canterbury!* Name but the three words, and what echoes are awakened, and wander through the corridors of time!

No place is really more intimately connected with Plymouth and Massachusetts Bay than is this. The invisible telegraph of momentous events—a continuous unbroken line—exists, and is as real as the material cable that reposes on the floor of the sea; and when all of them shall have become extinct, this, forever revivified and renewed, will increase in power and be an instrument for good, "till the angel, standing with one foot on the land and the other on the sea, shall declare that time shall be no more."

Not long before the accession of Queen Victoria to the throne in 1838, a most thorough repair of the cathedral was made, and it is now one of the most perfect in England.

In our examinations of these great structures, admiring each of them, we have at times tried to decide which one of all we would, if the thing were possible, transport to America. At times the elegant interior of Winchester, with its fine long nave, is in the front rank. Then appears the great Lincoln, splendid within and without. Next, these are crowded aside by imperial York Minster. Then comes antique but sublime old Durham; how can we part companionship with that? or Salisbury, with its commanding spire, 404 feet high, and its rich transept end? Next, rich gem-bedecked Ely comes well up in front. Finally we make one herculean move, and, as the waking giant shakes his locks and spreads his arms, we make an effort to be unsympathetic; and ignoring these grand old friends, all of whom with charms peculiar to themselves have wooed and captivated us,—leaving them, a noble army of martyrs,—we say *Canterbury*. The effort has cost us much sacrifice. "Not that we love Cæsar less, but that we love Rome more." The grounds about the structure are very fine and inviting, though they do not possess those charms that exist at Salisbury and Peterboro.

The cathedral was founded by Archbishop Lanfranc, and enlarged and consecrated by Archbishop Corbel in 1130, in presence of Henry I. of England, David, king of Scotland, and all the bishops of England. The roof, or exterior covering, of the stone vaulting is of wood, and was seriously troubled by fire in 1174, when the choir and other portions of the interior were greatly damaged; and as late as Sept. 3, 1872, a portion of the roof, 150 feet in length, was badly damaged by fire and water, but all is now in perfect condition of repair. The cathedral is in extreme length 514 feet, and is 159 feet wide at the transepts. It has a magnificent central tower, of elaborate decorations, which is 285 feet high; also two very beautiful western towers terminating in embattlements and lofty turrets. The stone is of a dark-gray tint, and the structure has a sublime and imposing appearance. The interior is indescribably grand, and has one especial peculiarity, which is that the choir, or head of the cross,—which is the plan of the cathedral,—is elevated some seven feet or so above the floor of the nave, and is reached by a flight of marble steps. The arrangement, if anything, adds to the grand effect.

Beneath is the crypt, or basement, which is common to but few cathedrals. Here are very ancient columns, and a solid stone, groined ceiling; all is but dimly lighted, and was once a chapel in which monks worshipped. A painful silence now reigns throughout; and all is still and solemn, save as the footfalls on its pavements, or our voice,—or it may be sounds from the great cathedral floor coming down through the stone vaulting, subdued and subduing,—break the spell. Except for these, a silence of the tomb prevails. More than half a thousand years are gone since here the fumes of incense and the sound of papal prayers and the repetition of the Mass were begun. Centuries now are passed since all ceased. Dust of many pious ones has been here laid in its last resting-place, and "after life's fitful fever they sleep well." Nations have risen since then, and kingdoms have been transformed. The great realm of thought has been enlarged and extended, and humanity has become enlightened and advanced. Then, monk and nun were the rule, but they are not now even the exception. All are forever gone, and a hard theology, one anticipating an everlasting triumph of evil over good; penance, tormenting the body for the good of the soul,—or, later advanced tenet, that of tormenting the mind for the soul's good,—are discounted. Personal accountability, divine sovereignty, the Golden Rule, progress never ending for the individual and the race, are in the ascendant; and so crypt and dark room are deserted, and only tell of human life and endeavor as they were.

This cathedral has many monuments, and well it may have. How long is her line of bishops and illustrious men! A history of 700 and more years of active work, must have made conditions of note and renown; but we leave these monuments as we must, and say a few things of two or three of the noted ones who here kept holy time. Every reader of history has anticipated the name we speak of first, Thomas à Becket. At the north cross-aisle, or transept, is a small alcove, or chapel, on the right side of which is a table-altar. On the 29th of December, 1170, but forty years after the cathedral's consecration, and more than 700 years ago, as he was kneeling at this altar, he was assassinated, killed on the spot; and now a small place, six inches square, is shown in the floor, where some of his blood fell. The stone was long ago cut out and sent to Rome.

Few mortals have had a history as eventful as his. Born in London, in the olden time of 1117, he was educated, and finally appointed Archdeacon of Canterbury; and, in turn, prebend of Lincoln, and of St. Paul's at London. Nothing short of distinguished abilities and intellect could have brought such honored conditions as these.

When at the age of forty-one, in 1158, Henry II. made him Chancellor of England. So powerful was he in influence over the King, that in 1162, on the death of Theobold the Bishop of Canterbury, the King pressed his election to this See. He was appointed, and so was the first native Englishman who held the archbishopric of Canterbury. He was first ordained a priest, and then made Primate of all England. He resigned his office of Chancellor against the desires of the king, and in retaliation was deprived of his archdeaconship which he wished to retain along with his archbishopric. He at once began to exercise great authority. He became reserved and austere, and soon acquired great renown for his sturdy defence of the prerogatives of the Church against the threatened encroachments of the crown and the nobility.

In 1164 he strongly opposed the famous constitutions presented by Clarendon, and bitter feuds arose between him and the King. The hostility of the King to him was great, and his persecutions increased. He became exceedingly unpopular with the nobility, and at length fled from England. He spent nearly two years in an abbey in Burgundy, and was encouraged by the Pope, who, refusing to accept his resignation of the See of Canterbury, reconfirmed him as Primate of all England, except the See of York.

The strife between King Henry and Becket increased, but after a long continuance of the quarrel, in 1170 a reconciliation took place, and on his return to England the people gave him an enthusiastic reception; but he soon revived his old troubles by publishing the suspension of the Archbishop of York, and the King taunted his attendants for remissness in revenging the overbearing prelate. This excited four barons of the court, Reginald Fitzurse, William de Tracy, Hugh de Moreville and Richard Brito, who undertook the work of his assassination. Dec. 28, 1170, they met at the castle of Ranulth de Broc, near Canterbury, accompanied by a body of armed men. The next day they went to the Archbishop's palace and there had a stormy interview, and on the same evening invaded the cathedral at vesper service. Becket prevented all opposition to their ingress by declining, as he said, "to convert a church into a castle," and implored the assailants to spare everybody but himself. They attempted to drag him from the church, so as not to desecrate it by bloodshed; but while manfully wrestling with De Tracy, Becket received a blow, inflicting a slight wound, which, falling obliquely, broke the arm of his cross-bearer, Edward Grimes. The Archbishop then kneeled at the altar, when the three other barons gave him the death blow, and his brains were scattered on the floor. The cathedral was then ordered by the Pope to be closed for one year.

In 1172 Alexander III. canonized Becket as St. Thomas of Canterbury. In 1221 his remains were deposited by Henry III. in a rich shrine, which became a great resort for pilgrims.

After the Reformation, Henry VIII. despoiled the shrine of its treasures of silver and gold, which were of incredible value; and he had the saint's name stricken from the calendar, and his bones burnt to ashes and scattered. The shrine was in the cathedral, back of the high altar, and now its only traces are in the marble floor where it rested, and in the worn and sunken line encircling it, made by the feet and knees of pilgrims who for three centuries had there paid tribute.

As we stood there we could in imagination see the incessant train coming in with demure look, and with a pious reverence kneel and offer their humble petition for the repose of his soul and for the prosperity of the religion he defended. Fearfully in earnest were these honest but superstitious ones, and so was Henry VIII. when he said to the enslaving service, "Thus far shalt thou go and no farther, and here shall thy proud waves be stayed." What determination, what intrepidity, were requisite for the inauguration of reform like this! What master-work to do! Becket and his adherents meant well, but they were superstitious and blind to truth and fact. Henry VIII. did a great work, but when he did it he also did unchristian things. So of Queen Mary, when to the stake must go Rogers and Hooper, Cranmer, Latimer, and Ridley. We cannot well stop there. Puritanism established, somebody was responsible for the persecutions of Roger Williams, of Marmaduke Stevenson, and others. Persecution for opinion's sake is not yet done, but "out of the bitter comes forth the sweet." Becket and his coadjutors, the kings and queens of England, Boston ministers and judges of old, form one long connected chain of defenders of the faith,—not always of clear vision, but outside of themselves governed and overruled; and so, by the work done, humanity steps up higher, and walks on towards the perfection attainable, and in the end sure to be attained.

That work, done in the time of Becket, was the transition period from the Papal Church to the Protestant. Our next man of renown was the noted Archbishop Laud; and his administration was the transition period, from intense formality and ritualism, into a somewhat similar form of Christian worship and work, out of which has come our New England's existence and element and life,—and so, indirectly, our Great West, which in its early days New England people and customs did so much to mould and establish.

William Laud was born at Reading in England, Oct. 7, 1573, but eighteen years after the death of the martyrs at Oxford. He nursed from his mother's breast the spirit of the time, or, like Laurence Sterne's *Tristram Shandy*, was able to date his nature and inclinations to acting and influencing elements at a day the very earliest in his history. He was educated at St. John's College, Oxford; obtained his fellowship in 1593, clerical orders in 1601; and in 1605 became chaplain to Charles, Lord Mountjoy, Earl of Devonshire; and here, he showed pliability of conscience which was ever a distinguishing feature of his life, for he was willing to perform the marriage ceremony between the Earl and Lady Rich, whose first husband was still living.

In 1608 he was made bishop of Nene, being then but thirty-five years of age. In 1611 he was president of the college at which he was educated. In 1616 he was Dean of Gloucester; was a prebendary of Westminster in 1620, and Bishop of St. David's in 1621. In 1624 he was member of the Court of High Commission; in 1626, Bishop of Bath and Wells, and in 1628 Bishop of London; and now begins his great life-work, for he became confidential adviser of Charles I. in ecclesiastical affairs. Succeeding Buckingham in the royal favor he began to play important parts in politics, and his first object and step was to force Puritans, and all Dissenters from the Established Church, into conformity. Macaulay says:—

Under this direction every corner of the realm was subjected to a constant minute inspection. Every little congregation of Separatists was tracked out and broken up. Even the devotion of private families could not escape the vigilance of his spies. Such fear did his rigor inspire, that the deadly hatred of the Church, which festered in innumerable bosoms, was generally disguised under an outward show of conformity.

In 1628 Robert Leighton, a Scottish prelate, published a book, "Sion's Plea against the Prelacy." At the instigation of Laud he was in 1630 brought before the Star Chamber, condemned to pay a fine of £10,000; and he was twice publicly whipped and pilloried in Cheapside, London, had his ears cut off, his nostrils split open, and his cheeks branded with S. S. (Sower of Sedition), and he was incarcerated ten years in the Fleet Prison.

Flattered with success, Laud, being present at the coronation of Charles in Scotland, urged the *forced* establishment of Episcopacy and uniformity in that country, which resulted in revolt; and, contrary to the ambitious and narrow-minded Bishop's anticipation, ended in the adoption of the National Covenant, and so Presbyterianism triumphed. On his return from the ceremonies of coronation, and doubtless in aid of their enterprise to "kill out Puritanism" and to "harry the Puritans out of the land," he was appointed to the See of Canterbury. He became a politician in the more odious sense of that word, and so worked himself in as one of the committee of the king's revenue, and in 1634 he became a commissioner of the treasury; and soon after, and finally, was made Censor of the Press under decree of the Star Chamber in 1637.

He was powerful, overbearing, and injudicious, and the public odium soon manifested itself largely against him. The Long Parliament in 1640, impeached him for high treason, and he was committed to the Tower. After an imprisonment of more than three years he was tried and condemned,— and, as now thought, according to the letter of the law, illegally,—and was executed in the Tower, Jan. 10, 1645, at the age of seventy-two.

Of the many other noted and eminent men of Canterbury's almost interminable list, we take but one, and that was the second Protestant bishop, Matthew Parker. He was eminent as a churchman, as much so as Laud, but was a man of good judgment, and more than any other person gave the character of worship which the Established Church of England now has. He was born at Norwich, Aug. 6, 1504, and entered Corpus Christi College at Cambridge in 1520; in 1533 was licensed to preach, and soon was made Chaplain to Anne Boleyn. He was Dean of Clare College in 1535; chaplain to Henry VIII. in 1537; Master of Corpus Christi College in 1544; and Dean of Lincoln Cathedral in 1552. Having married in 1547, on the accession of Queen Mary he was deprived of his office, and obliged to remain in obscurity. He then translated the Psalms into English verse, and wrote a treatise entitled "A Defense of Priests' Marriages."

His fortune at length turned, for on the accession of Queen Elizabeth, and a reform in the religion, he was chosen Archbishop of Canterbury, and Dec. 17, 1559, was consecrated in the chapel at Lambeth. He was successful in dispelling the Queen's lingering affection for images, and he filled all the vacant Sees with decided Protestants, and did all in his power to render the rites and ceremonies of the church uniform. He founded schools, made valuable presents to the colleges at Cambridge, was one of the first chosen to review the Book of Common Prayer; and was employed in the revision of the Bishop's Bible, which passed under his inspection, and was published at his own expense in 1568. He was the author of several other standard works, and at last, after a life of remarkable activity and usefulness, he died at London, May 17, 1575, at the age of seventy-one, deeply lamented.

1575! 200 years before the declaration of our American Independence, and almost half a century before the Pilgrims set sail for America! He did much towards establishing Protestantism, and making Puritanism possible; and so he was the John the Baptist to prepare for the bad work of Laud and his coadjutors,—which caused the persecution of the non-conformists, and, indirectly, the emigration to the New World, and the great good which is its outcome. Laud, thunder-storm-like, induced a clearer theologic atmosphere.

There is a thing yet untouched we would speak of, but must forbear a long recital. In speaking of the crypt, we strangely forgot to mention that, in the time of Queen Elizabeth, there were a company of French silk-weavers, who were driven from their native land, and sought refuge in England. They were called Walloons, and the crypt of the cathedral was granted them by the Queen as a place of worship. In the time of Charles II., who died in 1688, they were the most noted silk-weavers in England. The blood was strong; and, strange to tell, to this day the humble remnant, after the lapse of centuries, still claim and use this room as their place of worship. There is a tinge of melancholy that comes over one as he thinks of their devotion and humble sanctuary, but it is Sabbath home to them, and so is at once cathedral and gate of heaven.

At the Altar of Martyrdom, where Becket died, in 1170 was that appalling scene of riot, distress, and death. 129 years gone, and how changed! Then was gathered another crowd, and all was peace, happiness, and life, for Edward I. and Margaret were there to be married in 1299.

On the 8th of June, 1376, great commotion was in the Episcopal Palace near by, for there lay in the agonies of death their great-grandson, Edward the Black Prince, who was so called from the color of his armor. Two days after he was buried in the cathedral; and now, after 500 years, we look upon his effigy in bronze, old and black, but highly wrought, and once and for years of rich gilt. Above his tomb are suspended the helm, surcoat, shield, and gauntlet he wore on the field of Cressy. In this cathedral is the ancient chair in which all the old kings of Kent were crowned.

And so we might go on; and when many pages had been written, the door would but be opened, and an inexhaustible store of things of inexpressible interest present themselves, and be in waiting for consideration.

We must now begin to think of parting companionship with these cathedral towns, for we are to move on yet more southerly till Dover is reached; and so for a time is to end our good stay in historic Old England, the mother country of us all. We confess to a feeling of dislike, and at the same time to a consciousness of grand satisfaction of what we have enjoyed, and so that feeling, if permitted to prevail, would neutralize the anticipation of good to come.

We now, at 6 P. M., take cars for Dover. The ride is like that before it, very much like one over lands in New England, on the South Shore Road, towards Hingham and Cohasset. There are rocks, and even ledges, increasing as we advance. There are grand fields of hops, an incredible number of them, and gardens with the new vegetables of all kinds, as in our Old Colony at that time of the year.

Now at 7.30, after a ride of an hour and a half, we come in sight of the bluffs and chalk-cliffs and abrupt hills—a wonder to us indeed. "How extensive, how white!" we say.

And now comes the well-known odor of the heavily charged salt air of the sea. Cohasset, Nantasket, or Nahant, even at their best, could do no better. We are as it were in a new world of observation, feeling, and thought; and on landing there is opened to us a vast panorama of sea view, of high life and animation, a new paradise,—not an old one regained, for we never at home nor abroad had one like this to lose.

CHAPTER XXII.

DOVER—BRIGHTON—CALAIS.

Arrived at 7.30 P. M. and took room at Hotel de Paris—a high-sounding name; but not very Parisian was the institution; however, it was neat and every way good and worthy. Took tea, and then a walk out. As before intimated, we are now in a southern border-town, and the waters of the Channel wash its shore.

Dover is 62 miles southeast of London, and 21 miles northwest from the coast of France, being England's nearest seaport. The population is 28,270 of permanent residents, but it varies by reason of its large number of hotel boarders. It is situated on a small but beautiful bay, and is of an amphitheatre form, between lofty cliffs, and alongshore by the valley of a small river called the Dour. The older portion is rather poorly and irregularly built, and is principally on one street that runs parallel to the river, or valley, and having hills as a background. The newer part is along the shore of the bay, and consists of watering-place hotels, boarding-houses, and aristocratic private residences, many of which have fine grounds about them. These continue for a mile or more, and at the lower end terminate at lofty chalk-cliffs of a stupendous height,—producing a grand and unusual appearance, being very precipitous and of a chalky whiteness. In front of the buildings named is a grand watering-place promenade-avenue, in front of which, the entire length, is a pebbly beach, and this is washed by the waters of the bay. Thousands of people, old and young, were here, and much of gay life and fashion displayed. Never will be lost sight of the grand entertainment we thus had, and which was so unexpected to us. The harbor consists of three basins, though in general appearance but one; and the entrance of the harbor is sheltered by a pier or breakwater of stone, 1,700 feet long.

The castle of Dover is one of the interesting edifices in England. It stands on one of the great hills, a short distance from the town, and its walls inclose thirty-five acres. It is supposed to have been founded by the Romans; but some portions of it are Saxon, some Norman, and some belong to a later period. It contains a separate keep, as it is called, now used as a magazine, and other parts are barracks for 2,000 men. Within the castle precincts stands an octagonal watch-tower, interesting not only as the earliest specimen of Roman architecture in England, but also as one of the most ancient examples of mason-work in Great Britain.

This town is one of very great antiquity. In the neighborhood of Dover, Julius Cæsar made his first attempt to land on the British coast. The antiquity of this event is made more apparent by a remembrance of the fact that he died 44 years before Christ. We are informed by history that "he was induced to change his point of debarkation, owing to the abruptness of the shore and other difficulties." Under the Saxon kings it became a position of great importance in the defence of Kent, which was then all of the southern part of England.

In the reign of Edward the Confessor, who died in 1066, this was one of what were called the Five, or Cinque Ports; the others were Hastings, Romney, Hythe, and Sandwich. As these ports were opposite to France, they received peculiar advantages in the early days of English history, on condition of providing in times of war a certain number of ships at their own expense. They were governed by an officer called the Lord-warden of the Cinque Ports. The Duke of Wellington was lord-warden of them at the time of his death, which was at the official residence, Walmer Castle, near Deal, Sept. 14, 1852.

According to Camden, the first warden was appointed by William the Conqueror, who died in 1087, but their charter has been traced directly to the times of Edward the Saxon king, as before named. This port was considered as the key of the kingdom. After the establishment of Norman rule, it suffered the vengeance of William the Conqueror, to whom it made strong opposition. In 1213 King John performed at Dover the ceremony of submission to the Pope, giving up his authority to the papal nuncio.

In 1295 the French made a descent upon the place and committed great depredations; and so for centuries it was the theatre of attacks and defences, but we pass all, intimating, however, that no more interesting history exists than that relating to these invasions of the territory of England by the various people who had an eye to the possession of new territory,—for which practice England herself has for centuries been celebrated, and which found its last expression in obtaining possession of Cyprus.

In 1847 a mass from one of the chalk-cliffs scaled off and fell to the base. It was 254 feet in height, 15 feet thick, and was calculated to weigh 48,000 tons. Shortly after, another fell, of 10,000 cubic yards. The principal cliff is 350 feet high above the water, which is more than half as high again as our Bunker Hill Monument. Another, called Shakespeare's Cliff, is located just in the rear of, and is a background of, the town, and is perforated by the tunnel of the Southeastern Railway.

Nothing is or can be more picturesque and grand than these chalk-white, clean-faced, and very perpendicular walls, covered as they are on their top and rear slopes with a splendid grass verdure. The blue water of the bay; the old weather-beaten part of the city,—quite European, though not all antique; and the long line of fine beach; the grand avenue above it, so alive with gay teams and pleasure-seekers; the mile-range of hotels and mansions; and to the left, the lofty promontory land, with the castle on its top and the high lands extending well out into the sea, its waves beating at times grandly against these milk-white ramparts,—this group of things forms a scene of remarkable splendor and interest. Our stay here was exceedingly pleasant and was exhilarating in the extreme. We, the next A. M. at 9.30, took our steamer for Calais, which is the nearest port of France, 21 miles over the channel.

Before, however, closing our work, we will speak of one more place in England,—in a sense a counterpart of Dover. It is the famed watering-place, Brighton. Though we did not visit it for some months after this,—till on the 10th of August,—yet as it is the only place of England we visited not yet described, we take occasion to speak of it now, and so complete our record.

BRIGHTON.

We took cars at London for Brighton one Saturday night, and after a two hours' ride arrived at the famed watering-place. The first impression was that we were in a large and old place, and in anything but one to which people would resort for pleasure; for the place in the vicinity of the station, and especially for the entire length of a long street leading down from it, had a very commercial and business-like appearance; and, as we passed down its entire length and looked to the right and left, compactly built streets, houses, and shops, and even fine stores and warehouses, seemed to extend as far as the eye could reach; no tree nor garden, nor even front-yard anywhere, but one mass of solid buildings, and surely a great population.

Our only hope and tangible evidence that we had not mistaken this for the watering-place Brighton—as we had mistaken the little fishing-place Wells, for the cathedral town—was a very large lot of well-to-do, stylishly dressed people, all passing down this great main street. We of course followed, for just then we considered ourselves watering-place visitors, and so in a sense aristocratic. At length the end of the street gained, all fears were dispelled, for there in front lay the grand harbor, and for aught we could see to the contrary, thousands of miles of good ocean were stretching out from it.

Here, as at Dover, was a grand avenue, along for some two or three miles, with a most remarkable shore, and its fine beach extending for miles. A very good cut-stone wall is built the entire length of the city, dividing the beach from the grand avenue, and along these thousands were promenading. The style of hotels is quite in advance of those at Dover. They are many in number, and are of a quite similar appearance as compared to each other, none of them, however, being striking as works of art or architecture. They are of stone or brick, and of a cream-color; all are from three to five stories high, very plain, without porticos or much of any decoration; and while they had a neat and inviting look, yet none of them appeared to be very new or modern, but substantial, and, perhaps of most appropriate construction for their exposed situation. The land rises amphitheatre-like from the water, and, as before named, has a solid and very substantial look.

It has a population of 90,000, and extends for three miles along the coast, from Kemptown on the east to Hove on the west. It was not a place of especial resort till about a century ago, when Dr. Richard Russell published a work on the use of sea-water which attracted much attention; and its celebrity as a watering-place became established when George IV.—who at the time, 1784, was simply the Prince of Wales—made it his place of residence, and began the erection of a peculiar building, called the Pavilion, which was finished in 1787. The grounds were some five acres in extent, and finely laid out by the building of avenues, paths, lawns, flower-beds, and the setting out of good shrubbery and trees. The estate is very centrally located, and in the midst of a neighborhood of the best inhabitants. The town ultimately purchased it of the crown, for the sum of $265,000, and threw the premises open to the public as pleasure-grounds. In all our travels we saw no finer taste displayed in the arrangement of elegant colored-plant designs, nor on as large a scale, as we saw here. They were indeed marvels of genius and beauty. Our visit to these grounds was after tea Sunday night, when hundreds of people were enjoying the treat; and among the few very choice and pleasant hours in England, these are to be named.

For the pleasure of sojourners, two novel things exist. They are what are called *chain-piers*, and extend out into the sea; and are as exposed as would be similar structures built out into the ocean from our Chelsea or Nantasket Beach, for the relative situation is the same. One was erected in 1822-3, at an expense of $150,000. It is 1,134 feet long, and extends, of this length, 1,014 feet into the sea. As 5,280 feet are a mile, it will be seen that this is about one quarter of a mile in length. The other, which is located about half a mile or so from that named, was erected in 1867. It is 1,115 feet long. They are built in suspension-bridge style, with good stone towers, and iron-work for cords and suspension. They are frequented by thousands for the fine views and sea air.

The sea-wall before alluded to is a grand structure, varying in height as the rise or fall of the land requires; and is in height, above the beach, all the way from 20 feet,—which is about the average height, for a mile at the central part of the town,—and then rising to full 60 feet, as it extends towards the elevated land at the left. The broad avenue continues to this, and well up on the elevation, and from this the finest imaginable views of the ocean in front and the city are at hand, and to the rear and right may be had. At the base of this wall, and near the shore, is an aquarium, the buildings being low but large, tasty, and admirably adapted for their purpose. It was opened to the public in 1872. In the western quarter is a battery of six 42-pounders, erected in 1793. On the eastern side is Queen's Park, and on the western is a chalybeate spring.

There are twenty-five chapels and churches belonging to the established church, and thirty of other denominations. Of them all, none had so much charm to us as Trinity Chapel, where once the thoughtful and good Frederick W. Robertson preached, and sacrificed himself for humanity. We, as it were instinctively, on Sunday wended our way there, for although long since, as Cotton Mather would have said, he had "passed on to the celestials," yet it was our highest thought to see the place. We found it a very ordinary building, in a fair neighborhood. The edifice was of no especial pretension, outside or inside. It had a frontage of perhaps 45 feet, was of a debased Grecian architecture, with no look of chapel, save what was given to it by a very unpretending cupola, or bell-tower, resting on the roof. Inside it was quite as simple and in the same style; common galleries were on the two sides and the door end; and while all was neat, yet there was no display nor churchly look. Here the scholarly man thought and labored, and, as it were, died. Robertson was born at London, Feb. 3, 1816; graduated at Brazenose College, Oxford, 1840; and, after being curate at Winchester, Cheltenham, and Oxford, in 1847 he became minister here; and after a most laborious experience in his parish, and outside of it, and remarkably so for the working-men and the poor, he fell a victim of overwork and left the scenes of his earthly labors, Aug. 15, 1853, at the age of but 37. His broad views of the divine government and human destiny cost him the loss of sympathy he otherwise would have had. Conscientious to a remarkable degree, intellectual and finished beyond most others, and withal sensitive, he inwardly deplored his conditions and surroundings; but never yielded, and at last passed on, to be fully appreciated only when the spirit and body had parted companionship. Hardly had his sermons been issued from the press before their depth of thought, their comprehensive reach, their elegant diction, and sweet temper were appreciated; and now, no denomination, evangelical or unevangelical, is there whose clergyman will not speak in their praise. Wherever the English language is spoken, the fine productions of Frederick William Robertson will be spoken of as a choice thing, and an honor to the English tongue.

There are five banks and six newspapers in the town; and one hundred fishing-boats are owned and used, manned by 500 men. The principal fish taken, and in abundance, are mackerel, herrings, soles, brill, and turbot; and mullet and whiting are often caught. The place is very old, for in the old Doomsday Book it is spoken of, and there called by the name of Brighthelmstone.

Having before spoken of Doomsday Book, we will take time enough here to say that it is an old register of lands in England, framed by order of William the Conqueror, and was begun somewhere from 1080 to 1085, and was finished sure in 1086. The book is yet preserved in the chapter-house of Westminster. A facsimile was published by the government in 1783, having been ten years in passing through the press. It is a valuable and interesting work, and is in itself a sort of complete registry of English possessions.

Brighton under the longer name is there referred to. It, like Dover, and in fact all border towns, suffered often from invasions, and the French plundered and burnt it in 1513. During the reigns of Henry VIII. and Queen Elizabeth, fortifications were erected for its protection. Two hundred years ago it was a fishing-town, and had 600 families. Now, the fishing still continues, but its many hotels, its grand summer boarding-houses, and its population furnish a ready market at home.

On one portion of the Sunday we attended worship in the Quaker meeting-house. The word *church* cannot be used with propriety here, for the place was anything but that. We chanced in our walks to fall in with it,—and need we have asked who worshipped there?—a good stone building, unpretending but very neat, end to the road, and back full 100 feet from the street, with a beautiful park-like garden enclosed in front. We went in, and the same nicety was everywhere. Plain, but of a rather higher grade than we were used to seeing in places of worship of this sect. The house was quite large, and was nearly filled. Some four or five of the more elect ones were at their usual place on the high-seats, and facing the audience. All of them were moved by the spirit to speak, and to our pleasure did so. The tone of remark was to speak ill of themselves, and suggest the deplorable conditions incident to an earthly life; but the advice they gave was salutary, the opinion honest and sincere, and good was done. This was the extreme opposite of the ornate Episcopal service, and as we had had that first on entering England, it was well we had this last on leaving it. It was not our intention to furnish evidence against ourselves, and tell that after remaining but a short time in Trinity Chapel we were too uninterested to stay, and so quietly walked out, being near the door, and going we knew not exactly where, came in here; but we have now told the story, and so the reader will not be at a loss to know why we had nothing to say of service there.

Much more would we say of this Brighton,—its fine air, views, fashionable life, and desirable conditions, but we rest the case here. When we have written one of these articles, we find an abundance more material left than we have used. The task of omitting material is a great one. What *not* to say is what troubles us.

Although an account of the passage to Calais, and a description of that place would not ordinarily be in order in a work pertaining to the places here described; yet there being involved certain items of historical interest to

Americans we venture to say a few words pertaining to things across the channel, and with that end our work.

Having digressed this much, we now go back to old Dover, where the last accounts left us, and at 9.30 A. M. of Wednesday, June 19, are on board the steamer for a few hours' sail, across the channel to Calais.

Our voyage was far from being an unpleasant one. We were not entirely out of sight of land, as Dover was behind or Calais before us all the time, for in fair weather these are always in view. The steamers are strong and adapted for their work. They are about the size of those that ply in our harbor, the John A. Andrew if you please; but white paint for a steamer is quite distasteful to people of the region we are in. Black is to them the fine and good color. No money is to be expended for nice inside finish as in the Andrew; but everything is solid and neat, and we ought to be generous enough to say, "as good as need be," and we *will* say it.

Generally this Channel is rough and boisterous. Currents and winds through this great valley of the land and sea are so in conflict, that seldom is there a calmer or even as calm a time as we had. Now the two hours end, and we are nearing shore. England has been left behind, with pleasant memories that it wouldn't take much reflection to transform into regrets; yet all is lighted up with good anticipations, for we two Bostonians are soon to stand on the soil of Imperial France. The thought even now kindles peculiar emotions. Sunny France! an elastic people, brilliant in exploit; its great metropolis the epitome of a remarkable civilization! We thus thought of it then, and thus we think of it now. The steamer slackens her speed, and we are on the upper deck, ready to land at

CALAIS.

But two hours' sail across the Channel, and we are now, at 12 M. of Wednesday, June 19, standing on French soil, and though but 21 miles from England, and people of the two places have been for centuries crossing the Channel and communicating with each other, still, things here are peculiar and have an outlandish look. It is like Dover, somewhat of a watering-place; and there is a fine beach, with a large chateau-like hotel on the right shore as we enter. The wharf at which we land is an old wooden structure, and everything about it has an aged look. We did not go up into the city, but remained at the wharf for the departure of the train which was already there and in waiting. We now began to hear French talked as the rule, and English as the exception. The station was quite a large and substantial structure of brick, and here was what was called a *café*, or, as we should say, a restaurant. The art of restaurating is not well developed outside of America. Lager beer, sandwiches, and a few ordinary cakes are about all that can be found. In a distant part of the building dinner could be had at a cost of about a dollar. In fact people when they came into the car were complaining loudly: first, of the lack of things to eat; next, of quantity; and finally, of exorbitant prices. This was a fair sample of a majority of all we met with. A mild rain was falling, and we contented ourselves with remaining about the station nearly an hour.

Calais is one of the seaports of France, 19 miles from Boulogne, and 150 miles north of Paris, which—added to the 21 miles from Calais to Dover, and the 62 miles from there to London—makes the distance from the place last named to Paris 233 miles, or the same distance as between New York and Boston. Its population in 1866 was 12,727, or about double that of our Calais, Maine, that being 5,944. Both are border towns, with the English opposite. It is situated on a rather barren district, the surrounding country being of cheap land, and under poor cultivation. A great difference exists in these respects on the two sides of the water. The place is well fortified by a citadel and quite a number of forts; being one of the border towns, it has, like those of England, been subject to constant invasions.

The harbor is formed of long wooden piers, and is very shallow. It has a lighthouse 190 feet high, which is very commanding in effect, and adds much to the look of the place as one of commerce. Steamers ply daily, and at times quite often, across the Straits of Dover to England. The streets are broad and level, and so far as we saw, were well paved. The houses were neat, and mostly of stone or brick, though a portion of them were wooden. What are called the ramparts afford a good promenade, and it is said that, as a general thing, English is the spoken language. Among the noteworthy buildings is the old church of Nôtre Dame,—a favorite name for French churches,—the words meaning *Our Lady*, an allusion to the Virgin Mary. This church contains the celebrated painting of the Assumption by Vandyke.

The Hôtel de Ville is a very old and large structure containing the public city offices, and has a high tower and belfry, with clock and chime of bells. Another ancient structure is the Hôtel de Guise, an edifice erected for the wool-stapler's guild—an institution founded by Edward III. There are various statues and busts of distinguished men in the more public places; but what is a very conspicuous object is the Tower of Guet, which dates back to 1214, or 669 years ago. It was for centuries used as a lighthouse; and, though having a history of one third of the time from the Christian era, as Longfellow has said of the Belfry of Bruges, "still it watches o'er the town."

Prior to the twelfth century Calais was an insignificant fishing-village; but Baldwin IV., Count of Flanders, was especially pleased with the location, and realizing its importance as a seaport, and its possibilities as a place of resort for sea-bathing and summer residence, greatly improved it, and about the year 997, expended much money for its advancement. Philip of France,

Count of Boulogne, in the early part of the thirteenth century enlarged and strengthened its fortifications.

It was invaded by the English, and in 1347 it was, after a long siege, taken by King Edward II.; and in the negotiations for peace, Eustace St. Pierre, and five companions were accepted as a ransom for the entire population, and finally, they themselves had their lives spared by the intercession of the wife of Edward, Queen Philippa. From that time it remained in possession of the English a period of 211 years, when in 1558, it was besieged by the French under the Duke of Guise; and with the exception of the years 1596-8, when it was in the hands of the Spaniards, it has remained in comparatively quiet possession of the French.

It has been from first to last a somewhat memorable place, and has played an important part in history. Charles II. of England, after the battle of Worcester, Sept. 3, 1651, fled to France; but the peace of 1655 forced him to leave the country and he went to Bruges, and remained there and at Brussels till he heard of Cromwell's death in 1658, when, in order to avail himself of the great confusion it caused in England, he ventured to station himself at Calais, which he did in August of 1659; and, with this as his headquarters, he opened negotiations with General Monk, which ended in his being proclaimed king of England, May 8, 1660.

It was here also that James II. mustered his forces for the invasion of Ireland; and finally it is memorable as the place where Louis XVIII. landed, April 21, 1814, after his exile, and the spot is marked by a column and an inscription of the event.

There is a matter of such interest, more especially to us Bostonians, connected with the channel between Dover and Calais, we cannot well refrain from noticing it; and it is, that on the 7th of January, 1785, two men were here for the first time successful in conducting a balloon on any extended scale, and guiding it to a particular destination; and we are happy to be able to state that a very distinguished Bostonian was one of these, the celebrated physician Dr. John Jeffries, who was born in our Boston, Feb. 4, 1744, being at the time first named, a resident of London, and in a successful practice of his profession. Being largely interested in scientific pursuits, and especially those relating to atmospheric pressure, he was invited by one François Blanchard, a Frenchman and an aeronaut, to attempt with him the task of crossing this channel. They started from the cliffs of Dover at the time before named, and safely landed in the forest of Guines in France. The doctor, in consequence of his venture, received great attentions from learned and scientific men and societies in London and Paris. Blanchard, who had planned the voyage and furnished the balloon, was rewarded by Louis XVI.

with a gift of 12,000 francs, or $2,500, and a life-pension of 1,200 francs annually. He died in Paris, March 7, 1809, at the age of 71. Dr. Jeffries removed back to Boston in 1789, four years after the balloon passage, and died there Sept. 16, 1819, at the age 75, and was buried in the Granary burial-ground on Tremont Street.

There are two things of especial interest that may be named as we speak of Dr. Jeffries. One is that it was he and John Winslow of Boston who first recognized the body of General Warren who fell at the battle of Bunker Hill. It lay where it fell till the succeeding day, when, being recognized, it was buried on the same spot. The other fact is that he was one of the early permanent settlers of East Boston, at what is now—and long has been known as—Jeffries Point. Although in a degree foreign to our purpose, yet we extend our remarks and name an incident of connecting interest, which took place in this year of Dr. Jeffries' decease.

After the death of Blanchard in 1809, his wife, Marie Madeline Sophie Armant, who had accompanied him on many of the sixty-six voyages he had made, continued making like aerial excursions for the following ten years; till on a day of June in this year, 1819, she ascended from the Tivoli Garden in Paris, when her balloon, which was illuminated with fireworks, took fire while at a considerable height, and she, falling, was dashed to pieces. In a few months after, as named, died Dr. Jeffries, and so ended the earthly career of the trio most interested in that first great balloon enterprise between Dover and Calais, thirty-four years before.

There are yet a few places of interest, which, although not included in our journey, are so readily reached by detours from places we did visit, that we deem it advisable to name them. Conspicuous among them are the three cathedrals not described in our work: these are CHICHESTER, one of the five English cathedrals with a spire; WELLS, celebrated for its elaborately carved west façade and the wide grounds in front of it; and EXETER, having also a highly decorated west end, with the two transepts ending as towers.

Chichester is easily reached by a ride by rail of 28½ miles from Brighton; Exeter by one of 80 miles from Bristol; and Wells, by one of 19 miles from Bath.

LAKE WINDERMERE, in no way inferior in picturesque beauty to the lakes of Ireland or Scotland, may be visited by a ride of 15 miles from Lowgill, a station between Leeds and Carlisle.

GLASTONBURY ABBEY ruins are excelled in beauty and interest by none in England; they may be reached by a ride of 6 miles from Wells, and may be visited while making the tour to the cathedral.

TINTERN ABBEY, remarkable for its beauty, may be visited from Gloucester. It is a ride by rail of 40 miles to Chepstow, and then by coach for 14 miles further. It hardly need be added that these ruins are over the Welsh border.

FOUNTAIN'S ABBEY ruins, renowned and of indescribable beauty and interest, are 13½ miles from Harrowgate, a town that may be reached by a ride of 27 miles by rail from either York or Leeds. In the vicinity of both Fountain's Abbey and Harrowgate are the celebrated ruins of BOLTON PRIORY, and no day can be more interestingly employed than one devoted to these unusual and remarkable places.

In Scotland, 30 miles from Glasgow, is the town of AYR, in which are the ruins of the Kirk of Alloway, the scene of "Tam O' Shanter." Near-by is the cottage in which Robert Burns was born; and a fourth of a mile away, on the banks of his celebrated Doon, is a fine monument to his memory.

The famous ruins of JEDBURG ABBEY are reached by a carriage-ride of eight miles from Melrose. The town itself is peculiar in the quaintness of many of its streets and buildings, and it is a principle with the inhabitants to preserve these antiquities.

DRYBURG ABBEY ruins are beautiful in the extreme, and a fit resting-place for the remains of Sir Walter Scott. They are within four miles of Melrose.

But we find the theme lengthening, and must forbear; and in closing will simply say, that the GIANT'S CAUSEWAY may be reached to advantage by a jaunt from Dublin to Belfast, one of the chief cities of Ireland, 88 miles north of the capital; thence to Londonderry, one of the most finished and intelligent places of the Emerald isle; and thence to the northern border, and by steamer to the Causeway. The spot may also be reached direct by steamer from Belfast.

And now we take a respectful leave of our readers, trusting that our humble work may be acceptable, and that their knowledge has been increased, or their memory refreshed, as to things in England, Ireland, and Scotland.

FOOTNOTE:

[1] There is no uniformity in the spelling of this name. The oldest records of the family give it as *Shakspere*. In the poet's will it is spelled *Shakspeare*, and is so signed by him. Whenever he and his friend Ben Jonson caused it to be printed, they spelled it Shakespeare. In this form we find it in almost every book of that period where it appears at all. And so we have it on his wife's tombstone. The probabilities are, that the later spelling was the one most approved by the poet himself, as giving more correctly the usual pronunciation.